STATS™ 1994 BASEBALL SCOREBOARD

John Dewan, Don Zminda, and STATS, Inc.

Foreword by Bob Costas

Illustrations by John Grimwade

Statistical Compilations by Robert Mecca

Editorial Assistance by Rob Neyer
& Michael Coulter

Typesetting by Pat Quinn

HarperPerennial

A Division of HarperCollinsPublishers

STATS is a registered trademark of Sports Team Analysis and Tracking Systems, Inc.

FIRST EDITION

Cover Design by John Grimwade

ISBN 0-06-273230-7

94 95 RRD 3 2 1

Acknowledgments

For many of us at STATS, the *Scoreboard* is a particular labor of love, and our very favorite publication. It couldn't have been produced without the efforts of the STATS team, which we think is "championship caliber." Bob Mecca, famed manager of the New England Anarchists in the Ozark Mountain League, is the programmer who gathers most of the data we use in this book. Bob never fails to answer that "one last request" for additional information. Also helping on the programming side were Mike Canter, Stefan Kretschmann, Rob McQuown and David Pinto.

Rob Neyer, who broke all of Wilt Chamberlain's scoring records at the University of Kansas, is chief assistant to Don Zminda on the writing side. Along with managing many of the daily details on the book, Rob wrote 10 of the essays in top-level fashion. Also contributing essays were Steve Moyer, who produced his annual report on "long-shot prospects," and David Pinto, who wrote the excellent essay on the effects of expansion.

John Grimwade, one of the greatest players ever to come out of the Canterbury School of Art ("The Fighting Impressionists"), is our illustrator. He's a true franchise player.

Michael Coulter, the Mod Hatter himself, was the person primarily responsible for checking the stats for accuracy, and for pointing out other errors in the manuscript: "Hey, it's not the Sultan of *Sweat*, it's the Sultan of *Swat*." Assisting Michael in this important task were Chuck Miller and Steve Moyer.

Pat Quinn, our typesetter, doesn't know Robin Ventura personally, but he sure knows Ventura Publisher. Pat modestly calls one of his fantasy teams the "Rookies," but he's a great veteran when it comes to producing a fine-looking book.

Our appreciation also goes to the rest of the STATS staff: Art Ashley, Sue Dewan, Ross Schaufelberger, Jules Aquino, Stephanie Armstrong, Kevin Davis, Patti Foy, Jason Gumbs, Mike Hammer, Bob Meyerhoff, Marge Morra, Jim Musso, Kenn Ruby, Jeff Schinski, Allan Spear and Debbi Spence.

Thanks to Bob Costas for contributing the Foreword.

And special thanks to the "cheering section," which consists of Sharon Zminda, Mike and Steve Cacicoppo, and Jason and Erica Dewan. You're the best fans a team ever had.

— John Dewan and Don Zminda

Table of Contents

III. QUESTIONS ON OFFENSE 111

IV. QUESTIONS ON PITCHING 153

V. QUESTIONS ON DEFENSE 197

FOREWORD

By **Bob Costas**

October, 1985. Game 5 of the National League Championship Series between the Dodgers and Cardinals. The series is tied 2-2 and this game also is tied at two in the bottom of the ninth inning at Busch Stadium. With the bases empty, Ozzie Smith faces Los Angeles righthander Tom Niedenfuer. As the Wizard settles in, Ricky Diamond, then an associate producer at NBC, feels the time is right to let the audience in on a bit of information. And so a graphic appears: "Ozzie Smith has never hit a home run in 2,967 left-handed at-bats."

One pitch later, Ozzie smacks one over the right-field wall. And here he is, half sprinting, half dancing around the bases. (Having had, to that point, insufficient opportunity to develop a home run trot.)

The game is over. The ballpark is a madhouse, and as the Cardinals high-five Ozzie. . . Diamond is receiving similar treatment in the production truck for a clutch performance just as timely as Smith's.

The homer was high drama in any case, but for millions of viewers it was all the more incredible, all the more exciting and ultimately all the more memorable because the perfect stat, used at the perfect time, had placed it in context.

Next time you're watching a ballgame, and you nearly retch after being told that Cincinnati's Joe Plotz is "hitting .246...but only .229 against lefthanders. . . this despite hitting safely in three of the last five night games started by a lefty away from Riverfront Stadium." Just remember, would Ricky Diamond inflict that on you? Of course not.

Stats don't numb the brain. The people who misuse them do, and somewhere out there in the statistical wilderness there are a blessed few who don't just crunch numbers, they make sense of them. Pulling them together to make larger points, illuminating significant strengths and weaknesses. Offering objective evidence to support the game's verities. Putting the lie to the tired cliches that often pass for baseball wisdom.

The annual *STATS Baseball Scoreboard* is one of the best places to turn for some genuinely useful and just plain interesting baseball information. The research here is purposeful and meticulous. The topics lean more toward the accessible than the arcane. It may take more passion and persistence than most of us can muster to document the strategic efficacy of all the intentional walks issued in a season, but not to worry—the staff of happy zealots at *STATS Baseball Scoreboard* has done it for you. All you need do is soak it up.

When I'm broadcasting a game, I look for information that can be used in insightful and perhaps amazing ways. I am not interested in a deluge of numbers that if anything obscure the game—rather than enhancing our understanding and enjoyment of it.

With the information explosion in baseball, a broadcaster, writer, or dedicated fan must make discerning judgements. As I return to the baseball booth in 1994, the *STATS Baseball Scoreboard* is one place I'll be turning for fresh baseball perspectives, presented in a lively fashion.

As you know, I love baseball as much as anyone. So if you've bought this book, you've got a kindred spirit in Bob Costas. Still, I must draw the line someplace. So if you see me on a plane, please stop and chat. However, if you have a question about what moves to make with your rotisserie league team, ask the flight attendant.

INTRODUCTION

Hi, and welcome to *The STATS Baseball Scoreboard 1994*. This is our fifth edition, and our second for HarperPerennial. If you haven't seen this book before, we think you'll find it a one-of-a-kind publication, one that's both informative and fun to read. If you've read our book in the past, we think you'll find plenty of new items to intrigue you.

The format of the *Baseball Scoreboard* is pretty simple. Every year we present 101 essays, all based on a question-and-answer format, and all designed to unlock some of the mysteries of our favorite game. For instance, have you ever wondered whether rookies drop off "the second time around the league"? That's a question we address this year. Ever wondered how much the annual Gold Glove awards are influenced by a player's hitting stats? That's another one we look into. Ever wondered how the altitude in Colorado (and other places) affects the distance of a fly ball? You'll find a discussion of the subject in the *Baseball Scoreboard*, along with the pertinent figures.

To aid us in our investigations, we have one advantage available to no one else in the field: the STATS database. We have reporters at every major league game, recording not only what happens on every play, but on every pitch as well. That enables us to look into subjects like which players swing and miss the most, or which moundsmen throw the most pitches in a game. Our reporters also record the direction and distance of every batted ball, so we can tell you which fielders have the best "zone ratings" (outs recorded on balls hit into their fielding area), or which players hit the longest home runs of 1993. Last but not least, we have an extensive historical database, so we can look into subjects like whether there'll be another 300-game winner, or how the young Frank Thomas compares with the young Ted Williams.

We've divided the book into six sections: a section on teams, with an individual essay devoted to each major league club; a section of general baseball questions; one section each on hitting, pitching and fielding; and a section on major league managers. We try to add something new each year, and the managers section is our major new addition for 1994. We think you'll find our discussions on managerial tactics and strategy to be one of the best features of this year's book.

Like many of you, we are unabashed disciples of Bill James, and as usual, there are a number on essays which feature stats invented by Bill: runs created, secondary average, defensive efficiency ratings, and the like. We have even more "Bill James stats" than ever this year, as we delve into subjects like which managers have "quick or slow hooks" when removing a pitcher, and which active players are on track for the Hall of Fame.

We get into some pretty weighty subjects in this book, but don't worry: this is no unintelligible "stat book." Our discussions are down to earth, using a light touch, and often feature the informative and interesting graphics of our illustrator, John Grimwade. Our hope is that by the time you finish this book, you'll know a little more about the players, teams and managers in baseball, and about how the game is played. We also hope that the next time your favorite announcer says something like, "Good pitching always beats good hitting in the postseason," you'll have had access to some of the *real* information, so you can make your own judgement on the subject.

Have fun.

John Dewan and Don Zminda

I. TEAM QUESTIONS

BALTIMORE ORIOLES: IS THIS THE "GOLDEN AGE" FOR CATCHERS?

Orioles catcher Chris Hoiles isn't very well-known outside of Baltimore, but if he keeps playing like he did in 1993, he seems destined to become famous. Last year Hoiles batted .310, belted 29 homers and drove in 82 runs, despite the fact that he batted only 419 times.

We have another indicator of just how good Hoiles' season was. Hoiles had what we call a "3-4-5 season," meaning that he had a batting average over .300, an on-base average over .400, and a slugging average over .500—superior performances in three important categories. A "3-4-5 season" is an accomplishment for any player, but especially for a catcher. In fact, Hoiles was only the seventh catcher in history to accomplish the feat. Here's the complete list of catchers who have done it (minimum 400 plate appearances); Gabby Hartnett, Mickey Cochrane and Bill Dickey each did it three times:

Catchers with .300 Avg/.400 OBP/.500 Slg Seasons

Catcher	Year	Avg	OBP	Slg	HR	RBI
Bubbles Hargrave	1923	.333	.403	.521	10	78
Gabby Hartnett	1928	.302	.402	.523	14	57
Mickey Cochrane	1930	.357	.423	.526	10	85
Gabby Hartnett	1930	.339	.403	.630	37	122
Mickey Cochrane	1931	.349	.419	.553	17	89
Mickey Cochrane	1933	.322	.456	.515	15	60
Gabby Hartnett	1935	.344	.403	.545	13	91
Bill Dickey	1936	.362	.424	.617	22	107
Bill Dickey	1937	.332	.413	.570	29	133
Bill Dickey	1938	.313	.410	.568	27	115
Dick Dietz	1970	.300	.427	.515	22	107
Ted Simmons	1977	.318	.408	.500	21	95
Chris Hoiles	1993	.310	.408	.585	29	82

(Minimum 400 PA)

So Hoiles obviously had a superior season, but one would be hard-pressed to call it the best performance by a catcher in 1993. The Dodgers' Mike Piazza (.318-35-112), the Cubs' Rick Wilkins (.303-30-73), the Yankees' Mike Stanley (.305-26-84) and the Phillies' Darren Daulton (.257-24-105) all put up big numbers, and there were other good seasons from the likes of Chad Kreuter of the Tigers, Mike Macfarlane of the Royals, and several others. Hoiles was just one of many top performers at the position.

All those big seasons caused us to wonder where last year's catching crop stacked up in comparison with those of the past. So we chose the six best-hitting catchers from each season (minimum 400 plate appearances) and combined their figures, with on-base plus slugging average used as the criterion of performance. In some of the seasons, there were players who saw significant action at other positions aside from catcher; in those cases, we used their full-season totals, as long as they played the majority of their games behind the plate. Here are the best catchers'-hitting seasons of all time:

The Best Years for Catchers

Year	OBP +Slg	HR	RBI	Catchers
1993	.919	159	507	Daulton, Hoiles, Kreuter, Piazza, Stanley, Wilkins
1938	.876	90	498	Danning, Dickey, Ferrell, Lombardi, Pytlak, York
1977	.876	140	512	Bench, Carter, Ferguson, Fisk, Simmons, Tenace
1950	.875	133	481	Berra, Campanella, Cooper, Lollar, Seminick, Westrum
1970	.871	119	530	Bench, Dietz, Fosse, Munson, Sanguillen, Torre
1979	.865	120	490	Bench, Downing, Ferguson, Porter, Simmons, Tenace
1932	.859	77	451	Cochrane, Davis, Dickey, Ferrell, Hartnett, Lombardi
1956	.850	142	511	Bailey, Berra, Campanella, Lollar, Lopata, Triandos
1937	.847	81	485	Dickey, Phelps, Pytlak, Sewell, Todd, York
1931	.842	50	410	Cochrane, Davis, Dickey, Ferrell, Hartnett, Hogan
1975	.842	114	517	Bench, Munson, Porter, Sanguillen, Simmons, Tenace

(Best OBP+Slg—Top 6 catchers; minimum 400 PA)

We were right about 1993, and then some: in terms of production from the top six receivers, it was the best of all time, and by a good margin. It's a remarkable improvement in a short time; in 1988, the group of "top six" catchers combined for an OPS of .706 and had just 72 homers and 335 RBI. From a hitting standpoint, there's as much catching talent in the game today as at any time in history—and with top prospects like Javy Lopez and Carlos Delgado waiting in the wings, it could get even better. Hopefully, we'll get a break for a while from those tired old articles about "spoiled youth of today" who don't want to play this tough position!

A complete listing for this category can be found on page 246.

BOSTON RED SOX: CAN CLEMENS COME BACK?

Can Roger Clemens get back on track? The great righthander entered last season with a career record of 134-61, and he had won three straight American League ERA titles. But last year Clemens went 11-14, and his ERA rose by more than two runs to a career-high 4.46. Clemens' arm is said to be sound, and he's only 31. There's no reason to think he can't come back. Or is there?

To find the answer, we decided to look for pitchers whose careers roughly parallelled Clemens' to this point. That is:

1. They were between the ages of 29 and 31 (with age figured as of July 1 of each season).

2. They were superior pitchers, with at least 125 career wins (Clemens had 134 entering the 1993 season) and career ERAs under 3.50 (Clemens' was 2.80).

3. They had qualified for the ERA title during each of the previous three seasons, thus exhibiting no signs of arm trouble.

4. They ran into a sub-par season, with either 15-plus losses or an ERA of 4.00 or higher, while continuing to qualify for the ERA title.

The following pitchers had careers most parallel to Clemens prior to their off-seasons, in seasons since 1920. The "rest of career" totals include the sub-par year:

Pitcher	Year	Age	Prior Record			Sub-par Year			Rest of Career		
			W	L	ERA	W	L	ERA	W	L	ERA
Hooks Dauss	1921	31	138	113	2.96	10	15	4.33	84	69	3.93
Wilbur Cooper	1923	31	165	126	2.59	17	19	3.57	51	52	3.83
Burleigh Grimes	1925	31	139	108	3.24	12	19	5.03	131	104	3.84
Waite Hoyt	1929	29	155	99	3.43	10	9	4.23	82	83	3.82
Larry French	1938	30	138	112	3.48	10	19	3.81	59	59	3.37
Bob Feller	1948	29	158	83	2.92	19	15	3.57	108	79	3.70
Hal Newhouser	1949	29	170	119	2.84	15	13	4.33	37	31	4.20
Robin Roberts	1956	29	160	102	3.02	19	18	4.45	126	143	3.78
Don Drysdale	1966	29	164	118	2.96	13	16	3.42	45	48	2.92
Mel Stottlemyre	1972	30	128	98	3.28	14	18	3.22	36	41	3.22
Dave McNally	1972	29	135	69	3.15	13	17	2.95	49	50	3.44
Fergie Jenkins	1973	29	135	93	3.03	14	16	3.89	149	133	3.60
Vida Blue	1979	29	142	96	2.92	14	14	5.01	67	65	3.91

Not everyone here is a household name; you really have to know your baseball history to be aware of pitchers like Hooks Dauss and Wilbur Cooper. But you're probably familiar with most of the names on the list, since it includes several members of the Hall of Fame. Talent-wise, Clemens ranks with the very best on the list: Feller, Roberts, and Jenkins.

What do the numbers mean? Not all the seasons on the list were all that bad. Sometimes the pitchers continued to win; other times they maintained good ERAs. But there were definite signs of slippage in comparison to the numbers they'd been churning out. For instance, Dave McNally had gone 22-10, 20-7, 24-9 and 21-5 in the four seasons prior to his 13-17 year in 1972. He was still a good pitcher; he was no longer a great one.

There's a picture on the cover of an old *Baseball Digest* which sort of sums up what happened to most of these pitchers. It's from the winter of 1956-57, just following Robin Roberts' difficult '56 season. It shows Roberts sitting on the dugout steps, staring forlornly at the baseball he's gripping in his hand. The caption says, "Goodbye Fastball?" When a pitcher nears the age of 30, especially if he's been worked very hard, it's likely that he'll lose some velocity. That's not to imply that Clemens isn't still capable of throwing very, very hard. He can probably throw as hard as ever, much of the time. But he can't throw as hard inning after inning, 260 innings a year, as he once did. It's just part of growing older, and it requires some adjustment.

Some pitchers seem to make that adjustment better than others. While Feller, Roberts and Jenkins weren't as consistently good after this point in their careers as they were before it, they all won over 100 more games. Some of the others, though, wore out pretty quickly after this point, like McNally and Hal Newhouser; in several cases, their overworked arms simply gave out.

So Clemens' poor 1993 season simply can't be shrugged off by saying, "Every good pitcher has a bad year now and then." He's at an important transitional age for a pitcher, and he'll have to show he can make the transition. We still like his chances. As we noted a couple of years ago, Clemens' career numbers have been remarkably similar to Tom Seaver's at the same points in their careers. Despite his poor 1993 season, Clemens still compares very favorably with Tom Terrific:

	Age	W	L	IP	SO	BB
Seaver through 1975	30	168	96	2,447	2,099	656
Clemens through 1993	30	163	86	2,223	2,033	619

Seaver had his own sub-par season at around this point in his career, going 11-11 at age 29 in 1974. He recovered and went on to win more than 300 games. We can't guarantee that Clemens will win 300, but we do think he's an excellent candidate to make a strong comeback.

CALIFORNIA ANGELS: WOULD A BETTER RUNNING GAME GIVE THEM A BETTER CHANCE?

To understand how the Angels play the game, you have to know a little about Buck Rodgers' managerial history. The first time Rodgers piloted a club for a full season, his heavy-hitting 1981 Brewers finished 12th in the league in steals with only 39—a very low total even in that strike-shortened year. The '81 Brewers also had a terrible stolen base success rate, 52.0 percent. But they were also a good club, qualifying for that year's "division playoffs" with the best record in the American League East.

Rodgers was fired by the Brewers early in 1982, and in 1984 he went down to the minors to skipper the Cardinals' Triple-A farm club at Louisville. There he managed Vince Coleman, who stole 101 bases that year, along with some of the other speedsters in the St. Louis system. That experience—not his experience with the Brewers—has dominated the way he's managed ever since then. Since Rodgers returned to the majors as manager of the Montreal Expos in 1985, the only way to describe him would be as a "stolen base manager." In eight full seasons with the Expos and Angels—he was fired by Montreal early in 1991, and took over California later that year—his clubs have finished either first or second in the league in stolen bases five times, and never lower than fourth. The chart shows the results.

While the totals and league rankings since 1985 are impressive, there are two things wrong with the picture:

1. Rodgers' stolen base success rates have never been very good. Most statistical studies tell us that the break-even rate for stolen bases is about 65-67 percent,

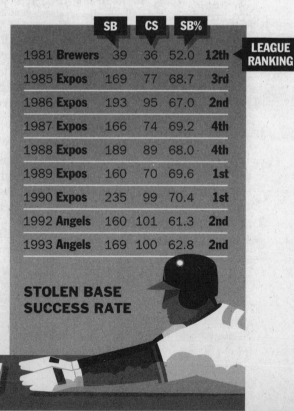

	SB	CS	SB%	LEAGUE RANKING
1981 **Brewers**	39	36	52.0	12th
1985 **Expos**	169	77	68.7	3rd
1986 **Expos**	193	95	67.0	2nd
1987 **Expos**	166	74	69.2	4th
1988 **Expos**	189	89	68.0	4th
1989 **Expos**	160	70	69.6	1st
1990 **Expos**	235	99	70.4	1st
1992 **Angels**	160	101	61.3	2nd
1993 **Angels**	169	100	62.8	2nd

STOLEN BASE SUCCESS RATE

meaning that if you're safe only two-thirds of the time, the damage caused by the caught stealings cancels out the benefits of the stolen bases. Even Rodgers' best clubs have been barely above that level, and his Angel teams have been well below it. No matter; Rodgers keeps sending them anyway.

2. The only Rodgers club which has qualified for postseason play is still the 1981 Brewers—the only one which didn't steal. With all those great basestealing clubs, he's won more than 85 games only once; the 1987 Expos won 91. Rodgers' defenders always say that he's had to compete with inferior talent, and that the stolen base is his most effective weapon. The part about lack of talent may be true to an extent, but there's also the way Rodgers *uses* his talent. Last year the Angels leadoff man for all but a handful of games was Luis Polonia; his number-two hitter was Chad Curtis. Rodgers had them running like crazy, and Polonia wound up tied for second in the league in stolen bases with 55, while Curtis was fifth with 48.

Why were they attempting to steal so often? To produce runs, by getting into scoring position for the club's power hitters. But again, there's something wrong with this picture. Polonia and Curtis were thrown out 24 times each, most in the league by plenty—Mark McLemore and Roberto Alomar, who tied for third, were tossed out only 15 times. As a result, the Angels weren't effective at all at getting players in scoring position for their "heart of the order." Here are the worst American League clubs in total plate appearances with men in scoring position for their 3-4-5 hitters:

Fewest Scoring Position PA for the "Heart of the Order"
American League—1993

Team	Tot
Orioles	591
Brewers	594
Rangers	596
Angels	598
Red Sox	609
AL Average	**634**

Of course, the caught stealings weren't the only reason why the Angels had so few men in scoring position. There was also the strategy of using the free-swinging Polonia as the leadoff man. Why did Rodgers have him batting leadoff? Because he's a "stolen base threat," a guy who "ignites the offense." Then why did he score only 75 runs?

We respect Buck Rodgers, but we'll have more respect for his "trying to win with inferior talent" when he stops putting inferior talent at the leadoff spot (we do like Chad Curtis). Isn't it time to admit that you can't steal your way to success—especially with guys who aren't good percentage stealers? Now that Polonia's back with the Yankees (where he's supposed to solve *their* leadoff problem), why doesn't Rodgers do something different, like look for a number-one hitter who can get on base?

A complete listing for this category can be found on page 247.

CHICAGO WHITE SOX: IS THOMAS THE NEW TED WILLIAMS?

Frank Thomas is a great young American League slugger whose biggest assets are his great power, his ability to hit for a high batting average, and his outstanding batting eye. Who does that remind you of? If you said Ted Williams, welcome to the club. Thomas is one of the few modern players whose stats can be compared to Williams without embarrassment.

So let's do it—not to see if Thomas looks better than Williams, because he won't, but to see how well he compares. The most useful comparison would be between the young Williams and the young Thomas. There are a couple of complications, however. For one thing, Williams made his debut on Opening Day, 1939, while Thomas started his career in the middle of a season, in August of 1990. If we compare Thomas' overall figures thus far with Williams' first three seasons, Ted will have fewer games and plate appearances. If we use Ted's first four seasons, he'll have too many. So let's compare Thomas (1990-93) with Williams (1939-42) using the Bill James tool called "seasonal notation," with the totals compiled per a Williams-era 154 games played. Since sacrifice flies were not counted during most of the Splinter's career, we'll use the simplest version of on-base percentage for each player, one which doesn't include sac flies:

Williams (1939-42) vs. Thomas (1990-93) per 154 games played

Player	AB	R	H	2B	3B	HR	RBI	BB	SO	Avg	OBP	Slg
Williams	553	142	197	41	9	33	135	130	52	.356	.481	.642
Thomas	543	104	174	36	2	30	111	121	89	.321	.446	.561

You can see the similarities, but Thomas comes out a decided second in the comparison. Williams bests him in every single category, and usually by a good margin. However, this system is a little unfair to Thomas, since Williams played in a generally higher-scoring era. Let's adjust each player's figures to the same environment, that of the 1993 American League:

Williams (1939-42) vs. Thomas (1990-93) per 154 games played (adjusted for 1993 American League context)

Player	AB	R	H	2B	3B	HR	RBI	BB	SO	Avg	OBP	Slg
Williams	553	142	196	42	6	39	137	117	87	.354	.468	.660
Thomas	544	110	182	38	2	32	118	122	94	.334	.453	.589

Using this type of comparison, the gap narrows in most categories. Interestingly, though, Williams' home run edge increases, as the early years of his career weren't as good for home runs as the early years of Thomas'. But Thomas is reasonably close in most categories, and ahead in walks. His performance in the comparison is especially impressive when you remember that the Williams figures include his legendary .406 season of 1941.

So we've established that Thomas is a great young hitter and comparable in many ways to Williams . . . but he's not as good, even when we even out the contexts they were playing in. We also can't forget that Williams made his debut at the tender age of 20; Thomas was 22 when he began his career with the White Sox. That tips the scales even more in Ted's favor. But one thing you might be wondering about is the "ballpark factor." Williams got to play at Fenway Park, a great park for batting average but not a good home run park for a left-handed hitter. Except for two months in 1990, Thomas has played in new Comiskey Park, a good one for hitters but not one with the reputation of the old Fenway. How do the players compare home and road? Here's how, restricting the Thomas numbers to the ones he's compiled at the new Comiskey:

	At Home			On the Road		
	Avg	Slg	Home Run Rate	Avg	Slg	Home Run Rate
Williams, 1939-42	.365	.639	1 per 18.6 AB	.347	.644	1 per 14.9 AB
Thomas, 1991-93	.333	.626	1 per 14.0 AB	.306	.503	1 per 22.8 AB

As it turns out, the new Comiskey helps Thomas more than Fenway helped Williams, in terms of batting average. And when it comes to home runs, Comiskey helps Thomas greatly, while Fenway hurt Williams.

Williams thus is even more the unquestioned king in this comparison, but that's what we expected. Think this about Frank Thomas: we compared him with a man generally regarded as one of the two greatest offensive performers of all time (along with Babe Ruth), and he doesn't disgrace himself. That's impressive.

CLEVELAND INDIANS: WILL THEIR NEW PARK BE THE GATEWAY TO SUCCESS?

For the first time in quite awhile, the Indians are feeling excited about their future. Not only does the Tribe have a number of good young players, but the club will have a brand new home. The new park, which was still unnamed as we went to press (Gateway Stadium was the likely name), will be the first new home for the Indians in 62 years.

Does a move into a new park create enthusiasm that spills over to the playing field? People have been espousing that theory since the early days of the century. To cite a few examples, the Pittsburgh Pirates (Forbes Field, 1909), Boston Red Sox (Fenway Park, 1912) and New York Yankees (1923, Yankee Stadium) all marked the first year in their new parks by winning the World Series.

But that was a long time ago, and if we really want to study the effects of a new park on a ballclub, it's better to examine data from more modern times. Let's start with the Giants' move to Candlestick Park in 1960, which was the first time a club had moved to a new park in the same metropolitan area since the Indians moved to Cleveland Stadium (then called Municipal Stadium) on a part-time basis in 1932. We won't consider clubs which moved to parks in new cities, since that's obviously a special situation. There are a few situations which we have to rule on:

1. In 1962, the Angels began sharing brand-new Dodger Stadium (which they called "Chavez Ravine") with the Dodgers—and had a great season. But the club was only a year old and had not established a real identity in its first park, Wrigley Field (the West Coast version). We won't count this as a move to a new park.

2. In 1966, the Angels moved from Dodger Stadium to Anaheim. L.A. is a great big freeway, and since the move was within driving distance, we'll consider it a move in the same metropolitan area.

3. In 1974-75, the Yankees shared Shea Stadium with the Mets while the new Yankee Stadium was being built. We won't count this, since it was coincidental and had nothing to do with the enthusiasm of moving to a new park.

4. In 1976, the Yanks moved back into the new Yankee Stadium. This had everything to do with the enthusiasm of a new park, and we'll count it.

5. Four clubs moved into new parks during the middle of a season: the Cardinals in 1966, the Reds and Pirates in 1970, and the Blue Jays in 1989. We will count all of those seasons as the first year in the new park.

With those ground rules established, we wind up with 16 park shifts in 33 years, from the Giants' move to Candlestick in 1960 to the Orioles shift to Camden Yards in 1992. The chart shows the clubs' composite record in the last year playing in their old park, and the composite record in the first year in their new parks. It also shows the number of first-place finishes in each venue.

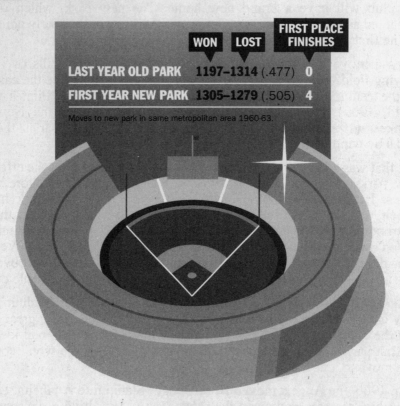

	WON	LOST	FIRST PLACE FINISHES
LAST YEAR OLD PARK	1197–1314 (.477)		0
FIRST YEAR NEW PARK	1305–1279 (.505)		4

Moves to new park in same metropolitan area 1960-63.

An Indians fan looking at these figures would have to feel pretty good. The average club increased its winning percentage by almost 30 points. That translates to a five-game improvement over a 162-game season. Projecting all strike-shortened and 154-game seasons to the current 162-game standard, the average record in the final year at the old park was 77-85; the average record in the first year in the new park was 82-80.

There's even more good news. Of the 16 clubs, 11 improved their won-lost percentage in the first year in the new park. Most of the drops were small (the biggest decline in performance was seven games by the 1991 White Sox), but many of the gains were big. The Orioles, for example, went from 67 wins in 1991 to 89 wins in 1992. The 1976 Yankees improved by 14 wins. The 1973 Royals improved by a dozen wins. The 1970 Reds improved by 13, though that is less significant since they didn't move to Riverfront Stadium until the end of June.

Best of all, four teams finished in first place in their first year in their new stadium: the 1970 Reds and Pirates, 1976 Yankees and 1989 Blue Jays. Three of those teams played at least part of the year in their old park, but if we can't count those, we ought to be allowed to count the 1967 Cardinals, who won the world title in their first full year in Busch Stadium, and the 1971 Pirates, who also won a world championship in their first full year at Three Rivers. There's also the 1962 Dodgers, who won 102 games and finished in a tie for first before losing to the Giants in a playoff.

The evidence seems pretty clear that the enthusiasm of a new park gives most clubs a boost, at least for the first year. That's good news for the Indians, a franchise which is long overdue for something good.

A complete listing for this category can be found on page 248.

DETROIT TIGERS: IS CECIL ABOUT TO SUFFER A POWER OUTAGE?

In 1990, Cecil Fielder joined the Tigers after a year in Japan. He became an instant hero—a folk hero, really—while belting 51 homers. Fielder has remained a major power source since then, but his home run totals have declined each year: from 51 to 44 to 35 to last year's 30.

Since Fielder has continued to drive in runs (thanks to Tony Phillips, et al), not too many people have noticed the home run decline. But Cecil turned 30 last September, and—in case you haven't noticed—he doesn't keep himself in the greatest physical shape. One thing we wondered was how unique this sort of steady home run decline is, and whether it's been a sign of future trouble.

The first answer is easy: this sort of decline has happened to many other hitters. We looked for players who had hit at least 40 home runs in the first year of a sequence, and then saw their home run totals decline for at least the next three straight seasons. It turned out that Fielder was the 27th player in history to suffer this kind of drop. Among the other members of the club were some of the greatest home run hitters of all time: Babe Ruth, Jimmie Foxx, Lou Gehrig, Willie Mays, Eddie Mathews, Ernie Banks, Willie McCovey, Harmon Killebrew, Willie Stargell, Henry Aaron. The Home Run Hall of Fame, practically. There were other good ones, too, like Orlando Cepeda, Frank Howard, and Jim Rice.

However, many of those players were fairly old when the decline began: for example, McCovey was 31, Killebrew 33, Ruth 35, Aaron 39. You can't really compare those situations with what's happened to Fielder, who was in an athlete's prime—his late 20s—when his dropoff began. So let's restrict the study to players who were closer in age to Fielder, say no older than 28 in the first year of the sequence. Including Fielder, 15 players fit that profile. Here are their totals for the years of the power drop, plus the next few seasons afterward:

Home Run Declines for 3+ Years After a 40-HR Season

Player	Age	Year	HR	HRs in Subsequent Seasons					
Jimmie Foxx	24	1932	58	48	44	36	41	36	50
Ralph Kiner	26	1949	54	47	42	37	35	22	18
Wally Post	25	1955	40	36	20	12	22	19	20
Willie Mays	24	1955	51	36	35	29	34	29	40
Eddie Mathews	23	1955	41	37	32	31	46	39	32
Ernie Banks	27	1958	47	45	41	29	37	18	23
Eddie Mathews	27	1959	46	39	32	29	23	23	32

Home Run Declines for 3+ Years After a 40-HR Season

Player	Age	Year	HR	HRs in Subsequent Seasons					
Norm Cash	26	1961	41	39	26	23	30	32	22
Orlando Cepeda	23	1961	46	35	34	31	1	20	25
Rico Petrocelli	26	1969	40	29	28	15	13	15	7
Darrell Evans	26	1973	41	25	22	11	17	20	17
George Foster	28	1977	52	40	30	25	22	13	28
Jim Rice	25	1978	46	39	24	17	24	39	28
Kevin Mitchell	27	1989	47	35	27	9	19	–	–
Cecil Fielder	26	1990	51	44	35	30	–	–	–

(Age 28 or younger in first season)

There's still a lot of great players on the list, including Foxx, Mays, Mathews (twice) and Banks. Three of them came back from their falloff to return to the 40 home run level, and one of those (Jimmie Foxx) returned to the 50 level. That's good news for Fielder fans.

However, there were a number of players who suffered this kind of falloff, and never were able to return to anywhere near their previous level. Sometimes that first big season was simply a fluke—Rico Petrocelli is the best example—and the player couldn't be expected to maintain that level of performance. In other cases, injuries were to blame: Orlando Cepeda, for instance, was plagued by bad knees, and back problems eventually ended Ralph Kiner's career. Sometimes the drop was a mystery, as in the case of George Foster.

Fielder hasn't been injured, but he *is* chronically out of shape, and that can lead to injuries or shorten a player's career. You can see some parallels between him and Kevin Mitchell, another overweight player whose production has suffered a big drop . . . often simply because he's out of the lineup.

That hasn't happened thus far to Fielder, who's been remarkably durable. He may be fat, but he's not particularly old, and by itself, his home run drop is not something that should cause major concern. Other players in the same situation have come back strong. Fielder may not hit 50 home runs again, but a return to 35 or more is a good possibility. He should remain a productive power hitter for the next couple of years, at least. In his condition, we can't predict he'll go on for years, but we *don't* think his power is about to go out.

KANSAS CITY ROYALS: WHAT ARE TURF FIELDS REALLY LIKE?

This will be the last season that Kauffman Stadium in Kansas City will have artificial turf. As Chicagoans and fans of Dick Allen, we've always agreed with the Allen maxim, "If a horse can't eat it, I don't want to play on it." (Although as we recall, sometimes Allen didn't want to play on grass, either.) Of course, they *do* play on it, and they've been playing on it in Kansas City for over 20 years. We thought this would be a good time to talk about turf fields in general, and the turf field at Kauffman Stadium in particular. Here's a turf field Q&A:

1. Do turf fields raise batting averages? When turf fields started becoming common in the early 1970s, we heard how, with the way the ball scooted through the infield, turf parks would "raise batting averages 10 or 15 points." Or more. People still say this; for instance, last year we got a call from a writer who kept insisting John Olerud was hitting over .400 "because of all the turf hits he gets in Toronto"—this despite the fact that Olerud was hitting much better on the road than he was at home. Last year the major league average in games on grass (.265) was a point higher than the average on turf (.264). Kauffman Stadium has been a good one for hitters over the years, but over the last three campaigns, it's increased batting averages by only two percent.

2. Do groundball pitchers have problems on turf? The ball scooting through the infield is supposed to be big trouble for groundball pitchers, but over the last five seasons, groundballers have had a .250 opponents average on grass, .250 on turf. The figures fluctuate from year to year, but there's no reason to think that groundballers have any special handicap on turf.

3. Do turf fields reduce errors? The "true hops" on turf fields are supposed to reduce the error rate, and in general they do. According to our ballpark indexes, which are based on the last three seasons unless a park has changed configuration, the error rate for turf teams was nine percent lower when they were playing at home. As we discuss in another essay, Kauffman Stadium has been a major exception. Over the last three years, the Royals and their opponents have committed 260 infield errors in Kansas City road games, 299 in Kansas City home games—15 percent more. Kauffman Stadium had by far the highest error rate among turf stadiums.

4. Do turf stadiums increase the number of doubles? The ball is supposed to scoot into the gaps on a turf field, with routine singles becoming doubles. In general, this particular stereotype is true. According to our park indexes, the doubles rate for turf teams has been 10 percent higher at home than it's been in their road games. Kauffman Stadium has been one of the premier doubles parks, with a doubles rate 18 percent higher than in Royals road games.

5. Do turf stadiums increase the number of triples? According to the park indexes, the triples rate for turf teams has been 13 percent higher at home than on the road. However, this one varies greatly from park to park. Two of the turf stadiums—Riverfront in Cincinnati and the Kingdome in Seattle—are terrible parks to hit a triple in. Others are above-average, and none is more above-average than Kauffman Stadium. For the 1991-93 period, the Royals and their opponents hit 142 triples at Kauffman, only 74 in Royals road games. The triples index of 187 for the Kansas City park was easily the highest among turf parks, and the second-highest overall to Mile High Stadium in Denver. Little wonder that the active career leaders at the end of the 1993 season were long-time Royals Willie Wilson (a Cub last year) and George Brett.

6. Are most turf stadiums poor home runs parks? What's plastic grass got to do with hitting a home run? Nothing, but artificial turf parks have been stereotyped as big stadiums where the double and triple are king, and the home run is hard to come by. In general, most turf stadiums *are* difficult home run parks, but as with the triples rate, it varies greatly from park to park. Two turf stadiums are very good for home runs, Riverfront Stadium and SkyDome. The rest are below-average, none more so than Kauffman Stadium, where the park index is a deadball-era 64. Over the last three seasons, the Royals and their opponents have hit 382 homers in Kaycee road games, only 251 in Kansas City home games.

While we won't miss the plastic grass at Kauffman, this has been a special park, one which has produced its own unique brand of ball. Word is that, along with ripping up the turf, the Royals will also reduce the dimensions of the park. We hope that, whatever they do, they won't destroy the park's special characteristic as a good park for hitters, without being a good park for home runs. That would be a pity.

A complete listing for this category can be found on page 249.

MILWAUKEE BREWERS: IS A GOOD SECOND HALF A GOOD SIGN FOR A ROOKIE?

Considering the sort of buildup people have given them, Dave Nilsson and John Jaha ought to be stars by now. Instead, each has been considered a bit of disappointment. However, the young Brewer players have shared one trait thus far in their major league careers: strong finishes. As a rookie in 1992, Nilsson hit a solid .281 after the All-Star break; then in 1993, he recovered from some early-season injuries with another nice finish. Jaha, who came up in July of 1992, wasn't technically a rookie last year, as he was three at-bats over the 130 at-bat limit in '92, but he was a rookie in everything but name. Like Nilsson, he recovered from a very slow start. Jaha hit 14 homers after the All-Star break to wind up with 19 for the season.

Those strong finishes caused us to wonder whether it's a good sign when a rookie has a weak first half, but then recovers to have a strong finish. Going back to 1988, we looked for rookies who met the following standards:

1. They batted at least 50 times during each half of the season, and at least 150 over the season as a whole.

2. They had poor first-half numbers: their on-base and slugging averages, combined, had to be less than .675, and their batting averages had to be less than .250.

3. They rebounded after the All-Star break with an OBP+SLG at least 15 percent better than their first-half mark, and a minimum second-half batting average of at least .270.

We found a total of 19 players who met those standards during the six seasons in question. As you can see, it's a very impressive list:

Rebounding Rookies, 1988-93

Player, Year	First Half			Second Half		
	Avg	OBP	Slg	Avg	OBP	Slg
Roberto Alomar, 1988	.237	.279	.342	.296	.375	.423
Carlos Baerga, 1990	.207	.248	.320	.309	.347	.463
Derek Bell, 1992	.189	.282	.289	.310	.380	.437
Steve Finley, 1989	.210	.270	.306	.301	.337	.333
Joe Girardi, 1989	.211	.243	.254	.279	.351	.395
Scott Hemond, 1993	.197	.293	.258	.282	.379	.483
Carlos Hernandez, 1992	.248	.316	.267	.278	.316	.431
Darrin Jackson, 1988	.248	.259	.389	.293	.329	.547

Rebounding Rookies, 1988-93

Player, Year	First Half			Second Half		
	Avg	OBP	Slg	Avg	OBP	Slg
Gregg Jefferies, 1989	.230	.284	.318	.287	.345	.470
Felix Jose, 1990	.243	.278	.349	.283	.337	.414
Carlos Martinez, 1989	.248	.296	.347	.321	.358	.430
Derrick May, 1992	.243	.280	.329	.296	.327	.407
Joey Meyer, 1988	.234	.261	.380	.284	.348	.447
Dave Nilsson, 1992	.200	.238	.320	.281	.395	.406
Tom Pagnozzi, 1988	.244	.287	.305	.310	.342	.345
Jody Reed, 1988	.237	.333	.333	.314	.399	.392
Scott Servais, 1992	.200	.262	.242	.294	.341	.341
Luis Sojo, 1991	.228	.263	.287	.285	.324	.363
Walt Weiss, 1988	.232	.291	.299	.273	.339	.348

There are many fine players on this list: Roberto Alomar, Carlos Baerga, Derek Bell, Steve Finley, Gregg Jefferies, Felix Jose, Tom Pagnozzi, Jody Reed. . . none of whom would have been earmarked as stars off their first-half rookie performances. Almost everyone has made at least some sort of major league impact, and shown some flashes of stardom. The only exceptions would be Carlos Hernandez, who hasn't received much playing time thus far; Scott Hemond, a 1993 rookie; Luis Sojo, who's had injury problems, and Joey Meyer, perhaps the only real dud, who played (naturally) for the Brewers.

For rookie-watchers, this has major implications: a player with a good second half deserves watching, whatever his overall figures look like. For Brewer-watchers, this has other implications: Nilsson and Jaha (who would have made this list, if not for those three at-bats) may turn out to be the real thing after all. Hopefully, they won't be exceptions to the group, like Joey Meyer.

A complete listing for this category can be found on page 251.

MINNESOTA TWINS: WILL KIRBY REACH 3,000?

The Twins had a pretty depressing season in 1993, and we hate being depressed, so we thought we'd talk about Dave Winfield and Kirby Puckett. Doesn't that cheer you up already? On September 16th, Winfield singled off Oakland's Dennis Eckersley for the 3,000th hit of his major league career. Puckett, who scored from third on that single, is still a long way from 3,000, but he appears to be on the right track. After less than a decade in the majors (he made his debut on May 8, 1984), Puckett has already amassed 1,996 hits.

Will Kirby eventually join Winfield in the 3,000-hit club? To estimate his chances, we'll use the old Bill James tool known as "The Favorite Toy." This is a mathematical projection of a player's chances to reach milestones like 3,000 hits or 500 home runs. The formula is a little complex (it's carried in the *1991 Scoreboard*, which is still available from us), but The Favorite Toy starts with a player's established levels of performance over the last couple of seasons. It then factors in his age, and estimates his chance of reaching the particular goal before the end of his career.

According to The Favorite Toy, the following players have a better than 10 percent chance to reach the 3,000 hit milestone:

		Chances for 3,000 Hits		
Player	Opening Day Age	Current Total	Projected Total	Chance
Eddie Murray	38.1	2,820	3,060	83.3
Kirby Puckett	33.1	1,996	2,806	30.7
Roberto Alomar	26.2	1,054	2,601	29.5
Ken Griffey Jr	24.4	832	2,500	26.9
Carlos Baerga	25.4	657	2,380	23.5
Cal Ripken	33.6	2,087	2,742	21.7
Ruben Sierra	28.5	1,307	2,432	16.5
Tony Gwynn	33.9	2,039	2,663	14.9
Don Mattingly	33.0	1,908	2,612	14.4
Travis Fryman	25.0	570	2,127	14.1
Gregg Jefferies	26.7	830	2,208	13.5
Frank Thomas	25.9	600	2,114	13.1
Paul Molitor	37.6	2,492	2,802	11.0

Puckett, as you can see, ranks second on the projection list to Cleveland's Eddie Murray, who's only 180 hits away from the goal. While Kirby's 30 percent chance seems low, The Favorite Toy takes into account that he'll be 33 years old at the start of this season; that means he'll need to remain productive until he's in his late 30s, which is difficult for any player. The longer he stays healthy and productive, the better his chances will be. Our estimate of Puckett's chances to reach 3,000 have been going up; in 1992, we gave him only a 22 percent chance.

Before we leave The Favorite Toy, we'll make a couple of comments. The first is that there's a number of very good young players on the list, headed by Roberto Alomar, Ken Griffey Jr. and Carlos Baerga. The Favorite Toy estimates that all three have a one-or-two percent chance to reach 4,000 hits—slim, but possible. There's also a good *old* player on the list in Toronto's Paul Molitor. Nearly 38, Molitor needs a couple more good seasons to have a realistic chance at 3,000. But the way he's playing, don't count him out.

Let's return to Puckett. Another way to estimate his chance to reach 3,000 is to compare his progress with the players who, like Winfield, wound up achieving the milestone. Puckett was 32 last season; here's how his hit total compares with the 3,000 hit men at the same age (age figured as of July 1 of a given season):

Hits Through Age 32—3,000 Hit Club, Plus Kirby

Player	Hits thru Age 32	Career Total	Player	Hits thru Age 32	Career Total
Pete Rose	2,152	4,256	George Brett	1,967	3,154
Ty Cobb	2,714	4,190	Paul Waner	2,036	3,152
Hank Aaron	2,434	3,771	Robin Yount	2,407	3,142
Stan Musial	2,223	3,630	Rod Carew	2,085	3,053
Tris Speaker	2,233	3,515	Lou Brock	1,808	3,023
Carl Yastrzemski	1,952	3,419	Dave Winfield	1,761	3,014
Honus Wagner	1,746	3,415	Al Kaline	2,228	3,007
Eddie Collins	1,978	3,310	Rob. Clemente	2,238	3,000
Willie Mays	2,033	3,283	Kirby Puckett	1,996	?
Nap Lajoie	1,909	3,242			

In case you're wondering about Cap Anson, our encyclopedia credits him with only 2,995 lifetime hits. (Sorry, Cap.) As for the others, Puckett has more hits at this point in his career than seven of the 18. However, many of the rest, especially the top five, wound up with a lot *more* than 3,000 hits, meaning that Kirby's in good shape. Puckett will have to watch his conditioning, but given that he's been injury-free during his career (he's never been on the disabled list), we like his chances.

NEW YORK YANKEES: IS YANKEE STADIUM "THE HOUSE THAT FORD BUILT"?

When the Yankees were winning pennants on an annual basis 30 or 40 years ago, their pitching ace was lefthander Whitey Ford. One of the best lefties in major league history, Ford still holds the all-time record for career winning percentage (200 or more decisions) with a mark of .690. But good as he was, Whitey was only continuing a tradition of great Yankee lefties, which began with Herb Pennock in the 1920s, continued with Lefty Gomez in the 1930s, and went on after Ford with Ron Guidry in the 1970s. Over the years, championship Yankee clubs have also had such left-handed stars as Ed Lopat and Tommy John, and lefty relief aces like Joe Page, Luis Arroyo and Sparky Lyle.

For someone pitching in the original Yankee Stadium, being left-handed was a major advantage. Because of the deep power alleys in left and left-center, a southpaw could give up a 430-foot drive, yet still record an out. The dimensions at the new Stadium, which opened in 1976, were a little less extreme, but they still worked considerably to a lefthanders' advantage.

However, the dimensions have changed since the new park opened. In its current configuration, the power alleys in left-center are much closer to the plate than in the past: it's currently 379 feet to the bullpen gate in short left-center field, vs. 387 feet in 1976 and a distant 402 feet to the same point in the old Stadium. To straightaway left center, it's now 399 feet, vs. 430 in 1976 (the famed "Death Valley") and an all-but-impossible 457 feet in the old park.

Given such sweeping changes, it's logical to ask whether the park still favors left-handed pitchers the way it once did. This is of particular interest to Yankee fans, since the club made a heavy investment a year ago by trading for lefty starter Jim Abbott, and signing southpaw free agent Jimmy Key.

To measure how the current park affects lefties, we bring out our old familiar tool, the "park factor." What we'll do is to measure the ERAs of all lefty pitchers (both clubs) in a team's home park, and compare that to lefties' ERAs in the club's road games. The chart on the following page shows the best and worst parks for a lefthander. A grade of 100 indicates a neutral park for a lefty; the farther the index is under 100, the more it favors a left-handed pitcher.

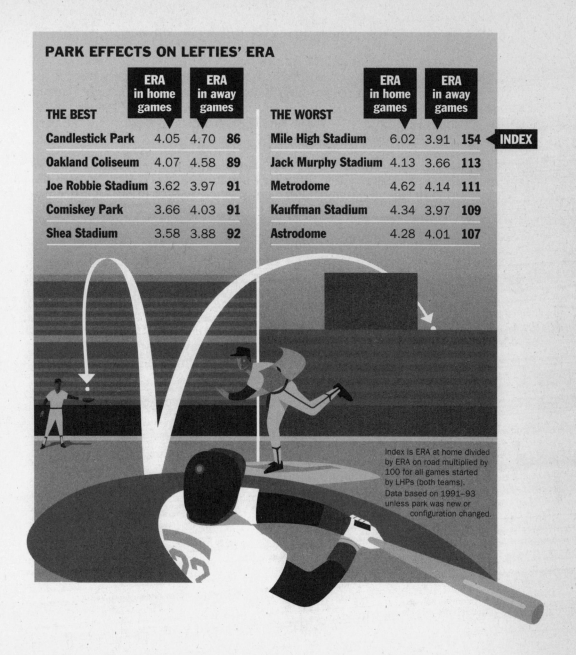

PARK EFFECTS ON LEFTIES' ERA

THE BEST	ERA in home games	ERA in away games		THE WORST	ERA in home games	ERA in away games	
Candlestick Park	4.05	4.70	86	Mile High Stadium	6.02	3.91	154 ◄ INDEX
Oakland Coliseum	4.07	4.58	89	Jack Murphy Stadium	4.13	3.66	113
Joe Robbie Stadium	3.62	3.97	91	Metrodome	4.62	4.14	111
Comiskey Park	3.66	4.03	91	Kauffman Stadium	4.34	3.97	109
Shea Stadium	3.58	3.88	92	Astrodome	4.28	4.01	107

Index is ERA at home divided by ERA on road multiplied by 100 for all games started by LHPs (both teams).
Data based on 1991–93 unless park was new or configuration changed.

As you can see, there are some very good parks for a lefty in the majors: Candlestick Park, the Oakland Coliseum, Comiskey Park and Joe Robbie Stadium head the list. The worst, by far, is Mile High Stadium in Denver, which is paradise for a right-handed hitter.

But where is Yankee Stadium? Smack dab in the middle, with an index of 100. Over the last three years, the Stadium has been completely neutral for lefties, neither helping nor hurting them. The park index for right-handed pitchers, which is included in the appendix, rates Yankee Stadium at 99, again about as neutral as you can get. Thus, the data indicates that the park favors neither lefties nor righties.

However, there is one good sign for Yankee rooters. While the park was neutral for lefties as a whole, both Key and Abbott had better ERAs at the Stadium last year than they did on the road, with Abbott significantly better:

	Home			Road		
	W	L	ERA	W	L	ERA
Key	8	2	2.75	10	4	3.20
Abbott	8	6	3.12	3	8	5.75

It's possible that Key and Abbott know how to use the Stadium better than most pitchers, and that they'll thrive there the way Ford and company did. But the odds are against it. Without "Death Valley," Yankee Stadium doesn't help a lefthander the way the old park did.

A complete listing for this category can be found on page 252.

OAKLAND ATHLETICS: WOULD AN ACROSS-THE-BAY RIVALRY BOOST ATTENDANCE?

Every time major league attendance or television ratings go down a little, someone will say, "What baseball needs is inter-league play." And then the speaker will talk glowingly about how "natural" rivalries like Cubs/White Sox, Dodgers/Angels and Mets/Yankees would be certain to arouse fan interest. A Bay Area Athletics/Giants rivalry, of course, would be one of the most appealing of all.

Of course, inter-league play would involve a lot more than those few appealing match-ups. But before we discuss some of the problems, let's test the general premise, which is that natural rivalries boost attendance. If that's the case, then attendance also ought to go up when appealing intra-league rivals battle each other. We picked out five of the best—Dodgers/Giants, Red Sox/Yankees, Cubs/Cardinals, Phillies/Pirates and White Sox/Brewers—and measured what happened to attendance in all games between the rivals since 1987. The chart shows the results.

Average Home Attendance (1987-93)

Home	Road	vs Rival	vs Rest of League	Avg Increase	Pct Increase
Dodgers	Giants	40,684	36,294	4,390	12.1%
Giants	Dodgers	35,459	23,605	11,854	50.2%
Red Sox	Yankees	33,753	30,363	3,390	11.2%
Yankees	Red Sox	36,652	26,749	9,903	37.0%
Cubs	Cardinals	29,289	28,206	1,083	3.8%
Cardinals	Cubs	37,203	33,819	3,384	10.0%
Phillies	Pirates	27,823	26,976	847	3.1%
Pirates	Phillies	21,458	21,151	308	1.5%
White Sox	Brewers	26,975	24,036	2,939	12.2%
Brewers	White Sox	28,738	21,830	6,908	31.6%

All the rivalries appeared to increase attendance at least a little, but as you can see, some rivalries create a lot more interest than others do. The Dodgers/Giants, Red Sox/Yankees and White Sox/Brewers rivalries all boosted attendance by at least 10 percent in each city. But the Cubs/Cardinals match-ups had less of an impact on attendance, especially in Chicago, and the Phillies/Pirates games—supposedly the sort of "dream match-up" that inter-league play would make possible—hardly increased attendance at all. We also checked the Phillies/Mets rivalry, because several Phillies fans told us it was an intense one. From the Philadelphia point of view, they're right; attendance at Veterans Stadium went up 22.5% for Mets games. But the Phils were certainly no draw in New York—attendance actually dropped four percent when the Phillies were in town.

The San Francisco and Milwaukee figures—way up when the Dodgers and White Sox, respectively, came to town—seem to support the notion that inter-league play would help the "have-nots," who need the boost of a natural rivalry in order to fill their stadiums. It's obvious that a club like the Giants, struggling to fill their stadium during most of this period, needed the boost they got from having their natural rival come to town. So inter-league match-ups against each other would have special appeal to both the A's and Giants.

That's great, but how many rivalries actually have such a big appeal? The Phillies/Pirates numbers are instructive; fans in Pittsburgh don't seem to have the same emotions about Philadelphia that fans in San Francisco have about Los Angeles. Some of these inter-league rivalries would click, but many wouldn't. And we're not the first to ask this practical question: who's the "natural rival" of the Seattle Mariners, anyway?

The other argument that inter-league proponents make—the one which says that fans in Seattle would flock to see Barry Bonds and other National League stars—is unproven, and has a built-in down side. If the Mariners are playing the Giants, they're *not* playing one of the American League clubs in their division, maybe a club that creates one of the most intense kind of rivalries: a battle for a championship. And the Mariners would also have to visit San Francisco, which might mean one less Dodger/Giant game. How's that going to boost attendance? Even an A's/Giants game, appealing as it would be, might deprive Giants fans of a game against the Dodgers.

All in all, it's hard to see how inter-league play would have much overall positive effect on attendance. There's just not enough of those Dodgers/Giants-type rivalries to exploit . . . and as we say, for every appealing game you create, you might be giving up another. The data we've presented, though, suggests that the really good match-ups like A's vs. Giants *would* create a lot of interest. For that reason, the idea of inter-league play will always have some appeal.

SEATTLE MARINERS: HOW IMPORTANT IS A GREAT CLOSER?

The Mariners were still hoping they could come back to win the AL West last August when they suffered a disaster: ace closer Norm Charlton went out for the season with a serious arm injury. Many thought the M's season—and perhaps their hopes for 1994—ended right there. After all, the conventional wisdom says, "you can't win without a great closer."

Or can you? This is one of those traditional statements that's repeated so many times that no one questions it; it's true because everyone says it is. If you've seen the way we work, you know that we're skeptical about "conventional wisdom." We like to examine the evidence before reaching *any* kind of conclusion.

So, let's look at some figures on closers. The average American League club converted 68 percent of its save opportunities last year. The club with the best rate, the White Sox, converted 83 percent of its opportunities; the one with the worst, the Brewers, converted only 56 percent. Here are the figures:

American League Relief Staffs—1993

	Saves	Opp	Pct
White Sox (best)	48	58	.828
Brewers (worst)	29	52	.558
League Average	42	62	.677

Let's do some simple arithmetic. Say the White Sox hadn't had such a fine bullpen. If their relievers had converted saves at the rate the average club did, the Sox would have only 39 saves instead of 48—nine fewer. If their staff had been as bad as Milwaukee's, they would have recorded *16* fewer saves. That would have given them 16 fewer wins, and only 78 victories instead of 94 . . . wouldn't it?

No, it wouldn't. This kind of approach is deceptive, for a couple of reasons. One is that many save opportunities go to middle relievers, not closers, coming as early as the sixth inning. This particularly applies to the Mariners, who had one of the league's worst save percentages last year (.640). Most of the blown saves were the fault of the M's shaky middle relief corps, not Charlton or the man who got most of the save opportunities after his injury, Ted Power:

	Saves	Opp	Pct
Charlton and Power	31	36	.861
Other relievers	10	28	.357

As we point out in the essay on save-plus-hold percentage, one of the Mariner middle men, Jeff Nelson, had only one save in 11 opportunities last year. But while his failures were costly, Nelson wasn't a closer; he was the last pitcher on the mound in only 13 of his 71 appearances.

A better way to look at the question is to compare a club which had a good closer with one that didn't. The major league closer with the best save percentage last year was the Giants' Rod Beck, who converted 48 of 52 opportunities for 92 percent. The worst regular closer—how the mighty have fallen!—was Cincinnati's Rob Dibble, who converted 19 of 28 for a 68 percent conversion rate. If Beck had been as ineffective as Dibble, he would have notched only 35 saves. That would mean 13 fewer victories for the Giants . . . wouldn't it?

Again, no it wouldn't. For one thing, a blown save isn't an automatic loss, as teams frequently come back to win the game anyway. A 1992 study we performed showed that, even when clubs blew saves in the ninth inning or later—closer's territory—they still wound up winning the game about one-fourth of the time. So make that 10 fewer victories for the Giants instead of 13. There's also the fact that no club would give 52 save opportunities to someone with a conversion rate as poor as Dibble's; Beck got all those chances simply because he was so good. Clubs with poor closers try to contain the damage by letting their starters and middle men work a little longer, or they try to find someone better. In a case like the hypothetical situation of the Giants, it's reasonable to think that would make a difference of another victory or two.

Summing up, the difference between a club with a great closer and a club with a poor one—or no real closer at all—is probably on the magnitude of six to eight victories over the course of a season. That's the difference between first and second place in most years. A top closer *is* important, especially in a tight pennant race. But by the same token, an average closer will only cost a team a few wins, so it's certainly possible to take a pennant *without* a top closer.

Oddly enough, the Mariners fared far better without Charlton last year than anyone had a right to expect. Charlton had converted 18 of 21 opportunities, 86 percent, before going down. His stop-gap replacement, the ancient Ted Power, converted 13 of 15 for 87 percent. There's no way that Power could be expected to perform like that over a full season. Finding an adequate replacement for Charlton, who's not being counted on for 1994, will be necessary if the Mariners expect to win the West.

A complete listing for this category can be found on page 254.

TEXAS RANGERS: CAN GONZALEZ (AND GRIFFEY) THREATEN AARON'S HOME RUN RECORD?

Last year Juan Gonzalez won his second straight American League home run crown, belting 46. He barely nosed out Seattle's Ken Griffey, who hit 45. That figures to be the first of many battles for the home run crown between these two exciting young sluggers. Amazingly, neither of them turned 24 until after the 1993 season was over.

Gonzalez and Griffey are so good at such a young age that it's logical to wonder how many home runs they'll hit before they're through. One tool we like to use is Bill James' "Favorite Toy." As we explained in the Minnesota essay, this is a formula which uses age and past performance to speculate what chances players have to achieve goals like 3,000 hits or 500 home runs.

The Twins essay lists the players with the best chances for 3,000 hits. The chart here shows the ones with the best chance at 500 home runs. Not surprisingly, the leaders are Gonzalez and Griffey. What *is* surprising is what a good chance the formula gives them to reach the goal: better than 50/50 for Gonzalez, and a solid 40 percent for Griffey. When we ran this chart a year ago, no player was given more than a 36 percent chance.

If you're wondering why The Favorite Toy gives Gonzalez a better chance than Griffey, it's because he's shown more consistency, with two-straight 40-home run seasons; until last year, Griffey had never hit more than 27. But obviously, both hitters have at least some chance to hit many more than 500 home runs. How much chance? The Toy shows four players with a better than five percent chance at 600: Gonzalez (31.4 percent), Griffey (20.5), Barry Bonds (13.0), and Frank Thomas (7.9).

	AGE	CHANCE	HOME RUNS
Juan Gonzalez	24	53%	121
Ken Griffey Jr.	24	40%	132
Barry Bonds	29	36%	222
Dave Winfield	42	26%	453
Fred McGriff	30	25%	228
Frank Thomas	25	23%	104
Albert Belle	27	16%	108

How about 700 home runs—a level reached only by Henry Aaron and Babe Ruth? Both Gonzalez and Griffey are long shots, but the projection system, which usually doesn't give anyone more than a one percent chance at reaching that level, lists Gonzalez with a 17 percent chance at 700, and Griffey an eight percent chance. Dare we talk about Aaron's seemingly-unbreakable record of 755 homers? We do. The Favorite Toy, which had never given anyone even a one percent chance at the record during our past studies over three years, has both Gonzalez and Griffey on the map, at least:

Chances for 756 Home Runs

Batter	Chance
Juan Gonzalez	11.4%
Ken Griffey Jr.	2.9%

The Favorite Toy even gives Gonzalez a seven percent chance to hit 800 homers!

Interesting stuff, and fun to speculate about; that's why Bill called it a "toy." But pure mathematics apart, do either Gonzalez or Griffey have a realistic chance to hit 500, 600 . . . or more? And which one has the better chance, looking at factors that don't show up in the numbers? One thing that will bring the discussion to a more realistic level is a list of all the players who have accomplished what Griffey and Gonzalez have done—that is, hit at least 120 homers by age 24. "Age" here is figured as of July 1 of a given season:

120+ Home Runs by Age 24

Player	HR by Age 24	Career Total	Player	HR by Age 24	Career Total
Eddie Mathews	190	512	Joe DiMaggio	137	361
Mel Ott	176	511	Hal Trosky	136	228
Jimmie Foxx	174	534	Ken Griffey Jr.*	132	132
Mickey Mantle	173	536	Boog Powell	130	339
Frank Robinson	165	586	Jose Canseco*	128	245
Orlando Cepeda	157	379	Ted Williams	127	521
Johnny Bench	154	389	Al Kaline	125	399
Hank Aaron	140	755	Tony Conigliaro	124	166
Bob Horner	138	218	Juan Gonzalez*	121	121

* Active player

Lots of players have hit more home runs than Gonzalez and Griffey at the same age, and some have hit *a lot more*. Will Gonzalez and Griffey be like Aaron, who went on and on, or like Eddie Mathews and Jimmie Foxx, who faded out as great sluggers when they were in their early 30s? Hopefully they'll be more fortunate than Hal Trosky and Tony Conigliaro, whose careers were derailed by injuries.

Looking at the list, it's not easy to pick out Aaron as the man who would set the record; in his early days with the Braves, he was decidedly second-fiddle to Mathews as a home run hitter. Compared to Mathews, Aaron was not overly imposing physically, and neither was Willie Mays, who, due to time in the military, had only 116 homers by this age. Frank Robinson didn't look especially muscular, either. Many people feel that a looser body type like theirs is better suited for the long haul than a muscular body like Foxx' or Orlando Cepeda's. Gonzalez and Griffey are both 6-3 and over 200 pounds; but while their "program weights" are only five pounds apart, Gonzalez is the more muscular, and likely to get even bigger. That could lead to physical problems in the future. Gonzalez is already having back problems, and a bad back can be deadly to a slugger: look at Darryl Strawberry, or for those who remember the 1950s, Ralph Kiner.

Griffey is also a better all-around athlete than Gonzalez, a .300 hitter, a fast runner, and a Gold Glove center fielder. Built to last, we think, more than Gonzalez is. Mathematical projections aside, we think Griffey is the better bet to have a long career, and hit 600 home runs or more. That's not to knock Gonzalez, a tremendous player. He and Griffey should be waging some epic duels over the next few seasons.

A complete listing for this category can be found on page 255 .

TORONTO BLUE JAYS: HOW TOUGH WILL IT BE TO MAKE IT THREE?

How times have changed. Remember a few years ago, when the Toronto Blue Jays were known to some as the "Blow Jays," and being labeled a club which could never make it past the playoffs? The Jays have overcome that reputation, and then some: last year they became the first team since the 1977-78 New York Yankees to win consecutive world championships. This year, they could become the first club in 20 years to win three straight world titles.

How difficult is it to win three straight world championships? Well, it hardly ever happened even in the old days, when there were only 16 teams and no playoff series to precede to the World Series. Here's the very short list of the clubs which won at least three straight world titles:

Three or More Consecutive World Championships, 1903-93

Team	Years	Championships
New York Yankees	1936-39	4
New York Yankees	1949-53	5
Oakland Athletics	1972-74	3

That's it, the entire list, in 90 years of World Series. How about the other teams which had won two straight Series, like the Jays? Here's how they fared in their quest for number three, including the above teams:

Going for a Third Straight World Championship

Team	Year	W	L	Result	
Chicago Cubs	1909	104	49	2nd	6.5 GB
Philadelphia Athletics	1912	90	62	3rd	15.0 GB
Boston Red Sox	1917	90	62	2nd	9.0 GB
New York Giants	1923	95	58	1st	lost WS in six games
New York Yankees	1929	88	56	2nd	18.0 GB
Philadelphia Athletics	1931	107	45	1st	lost WS in seven games
New York Yankees	1938	99	53	1st	won WS in four games
New York Yankees	1951	98	56	1st	won WS in six games
New York Yankees	1963	104	57	1st	lost WS in four games
Oakland Athletics	1974	90	72	1st	won WS in five games
Cincinnati Reds	1977	88	74	2nd	10.0 GB
New York Yankees	1979	89	71	4th	13.5 GB

All 12 of these clubs had fine teams in the year they attempted to win a third straight title. Six of them made it to the World Series again, four more finished in second place, and no one won fewer than 88 games. Judging from that, the Blue Jays can be expected to have a contending team, with an excellent chance to reach the postseason again.

One note of caution: the two teams with the *worst* won-lost records in year three were the two clubs in the free agent era, the 1977 Reds and the 1979 Yankees. One thing that happens when teams win championships is that the players can justifiably demand hefty salary increases. Before the free agent era, ownership had most of the power, so those demands were kept in check somewhat. Now that players have more freedom of movement, the salary spiral is harder to control. The 1977 Reds, facing a skyrocketing payroll, traded a key high-salaried veteran, Tony Perez, and lost one of their best starting pitchers, Don Gullett, to free agency. The '79 Yankees had much deeper pockets, but even they dealt a couple of star players at least partly for salary reasons (Sparky Lyle, Mickey Rivers). Of course, those Yankees also ran into some very bad breaks, like Thurman Munson being killed and Catfish Hunter suddenly breaking down completely. Winning three straight involves continued luck, as well as a lot of skill.

The Blue Jays, like the 1979 Yankees, are one of the richest clubs in baseball, and seem as well-equipped as anyone could be to deal with the financial pressures that come with having a champion. They also have another potential advantage. If we assume the new three-division plan is in effect, qualifying for postseason play would be easier than in the past, since the Jays could make it as a second-place "wild card." But once they did that, they'd have to win *three* rounds of playoffs, instead of one or two as in the past.

Let's put this in perspective: if the Jays make it all the way to victory in the World Series, they will have won *seven* consecutive best-of-five or seven-game series, including the playoffs, over three years. And only one team has won that many series in a row: the New York Yankees, who won seven World Series over an 11-year period from 1943 to 1953, a situation not really comparable to the Toronto's. The A's won six straight series from 1972 to 1974 (three playoffs, three World Series), but failed in their chance at seven in the 1975 ALCS against the Red Sox. "To boldly go where no club has ever gone before"—that's the challenge for the Blue Jays this year.

ATLANTA BRAVES: HAVE THEY STARTED A PITCHING REVOLUTION?

Everyone knows about the talents of Atlanta's "Four Aces": Greg Maddux, Tom Glavine, Steve Avery and John Smoltz form the strongest rotation in baseball. They're not only very good, they're very young; Maddux, the oldest, will turn 28 in April. Those are four great young arms, and the Braves are trying to keep them healthy for years to come.

The Braves' method of protecting their pitchers is pretty simple: they limit the number of high-pitch outings their starters make. Last year Smoltz and Glavine had only two starts all season with 130 or more pitches. Avery and Maddux, a man who's shown his durability by leading the National League in innings pitched during each of the last three years, each had zero starts—none—with over 130 pitches. Here's the number of 130-pitch outings the Four Aces have had in their careers; Maddux was with the Cubs until 1993, of course, but the careful usage the Cubbies gave him may have been a big factor in Atlanta's decision to pursue him:

Pitcher	1987	1988	1989	1990	1991	1992	1993	Total
Steve Avery	-	-	-	0	2	1	0	3
Tom Glavine	0	0	0	0	2	0	2	4
Greg Maddux	0	4	2	2	0	3	0	11
John Smoltz	-	0	3	6	0	4	2	15

130+ Pitch Starts Per Season

Is this a fundamental change in baseball? We don't have the complete answer, as we've only been keeping pitch counts since 1987. But let's look at a list of 20 of the best young starters since then. None of the pitchers were older than 26 years old in the first season of the sequence; here are the number of 130-plus-pitch starts they made each year:

130+ Pitch Starts Per Season

Pitcher	1987	1988	1989	1990	1991	1992	1993	Total
Kevin Appier	-	-	0	2	1	1	3	7
Andy Benes	-	-	-	1	2	3	0	6
Kevin Brown	-	1	2	0	1	2	4	10
Roger Clemens	10	13	12	3	7	9	4	58
David Cone	0	4	7	6	7	11	9	44
Doug Drabek	0	1	0	1	0	5	1	8
Cal Eldred	-	-	-	-	0	1	11	12
Alex Fernandez	-	-	0	3	2	1	2	8
Chuck Finley	0	3	3	9	8	6	6	35
Dwight Gooden	3	2	3	1	1	0	2	12

130+ Pitch Starts Per Season

Pitcher	1987	1988	1989	1990	1991	1992	1993	Total
Juan Guzman	-	-	-	-	0	1	4	5
Pete Harnisch	-	-	4	4	3	0	2	13
Randy Johnson	-	1	4	9	4	11	13	42
Mark Langston	9	9	11	5	4	3	3	44
Ramon Martinez	-	1	3	8	3	2	3	20
Jack McDowell	0	0	-	3	3	6	1	13
Jose Rijo	2	2	0	5	0	0	5	14
Bret Saberhagen	8	2	3	2	0	0	0	15
Kevin Tapani	-	-	0	0	0	1	0	1
Fernando Valenzuela	15	4	3	4	0	-	0	26

In 1987, Mark Langston and Fernando Valenzuela were 26 years old, Roger Clemens was 24, and Bret Saberhagen was 23 (ages as of July 1). Yet each one of them threw 130-plus pitches on at least seven occasions; Valenzuela, the "horse," did it 15 times in 34 starts. In eight of those 15 games, he threw more than *150* pitches; in one four-start sequence, he threw 156, 168, 173 and 160 pitches. Unbelievable.

Valenzuela's subsequent arm problems, and those of Dodger teammate Ramon Martinez, who broke down after being given a lot of high-pitch starts at age 22 in 1990, seemed to make managers more cautious about letting their pitchers, particularly the young ones, throw more than 130 pitches. The Braves may not have invented the notion of lifting a young starter before he reached the 130-pitch mark, but they did an awful lot to popularize it.

Looking at the start-by-start data for individual pitchers, it's clear that many, if not most, are on a 130-pitch limit except on rare occasions, and get lifted before they reach 130, even if they're pitching a brilliant game. The Brewers' Cal Eldred, who had 11 high-pitch outings at age 25—including five with more than 140—was almost in a world by himself last year. (Randy Johnson has *always* been in world by himself.)

Will this sort of caution save arms? The truth is that no one knows; the science is too new. Charles Nagy of the Indians had only four 130-pitch starts in 1992, and none with more than 135, yet his arm blew out anyway. If the Four Aces stay healthy while Cal Eldred's arm falls off, then we'll know a little more. Until then, the Braves will stay cautious and hope for the best.

A complete listing for this category can be found on page 256.

CHICAGO CUBS: ARE HIGH SAVE SEASONS DANGEROUS?

In 1984, Bruce Sutter set a National League save record with 45. A year later, he had only 23 saves and his ERA was 4.48. The year after that, his arm broke down completely and his save total was three.

In 1986, Dave Righetti saved 46 games, a major league record. A year later, his save total was 31 and his ERA rose by over a run to 3.51. The year after that, his save total dropped to 25.

In 1990, Bobby Thigpen saved 57 games, breaking Righetti's record. A year later, his save total dropped to 30 and his ERA was 3.49. The year after that, he had only 22 saves, and a 4.75 ERA. In 1993, he had only one save all year, and an ERA of 5.83.

In 1991, Lee Smith set a National League save record with 47. He continued to pile up the saves the next two years, but his rising ERA indicated deterioration: 2.34 in 1991, 3.12 in 1992, 3.88 in 1993.

In 1992, Dennis Eckersley became the second pitcher in history to post a 50-save season. A year later, his save total dropped to 36, and his ERA was 4.16.

In 1993, Randy Myers set a National League save record with 53. Complete the rest of this picture.

We can't complete the picture, of course, because 1994 hasn't happened yet, but the stories of some of the saves record-holders have to give one pause. Other pitchers have had big problems after a high-save season. For instance, Bryan Harvey went from 46 saves in 1991 to a sore arm and only 13 saves in 1992. Mark Davis went from 44 saves and the Cy Young Award in 1989 to six saves and a 5.11 ERA in 1990. Doug Jones went from 43 saves in 1990 to seven saves and a 5.54 ERA in 1991.

Does this evidence prove that high-save seasons lead to big trouble? Not by itself. For one thing, we've chosen selective horror stories out of a bigger picture. Some pitchers, notably Eckersley until 1993, have recorded high save totals year after year without many signs of deterioration. More importantly, the usage pattern for relief pitchers is evolving so rapidly that we don't really have much evidence to go on. High-save seasons are a product of the very recent past, and we mean *very* recent. There have been only 24 pitcher-seasons of 42-plus saves; eight of them came in 1993.

We do, however, have some evidence to present on the subject. Here's a listing of the 16 best save seasons prior to 1993. We'll show you the pitcher's save total and ERA during that season (Year One), and then the figures for the next three years:

Highest Save Totals—One Season—Through 1992

Pitcher, Year	Year 1		Year 2		Year 3		Year 4	
	Sv	ERA	Sv	ERA	Sv	ERA	Sv	ERA
Bobby Thigpen, 1990	57	1.83	30	3.49	22	4.75	1	5.83
Dennis Eckersley, 1992	51	1.91	36	4.16	--	----	--	----
Dennis Eckersley, 1990	48	0.61	43	2.96	51	1.91	36	4.16
Lee Smith, 1991	47	2.34	43	3.12	46	3.88	--	----
Dave Righetti, 1986	46	2.45	31	3.51	25	3.52	25	3.00
Bryan Harvey, 1991	46	1.60	13	2.83	45	1.70	--	----
Bruce Sutter, 1984	45	1.54	23	4.48	3	4.34	--	----
Dennis Eckersley, 1988	45	2.35	33	1.56	48	0.61	43	2.96
Dan Quisenberry, 1983	45	1.94	44	2.64	37	2.37	12	2.77
Mark Davis, 1989	44	1.85	6	5.11	1	4.45	0	7.13
Dan Quisenberry, 1984	44	2.64	37	2.37	12	2.77	8	2.76
Lee Smith, 1992	43	3.12	46	3.88	--	----	--	---
Dennis Eckersley, 1991	43	2.96	51	1.91	36	4.16	--	----
Doug Jones, 1990	43	2.56	7	5.54	36	1.85	26	4.54
Jeff Reardon, 1988	42	2.47	31	4.07	21	3.16	40	3.03
Rick Aguilera, 1991	42	2.35	41	2.84	34	3.11	--	----

Eckersley's name appears several times, and those of Lee Smith and Dan Quisenberry also appear more than once. That alone is a sign that a high-save season doesn't inevitably lead to a breakdown. In all but two of the seasons, the pitcher's save total declined in Year Two, but that's to be expected, since we're talking about pitchers' career years. However, as you can see, some of the drops were huge; seven of the 16, or nearly half, saw their save totals decline by 15 or more. The rise in ERA is more disturbing: in over half the seasons—nine—the pitcher's ERA rose by more than a run. Nearly a third of the pitchers (five) had ERAs higher than 4.00 in Year Two, and an ERA that high for a closer basically defines a lousy year.

Again, this "proves" nothing as far as Randy Myers is concerned. Whatever their save totals, relief pitchers are subjected to varying amounts of abuse. In the 1980s, pitchers like Bruce Sutter, Dave Righetti and Dan Quisenberry recorded high save totals while working well over 100 innings a year. That sort of workload is almost unheard of now, as too many pitchers broke down under the strain. Tony La Russa pioneered the idea of "protecting" his closer by limiting his usage until the ninth; other managers followed suit, and it's possible that relievers will now be able to post high save totals year after year without deterioration. But it's a new science, and the danger for pitchers like Myers is that the use patterns of the future will be determined by the mistakes of the past.

CINCINNATI REDS: WHY DOESN'T RIJO WIN MORE?

By most statistical measurements, Jose Rijo is one of the best starting pitchers in baseball. Over the last four seasons, a total of 33 pitchers have worked at least 800 innings—among them Roger Clemens, David Cone, Tom Glavine, Randy Johnson, Mark Langston, Greg Maddux, Dennis Martinez and Jack McDowell. The cream of the crop, in other words. Here are a few of the leaders boards for that group:

Baseball's Best Starters, 1990-93

Earned Run Average		Fewest Hits/9 Inn		Fewest Baserunners/9 Inn	
Jose Rijo	2.56	Randy Johnson	6.74	Jose Rijo	9.93
Roger Clemens	2.77	Jose Rijo	7.44	Roger Clemens	10.04
Kevin Appier	2.80	David Cone	7.47	Dennis Martinez	10.05
Greg Maddux	2.82	Roger Clemens	7.58	Greg Maddux	10.08
Dennis Martinez	2.91	Dennis Martinez	7.62	Doug Drabek	10.44
(Minimum 800 IP)					

Clearly, Rijo is among the very best. We have even more evidence of that. Over those four seasons, Rijo has a strikeout/walk ratio of 3.02, third-best after Greg Swindell (3.56) and Roger Clemens (3.30). He also has a .637 winning percentage, fourth-best in the group after Glavine (.661), McDowell (.652) and John Burkett (.642).

There's only one problem: Rijo has only 58 wins over the four seasons, a figure that doesn't even make the top 10 for the period. After 10 years in the majors, he still hasn't won more than 15 games in a season. Why doesn't he win more? After all, he's not one of those pitchers with great stuff, but a .500 record; his winning percentage proves that. One problem is that Rijo gets an amazing number of no-decisions. Over the last four years, he's gone without a decision in 28.9 percent of his starts, second-most in the group of 33 after Houston's Pete Harnisch (33.6 percent). Okay, but *why doesn't Rijo win more?* That's tonight's subject on *Nightline*.

The Rijo Theories

1. He doesn't get enough run support. Over the last four seasons, the Reds have scored an average of 4.6 runs per nine innings for Rijo. While he probably wishes he had Jack McDowell's support (5.4), he ranks in the top half—15th—in run support among the group of 33. It could be a lot worse. Think how Tom Candiotti and Andy Benes, both of whom have received only 3.6 runs per nine innings over the period, must feel.

2. His bullpen lets him down. Over the four-year period, Rijo has left a total of 54 games with a lead, and has wound up with either a loss or a no-decision in 11 of them. Does that constitute being victimized? Not at all. Over the same period, Harnisch left 51 games with leads, and wound up with either a loss or no-decision in more than a third of them (19). Eric Hanson has left 46 games with leads, and been saddled with a loss or a no-decision 14 times. In fact, 19 of the 33 pitchers had more losses or no-decisions in games they left than did Rijo. So don't pity Jose.

3. He needs careful handling because he's prone to arm problems. Early in his career, Rijo had arm troubles and spent some time on the disabled list. When the Reds made him a full-time starter, they were understandably cautious, and they also had the superb "Nasty Boys" bullpen to protect him. But there's little reason to worry about his arm any more. Last year Rijo tied for the N.L. lead in games started, and ranked second to Greg Maddux in innings pitched.

4. He's not durable enough. During the four seasons, Rijo has pitched seven or more innings in 78 of his 128 starts (60.9 percent). Is that bad? Well, it can't compare with Clemens (74.0 percent), Cone (71.1) or Langston (70.2), but it's a lot better than Harnisch (46.6%), Burkett (47.0) or Key (47.0). Among the group, his seven-inning percentage ties him for 13th place with Jim Abbott. He'd probably rank much higher, if the Reds weren't being so cautious with him.

If Rijo's arm is fine, and the Reds have a shakier bullpen with the Nasty Boys no longer operating, why not stick with him a little longer? The notion that he needs to be protected gets a jolt with these numbers from the *STATS 1994 Player Profiles* book:

Jose Rijo, Opponents Batting Avg—Last Five Years

	Opp. Avg.
First 75 Pitches	.231
Pitches 76-90	.219
Pitch 91-105	.228
Pitch 106+	.217

The evidence strongly suggests that Rijo could handle being left in games a little longer without any loss of effectiveness. Since his arm seems strong and healthy, what do they have to lose? After all, Rijo has that 58-33 record in his 128 starts over the last four seasons; the Reds pitchers who have taken over for him have a record of 14-23. Given a little less tender usage, Rijo could win a lot of those games. . . and be a big winner at last.

A complete listing for this category can be found on page 257.

COLORADO ROCKIES: HOW DAMAGING IS THE "MILE HIGH FACTOR"?

By any account, the Colorado Rockies had a memorable first season. They won 67 games, three more than their expansion rivals, the Florida Marlins. They finished strongly, going 31-21 from August 8 through the end of the season. Their first baseman, Andres Galarraga, won a batting title. And they set an all-time attendance record.

However, any discussion of the Rockies has to begin with their ballpark, Mile High Stadium. With the Denver altitude giving flyballs a boost (see essay on page 96), everyone thought that Mile High would be a very friendly park for hitters. And it was. But what happened surpassed almost all expectations, including ours. We keep a "ballpark index" for each major league park, comparing the home and road figures (both teams), with an index of 100 indicating a neutral park, and numbers higher than 100 indicating one friendly to hitters. The higher the number, the friendlier the park.

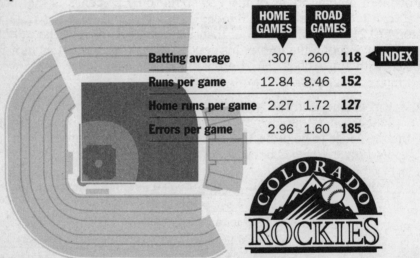

	HOME GAMES	ROAD GAMES	INDEX
Batting average	.307	.260	118
Runs per game	12.84	8.46	152
Home runs per game	2.27	1.72	127
Errors per game	2.96	1.60	185

The chart shows the park indexes for Mile High Stadium in various categories. In terms of positive effect on batting average and runs scored, it was the best hitters' park in baseball; for home runs, it was second-best to Toronto's SkyDome. But you don't need to know anything about park indices to get an idea of how hitter-friendly Mile High was. Just look at that first number, which shows that the average hitter batted .307 there last year—and that's pitchers included. By itself, the Denver park raised the National League batting average four points; the league hit .260 without the games at Mile High, .264 with it.

The result was that Rockies hitters looked a lot better than they really were, and their pitchers a lot worse. At home, the Rockies ranked first in both batting average and runs scored; in their road games, they ranked dead last. The park was particularly favorable for right-handed hitters like Andres Galarraga, Charlie Hayes and Dante Bichette. Here are home/road breakdowns for those three, along with a few others:

Batter	Home			Road		
	Avg	HR	RBI	Avg	HR	RBI
Andres Galarraga	.402	13	64	.328	9	34
Freddie Benavides	.387	3	21	.208	0	5
Dante Bichette	.373	11	51	.252	10	38
Charlie Hayes	.338	17	66	.271	8	32
Jerald Clark	.322	8	40	.247	5	27
Vinnie Castilla	.305	5	19	.206	4	11
Eric Young	.303	3	33	.238	0	9

So the park made a lot of the Colorado hitters look good; at the same time, it made a lot of their pitchers look very bad. Rookie Steve Reed, for example, had a 1.60 ERA on the road; he had a 6.39 ERA at Mile High. Reliever Darren Homes had a 2.10 ERA on the road, a 5.65 mark at home. Gary Wayne was 2.54 on the road, 7.15 at home. Most of the Rockies pitchers were lousy on the road as well as at home, but you have to think it was confidence-shattering to pitch in that park. Rockies pitchers wound up giving up 551 runs in their home games, the most for any major league club since the 1939 St. Louis Browns, and the most for any National League team since the legendary 1930 Phillies.

To complete the picture, there was the effect on the Denver fielders. The park index shows that the error rate at Denver was almost twice as high as in Rockies road games, apparently because of the dry, rocky (good nickname, guys) soil. So the fielders looked much more inept than they really were, and Lord knows what havoc this wreaked with sinkerballers like Steve Reed, who depends on his infield to turn groundballs into outs.

The Rockies will return to Mile High in 1994, and then are scheduled in 1995 to move into their new park, Coors Field—where the power alleys are supposed to be deeper. In '94, though, it'll be more of the same: average hitters looking great, good pitchers looking bad, and almost all fielders looking lousy. It's hard to evaluate talent under conditions like that, and the real potential damage in the "Mile High factor" is that the Rockies and their fans will overrate some mediocre players, and give up on some good ones.

FLORIDA MARLINS: WHAT'S THEIR FIRST-YEAR REPORT CARD?

The Florida Marlins' first season, according to most accounts, was a very successful one. The Marlins won 64 games, four more than the average total for the 12 expansion clubs since 1961. They avoided last place, finishing ahead of an established team, the New York Mets. They had quality players at several positions: third baseman Gary Sheffield, left fielder Jeff Conine, center fielder Chuck Carr, shortstop Walt Weiss (now departed), relief ace Bryan Harvey. They had several other decent players. And they began to develop what most people consider to be a very solid farm system.

How did the club the Marlins put on the field compare with the other 11 expansion clubs, including last year's Colorado Rockies? Here's a comparison chart:

First-Year Expansion Teams

Year	Team	W	L	Pct	Runs	OpRns	Avg	HR	ERA
1961	Los Angeles Angels	70	91	.435	744	784	.245	189	4.31
1969	Kansas City Royals	69	93	.426	586	688	.240	98	3.72
1993	Colorado Rockies	67	95	.414	758	967	.273	142	5.41
1962	Houston Colt .45s	64	96	.400	592	717	.246	105	3.83
1969	Seattle Pilots	64	98	.395	639	799	.234	125	4.35
1977	Seattle Mariners	64	98	.395	624	855	.256	133	4.83
1993	Florida Marlins	64	98	.395	581	724	.248	94	4.13
1961	Washington Senators	61	100	.379	618	776	.244	119	4.23
1977	Toronto Blue Jays	54	107	.335	605	822	.252	100	4.57
1969	Montreal Expos	52	110	.321	582	791	.240	125	4.33
1969	San Diego Padres	52	100	.321	468	746	.225	99	4.24
1962	New York Mets	40	120	.250	617	948	.240	139	5.04

Some observations on these figures:

1. The Marlins' 64 wins, while above-average, were nothing exceptional, as the average is brought down by the terrible performance of the 1962 Mets. It's the same total recorded by the Houston Colt .45s, Seattle Pilots and Seattle Mariners, none of whom had exceptional success in their early years. The two franchises which won the most games in Year One, the Angels and Royals, were also the quickest to reach respectability. The Angels reached the .500 mark in their second year, the Royals in their third; by contrast, it took the Colt .45s (by then the Astros) eight seasons,

the Pilots (by then the Milwaukee Brewers) 10, and the Mariners 15. The moral: 64 wins are nothing to get excited about.

2. The Marlins seemed to concentrate on building a respectable pitching staff, and succeeded. Their 4.13 team ERA was the third-best by an expansion club, and was achieved in a season that was a very good one for hitters. In terms of "relative ERA"—team ERA compared to the league average—the Marlins, 0.09 runs above the 1993 National League norm, had the second-best performance next to the 1962 Colt .45s, who were 0.11 runs under. And the .45s played in a much better park for pitchers than Joe Robbie Stadium, which slightly favored the hitter in its first year.

3. The Marlins offense, though, was very weak, despite the presence of a number of veteran hitters. Only the anemic 1969 Padres scored fewer runs than the Marlins' 581, and Florida's home run total of 94 was the lowest of anyone's.

4. In terms of a "club profile," the team which the Marlins most closely resembled was the 1962 Houston Colt .45s. The .45s went 64-96, batted .246, scored 592 runs and gave up 717; the Marlins went 64-98, batted .248, scored 581 runs and gave up 724. Given the difference in ballparks, the match isn't quite as close as it looks, but it's still the closest. Those Colt .45s, of course, took a long time to achieve success. Houston finally reached .500 at 81-81 in 1969, its eighth season; finally had a winning record in 1972, its 11th; and won its first division title in 1980, its 19th. Houston has never made it to a World Series.

This is not to say that the Marlins will be a mirror image of the Houston Astros, or that they won't be able to match the success of, say, the Kansas City Royals. They're off to a reasonably good start, and they seem to know what they're doing. But they're not off to sensational start. They have a long, long way to go.

HOUSTON ASTROS: HOW IMPORTANT IS MANAGERIAL EXPERIENCE?

The Astros, who hope to contend this year either in the new National League Central (if the proposed realignment plan is approved) or the old National League West (if it isn't), begin the season with a brand-new manager, Terry Collins. Collins is not only new to the Astros; he's never managed in the major leagues. Managerial experience is supposed to be important; will Collins' rookie status work against him?

We decided to scan the record books, going back to 1946, first identifying all the skippers who were in their first year with a club. Then we split them into two groups: those who previously managed in the majors, and those who hadn't, like Collins. There are always a few gray areas in a study like this, so we had to establish some ground rules. First, if the manager had piloted a club very briefly in the past, for 25 games or fewer—like Tom Kelly with the 1986 Twins—we decided to count his first full year as his "rookie" season. If he took over a club in midseason, we didn't make him part of the study unless he piloted that club for at least 130 games. And if he took over a team at the start of a season, and then got fired, like Whitey Herzog with the 1973 Rangers, we counted his figures up until the time he got the axe.

Let's look at the data, first for the experienced managers, those who had previously piloted a club in the major leagues. Here's a comparison of their club's record the year before they took over, and then the record in the manager's first year:

Managers with Previous Major League Experience

	W	L	Pct
Club Record in Previous Season	7,040	7,732	.477
Club Record in Manager's First Year	7,176	7,316	.495

Most managers take over clubs which had losing records in the previous season—that's why the old manager got fired. The experienced managers, as a group, improved the club's record in their first year by 18 percentage points. Over a 162-game season, an 18-point improvement would mean about three additional victories, from 77-85 to 80-82. That's not a big improvement, but it *is* progress, and seems to indicate that experience is a benefit.

Or is it? Let's look at the managers who had no previous major league experience:

Managers without Previous Major League Experience

	W	L	Pct
Club Record in Previous Season	7,960	8,694	.478
Club Record in Manager's First Year	7,872	8,043	.495

The results are almost identical: the rookie skippers took over losing clubs, and improved them by an average of 17 percentage points, which again would be from 77-85 to 80-82. Previous managerial experience, one is led to conclude, doesn't make any difference.

Scanning the record of individual managers in the study, we find all kinds of success stories for rookie skippers. For example, in 1967, Dick Williams took over a Red Sox club which had gone 72-90 and finished ninth the previous year, and led them to the American League pennant with 92 wins. In 1969, Billy Martin took over a Twins team which had gone 79-83 the year before, and led them to 97 wins and the AL West title in his first try at managing. In 1970, Sparky Anderson took over a Reds club which had finished third the year before (89-73) and led them into the World Series with 102 wins. In 1980, *both* American League division champions—Dick Howser's Yankees and Jim Frey's Royals—were piloted by rookie skippers. There are several other cases where a rookie pilot has won a championship in his very first year at the helm, including the likes of Ralph Houk, Bill Virdon and Tommy Lasorda.

Collins might not be able to win a pennant, or match the managerial exploits of Sparky Anderson or Tommy Lasorda. But his lack of experience, by itself, doesn't figure to be a major detriment.

LOS ANGELES DODGERS: CAN AN OLDER MANAGER RELATE?

Tommy Lasorda has managed the Dodgers for 17 seasons, one of the longest stints for one manager with one club in major league history. Lasorda is also 66 years old, which makes him one of the few skippers to pilot a major league club past the age of 65. It's legitimate to ask whether, at that age, a man can relate to players two generations younger than he is. So we decided to look at the record.

The first thing we discovered was that very few men had managed past the age of 60, much less 65. Counting only seasons in which a manager worked at least 50 games, there have been only 31 men who managed at age 60 or older (age figured as of July 1 of each year). More than one-third of those seasons—42 of 119—were skippered by two men, Connie Mack and Casey Stengel. This just doesn't happen very often.

The number of those seasons is so small that we can show you the complete list. Here it is, with the position in the standings at the end of each year, except if the manager was replaced before the season ended. In that case, the position is the place the club was in when the manager was replaced:

Managers 65 or Older (50-Plus Games)

Manager	Year(s)	Team	Age(s)	Position in Standings
Chuck Dressen	1965	Det	65	3*
Leo Durocher	1971-72	Cubs	65-66	3-4
Leo Durocher	1972	Cubs	66	4*
Leo Durocher	1972	Hou	66-67	2*-4
Herman Franks	1979	Cubs	65	5
Tommy Lasorda	1993	LA	65	4
Connie Mack	1928-50	A's	65-87	2-1-1-1-2-3-5-8-8-7-8-6-8-8-8-8-5-8-8-5-4-5-8
Bobby Mattick	1981	Tor	65	7
Paul Richards	1976	WSox	67	6
Wilbert Robinson	1928	Bkn	65-68	6-6-4-4
Tom Sheehan	1960	SF	66	5
Burt Shotton	1950	Bkn	65	2
Casey Stengel	1956-60	Yanks	65-69	1-1-1-3-1
Casey Stengel	1962-65	Mets	70-73	10-10-10-10*

* Incomplete season

Mack managed until the end of the 1950 season, when he was nearly 88 years old; it helps when you own the team. That's 14 years past anyone else. Casey Stengel is the only other man to pilot a club past the age of 70.

A Q&A about the list:

Can you win past the age of 65? You sure can. Mack managed the 1929-31 Athletics, who won three straight pennants; he was 68 at the end of the 1931 season. Casey Stengel won four pennants after turning 65, the last one at age 69. Those were the only elderly managers who won, but Burt Shotton's 1950 Dodgers just missed, losing the flag on the last day of the season, and Mack's 1948 Athletic club, when Connie was a kid of 85, contended for much of the season.

Is a manager this old reluctant to put younger players in the lineup? It depends on the manager, but the best answer is: the good ones aren't. During the late 1950s, Stengel was able to break in young players like Bobby Richardson, Tony Kubek and Clete Boyer while continuing to win. Throughout his life, Mack was *always* breaking in younger players, in part because he was smart enough to know that younger players are cheaper. Chuck Dressen's Detroit Tigers included great young players like Bill Freehan, Willie Horton, Denny McLain and Mickey Lolich, all of them broken in by the elderly Dressen. The good ones recognize young talent, and nurture it.

Are an older manager's values so different from his young players that he'll be unable to relate to them? It can be a problem. Some of the hipper members of the 1976 White Sox, like Goose Gossage, Terry Forster and Pete Vuckovich, tended to think of their manager, Paul Richards, as some sort of visitor from Mars. By the end of his career, Leo Durocher was clearly out of touch with many of his players, though Durocher was such a good manager that he had winning records anyway. Stengel had problems relating to some of his younger players, and that was one reason why the Yankees fired him.

The Dodgers have high standards as well, which leads us to Lasorda. One of the knocks on him in recent years was that he didn't want to play his younger players, but then a lot of those younger players were no good, and he found a place for guys like Eric Karros and Mike Piazza (with perhaps some "encouragement" from the Dodger management). Every older manager faces this dilemma: young players take time to develop, at a time when the manager is thinking in terms of "one more pennant." Is that how the Dodgers wound up banking their future on Darryl Strawberry and Eric Davis? These Dodgers aren't the 1957 Yankees or the 1929 Athletics; they'll probably take several years to develop, and by then Lasorda will be pushing 70. In the meantime, he'll have to go with younger players, something he's generally shown a reluctance to do.

A complete listing for this category can be found on page 259.

MONTREAL EXPOS: WHAT IF THEY'D HAD GALARRAGA?

One of the games baseball fans love to play is the game of "What If?" What would have happened if the Red Sox had kept Babe Ruth? What would Joe Jackson have done if they had let him keep on playing? How many games would Dizzy Dean or Herb Score have won if they hadn't been hit by those line drives? What if Ted Williams had played in Yankee Stadium, and Joe DiMaggio had played in Fenway Park? Love the game, and you've played *this* game.

We love the game too, and though our job usually consists of reporting what happened and trying to explain why it happened, we like to speculate as much as the next fellow. Which brings us to the Montreal Expos, and an irresistible bit of speculation. Last year the Expos had a very fine season, winning 94 games and mounting a serious challenge to the Philadelphia Phillies for the National League East title. But the Expos fell three games short because they had a few holes in their lineup, and the biggest hole by far was at first base. Last year the average National League first baseman batted .291 and drove in 90 runs; the Montreal first basemen, combined, batted .225 and drove in 69 runs.

You "what if" fans are way ahead of us. You're thinking, what if the Expos still had Andres Galarraga at first base last year?

We've thought the same thing. After all, the Expo first basemen had that .225 average; Galarraga had a .370 average. The Expo first basemen drove in 69 runs in 162 games; Galarraga drove in 98 while playing only 120 games due to injuries. Why, if the Expos had Galarraga, they'd have gone 162-0. Or something close to it.

Well, not quite. We're professional statisticians, and if we're going to make speculations, they have to be grounded in reality. Great as Galarraga's numbers were, they were accomplished in the Colorado ballpark, which is paradise for a right-handed hitter; the Montreal ballpark, on the other hand, is extremely difficult for a right-handed hitter.

So we'll work on this basis: we'll adjust Galarraga's 1993 home figures for the difference in parks, using the ballpark indexes for batting average, doubles, triples and home runs; we'll base the Olympic Stadium figures on the last three seasons, since a several-season index is generally more accurate. We'll also assume that Galarraga would have only been able to play 120 games, as he did for the Rockies, and that the numbers for the other 42 contests would have been on the level of what the Expo first basemen actually produced last year.

Okay, then . . . how many more games would the Expos have won with Galarraga at first? We'll use Bill James' runs created formula to estimate that. Basically, about every additional 10 runs created will result in an additional victory for a club. The chart shows Galarraga's offensive percentages adjusted to the Montreal park, and the number of runs created the club would have produced had Galarraga been the first baseman in 120 of them.

The results, which also took into account that he would have been playing six road games at Denver instead of six at Montreal, are a lot less sensational than the numbers The Big

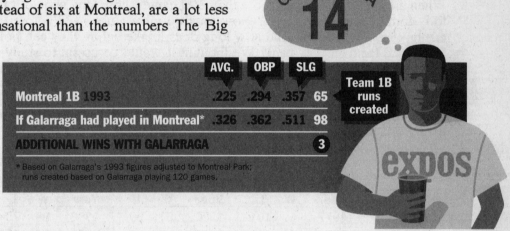

	AVG.	OBP	SLG	
Montreal 1B 1993	.225	.294	.357	65
If Galarraga had played in Montreal*	.326	.362	.511	98
ADDITIONAL WINS WITH GALARRAGA				3

GALARRAGA
14

Team 1B runs created

* Based on Galarraga's 1993 figures adjusted to Montreal Park; runs created based on Galarraga playing 120 games.

Cat produced at Mile High. Our estimate is that, playing the same number of games, he would have batted .326 instead of .370; hit 17 homers instead of 22; and had a .511 slugging average instead of his actual .602 mark. Those are still very good figures, and they're especially good compared with those produced by the other Expo first basemen. Those Expo first sackers created 65 runs; 162 games of Galarraga, even after adjusting for the ballpark figures, would have created 109 runs.

But the Rockies only had Galarraga for 120 games, not 162, so we have to reduce the runs created total based on the weak-hitting Expo first basemen playing the other 42 games. It makes a difference; the runs created total would have been only 98, not 109, which is still a net increase of 33 runs.

How many additional wins would that have given the Expos? The rule of thumb, remember, is one win for each 10 runs created. Galarraga for 120 games would have probably meant an additional three victories; Galarraga for 162 games at least one more. If you're a Montreal fan, remembering that your club only finished three games behind the Phillies, you might be "what if-ing" forever.

NEW YORK METS: HOW LONG WILL THE RECOVERY TAKE?

What a depressing club. The Mets, with one of the highest payrolls in baseball, lost 103 games in 1993—their worst season since way back in 1965, when they were in the fourth year of their existence and Casey Stengel was still their manager. The Mets also engaged in numerous "extracurricular activities," but we won't get into *that* stuff. The club's problems on the field are enough to occupy us.

When a modern team loses more than 100 games, how long should it take to become competitive again? How long do most clubs need before they can have a .500 season? And how long does it take before they can field a first-place team (if they can)? We thought it would be useful to study the history of clubs which have lost 100 games in the recent past—going back to the 1977 expansion season. We eliminated the early Mariner and Blue Jay clubs from the study; expansion clubs just starting out are clearly in a special category. So not counting the 1977-81 Toronto and Seattle teams, here is a list of the clubs which lost 100 games from 1977 to 1992:

100+ Losses in a Season, 1977-92

Team	100-Loss Yr			Next .500 Yr			Next 1st Place Tm		
	Year	W	L	Year	W	L	Year	W	L
Braves	1977	61	101	1980	81	80	1982	89	73
Athletics	1979	54	108	1980	83	79	1981	64	45
Twins	1982	60	102	1984	81	81	1987	85	77
Reds	1982	61	101	1985	89	72	1990	91	71
Mariners	1983	60	102	1991	83	79			
Indians	1985	60	102	1986	84	78			
Pirates	1985	57	104	1988	85	75	1990	95	67
Giants	1985	62	100	1986	83	79	1987	90	72
Indians	1987	61	101						
Orioles	1988	54	107	1989	87	75			
Braves	1988	54	106	1991	94	68	1991	94	68
Tigers	1989	59	103	1991	84	78			
Indians	1991	57	105						

(Expansion teams' first five seasons not counted)

One thing that's striking about these figures is how quickly some of the clubs were able to recover. The 1979 A's, for example, lost 108 games, a performance a lot worse than last year's Met club—yet they had a winning record by the very next season. The 1985 Indians, 1985 Giants and 1988 Orioles were also able to post winning records the year after losing 100 games. The 1982 Twins were a .500 club two years after losing 102 games.

It took a lot longer for most teams to field a first-place team, and almost half the teams on the list (six) still haven't done so. But the 1979 A's and 1985 Giants were in the playoffs within two years after losing 100 games, the 1988 Braves made it in three years, and the 1977 Braves, 1982 Twins and 1985 Pirates all did it in five seasons. A complete recovery doesn't have to take a long time.

Of course, some of the clubs on the list have made only tentative moves toward respectability since losing 100 games—namely the Seattle Mariners and the Cleveland Indians. The year after losing 102 contests in 1985, the Tribe had a winning record, but the year after *that* they dropped 101, and in 1991 they lost 105. Cleveland is still working on its "recovery plan."

The current Met club, however, doesn't suffer from the lack of resources which plagued the M's, Indians and many of the other teams on the list. *Their* poor record was mostly due to bad management at the front-office level, and they appear on the way to solving that problem. There seems to be an unusual amount of volatility in baseball these days, with clubs moving quickly from the bottom to the top, and vice versa. Some of that is due to free agency, where the right signings can lead to instant respectability, and the wrong ones can lead to disaster (just ask the Mets). It's not always necessary to break the bank to bring in one or two good players to help accelerate a recovery; Terry Pendleton, for instance, did wonders in helping the Atlanta Braves go from worst to first in a short time. A few smart trades can also make a big difference, as can the development of two or three young players.

If the low-budget 1985 Giants and 1988 Orioles could quickly return to competitiveness, there's no reason why the well-heeled Mets can't. New York is supposed to have talent in the low- and mid-minors, and in Joe McIlvaine they have a general manager with a solid reputation. If they make the right moves, there's no reason why the Mets can't get back over .500 within a year or two, and be contending for pennants a short time after that.

PHILADELPHIA PHILLIES: WHY DO WE THINK THEY'RE BEAUTIFUL?

The Phillies . . . ya gotta love 'em. Along with winning the National League pennant last year, the Phils established themselves as one of the most colorful group of characters on the major league scene in recent years. Lenny Dykstra. Pete Incaviglia. Mitch Williams. And the man who became his club's symbol, John Kruk. With Kruk's fat belly pointing the way, the Phils gave a new dimension to the term, "Winning Ugly."

We loved them, too, but all the focus on "characters" got in the way of what the Phillies were accomplishing on the field—most especially, the accomplishments of the club's offense. The Phils scored 877 runs last year, the most for a National League club since the 1962 Giants, with Willie Mays, Willie McCovey and Orlando Cepeda, scored 878. How'd they do it? The Phils didn't lead the National League in team batting (they ranked second to the Giants), and four other National League clubs hit more home runs. Why were they so good?

To understand the Phils' success, you have to realize that strengths in certain areas correlate much better with scoring runs than others do. We went all the way back to 1901, and asked our computers to analyze which statistics correlated best with scoring: batting average, on-base average, home runs, stolen bases, whatever. The chart shows the results; a high positive number indicates a high correlation, with 1.00 being a perfect correlation, zero no correlation—a negative number indicates a negative correlation:

Correlation With Runs Scored	
Slugging Percentage	0.86
On-Base Percentage	0.84
Batting Average	0.76
Double	0.72
Base on Balls	0.55
Home Run	0.49
Triple	0.21
Stolen Base	−0.11
(Major Leagues, 1901-93)	

As you can see, the stats which correlate most highly with scoring runs are slugging percentage and on-base percentage. Batting average ranks next, but batting average, in effect, is part of the other two stats, so if you want to study the most efficient offenses—and the players who contribute the most to winning—you need to start with SLG and OBP. That's why players like Barry Bonds and Frank Thomas (and in the old days, Babe Ruth and Ted Williams)—ones who combine the ability to get on base with the ability to hit with great power—rank so highly in our measurements. They're the guys who help you score the most runs.

Other stats, like doubles, walks, home runs and triples, correlate less highly with scoring, which doesn't mean they're unimportant; they're some of the building blocks of slugging and on-base percentage. Stolen bases actually have a negative correlation, which is not as curious as it may seem. For one thing, teams that do a lot of running are often bad clubs with weak offenses. In addition, clubs which steal a lot of bases often have a lot of caught stealings as well; unless they have a high success rate, they're actually costing themselves runs. If you steal at the rate of the Montreal Expos (80 percent) or the Toronto Blue Jays (78 percent), it helps, but very few teams can do that.

How do the Phillies fit in with all this? Very well, indeed. The key hitters in their attack—Lenny Dykstra, John Kruk, Darren Daulton and Dave Hollins—are players who have both power and on-base ability. As a team, the Phils ranked first in the National League in on-base percentage and second in slugging percentage—by one point. They were first in the league in walks (with the most for any National League team since the 1976 Reds), first in doubles, second in triples. Jim Fregosi seems to know that the stolen base doesn't carry a big payoff, and won't send his runners unless he's pretty sure they can succeed. The Phils ranked 13th in the league in steals, but second in success rate (74 percent).

The result of all this was a remarkably efficient offense, and it's no wonder the Phils scored so many runs. To people who admire a perfectly-designed attack, these Phils weren't ugly at all; they were absolutely beautiful. And we salute them.

PITTSBURGH PIRATES: WHAT IF THE "BIG THREE" HAD STUCK AROUND?

Talk about the "evils of free agency" usually leaves us cold, but there's no doubt that free agent losses have had a devastating effect on the Pittsburgh Pirates. Over two winters the Pirates lost three of the cornerstones of their franchise—Bobby Bonilla, Barry Bonds, and Doug Drabek. From 1990 to '92 they were National League East champions. Now they're coming off a 75-87 season, and rebuilding.

It's easy to blame free agent losses for the collapse of the Pirates, but is that all there was to it? Certainly the club had a lot of other problems, as well: a deteriorating pitching staff, no real closer, the injury to Andy Van Slyke. Would they still be champions with Bonilla, Bonds and Drabek around, or would those other problems have prevented a fourth straight title in 1993? We thought we'd play the same sort of "what if" game that we played in the Expos essay, when we wondered how Montreal would have performed had they still had Andres Galarraga.

Let's assess the impact of each of the free agent losses, estimating how many runs—and wins—the Pirates lost:

1. Bobby Bonilla. Bonilla, who left the Pirates after the 1991 season, hasn't found much peace in New York, but he hasn't been a total disaster, either—not with 34 homers last year. Would he have done the same thing playing in Three Rivers Stadium? The answer is yes, he probably would have. Unlike the big ballpark difference between Montreal and Denver that we found in the Expos essay, the Mets and Pirates parks have had very similar effects on hitters in recent years. After making that slight park adjustment, we'll do what we did in the Expos essay: estimate how many runs Bonilla would have created playing in Pittsburgh, factor in the fact that other Pirate players would have been playing some of the time in right field—he appeared in 139 contests last year—and compare the team's RF runs created with and without Bonilla:

	Avg	OBP	Slg	Pit RF Runs Created
If Bonilla had played in Pittsburgh	.265	.352	.524	106
1993 Pirate right fielders	.276	.361	.410	90

The Pirates would have created 16 additional runs with Bonilla as their right fielder.

2. Barry Bonds. Now *this* was a loss. One of the many amazing things about Bonds' 1993 season is that he produced those great numbers in a park that is poorly suited for a left-handed hitter. Three Rivers Stadium is about average, and if Bonds had been playing there last year, he probably would have produced even greater numbers. Our estimate is that he would have hit 52 home runs and had a slugging average of .733! Since he played all but three games, we can simply compare his projected figures with those of the Pirate left fielders:

	Avg	OBP	Slg	Pit LF Runs Created
If Bonds had played in Pittsburgh	.354	.473	.733	192
1993 Pirate left fielders	.278	.364	.450	102

The Pirate left fielders, mostly rookie Al Martin, weren't bad. But they couldn't hope to match one of the great players in history, having one of his greatest seasons. A difference of 90 runs is a bunch, about nine wins. That's the impact of losing an immortal.

3. Doug Drabek. An ace in Pittsburgh, Drabek was a dud with the Astros, going 9-18. But his season wasn't really as bad as the record would indicate. His earned run average was a respectable 3.79. And the Pirate starting staff, without him, had a ERA of 4.78, nearly a run higher. After adjusting for the difference in ballparks, which would have raised his ERA to 3.94, we'll assume that his 237.2 innings would have replaced the club average for starting pitchers, and simply compare runs allowed:

	IP	Runs
If Drabek had pitched in Pittsburgh	237.2	112
Average Pirate starter—1993	237.2	134

Having Drabek, even if he was pitching as he had in 1993, would have saved the Pirates 22 runs. That means about two additional victories.

Summing up. Our estimate is that, with Bonds and Bonilla, the Pirates would have scored 106 more runs. With Drabek in their rotation, they would have allowed 22 fewer. Using Bill James' Pythagorean Theorem, which projects winning percentage on the basis of runs scored and runs allowed, we estimate that the Bucs would have won 15 more games than they did.

That would have given the Pirates a 90-72 record, very respectable but not a serious challenge to either Philadelphia (97-65) or Montreal (94-68) in their division last year. Even if we assume that some of the additional wins would have come against the Phils and Expos, they still probably would have fallen short. The Bucs had so many problems last year that even Bonds, Bonilla and Drabek probably wouldn't have meant a pennant for them. Now, if they'd had Honus Wagner and Roberto Clemente . . . .

ST. LOUIS CARDINALS: WILL THEY BE KINGS OF THE CENTRAL?

What a race; they'll be talking about it for years. Three teams, fighting down to the last weekend, everyone with a chance. But in the end, it was those mighty Redbirds, champions again. What race are we talking about—1964, 1930, 1926, all of them won by the St. Louis Cardinals in the final days? No, we're talking about the thrilling National League Central Division race of 1993:

National League Central Division—1993

Team	W	L	GB
St. Louis	87	75	--
Houston	85	77	2
Chicago	84	78	3
Pittsburgh	75	87	12
Cincinnati	73	89	14

If you missed this race, you're not the only one, because it never took place. The major leagues' "three-division plan" isn't scheduled to go into effect until 1994, and it still wasn't definite as we went to press. But the word from the moguls is that this is the future of baseball, so why don't we warm up to the idea by pretending it's been around for awhile?

What we'll do is reconstruct the pennant races as though the NL Central came in with divisional play in 1969. We did this a year ago for the AL, and what we found was that there would be, as claimed, more close races than under the old two-divisional set-up. The only problem was that a lot of these races would be pretty irrelevant, since the runner-up would qualify for the playoffs anyway as a "wild card." In addition, the three-division plan guarantees that sometimes a mediocre club would qualify for postseason play. Just look at that '93 Central Division. Weren't the Cards, Astros and Cubs considered disappointments last year? Under this set-up, they would have been fighting for a flag. Perhaps that disturbs you; perhaps it would increase your interest. Baseball is counting on the latter.

Anyway, back to 1969. Our American League study last year worked out pretty neatly, since the AL has had 14 clubs for a long time, and since it's also been using a balanced schedule for quite a few years. But the NL didn't expand until a year ago, and before that its schedule was decidedly imbalanced. So this reconstruction of the races is just to get a feel for how the division might have looked if these five teams had been competing against each other. Here is the "winner," its margin of victory, and how the Cardinals would have fared. We'll assume, for the sake of simplicity, that there would have been no split season in the 1981 strike season:

National League "Central Division," 1969-93

Year	Winner	W	L	Margin	Cardinals			GB	
1969	Cubs	92	70	3.0	87	75	4th	5.0	
1970	Reds	102	60	13.0	76	86	5th	26.0	
1971	Pirates	97	65	7.0	90	72	2nd	7.0	*
1972	Pirates	96	59	0.5	75	81	5th	21.5	
1973	Reds	99	63	17.0	81	81	3rd	18.0	
1974	Reds	98	64	10.0	86	75	3rd	11.5	
1975	Reds	108	54	16.0	82	80	3rd	26.0	
1976	Reds	102	60	10.0	72	90	5th	30.0	
1977	Pirates	96	66	8.0	83	79	3rd	13.0	
1978	Reds	92	69	4.0	69	93	5th	23.0	
1979	Pirates	98	64	7.5	86	76	4th	12.0	
1980	Astros	93	70	3.5	74	88	4th	18.5	
1981	Reds	66	42	4.0	59	43	2nd	4.0	*
1982	Cardinals	92	70	8.0	92	70	1st		
1983	Astros	85	77	1.0	79	83	4th	6.0	
1984	Cubs	96	65	12.5	84	78	2nd	12.5	*
1985	Cardinals	101	61	11.5	101	61	1st		
1986	Astros	96	66	10.0	79	82	3rd	16.5	
1987	Cardinals	95	67	11.0	95	67	1st		
1988	Reds	87	74	1.5	76	86	5th	11.5	
1989	Cubs	93	69	7.0	86	76	2nd	7.0	
1990	Pirates	95	67	4.0	70	92	5th	25.0	
1991	Pirates	98	64	14.0	84	78	2nd	14.0	
1992	Pirates	96	66	6.0	83	79	3rd	13.0	
1993	Cardinals	87	75	2.0	87	75	1st		

* Wild-card playoff qualifier

As it turns out, the Cards' 1993 "championship" would have been the first they wouldn't have won anyway under the old format. However, they would have qualified as the wild-card team on three occasions, including 1981, when they and the Reds were left out of the playoffs despite having the league's best winning percentages. In '91, the Cards had the same second-place record as the Padres, but San Diego beat the Redbirds nine times in 12 meetings, and we made that the tie-breaker.

The hypothetical Central would have been well-balanced. The Reds would have had eight titles, the Pirates seven, the Cardinals four, the Astros and Cubs three (including 1969!); decent representation for everyone. This is what baseball is hoping will happen, and it won't bother them to have 84-78 teams qualifying for the playoffs. If it bothers you, you're probably one of those "purists" that baseball doesn't seem to care about.

SAN DIEGO PADRES: WHAT HAPPENS AFTER A CLUB HOLDS A "FIRE SALE"?

To hear some people tell it, the sun dropped out of the sky over San Diego last year. In an unvarnished attempt to cut the payroll, the Padres traded Fred McGriff, Gary Sheffield, Darrin Jackson, Greg Harris, Bruce Hurst and just about everyone else who was earning a high salary, or breathing. By season's end, the club had "succeeded," as the payroll was one of the majors' lowest. But of course, the Padres had also lost 101 games and fallen to last place.

On top of things as always, the nation's sporting press either jumped all over San Diego owner Tom Werner for his "outrageous" behavior, or warned that other "small-market clubs" would be forced to do the same thing in order to survive. What hardly anyone did was point out that the sort of "fire sale" held by the Padres had occurred several other times during baseball history, with clubs like the Athletics (three times) and the Red Sox playing featured roles. Let's take a look at how it was done in the past, and what happened to those clubs:

Philadelphia Athletics, 1915-18. The Athletics were a great dynasty in the early days of the American League, winning six pennants in the league's first 14 years, and four in the five seasons between 1910 and 1914. The 1914 club featured the "$100,000 infield" (big money back then) of Stuffy McInnis, Eddie Collins, Home Run Baker and Jack Barry, a star catcher in Wally Schang, and an outstanding pitching staff with Chief Bender, Eddie Plank, Bob Shawkey, Bullet Joe Bush and Herb Pennock. This was a truly great club, and a fairly youthful one as well, with most of the players still in their 20s.

But 1914 was the year the Federal League opened as a rival to the two established leagues, and the new league began attempting to sign some of the star players. In truth, the threat was somewhat overrated, as most of the stars who went over were pretty old, like the 39-year-old Plank and the 31-year-old Bender. But salaries began to rise as a result of the competition, and thrifty A's owner/manager Connie Mack couldn't handle that. He began selling or trading (usually selling) most of his stars: Collins and Eddie Murphy to the White Sox, Baker and Shawkey to the Yankees, McInnis, Barry, Schang, Pennock and Bush to the Red Sox. *Those* clubs became powers; the A's fell from first in 1914 to last in 1915, and stayed there for seven straight years.

Boston Red Sox, 1919-22. The Red Sox succeeded the A's as the American League's dominant team, winning pennants in 1915, 1916 and 1918. Some of the stars were home-grown, like Tris Speaker and Babe Ruth; some were former Athletics. But by 1919, Red Sox owner Harry

Frazee, a Broadway producer, started to become strapped for cash; so like Mack, he began selling or dealing away most of his stars. Speaker and Smokey Joe Wood went to the Indians and Harry Hooper went to the White Sox, but most of the good Boston players went to the Yankees, with Ruth obviously the biggest name. Know how the Yankee dynasty began? It began with players from the A's and Red Sox dynasties. And what happened to the Red Sox? The same thing that happened to the A's; they finished last in all but one season between 1922 and 1930.

Philadelphia Athletics, 1932-35. Give Connie Mack credit: he had a great eye for talent, and he was eventually able to rebuild his Athletics into a powerhouse that won pennants in 1929, 1930 and 1931. This was another outstanding team, with Jimmie Foxx, Mickey Cochrane, Al Simmons and Lefty Grove the biggest stars. But it was also an expensive club, especially by Mack's standards, and the 1930s brought the Great Depression and lower attendance. A's attendance dropped from 839,000 in 1929 to 405,000 in 1932, so Mack once again began unloading his stars. Cochrane went to the Tigers; Simmons, Mule Haas and Jimmy Dykes went to the White Sox; but most of the A's stars ended up with the Red Sox, as Boston owner Tom Yawkey—like an early free-agent era owner—picked up Grove, Foxx and others in an attempt to "buy a pennant." That didn't work, as Boston failed to win a flag, but what happened to the A's was predictable by now: they fell to the bottom of the standings, finishing either seventh or eighth every year from 1935 through 1943.

Oakland Athletics, 1976-77. What's with these A's? It seems that every time they build a good team, they tear it apart. Charlie Finley's Oakland club won five straight division titles from 1971 to 1975, and three straight world titles from 1972-74. The talent was again outstanding, with Reggie Jackson, Catfish Hunter, Rollie Fingers, Sal Bando and Vida Blue the leading stars. But 1976 was the last year before free agency came in, and Finley knew he would have to ante up big-time, if he wanted to keep his players. Like Mack, Finley was either unwilling or unable to do that. So he traded Jackson and Ken Holtzman to the Orioles, and attempted to sell off Blue, Fingers and Joe Rudi until commissioner Bowie Kuhn voided the deals. As a result, most of the Oakland stars left via free agency, and Finley had little to show for it. As with the other clubs, the A's dropped in the standings, finishing either sixth or seventh from 1977 to 1979. Fortunately, they were able to rebuild fairly quickly under their new ownership, reaching postseason play again in 1981.

So what the Padres did last year was hardly unique: there's nothing new about clubs trading and selling stars for economic reasons. It wasn't just the ones we mentioned, either. Other clubs, like the St. Louis Browns in the 1930s and '40s, and the Phillies in the '20s, were notorious for selling off a good player when he reached the point where he could finally start to demand some big money. There's little new in baseball.

What does this mean for the Padres? Well, they're already a last-place club, and historical precedent says they'll probably remain at the bottom of the standings for at least the next couple of years. However, the sort of thing the A's and Red Sox went through—being a doormat for seven or eight years—is less likely these days. Why? The economic forces are different nowadays. In the twenties and thirties, salaries were very low, and a club could eke out an existence without being competitive; heck, that's the entire history of the St. Louis Browns. That's less possible with today's higher salaries, and it's also probably true that the fans and press are less patient than in the past. If Tom Werner had a last-place club for five straight years, he wouldn't just sit around, losing money: most likely he'd sell the team to someone with more money, and reap a big profit. Then presumably the new ownership would have the resources to field a more competitive team. But that's about all the comfort a Padres fan can gain from their current situation.

SAN FRANCISCO GIANTS: HOW GOOD IS BARRY BONDS?

Barry Bonds' picture graces the cover of this book, with good reason: he's the greatest player in the game today. What Bonds has accomplished the last few years is so extraordinary that his performance deserves some historical perspective. Just how good *has* he been, compared to other players in major league history, and especially, National League history? We thought we'd use a few of the measuring tools developed by Bill James to look into the subject. Here's a rundown on some of them:

Runs Created. According to Bill's widely-accepted measurement of offensive production, Bonds created 172 runs in 1993. This means that, by himself, he produced more than one run per game for the Giants last year! When was the last time a player created more runs? Interestingly, it was another expansion year, 1961, when Norm Cash created 178 runs and Mickey Mantle 174. When was the last time a National League player created more runs? You have to go all the way back to 1949, when Stan Musial had 173. During the last 60 years, there was only one other season in which a National League player created more runs than Bonds did last year: Musial again, with 191 in 1948.

Offensive Winning Percentage. This is a refinement of runs created, which answers the question, "If a team of Barry Bondses took the field

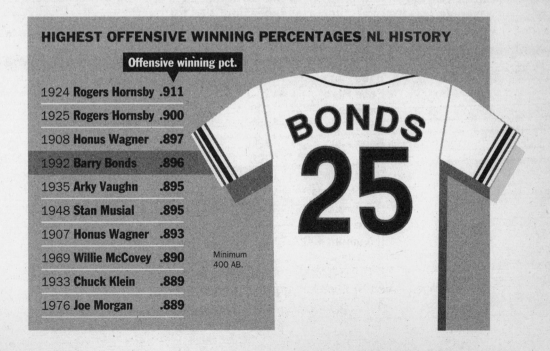

HIGHEST OFFENSIVE WINNING PERCENTAGES NL HISTORY

Offensive winning pct.

Year	Player	Pct.
1924	Rogers Hornsby	.911
1925	Rogers Hornsby	.900
1908	Honus Wagner	.897
1992	Barry Bonds	.896
1935	Arky Vaughn	.895
1948	Stan Musial	.895
1907	Honus Wagner	.893
1969	Willie McCovey	.890
1933	Chuck Klein	.889
1976	Joe Morgan	.889

Minimum 400 AB.

BONDS 25

against an average National League opponent from 1993, what would their winning percentage be?" Since the stat is measured relative to the league average of runs scored in a particular year, it's more useful for comparative purposes than simple runs created, where players from big-hitting years have an advantage.

As it turns out, the healthy offensive figures from 1993 make Bonds' offensive winning percentage (.877) a little less sensational than we thought. Bonds had a better mark himself (.896) in 1992, when the scoring rate was lower. But his 1992 figure was the best since Ted Williams (.939) and Mickey Mantle (.930) in 1957. And as the chart shows, no National League player has had a better offensive winning percentage than Bonds' 1992 mark since Rogers Hornsby in 1925 (.900), and only Hornsby (twice) and Honus Wagner have bettered it. Now you have an even better idea of just how extraordinary Bonds has been.

Secondary Average. This is another James tool, a way of looking at how many extra bases a player produces, independent of batting average; it takes into account extra-base hits, walks and stolen bases. The formula we use in the essay on secondary average subtracts caught stealings before computing the average, but we can't do that in a historical study, as caught stealing totals are not available for every year. This actually works to the disadvantage of Bonds, whose stolen base success rate is much higher than most players of the past. With that in mind, here are the top secondary average seasons of all time, using the simplified formula:

Best Secondary Averages—Single Season

Batter	Year	Secondary Avg
Babe Ruth	1920	.825
Babe Ruth	1921	.767
Babe Ruth	1923	.730
Babe Ruth	1927	.685
Babe Ruth	1926	.679
Barry Bonds	1992	.664
Babe Ruth	1930	.654
Ted Williams	1941	.651
Babe Ruth	1924	.647
Babe Ruth	1928	.646
(Minimum 400 AB)		

Eight seasons of Babe Ruth, one of Ted Williams—and one of Barry Bonds. Wow. We think we can quit right here.

A complete listing for this category can be found on page 260.

II. GENERAL BASEBALL QUESTIONS

DOES HARRY HELP THE CUBS GET RUNS?

The Fans Speak Out:

Dear Baseball Scoreboard,

Does Harry Caray help the Cubs get runs? How often do the Cubs score in the bottom of the seventh in home games? Is it higher than their average inning? The reason I ask this is that, with Harry singing, he gets the crowd all excited (more excited than most 7th-inning stretch crowds) and then screams, "LET'S GET SOME RUNS!"

A Loyal Cub Fan

This authentic question, which was the landslide winner in our annual "pick a question for the *Scoreboard*" competition, is what this book is all about. Haven't you heard at least 1,000 general managers say, "What this club needs is a really good announcer"? Was it just a coincidence that the Yankees started floundering after they fired Mel Allen? When the Padres needed a manager in 1980, didn't they look to the broadcast booth and Jerry Coleman? So why wouldn't Harry be able to help the Cubs get runs?

Let's look at the evidence. The following chart, a *Baseball Scoreboard* exclusive, shows the clubs which scored the highest number of runs in the bottom of the seventh the last three years:

Most Runs—Bottom of 7th, 1991-93

Team	Runs
Blue Jays	146
Cubs	138
Yankees	137
Padres	136
Phillies	136

He *does* help them score runs! . . . not that we ever had any doubt. Next to those Blue Jay announcers, Don Chevrier and Tommy Hutton, who whip those Canadian fans into a frenzy when they sing "Alouette" or "I'm a Lumberjack and I'm Okay" or whatever it is they do up there, Harry was the best (and he *is* the best in the good old USA). You'll also notice that other great broadcasters step to the fore in the bottom of the seventh: the legendary Phil Rizzuto (Yanks), Jerry Coleman (Padres) and Harry Kalas (Phillies). The bottom of the seventh—it's when the great ones show their stuff.

As for the reader's other burning question, about whether the inspired Cubbies score more runs in the bottom of the seventh than they do in other innings, we're embarrassed to say that the answer is no. Harry's best inning, and the Cubs', over the last three years, was the first. The Cubbies' next-best inning was the fourth (hmm, isn't that when that nice young man, Thom Brennaman, takes over?). The bottom of the seventh was only the third-best for the Wrigleys:

Cubs Run Scoring by Inning at Home, 1991-93

1st	2nd	3rd	4th	5th	6th	7th	8th	9th	10+
169	83	115	143	101	132	138	107	60	34

Our professional statisticians would have us believe that this is a fairly normal progression. They say that most clubs have their best innings in the first, the only one in which the batting order is guaranteed to come up exactly the way the manager designed it. National League clubs tend to drop off in the second, when the number-eight hitter and the pitcher will usually bat for the first time, then pick it up again in the third and fourth.

Well, that's what *they* say, anyway. We prefer to think of the Cub pattern this way: in the first, Harry's full of energy, the mere sight of him whips the crowd into a frenzy, and naturally the Cubs will score a lot of runs. They slough off a little in the second and third—a man's gotta conserve his energy, you know—but fans, broadcaster and club get re-inspired in the fourth, when Harry "goes over to the radio booth." Many is the time Ryne Sandberg has looked up from the batter's box in the bottom of the fourth, and thought, "Hey, there's Harry in the radio booth. I think I'll hit a home run." Then the tension builds, builds, builds over the next couple of innings, until it's time for Harry to grab the microphone and start singing . . . and also time (no coincidence here) for the Cubs to have another great inning.

Let's Get Some Runs!

WHO DO YOU WANT BEHIND THE PLATE WHEN YOU'VE GOT A PLANE TO CATCH?

It's a Sunday afternoon in New York, and you've got this *really* important plane to catch. Your buddy Joe says, "Let's see the Mets game before we get that plane." You hesitate to say yes, because one of your rules is to never leave a ballgame before it's over. But then Joe says, "Hey, don't worry. Frank's workin' the plate." You both smile and start heading for Shea.

It's a week later, and wouldn't you know it, you have *another* important plane trip coming up. You're buddy Ralph says, "The Yanks are in town. Let's go." You'd love to, but you've checked the paper and this time you say, "Sorry, buddy, not with Chuck back there."

You probably don't stop to think about it much, but when you go to a baseball game, one of the things which will have a major effect on the experience is which umpire is working the plate. Over the past few years, we've presented data which has shown that there's a big difference in how umpires call a game. Some umps shrink the strike zone, others enlarge it; some umps are great for hitters, others are their worst enemy.

And some umps make a game go faster than others do. One of the few studies we've never done is on the effect that umpires have on the time of a game. We'll correct that oversight right now. Here are the fastest and slowest-working umps in the American League over the last five years, based on a minimum of 100 games behind the plate:

American League Umpires, 1989-93

Fastest	#Gms	Avg Time	Slowest	#Gms	Avg Time
Tim Welke	159	2:48:03	Chuck Meriwether	109	2:55:06
Larry McCoy	155	2:48:44	Rocky Roe	163	2:54:56
Ken Kaiser	139	2:48:57	Rick Reed	158	2:54:50
Al Clark	160	2:49:14	Dan Morrison	159	2:54:30
Dale Scott	138	2:49:18	Derryl Cousins	155	2:54:23
AL Average	**5,164**	**2:51:21**			

"Chuck"—Meriwether, that is—is not the man you want behind the plate when you have an important appointment. Meriwether was a substitute umpire for a number of years before finally landing a regular gig, and our guess is that he wants to stretch things out and enjoy them. (But what about *our* enjoyment?)

The other group is represented by Tim Welke and company, who make an average game go six or seven minutes faster than Meriwether and friends do. Most of the "fast" umpires have shown up in previous studies as ones who feature a generous strike zone and don't call a lot of walks. In the umpire trade, there's an old saying which goes, "Strikes and outs will get you home faster." Here's proof.

Here are the National League leaders:

National League Umpires, 1989-93

Fastest	#Gms	Avg Time	Slowest	#Gms	Avg Time
Frank Pulli	156	2:40:28	Dana DeMuth	159	2:47:56
Joe West	155	2:41:49	Charlie Reliford	105	2:47:40
Mark Hirschbeck	119	2:42:08	Jerry Crawford	167	2:47:26
Greg Bonin	154	2:42:12	Dutch Rennert	107	2:46:38
Steve Rippley	164	2:42:38	Gerry Davis	161	2:46:26
NL Average	**4,492**	**2:44:22**			

"Frank"—Pulli—is the man you'd like to see behind the plate when you've just got to catch that flight. National League games generally move more quickly than American League games do, and none move more quickly than Pulli's; his average game over the last five years was fully 15 minutes faster than Chuck Meriwether's in the other league. Surprisingly, Pulli doesn't usually rank near the top in the categories that indicate a "pitcher's umpire," like a generous strike zone. He just seems to know how to move a game along.

And Dana DeMuth, a premier "hitter's ump" in most of our studies, knows how to slow it down. Batting averages and scoring rates seem to go up when DeMuth is behind the plate, so his leadership in this category is not a real surprise. He seems like a man trapped in the wrong league.

Dutch Rennert: at least 10 minutes of every one of his games must be taken up with his dramatic "Steeeeeeee-riiiiike!!!" calls, which are worth the price of admission. A great entertainer; in his case, the extra time is worth it.

A complete listing for this category can be found on page 261.

IF YOU HIT .450 FOR A MONTH, CAN YOU HIT .450 FOR A YEAR?

John Olerud began his great 1993 season with a dream month of April. Olerud batted .450 during the first month, the best monthly average of the year. Thus began the most serious challenge at a .400 season since George Brett hit .390 in 1980. Olerud was still over the .400 mark in early August before cooling off to a final mark of .363.

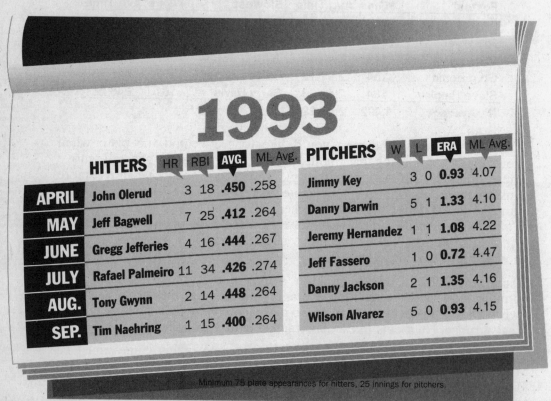

1993

HITTERS		HR	RBI	AVG.	ML Avg.
APRIL	John Olerud	3	18	.450	.258
MAY	Jeff Bagwell	7	25	.412	.264
JUNE	Gregg Jefferies	4	16	.444	.267
JULY	Rafael Palmeiro	11	34	.426	.274
AUG.	Tony Gwynn	2	14	.448	.264
SEP.	Tim Naehring	1	15	.400	.264

PITCHERS	W	L	ERA	ML Avg.
Jimmy Key	3	0	0.93	4.07
Danny Darwin	5	1	1.33	4.10
Jeremy Hernandez	1	1	1.08	4.22
Jeff Fassero	1	0	0.72	4.47
Danny Jackson	2	1	1.35	4.16
Wilson Alvarez	5	0	0.93	4.15

Minimum 75 plate appearances for hitters, 25 innings for pitchers.

The chart lists the top monthly batting and pitching performances of 1993, based on batting average and ERA. Along with that .450 April, Olerud batted .427 in June, and .389 in July. What kept him from challenging the .400 mark for the full season was the way he finished: a .310 average in August, and a .269 mark in September/October. Comparing Olerud's figures with the last .400 season, Ted Williams' .406 in 1941, and with the three highest averages since then, it's obvious that what enabled Williams to surpass the .400 mark in '41 was his remarkable consistency. Unlike all the other challengers, including Williams himself in 1957, the Splendid

Splinter had no prolonged slumps in his .400 season; he never hit below .372 in any month:

Month	Ted Williams 1941	Ted Williams 1957	Rod Carew 1977	George Brett 1980	John Olerud 1993
April	.389	.426	.356	.259	.450
May	.436	.402	.372	.329	.348
June	.372	.295	.486	.472	.427
July	.429	.440	.304	.494	.389
August	.402	.355	.363	.430	.310
Sept/Oct	.397	.632	.439	.324	.269
Final	.406	.388	.388	.390	.363

In case you're wondering, that .632 mark for Williams in September of '57 is no misprint. However, he was injured for much of that month and got only 19 at-bats, so he had no real chance to reach the .400 mark.

Neither did Olerud, who batted "only" .324 after the All-Star break. But he had a great run, as did NL batting champ Andres Galarraga, who batted over .400 much of the first half and was still hitting .391 at the All-Star break. Want more evidence that 1993 was a remarkable year for offensive feats? In 1992, players batted .400 or better for a month (75 or more plate appearances) on only six occasions. In 1993, players did it 19 times.

Compared with that, the best monthly pitching performances were pretty dull stuff, though Wilson Alvarez' September was a key to the White Sox winning the American League West. Even in a hitters' year, however, there will be a number of major slumps. These were the **worst** monthly performances of 1993:

	Player, Team	HR	RBI	Avg	Pitcher, Team	W	L	ERA
April	Darryl Strawberry, LA	3	8	.152	Craig Lefferts, Tex	1	4	8.28
May	J.T. Snow, Cal	4	11	.124	Butch Henry, Col	1	4	9.09
June	Leo Gomez, Bal	2	4	.111	Mike Moore, Det	2	4	7.64
July	Chad Kreuter, Det	3	7	.149	David Wells, Det	1	4	8.28
Aug	Omar Vizquel, Sea	0	2	.128	Chris Hammond, Fla	0	3	8.23
Sept	Mike Bordick, Oak	0	11	.144	Bill Gullickson, Det	1	3	9.24

Darryl Strawberry's horrible start last year helped seal his fate with the Dodgers. And J.T. Snow's month of May highlighted what a crazily up-and-down rookie season he had. Snow's monthly averages last year (September/October included together): .343, .124, .292, .159, .222, .297.

A complete listing for this category can be found on page 262.

WHO'S THE BEST G.M.?

In baseball, signing and developing young talent is only part of the story. A general manager who can make good trades or sign the right free agents can improve a club in a hurry, or keep it competitive on a small budget. We thought we'd go back to the winter before the 1988 season and pick the clubs which made the best trades and best free agent signings of each year . . . and sometimes, the worst. (Unless noted, a trade or free agent move after the season will be counted as one for the next year.) Pay attention: where your club is today is often the result of what happened back then.

1988

Best trades: Baltimore Orioles The O's, suffering through an 0-21 start and a 107-loss season, began their recovery with several great deals. They traded Mike Boddicker to Boston, getting Brady Anderson and Curt Schilling. They dealt aging Fred Lynn to Detroit, getting a minor leaguer named Chris Hoiles in the deal. And in a swap of minor leaguers with the Pirates after the season, they gave up Pete Blohm and got Randy Milligan. The next year, the O's won 87 games.

Worst trade: Cincinnati Reds You could also see this one as the best, from the Kansas City Royals' standpoint: the Royals gave up Van Snider, a career minor leaguer, and got Jeff Montgomery from Cincinnati. Runner-up: the Cubs traded Lee Smith to the Red Sox for Calvin Schiraldi and Al Nipper. Jim Frey *still* thinks this was a good deal.

Best free agent signing: Kirk Gibson, Los Angeles Dodgers. All he did was win the MVP Award and lead them to the world championship.

1989

Best trades: Philadelphia Phillies On June 2 of '89, the Phillies got John Kruk from the Padres, along with Randy Ready, for Chris James. Then on June 18, they traded Steve Bedrosian to the Giants, picking up Terry Mulholland. That same day, they got Lenny Dykstra, Roger McDowell and Tom Edens from the Mets for Juan Samuel. When the season ended, Phillies general manager Lee Thomas stole Dave Hollins from the Padres in the Rule 5 draft. We'd call Thomas lucky, except he's been "lucky" too many times for us to buy that one.

Worst trade: Texas Rangers On July 29, the Rangers traded Scott Fletcher, Sammy Sosa and Wilson Alvarez to the White Sox for Harold Baines and Fred Manrique. Baines was an excellent player, but it was too much to give up for an aging star with bad knees, and he lasted barely a year in Texas.

Best free agent signing: Nolan Ryan, Texas Rangers. From a public relations standpoint alone, this was a brilliant move, grabbing a Texan from the Houston Astros. Ryan added a lot of brilliant pitching.

1990

Best trade: Houston Astros They let Ryan get away, but on August 30, the Astros traded relief pitcher Larry Andersen to the Red Sox for Jeff Bagwell. Even though Andersen helped the Red Sox win a division title, it was a steal for the Astros.

Best free agent signing(s): Tony Phillips and Cecil Fielder, Detroit Tigers. Who thought these were big moves at the time?

Worst free agent signing: Mark Davis, Kansas City Royals. Runner up: Keith Hernandez, Cleveland Indians. Ouch!

1991

Best trade: Toronto Blue Jays In the biggest deal in years, the Jays traded Tony Fernandez and Fred McGriff to the Padres for Joe Carter and Roberto Alomar. They gave up a lot; they got back more, and it paid off in two world championships.

Worst trades: Baltimore Orioles How did the O's, so smart in 1988, get so dumb in 1991 as to make these deals on consecutive days: Pete Harnisch, Curt Schilling and Steve Finley to the Astros for Glenn Davis, and Mickey Tettleton to the Tigers for Jeff M. Robinson? That's baseball.

Best free agent signing: Jack Morris, Twins. Runner-up: Terry Pendleton, Atlanta Braves. These two signings helped put their clubs in the World Series.

Worst free agent signing: Darryl Strawberry, Los Angeles Dodgers. His first season with the Dodgers was pretty good (though not great), but after that it was one disaster after another.

1992

Best trade: San Francisco Giants In one deal, the Giants got almost one-third of a pitching staff—Bill Swift, Mike Jackson and Dave Burba—for Kevin Mitchell and Mike Remlinger. The deal would help make them contenders a year later.

Worst trade: Chicago White Sox Before the season, the Sox thought they sewed up the pennant when they acquired Steve Sax from the Yankees for pitchers Melido Perez, Bob Wickman and Domingo Jean. Even though the Sox had plenty of pitching, it was still a terrible deal.

Best free agent signing: Mike Morgan, Chicago Cubs. For one year, anyway; in 1993, Morgan proved to be miscast as the Cubs' staff ace.

Worst free agent signing: Bobby Bonilla, New York Mets. He was much better in his second season, but when a guy hits 34 homers and people still think his club made a bad deal, maybe they're right.

1993

Best trade: Atlanta Braves Hopelessly behind the Giants, the Braves won themselves a pennant by acquiring Fred McGriff from San Diego for minor leaguers Mel Nieves, Donnie Elliott and Vince Moore. That trio will have to be awfully good to be worth McGriff.

Worst trade: Boston Red Sox Phil Plantier for Jose Melendez?

Best free agent signing: Barry Bonds, San Francisco Giants. Runners-up: Paul Molitor, Toronto Blue Jays, Greg Maddux, Atlanta Braves and Andres Galarraga, Colorado Rockies.

Worst free agent signings: Doug Drabek and Greg Swindell, Houston Astros. They seemed to spook each other out, each one piling his failure on top of the other's. They're good pitchers; they could recover.

Going through this exercise, we were struck by several things. One is that many deals or free agent signings that are considered "minor" at the time turn out to be anything but. Another is that, despite what you may hear, big-money free agent signings often *do* make a dramatic difference for a club, though they seldom make the entire difference by themselves. And last but not least, there's a lot of luck involved in all this; clubs which seem to have a great eye for talent one year, like the Orioles, often end up seeming stupid a year or two later.

If we were going to pick a "best G.M." for this period, the choice would have to be Thomas of the Phillies, who, as we said, is one of the few G.M.s whose moves have paid off year after year. Not only was there Kruk, Dykstra, Mulholland and Hollins in '89; there was Mitch Williams, Wes Chamberlain and Tommy Greene in 1991; Curt Schilling and Mariano Duncan in '92; David West, Danny Jackson, Pete Incaviglia, Milt Thompson and Jim Eisenreich in '93. And others: mostly little moves that paid off big, players that other clubs didn't want. It's not always the "big" deals, and the big free agent signings, which pay off the biggest dividends.

WILL THINGS BE BACK TO NORMAL IN "EXPANSION YEAR PLUS ONE"?

Expansion years always seem to produce some extraordinary performances, from Roger Maris hitting 61 homers in 1961 to Maury Wills stealing 104 bases in 1962 to Rod Carew hitting .388 in 1977. It's not just the hitters, either: Whitey Ford (1961), Don Drysdale (1962) and Tom Seaver (1969) all had their best victory totals—25 wins—during expansion campaigns. The 1993 season was no different, with Barry Bonds, John Olerud and Andres Galarraga among the players having memorable seasons.

More than just a few players had great seasons last year. One way to show that is to count how many players achieved either a .300 average, 30 home runs, 100 RBI or 18 victories last year, then compare those totals with 1992. This chart shows the improvement:

	AL		NL	
	1992	1993	1992	1993
.300 hitters (250+ AB)	9	25	18	28
30 or more home runs	7	12	3	10
100 or more RBI	12	15	5	10
18 or more wins	5	6	2	6

Has the same thing happened during previous expansions? In general, yes—particularly in regard to the number of .300 hitters and players with more than 100 RBI. Leaving out the 1969 expansion, which was accompanied by rules changes to help improve offense, here are the before-and-after results from the 1961, 1962 and 1977 expansions:

	AL		NL		AL	
	1960	1961	1961	1962	1976	1977
.300 hitters (250+ AB)	6	11	13	17	11	23
30 or more home runs	5	6	7	7	1	9
100 or more RBI	4	7	6	10	3	14
18 or more wins	2	3	6	9	7	6

This seems to support the notion that numerous players have career years during expansion seasons, as they take advantage of the presumably diluted level of competition. But what happens the year *following* an expansion season? Is there a leveling off in the number of superior performances, or do they stay about the same? Let's look at what happened in the past; this time we'll have to skip 1963, since that season was accompanied by rules changes to help pitchers (the same ones which were tossed out in 1969). Let's discuss them one season at a time:

	AL	
	1961	1962
.300 hitters (250+ AB)	11	11
30 or more home runs	6	7
100 or more RBI	6	8
18 or more wins	3	6

The overall level of offense in the American League remained about the same in 1962 as it had been in 1961. And the number of players who topped 30 homers, 100 RBI and 18 victories all increased, which suggests that they were continuing to take advantage of expansion-diluted competition. However, there were no performances to approach Maris' 60 home runs and 142 RBI. In 1961, six players hit at least 40 homers; in 1962, only one (Harmon Killebrew, with 48) did. In 1961, four players drove in over 130 runs; in 1962, no one did (Killebrew led with 126). In 1961, the leader in pitching victories, Whitey Ford, was 25-4; in 1962, the leader, Ralph Terry, was 23-9. There continued to be many outstanding performances, but there was a definite leveling off at the top.

	AL		NL	
	1969	1970	1969	1970
.300 hitters (250+ AB)	7	15	15	24
30 or more home runs	10	7	7	12
100 or more RBI	7	8	6	13
18 or more wins	8	8	11	8

As in 1961 and '62, the 1969 expansion produced many extraordinary performances, like Harmon Killebrew's 140 RBI, Tom Seaver's 25 wins and Rico Petrocelli's 40 homers (Rico Petrocelli?). The offensive onslaught continued in 1970, especially in the NL; three National League players topped 40 home runs, Johnny Bench drove in 148 runs, Rico Carty batted .366. American League figures were a little less extreme than in 1969, a year in which Killebrew, Frank Howard and Reggie Jackson all hit at least 47 homers. But three players still hit 40-plus, and there were all sorts of weird, unexplainable performances. For instance, Bert Campaneris, who hit a total of 79 homers in 19 seasons, hit 22 of them in 1970; his next-best total was eight. Luis Aparicio, who was 36 years old and who had never batted higher than .280 in 14 previous seasons, batted

.313. If you didn't know better, you'd think *this* was the expansion year.

	AL	
	1977	**1978**
.300 hitters (250+ AB)	23	7
30 or more home runs	9	7
100 or more RBI	14	4
18 or more wins	6	11

The 1977 expansion season was another which featured outstanding performances. Carew batted .388 and had 239 hits. Hal McRae belted 54 doubles. Even the National League, which hadn't expanded, got into the act, as Cincinnati's George Foster had 52 homers and 149 RBI. By contrast, the 1978 season was much more of a pitchers' year, the season that Ron Guidry went 25-3 with a 1.74 ERA—one of the best pitching years ever. But there was one truly extraordinary offensive performance: Jim Rice hit 46 homers and slugged 406 total bases, the highest total for an American Leaguer since 1937.

Can we predict anything about 1994 from all this? The figures have fluctuated in other post-expansion years, but in general they have remained very good for offense. There continued to be numerous outstanding individual performances, but usually not quite on the level of what took place in the expansion campaigns. So, 1994 probably won't be *quite* as wild as 1993 was. However, there will probably again be a number of exciting performances, which means more treats for the fans.

A complete listing for this category can be found on page 263.

DO THROWS TO FIRST THROW OFF THE HITTER?

The running game, ain't it wonderful? We're always hearing about how a runner dancing off first will divide the pitcher's attention, making him think more about the man on first than he does about the man at the plate. He makes a throw to first, then another. Then maybe another. Pretty soon he's so distracted that he serves up a fat offering, and the hitter creams one. Rally time!

This is another of those notions which is repeated so often that no one questions it any more. By now, you should know that we don't accept things simply because "everybody" says they're true; we want to know what the *real* evidence says. While it may seem logical that throws to first would distract a pitcher's attention, wouldn't they also distract the hitter from doing his job effectively? We're reminded of Frank Thomas of the White Sox, who used to get visibly upset when Tim Raines was doing his dancing-off-first routine. We also know that a study we did last year showed that hitters' averages went down, not up, during at-bats in which a runner attempted a stolen base.

So let's look at the distracting effects of throws to first. While a pitcher might occasionally make a throw to first with the bases loaded or with runners on first and second, the situations we want to look at are those in which second base is unoccupied, inviting a steal attempt. That means plate appearances in which there's either a runner on first base only, or runners on first and third. With a hole on the right side because the first baseman is holding the runner, this is usually an excellent situation for a hitter:

MLB Avg—Runner on 1st Only—or 1st & 3rd

Avg	OBP	Slg
.284	.335	.423

(All major league games, 1993)

You might think these numbers, by themselves, are a good indication of how much the baserunner is dividing the pitcher's attention. And there's probably some truth in that. But look at what happens when the "distracted" pitcher gets his attention divided even more and begins throwing to first. The chart shows the major league average last year with zero throws to first, one throw, or two-plus throws.

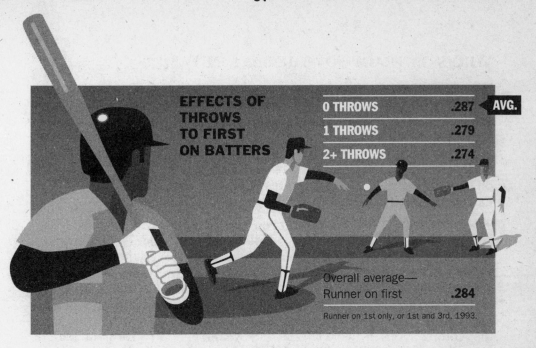

EFFECTS OF THROWS TO FIRST ON BATTERS		
0 THROWS	.287	AVG.
1 THROWS	.279	
2+ THROWS	.274	

Overall average—
Runner on first **.284**

Runner on 1st only, or 1st and 3rd, 1993.

As you can see, the results are exactly the opposite of what the announcers are always telling us. The hitter is most effective when *he's* not distracted, and the pitcher doesn't throw to first. But the average goes down eight points with even a single toss to first. If the pitcher throws to first twice or more, the hitter's average goes down an additional five points.

The results are even more damaging than this drop in batting average indicates. Slugging average goes down drastically when there are two or more throws to first, perhaps because the hitter starts thinking that he needs to "protect" the runner, and shortens his stroke:

Effects of Throw to First on Slugging Average

0 Throw	1 Throw	2+ Throws
.429	.423	.395

The evidence is pretty conclusive that while the running game does have a "distracting" effect, the one who gets distracted the most is the batter, not the pitcher. Naturally, there are going to be player-to-player variations; some hitters aren't going to be affected at all by throws to first, and some pitchers are going to be adversely affected by a dancing baserunner. But the next time you hear a broadcaster start going on about the "benefits" to an offense when a runner is dancing off first and drawing throws from the pitcher, here's our advice: don't believe him.

A complete listing for this category can be found on page 264.

WHO'S ON TRACK FOR THE HALL OF FAME?

Way back in 1980, Bill James wrote an article in the *Baseball Abstract* called "Discerning the De Facto Standards of the Hall of Fame." As Bill put it back then: "Understand, I am not the least talking about what the Hall of Fame standards *should be*. I am talking about what they *are*. *De facto* standards, inferred from a study of who has made it and who hasn't." He then presented two formulas, one for hitters and one for pitchers, based on past Hall of Fame voting patterns. One hundred points and you'd be in, the formula predicted; fall short, and you wouldn't make it.

These formulas, which have been periodically revised, are pretty complicated; if you're interested, Bill James has a book out this spring called *The Politics of Glory*, which should tell you everything you want to know about the Hall. Anyway, players earn points for various accomplishments, like one point for hitting 35 doubles in a season or 15 points for achieving 2,500 career hits. You get points for just playing on a championship team—not because it makes sense, but because it impresses the voters. Does it work? Well, 14 years ago, the formula had the following pitchers, all active in 1979, making the Hall: Tom Seaver, Jim Palmer, Gaylord Perry, Ferguson Jenkins, Catfish Hunter, Jim Kaat, Steve Carlton. All but Kaat made it.

That's enough of an intro; this ain't rocket science, it's just fun. According to the formulas, the following players, all active in 1993, had 75 or more Hall of Fame points through the end of last season:

Hall of Fame Potential Points—1993 Players

Player	HOF Pts	Player	HOF Pts
Nolan Ryan	189.5	Rickey Henderson	110.0
Wade Boggs	189.0	Cal Ripken	105.0
George Brett	182.0	Jack Morris	104.5
Roger Clemens	140.0	Dale Murphy	102.5
Tony Gwynn	129.5	Andre Dawson	101.5
Dave Winfield	123.0	Jeff Reardon	100.0
Robin Yount	123.0	Eddie Murray	98.0
Kirby Puckett	117.5	Paul Molitor	95.0
Dennis Eckersley	116.0	Carlton Fisk	94.5
Don Mattingly	115.5	Alan Trammell	83.0
Goose Gossage	114.0	Barry Bonds	82.0
Ryne Sandberg	113.5	Ozzie Smith	81.5
Lee Smith	112.0	Dwight Gooden	78.5

There are some surprises here—starting with the high ranking given to Wade Boggs, who is considered about as much of a lock as Nolan Ryan or George Brett. The problem for people in 1994 is that we're looking at the declining years of Boggs' career; the voters will focus more on his five batting titles, his extraordinary lifetime batting average, and all the other accomplishments of his prime. He's a lock. Some other players, like Carlton Fisk and Ozzie Smith, seem underrated by the formula, and probably are. Fisk will pick up support because he ranks at the top of so many catchers' career lists, something not really covered by the formula. The formula has seldom had to deal with a player of Smith's enormous defensive reputation. He's probably closer than these numbers indicate, although you could hardly call him a sure thing. Luis Aparicio, another extraordinary defensive shortstop, had to struggle for several years to make the Hall.

According to the formula, a total of 19 active players are sure things for the Hall, and that's not including players like Eddie Murray—who will probably pass 100 points this year—Fisk and Smith. This total seems high, and it probably is. One thing you need to know is that players can *lose* points in their declining years, if their averages or winning percentages or lifetime ERAs slide a bit. More importantly, the formulas are based on the voting standards of the past and present, and those standards undoubtedly will change. For instance, Jeff Reardon may be qualified for the Hall based on his career record and the current standards for relievers set by Hoyt Wilhelm and Rollie Fingers. But if he's competing for votes with Dennis Eckersley, Lee Smith and Goose Gossage, as he will be, he's going to have a tough time.

How are some of the younger players doing? Barry Bonds is certainly well on the way with 82 points, but others like Frank Thomas (46 points), Ken Griffey Jr. (34.5) and Juan Gonzalez (31.5) are really just beginning the trek to Cooperstown. Jose Canseco (62.5) and Darryl Strawberry (34.0), who once seemed headed there, have fallen off the pace, and will need to turn their careers around quickly to have a chance. As for Bo Jackson (6 points) and Neon Deion Sanders (1 point), our advice is: try the *Football Hall of Fame*.

A complete listing for this category can be found on page 265.

WILL HALL BE GOOD FOR THE LONG HAUL?

For our third annual "long-shot prospects" essay, we decided to go half-and-half with pitchers and hitters, rather than hitters only as we've done in the past. Last year, we maintained our 25 percent success rate by pegging Troy Neel, who, despite a brief midseason demotion to the minors, still managed a .290 average with 19 dingers. And when you play the long shots, one out of four isn't bad.

Billy Hall, 25, Boston, 2B

	AB	R	H	2B	3B	HR	RBI	BB	SO	SB	Avg	OBP	Slg
AA Wichita	486	80	131	27	7	4	46	37	88	29	.270	.323	.379
MLE	469	64	114	21	4	3	37	25	94	20	.243	.281	.324
Avg Minor Yr	420	71	130	18	6	3	38	42	73	34	.310	.372	.379
93 Winter Lg*	155	27	40	4	0	0	3	31	28	16	.258	.382	.284

*Mexican Pacific League

Although the Padres aren't overloaded with hot young second basemen, Billy Hall never seemed to be a big part of their future plans despite some impressive numbers in the low minors. Left unprotected in the Rule 5 draft, Hall was chosen by the Red Sox.

In order to keep Hall, the Sox must keep him in the majors for the entire 1994 season. That means that if perennially-wounded Tim Naehring has his usual abbreviated season and Scott Fletcher finally plays like the 35-year-old he is, Hall could get a shot. Hall definitely has minuses—he's not a great fielder and he's never played above Double-A—but hey, this isn't an article about blue-chippers. Some say that Boston will return Hall to the Padres shortly, but others say he was the steal of the draft. Keep your eyes open.

Luis Lopez, 23, San Diego, 2B

	AB	R	H	2B	3B	HR	RBI	BB	SO	SB	Avg	OBP	Slg
AAA Las Vegas	491	52	150	36	6	6	58	27	62	8	.305	.346	.440
MLE	458	33	117	26	2	4	46	17	65	5	.255	.282	.347
Avg Minor Yr	359	41	96	15	3	2	33	17	57	8	.268	.301	.341
93 Winter Lg*	122	6	28	5	2	1	9	10	20	0	.230	.288	.328

*Puerto Rican League

Speaking of hot young Padre second basemen, here's the reason Billy Hall's with the Red Sox. While Hall's defense is suspect, Lopez' is superb. *Baseball America* calls him the best defensive infielder in the Padre system. Lopez turned 23 last September and his hitting is coming along, evidenced by the 36 doubles he totaled at Las Vegas in 1993. He's not

Roberto Alomar, but experts say Lopez has the inside track on the Padre starting second base job for 1994. He's surprisingly unnoticed for a youngster with such a golden opportunity.

Carlos Reyes, 25, Oakland, P

	IP	H	BB	SO	W	L	Sv	ERA
AA Greenville	70.0	64	24	57	8	1	2	2.06
AAA Richmond	28.2	30	11	30	1	0	1	3.77
Avg Minor Yr	81.2	75	22	71	5	2	5	2.28
93 Winter Lg*	48.0	25	11	22	5	0	0	1.31

*Puerto Rican League

Our first shot at tabbing a pitcher is another Rule 5 draftee, Carlos Reyes. Reyes was lost among the Braves' barrel-full of pitching prospects until the A's rescued him as the very first pick of the 1993 draft. He's no fireballer, possessing just an average fastball, but he throws an excellent change-up, as well as a curve and slider.

Reyes has always been a reliever in the minors, yet he's never been a closer, with a high of seven saves in two 1992 stops. The Braves had him starting in the Puerto Rican League over the winter (seven games, seven starts) and he put up tremendous numbers, albeit in a pitchers' league. The A's cut Reyes' 1993 winter season short, so his big test will come in spring training.

Tom Wegmann, 25, New York Mets, P

	IP	H	BB	SO	W	L	Sv	ERA
AAA Norfolk	86.1	68	34	99	5	3	2	3.23
Avg Minor Yr	103.2	75	33	119	8	4	1	2.62
93 Fall Lg	46.0	41	18	59	5	1	2	2.70

The Mets admit that they haven't taken Wegmann's ability to get hitters out at every level too seriously. But their attitude is changing. Wegmann followed up a nice first full season at Triple-A Norfolk with a dominating performance in the Arizona Fall League. He led the league in strikeouts and was voted top right-handed pitching prospect by the league's managers.

Like Reyes, Wegmann's best pitch is the change-up, and he's been used mostly as a set-up man. As the Mets' 4.53 relief ERA was fourth-worst in the league in 1993, Wegmann could get his next big test in the Show if he can continue to impress in spring training.

CAN A SALMON SWIM UP A FENCE?

This works best on radio: "There's a long drive, *deep* to center, could be out of here. Back goes Lofton, wayyyyy back . . . to the fence . . . it's . . . caught! SENSATIONAL CATCH BY KENNY LOFTON!!! I DON'T BELIEVE IT! He really robbed Ripken on that one!"

Few events in baseball stir the emotions like a grab at the fence to rob the other team of a home run. According to statistics carefully kept by Harry Caray when he was broadcasting for the Cardinals in the 1960s, Curt Flood routinely saved 200 home runs a year, and probably more, with his fence-leaping grabs. Willie Mays, they say, was twice as good.

We at STATS love to have fun with statistics almost as much as we love to *keep* statistics. So last year, every time a ball was hit far enough to be close to an outfield fence, our software program would prompt our reporters to answer the question, "Prevented HR?" That enabled us to total up a count of exactly how many home runs were saved by outfielders over the course of the season.

As it turned out, no outfielder saved 200 home runs last year, which only goes to show that none of these modern ballplayers is as good as Willie Mays and Curt Flood were. But hey, you already knew that. As it turned out, the co-leaders in "home runs saved" were Mark McLemore of the Orioles and Tim Salmon of the Angels, with four apiece. Kenny Lofton had three, all of which were broadcast on radio. The (short) leaders list:

1993 Leaders—Home Runs Saved

Outfielder, Team	Saved
Mark McLemore, Bal	4
Tim Salmon, Cal	4
Dion James, Yanks	3
Kenny Lofton, Cle	3
9 tied with	2

The 1993 leaders in home runs saved, McLemore and Salmon, will probably not be confused with Willie Mays. (Lofton, at least, might be confused with Curt Flood.) One thing we hadn't considered was that, in order to prevent a home run, it has to be physically possible. And in some major league parks, the fences are 12 feet high, or higher. Even Michael Jordan would have problems preventing a home run in a park like that, though if he has a good spring training he might get his chance. In Baltimore and California, though, the fences are a user-friendly seven or eight feet high. And that makes all the difference, as anyone who has ever slam-dunked on one of those eight-foot baskets can attest.

The height of the fences is a crucial factor in how many times players on each team either robbed the other club of a home run, or were robbed themselves. Here's a list of the total home runs robbed and saved by each team, and the total number of homers prevented in each park:

Home Runs Robbed/Saved by Team—1993

Team	Robbed	Saved	Total At Park	Team	Robbed	Saved	Total At Park
Orioles	8	7	11	Braves	1	0	0
Red Sox	5	4	6	Cubs	0	1	0
Angels	3	6	7	Reds	2	1	3
White Sox	6	3	4	Rockies	0	1	0
Indians	5	5	5	Marlins	3	2	2
Tigers	3	1	1	Astros	2	0	0
Royals	2	1	0	Dodgers	3	1	2
Brewers	3	4	1	Expos	0	1	0
Twins	3	5	3	Mets	1	4	4
Yankees	5	5	8	Phillies	0	1	0
Athletics	2	4	2	Pirates	1	0	0
Mariners	1	1	0	Cardinals	1	0	0
Rangers	2	0	0	Padres	2	3	3
Blue Jays	1	3	1	Giants	3	4	5

It's obvious that the relatively short fences (seven feet) most of the way around at Baltimore's Camden Yards make for more fence-grabbing catches than at any other major league park. Yankee Stadium (eight home runs saved) and Anaheim Stadium (seven) are similar venues. So it makes perfect sense that the outfielders who saved the most home runs included ones from Baltimore (McLemore), California (Salmon) and the Yankees (James). Similarly, the hitters who were robbed of the most home runs last year were Cal Ripken (Orioles) and Mike Stanley (Yankees) with three each, while the pitcher whose outfielders prevented the most homers was Jamie Moyer of the Orioles, also with three.

Nice symmetry here: among the outfielders who "robbed" opposing hitters of home runs were Robin Yount (two) and Rob Deer; among the hitters who were "robbed" were Rob Ducey, Robin Ventura and Yount.

A complete listing for this category can be found on page 266.

ARE THERE TOO MANY OLD GUYS IN THE GAME?

While winning their second straight world championship last year, the Toronto Blue Jays received major contributions from Paul Molitor, who turned 37 in August, and 36-year-old Dave Stewart. Dave Winfield, who was 41 last year (he turned 42 on October 3), performed well for the Twins and belted the 3,000th hit of his career. Ozzie Smith, 38, continued his brilliant play for the Cardinals. Eddie Murray, who was 37, drove in 100 runs. Lee Smith, who was 35, had his third straight 40-save season. We could go on, but you probably get the point: a lot of veteran players had great years.

When the free agency era began in the late 1970s, many predicted that players would have shorter careers; they'd make their millions and then retire, because they wouldn't need to work any more. But this has not been the case. With a chance to keep earning those big paychecks, numerous players have stayed in shape and stuck around. The chart shows the number of players 35 and up, by 10-year intervals; ages are as of July 1 of each year:

Total Players—35 and Older

Year	#	Year	#
1993	75	1943	63
1983	78	1933	51
1973	43	1923	31
1963	48	1913	22
1953	52	1903	16

The chart shows an interesting pattern: not many older players in the early years of the century, a big jump in the thirties, forties and early fifties, a decline, and then another jump after free agency came in. There are more teams now, and on a per-team basis, there were actually more older players in the 1933-53 time frame than there are now. Why was that? The Great Depression and World War II. In the Depression, jobs were hard to find, and a guy would be a fool not to keep playing ball if he could. During the war, veteran 4-Fs were filling a lot of the roster spots. And in the early 1950s, a lot of the older players were ones who had lost time to the war, hanging around a little longer.

So the presence of a lot of veteran players isn't all that unique; it's happened before, when the circumstances were favorable. But how about the quality of the veteran players? Are today's veterans more effective because of better conditioning? Here's a performance chart, again by 10-year intervals:

Year	# of Batters 35+	Avg	OBP	Slg	AB
1993	31	.273	.336	.404	9,520
1983	47	.272	.344	.405	13,633
1973	24	.260	.335	.399	7,344
1963	26	.248	.313	.356	6,283
1953	31	.275	.358	.406	5,453
1943	31	.260	.337	.339	6,735
1933	23	.266	.339	.351	4,319
1923	22	.305	.374	.426	6,019
1913	17	.289	.364	.378	2,402
1903	13	.277	.323	.357	4,105

Today's crop of oldsters *is* good, but no better in level of performance than the 1983 group, which included Rod Carew (.339), Jose Cruz (.318-14-92) and Carlton Fisk (.289-26-86), who was an old guy in both the 1983 and 1993 groups. Or the 1953 group, which included American League batting champion Mickey Vernon. Or the 1923 group, which included Ty Cobb (.340), Eddie Collins (.360) and Tris Speaker (.380). There is, however, probably more depth of talent today than many years ago. The 1993 group averaged 307 at-bats per man; the 1953 group averaged only 176 at-bats.

How does the pitching talent compare? Here's another chart:

Year	# of Pitchers 35+	ERA	W	L	S	IP
1993	44	4.41	218	261	219	3,942.2
1983	31	3.90	229	261	58	4,422.0
1973	19	3.53	127	117	100	1,886.1
1963	22	3.24	143	142	127	2,525.1
1953	21	3.73	148	146	105	2,547.1
1943	32	3.17	247	198	43	4,113.0
1933	28	3.75	157	150	58	2,814.1
1923	9	3.87	91	84	18	1,528.1
1913	5	2.90	33	37	13	606.0
1903	3	2.58	45	25	2	614.1

There were more veteran pitchers working last year than ever before, though on a per-team basis, 1933 and 1943 still beat it. But the level of talent was not impressive; in fact, it was probably the worst group ever, looked at on the whole. It sure can't compare with the 1963 group, which was led by 42-year-old Warren Spahn (23-7, 2.60). So are there too many old guys in the game today? We'll qualify our answer: there are too many old *pitchers*. Why don't the owners, always whining about player salaries, try some younger arms?

A complete listing for this category can be found on page 267.

WHAT DOES EXPANSION AFFECT MORE: PITCHING OR HITTING?

When the 1993 season began, there was considerable speculation that, since it was an expansion year, teams would be short of pitching. With the explosion of offense in 1993, the pundits seemed to be correct. But is this falloff in pitching the norm for an expansion season? And what *should* we expect from expansion?

In the past, it's often been difficult to judge the effect of expansion, as other significant changes were taking place at the same time. In 1969, the pitching mound was lowered and the strike zone reduced. A new ball was manufactured in 1977. Even in 1961, two hitters' parks were added to the American League (Wrigley Field in Los Angeles and Metropolitan Stadium in Minnesota); all by themselves, the two parks were responsible for that year's increase in home runs.

However, those changes don't affect the relative abilities of ballplayers. In comparison to each other, the worst, average and best ballplayers should be the same, regardless of whether the league batting average is .240 or .300. The "standard deviation" of a statistic measures this variation, and should have a predictable response with respect to expansion.

Major league baseball players represent a minuscule percentage of the population; that is, they are pulled from the extreme high end of the talent curve. If you keep the number of baseball jobs the same while the population increases, this percentage grows ever smaller, and the worst major leaguers are culled from ever higher levels of ability on the normal curve; in other words, as the population increases, the average player gets better. In terms of relative ability, differences between the best and worst players get smaller—or technically, the standard deviation shrinks.

Let's take a look at how the standard deviation of pitching has changed with each expansion; an increase in the standard deviation indicates a dilution of talent:

ERA Qualifiers

Year	Mean ERA	Standard Deviation	Year	Mean ERA	Standard Deviation
1960	3.56	.53	1976	3.30	.51
1961	3.77	.58	1977	3.77	.67
1962	3.71	.65			
			1992	3.51	.69
1968	2.83	.60	1993	3.97	.77
1969	3.35	.68			

The theory holds well for pitching. In each case, the spread between the best and worst ERA qualifiers became larger. Here's the data for batting average:

Batting Average Qualifiers

Year	Mean BA	Standard Deviation	Year	Mean BA	Standard Deviation
1960	.275	.023	1976	.272	.029
1961	.281	.028	1977	.281	.025
1962	.280	.025			
			1992	.274	.027
1968	.262	.028	1993	.281	.027
1969	.272	.027			

The theory does *not* hold well for batters. In three of the five expansions, the standard deviation among batting title qualifiers actually went down. Last year, the change was nonexistent. How can we explain this unexpected finding?

The simplest explanation supported by the data is that it is easier to find hitters than pitchers. The standard deviations among batting title qualifiers range from about eight to 10 percent of the mean; ERA standard deviations, on the other hand, range from 15 to 20 percent of the mean, indicating that pitching talent is more spread out, or thinner, than batting talent. When baseball increases the number of teams, this divergence becomes even greater; hitters take advantage of weak pitchers, offense goes on the rise, and the effect can be so great as to mask an actual dilution of offense!

One last point; it's not going to get better any time soon. We are in the middle of a "baby bust" in which the number of 18-24-year-olds has shrunk over the last 10 years. The Census Bureau reports that in 1980, there were 30.5 million people in the United States in this age group, while in 1990 there were only 26.7 million, about one-sixth less. The Census Bureau does not expect a return to the 1980 level until 2010; even though baseball could heighten the search for talent in places like Latin America, Australia or Japan, we still figure to have at least another 15 years of higher diversity among players. Couple this with the likely expansion to 32 teams by the end of the century, and we could possibly be in for a decade of offense unmatched since the 1930s.

WHAT KIND OF TEAM GOES OFF ON A STREAK?

Few things in baseball are as satisfying as a long winning streak. Conversely, it's hard to match the depression of a long losing streak, when it seems like your favorite club is *never* going to win another game.

Who put together the longest winning streaks of 1993? You'd think it would be the elite teams, the four division winners plus the San Francisco Giants, who won 104 games. But you'd be wrong. The only winnings streaks of 10 games or more last year belonged to the L.A. Dodgers, Boston Red Sox and Baltimore Orioles, none of them exactly powerhouses. Here are the six longest streaks:

Longest Winning Streaks, 1993

Team	Start	End	Streak
Dodgers	May 17	May 29	11
Red Sox	July 16	July 25	10
Orioles	June 2	June 12	10
Expos	August 25	September 4	9
Braves	August 8	August 18	9
Blue Jays	September 10	September 21	9

How was it that such clubs as the Dodgers, Red Sox and Orioles could put together the longest streaks? Momentum is always hard to explain, but one thing which helps build a winning streak is a string of games against sub-par opponents. The Dodgers' winning streak came against the Reds, Rockies, Padres and Pirates; the Red Sox' streak came against the Mariners, Angels and A's; and the Orioles' streak came against the A's, Mariners and Red Sox. The best record among all those clubs was the Mariners' 82-80. But of course, you'd still expect the great teams to have the best streaks, not three clubs whose best record was Baltimore's 85-77.

As for the longest losing streaks, you'd expect the patsies in both leagues to have the longest streaks. But the only two clubs to lose 100 games—the Mets and Padres—didn't make the list, and one club with a respectable 85-77 record, the Detroit Tigers, did make it:

Longest Losing Streaks, 1993

Team	Start	End	Streak
Rockies	July 25	August 6	13
Reds	September 10	September 22	12
Tigers	June 22	July 1	10
Angels	July 17	July 26	10
Athletics	August 21	August 28	9
Twins	June 15	June 23	9

Another way to look at streaks is to examine which clubs put together streaks of three games or more on a consistent basis. This list is about what we'd expect, but again there's a surprise in the Houston Astros, who had a total of 18 winning streaks of three games or more. The chart shows the leaders in both winning and losing streaks.

THE STREAKERS 3-PLUS GAMES	
MOST WINNING STREAKS	
Phillies	19
Astros	18
Braves	17
Giants	15
MOST LOSING STREAKS	
Padres	15
Brewers	14
Marlins	14
3 with	13

While many of these winning streaks were only three games long, it's still interesting that clubs would have so many spurts like this. The Astros, for example, won only 85 games all year, and 62 of those wins came in spurts of three (12 times), four (four times) and five (twice).

What kind of club is best at avoiding losing streaks of three games or more? You'd think it would be clubs with strong pitching, since one man throwing a well-pitched game can end a losing streak almost by himself. The Braves, as expected, were good in this department, with no losing streaks longer than five games. But the Cubs, Expos and Phillies, whose staffs weren't as good, were even better, with no losing streaks longer than four.

A complete listing for this category can be found on page 268.

DO BALLPARKS HAVE AN EFFECT ON WALKS?

We've all heard the phrase, "He's walking the ballpark." But do batters do more walking at some ballparks than at others? The idea seems reasonable. A pitcher working in a hitters' park like Wrigley Field or Mile High Stadium figures to be more reluctant to challenge the hitters; thus the walk rate should go up. Someone pitching in a spacious yard like Kauffman Stadium, on the other hand, would have fewer fears, and thus issue fewer walks. That's the theory, anyway.

So let's look at whether there are significant differences in the walk rates at major league parks. As we usually do when studying park effects, we'll create an index based on the walk rate for both teams (home and visitors) during each club's home games, and compare it with the walk rate during the club's road games. An index of 100 means a neutral park; one over 100 means that the walk rate is higher than normal. Here are the figures for the American League, based on the last three seasons unless the club moved to a new park or the old one changed configuration:

American League Park Effects on Bases on Balls

Team	Home BB/AB	Road BB/AB	Index	Team	Home BB/AB	Road BB/AB	Index
Tigers	.119	.110	108	Blue Jays	.102	.100	101
Brewers	.097	.090	107	Twins	.091	.090	101
Indians	.096	.090	106	Athletics	.118	.119	99
Red Sox	.103	.098	105	White Sox	.107	.108	98
Orioles	.110	.108	103	Angels	.091	.096	94
Mariners	.109	.106	103	Rangers	.100	.106	94
Yankees	.100	.098	102	Royals	.086	.095	90

(1991-93 unless park was new or changed configuration)

Most of the numbers are in line with our expectations—for instance, Tiger Stadium is at the top and Kansas City's Kauffman Stadium is at the bottom. There are some surprises, however, particularly the high walk rate at Milwaukee County Stadium, a tough home run park. Do pitchers fill up on beer and bratwurst before the game, and then have trouble getting the ball over the plate? Seems unlikely, but it *could* have something to do with the mound at County Stadium, considered one of the more poorly groomed surfaces in the majors. Or it could just be a fluke.

The low rating at California's Anaheim Stadium is another surprise, since this has been a good home run park in recent years. For the most part, though, the data supports the notion that when a park is good for offense, the walk rate will go up.

Here is the National League data:

National League Park Effects on Bases on Balls

Team	Home BB/AB	Road BB/AB	Index	Team	Home BB/AB	Road BB/AB	Index
Rockies	.096	.082	117	Padres	.086	.087	99
Reds	.099	.088	113	Braves	.093	.094	98
Marlins	.105	.095	110	Cubs	.086	.088	98
Pirates	.093	.092	102	Astros	.091	.093	98
Expos	.096	.095	101	Mets	.088	.092	96
Dodgers	.097	.098	99	Giants	.085	.089	96
Phillies	.103	.105	99	Cardinals	.081	.086	94

This data is also pretty much in line with the theory, but not completely. Colorado's Mile High Stadium has been the best park for offense in recent times, and Cincinnati's Riverfront Stadium is tops for home runs. Busch Stadium in St. Louis, which ranks last, is a very tough home run park. But again, there are some mysteries, like the very high ranking of Florida's Joe Robbie Stadium—a neutral home run park last year, and one which slightly favored offense overall. (Is it the mound?) The below-average rankings for Wrigley Field and Jack Murphy Stadium, both very good home run parks, are also very surprising.

On balance, it does seem that the type of park has an effect on the walk rate—particularly a hitters' paradise like Colorado. Some of the baffling figures, however, indicate that we'll have to study the figures over several more seasons before we can clear up some of the mysteries.

HOW MUCH DOES ALTITUDE AFFECT HOW FAR A BALL TRAVELS?

Until 1993, almost every major league team played on a "level playing field," at least in one sense: there was little difference in the altitude—the distance above sea level—of the major league parks. With one exception, all the major league cities were less than 1,000 feet above sea level.

What difference does altitude make? Well, one clue might have come from the major league city which had the highest altitude prior to 1993. Fulton County Stadium in Atlanta, where the altitude is 1,050 feet, was long known as "The Launching Pad" for home runs, despite the fact that its park dimensions weren't any different than many other major league parks. As Dick O'Brien noted in a pioneering 1986 article in *The Baseball Analyst*, "altitude . . . [has] a significant effect on home run production." O'Brien relied mainly on home run data from minor league parks with high altitudes. Yale physicist Robert K. Adair got a little more scientific in his book, *The Physics of Baseball*. Adair stated that a 400-foot fly ball at Yankee Stadium could be expected to travel 408 feet in Atlanta.

Adair's book was published in 1990, three years before the major leagues finally got a park with *really* high altitude: Mile High Stadium in Denver. Adair felt that flyballs hit in Denver could be expected to travel as much as 10 percent farther than balls hit in parks with normal altitudes. Was he right? We can shed some light on the subject, using our extensive database. Our reporters calculate the distance of every batted ball; by comparing the average distance of a flyball hit by both clubs (home and road) in each team's home games, and then comparing it with the average distance a flyball traveled in the same club's road games, we can come up with a "flyball ballpark index." Here are those indexes, based on 1991-93 games, unless a club moved into a new park or its old park changed configuration:

Average Distance of Flyballs in Clubs' Home and Road Games

AL Team	Home	Away	Index	NL Team	Home	Away	Index
Baltimore	313	315	99	Atlanta	320	313	102
Boston	311	313	99	Chicago	310	314	99
California	316	313	101	Cincinnati	319	314	102
Chicago	316	313	101	Colorado	335	316	106
Cleveland	304	316	96	Florida	313	316	99
Detroit	311	317	98	Houston	319	315	101
Kansas City	315	313	101	Los Angeles	315	313	101
Milwaukee	313	314	100	Montreal	312	313	100
Minnesota	322	315	102	New York	308	315	98

Average Distance of Flyballs in Clubs' Home and Road Games

AL Team	Home	Away	Index	NL Team	Home	Away	Index
New York	313	317	99	Philadelphia	313	315	99
Oakland	308	316	98	Pittsburgh	317	314	101
Seattle	319	314	102	St. Louis	321	313	102
Texas	323	315	103	San Diego	305	315	97
Toronto	316	314	101	San Francisco	304	317	96

(1991-93 unless park or park configuration changed)

The data clearly suggests that the ball travels much farther in Denver than in any other park. The park index for Mile High was 106; only one other park had an index higher than 102, the now-defunct Arlington Stadium in Texas. Atlanta's index of 102 was higher than most, though several other parks matched it. One thousand feet above sea level isn't all *that* high.

Though the difference between Denver and the other parks was less than Adair's prediction of 10 percent, that doesn't mean he was wrong. There are other factors which affect how far a ball travels, including temperature, humidity and wind. The low indexes for two notoriously cold, windy stadiums—Candlestick Park in San Francisco and Cleveland Stadium (also defunct as of 1994)—is a strong indication of those effects. On the other hand, the domed stadiums at Minnesota, Seattle, and Houston, as well as the often-enclosed SkyDome in Toronto, all had indexes over 100—indicating that the lack of wind may have helped the flight of the ball. The domed stadium in Montreal, which was sometimes open, sometimes closed during the period, was a neutral 100.

Then there's humidity, a factor that Dick O'Brien thought might be as significant as altitude. In an article in last year's *Scoreboard*, "Does Humidity Affect Scoring?" we concluded that there was no reason to think that high humidity, by itself, would decrease the home run rate. Adair agrees with the basic premise, stating, "the humidity, per se, has little effect on the ball's flight." He even noted that, all other things being equal, "a ball will travel slightly *farther* (italics his) if the humidity is high."

However, Adair also noted that high humidity has an effect on the elasticity of the baseball, and felt that balls stored in humid conditions would be heavier, and thus not travel as far. There's the famous story of the White Sox refrigerating baseballs in the late 1960s—or at least keeping them in a cold, damp place—in order to help their pitching staff. Which it would. Factors like that are hard to pin down, but might have an impact on the park indexes presented above. However, no other factor would have quite the influence that Denver's high altitude does. This is the true "Launching Pad."

WHAT HAPPENS WHEN A PLAYER SWITCHES LEAGUES?

In 1973, outfielder Jay Johnstone was released by the Oakland A's after spending eight years in the American League. Johnstone had never batted higher than .270. But then he signed with the Phillies, and for the next four years he batted .295, .329, .318 and .284. Thus would begin one of the weirdest career patterns ever. Johnstone, who wound up spending 20 years in the majors, switched back and forth between leagues, and the story was this: in the NL he hit (lifetime .288), in the AL he didn't (.243). Heck, people even said that, for the first few seasons he was broadcasting, Johnstone *announced* NL games better. Seems a little far-fetched, but . . .

Johnstone was a legendary fastball hitter, and his career is often cited as evidence that a switch from the National League (the "fastball league") to the American (the "breaking-ball league") can wreak havoc with a player's career. If you wanted testimonial evidence, you could point to players like Wally Backman, who batted .303 for the 1988 Mets, went to the Twins the next year and hit .231, then moved back to the NL with the Pirates and saw his average move back up to .292. National League boosters could cite the case of Eddie Murray, who after hitting .284 with the 1988 Orioles, batted .248 for the '89 Dodgers. Or Dan Gladden, who went from .276 with the '86 Giants to .249 with the '87 Twins. And on and on.

Testimonial evidence is interesting, but what does the *complete* evidence say about what happens when a player switches leagues? To find the answer, we decided to go back to the start of the 1977 season, which was when free agency came in, making it easier for a player to change leagues. That was also the year the American League expanded to 14 teams, so it's a good place to start. What we did was to compare players who switched leagues from one season to the next, with a significant amount of action in each season: at least 250 plate appearances, or 100 innings pitched for pitchers. That way, we'd be making our comparisons based on a reasonable amount of evidence. The chart summarizes the results:

Batters Who Switched					Overall	
Year One	**Avg**		**Year Two**	**Avg**		**Avg**
American	.266	to	National	.268	National	.270
National	.265	to	American	.264	American	.270

Pitchers Who Switched					Overall	
Year One	**ERA**		**Year Two**	**ERA**		**ERA**
American	3.93	to	National	3.58	National	3.57
National	3.74	to	American	3.82	American	3.91

(Year Two range is 1978-93. Based on players with a minimum 250 PA or 100 IP in each of the two seasons.)

At first glance, the data seems to indicate that the American League is better; when a typical player goes from the AL to the NL, his average goes up, while when he switches the other way (NL to AL), his average drops. For pitchers, the change is even more dramatic. American League pitchers switching to the NL saw their ERAs go down significantly, while National League pitchers changing to the American saw their ERAs go up.

However, those numbers are deceptive unless put into a league perspective. The biggest difference in the leagues is that the American League has the DH rule, while National League pitchers have to hit. In addition, National League parks—at least until the addition of Mile High Stadium—have tended to be bigger, and better for the pitcher. Because of that, there's more scoring in the AL, and any pitcher switching from the National League to the American would be expected to have his ERA rise.

For the period, the ERA difference between the leagues for similar pitchers (100-plus innings a season) was 0.34 runs. American League pitchers switching to the National League saw their ERAs drop by 0.35 runs, or virtually no difference. However, the National League pitchers who shifted to the American League saw their ERAs rise by only 0.08 runs. These pitchers were worse than the NL average before they switched leagues; they were better than the AL average after the switch. National League pitchers actually thrived in their new environment.

The story is a little different for the hitters. The "overall" group, which consists of the hitters who had at least 250 plate appearances in each season, showed no difference—the average for each league was .270. However, American League hitters switching to the National League saw their average rise by two points; National League hitters switching to the American saw their batting average drop by a point. This difference is very slight, and probably not very significant, but it does suggest that National League hitters switching leagues have more difficulty making the adjustment than their pitching counterparts do.

So what happens when a player switches leagues depends a lot on whether he's a hitter or a pitcher. The evidence indicates that National League pitchers moving to the American League generally find the move to their liking. For hitters, it doesn't seem to make a lot of difference . . . except maybe for Jay Johnstone.

A complete listing for this category can be found on page 269.

DOES GOOD PITCHING BEAT GOOD HITTING IN THE POSTSEASON?

Every baseball fan has heard this one several thousand times: "In a short series, good pitching beats good heating" . . . I mean, hitting. We'll undoubtedly keep hearing it, despite all the times it doesn't happen. If you don't believe us, just ask the Atlanta Braves.

Exactly how often *does* good pitching beat good hitting in the postseason? The question occurred not only to us, but to a fine baseball analyst named Don Coffin, who wrote about the subject in the SABR newsletter, *By the Numbers.* Coffin studied all the playoffs and World Series going back to 1969, and to quote him, "I find nothing to suggest that we should expect teams with stronger pitching to do exceptionally well against other championship-caliber teams." We decided to go back to the start of the modern World Series, 1903, to see if those conclusions held up.

We'll stick with Coffin's basic methodology, which begins with forming a pitching and batting index for each team. To calculate the pitching index, you simply divide the team's ERA by the league ERA for that season, and multiply it by 100. To find the hitting index, you divide the team runs-per-game average by the league average for that season, and again multiply by 100. An average team in each category would have an index of 100; a team with above-average hitting or pitching would have an index above 100.

Using those indexes, Coffin then identified four types of teams which would be central to the study. A "dominant hitting" team, one which relies on its offense to win, is one with a batting index greater than 100 and a pitching index less than 100. A "dominant pitching" team is just the opposite: pitching index over 100, hitting index under 100. A "stronger hitting" team is one which doesn't qualify as dominant, but whose hitting index in greater than its pitching index. A "stronger pitching" is just the opposite, a non-dominant team whose pitching index is greater than its hitting index. There's one additional rule: to qualify for any category, the difference between the indexes must be a least five points. Many clubs would qualify for none of the categories, and would rank as "neutral."

This probably sounds complicated, but it really isn't. Here are four recent teams, and where they would rank:

Team	Pitching Index	Batting Index	Category
1969 Mets	120.5	96.2	Dominant Pitching
1993 White Sox	116.5	101.8	Stronger Pitching
1975 Red Sox	95.0	115.7	Dominant Hitting
1993 Blue Jays	102.7	111.1	Stronger Hitting

Now for the match-ups. What happens in the classic case, when a "hitting" team (dominant or stronger) meets a "pitching" team (same criteria)? This has happened 29 times in either the World Series or the championship series ("LCS" below also includes the pre-LCS "division series" of 1981):

Dominant/Stronger Hitting Teams vs Dominant/Stronger Pitching Teams

	Hitting	Pitching
World Series Won	12	7
LCS Won	6	4
Total	**18**	**11**

So "good pitching beats good hitting," eh? The hitting-dominated clubs won 18 of the 29 match-ups, including both of the 1993 playoff series. The last pitching-oriented club to win a World Series was the 1989 Athletics.

Of course, there are other possible match-ups, which involve a hitting- or pitching-dominated club taking on a neutral team. "Neutrality" turns out to be a good policy:

Dominant/Stronger Hitting or Pitching Teams vs Neutral Teams

	Hitting vs. Neutral		Pitching vs. Neutral	
	W	L	W	L
World Series	3	10	6	10
LCS	8	6	10	6
Total	**11**	**16**	**16**	**16**

The hitting-oriented clubs had a lot of problems with neutral teams, while the pitching-oriented clubs played dead even. Overall, the hitting-oriented clubs met either neutral or pitching-oriented clubs in a total of 56 series, and had a record of 29-27. Pitching-oriented clubs met either neutral or hitting-oriented clubs in 61 series, and had a record of 27-34. And neutral teams met clubs of either stripe in 59 series, and had a record of 32-27.

In summary, there's no reason to think that "good pitching beats good hitting in a short series." Any advantage which a pitching-oriented club has seems to be in *getting* to the postseason. Of the 240 teams which have finished in first place since 1901 (including the half-seasons in 1981), 96 have been pitching-oriented, 71 hitting-oriented and 73 neutral. So pitching may be an advantage in getting to the postseason, but it seems to offer no special advantage from then on.

A complete listing for this category can be found on page 270.

DO THOSE 3-AND-2 FOULS PAY OFF?

Our friend Bill Brown, the Detroit Tigers' traveling secretary, is good for at least one *Scoreboard* study per year, and this year he wanted to know about all those foul balls on 3-and-2 counts. Is it true, as Bill says the Tiger announcers always report, that the most common result of a 3-and-2 pitch is a foul ball? Our hunch is that the Detroit broadcasters are especially "tuned in" to those foul balls, since the Tiger Stadium broadcast booth is extremely—some would say dangerously—close to home plate. So fellows, this one's for you.

Let's look at an event breakdown from every major league game over the last three years, according to the ball-and-strike count:

Results by Ball-and-Strike Count, 1991-93 in Percentages

Count	Ball	Taken Strike	Swung & Missed	Fouled	Hit Into Play
0-0	43.6	25.6	6.2	11.0	13.6
1-0	35.1	20.7	8.1	15.8	20.3
2-0	32.3	25.4	6.3	15.2	20.9
3-0	37.7	52.9	1.4	3.4	4.5
0-1	44.2	10.7	9.8	15.9	19.5
1-1	36.7	11.0	10.4	18.6	23.3
2-1	29.2	10.0	9.8	22.3	28.7
3-1	27.3	14.4	6.8	19.8	31.6
0-2	49.0	4.8	11.1	16.5	18.5
1-2	37.5	4.5	12.7	20.7	24.6
2-2	29.7	4.4	12.4	24.1	29.4
3-2	22.3	4.0	10.6	27.6	35.6

The announcers were off by a little. The most common result from a 3-and-2 two pitch isn't a foul ball, but a ball being put into play. However, the next most common result *is* a foul ball, and a greater percentage of pitches are fouled off on 3-and-2 than on any other count.

Why are there so many fouls on full counts? Well, the pitcher needs to throw a strike to avoid giving up a walk, and the batter needs to swing at anything marginal in order to avoid being called out on strikes. The hitter is often content to "just get a piece of the ball" and foul it off; after all, it's not costing him anything.

And in fact, it might be gaining him something substantial. A study we did several years ago showed that the more two-strike fouls a batter hits, the better he will perform. This chart shows that, on a 3-and-2 pitch, a foul ball is anything but a waste of time:

3-2 Count Results by # of Fouls

#Fouls	Avg	OBP	Slg
0	.220	.455	.341
1	.235	.475	.370
2+	.240	.474	.394

(Major Leagues, 1991-93)

Over the last three years, hitters improved their batting average by 15 points, and their slugging average by a whopping 29 points, when they hit even a single foul on a 3-2 count. If they hit two foul balls, there was still further improvement. Two-strike fouls in general, we should point out, improve a batter's chances of getting a hit, whether the count is 3-and-2 or not. They force the pitcher to keep throwing more strikes, and thus improve the batter's chances of ultimate success.

So a note to you in Detroit and elsewhere: those 3-and-2 fouls may drive you so crazy that you think there are more of them than there actually are. But if your club's hitter is the one fouling them off, you ought to be glad (as long as you can keep out of the way!).

A complete listing for this category can be found on page 272.

IS THERE REALLY A "SOPHOMORE JINX"?

In 1949, Roy Sievers was the American League Rookie of the Year, hitting .306 and driving in 91 runs. In 1950, Sievers batted .238 and drove in 57 runs. People said that Sievers was a victim of the "Sophomore Jinx."

In 1959, Willie McCovey made a sensational debut with the San Francisco Giants, hitting .354 and belting 13 homers in only 52 games. That winter, he was rewarded with the National League Rookie of the Year award. But the next year, McCovey hit only .238, and even spent some time back in the minor leagues. People said that McCovey was a victim of the "Sophomore Jinx."

In 1980, "Super Joe" Charboneau was the toast of Cleveland, hitting .289 with 23 homers and winning the American League Rookie of the Year award. In 1981, Charboneau batted just .210 with four homers, and his major league career would be over after 22 games (with a .214 average) in 1982. People said that Charboneau was *really* a victim of the "Sophomore Jinx."

What's the "Sophomore Jinx"? It comes when a player has a good rookie year, then struggles through the next, supposedly because the pitchers (or hitters) have "figured out his weakness." Sometimes the player will recover and go on to have a fine career, as did Sievers and McCovey. Sometimes he won't recover and his career will end quickly, as was the case with Charboneau. Does the Sophomore Jinx happen to everyone? Well maybe we should ask the 1984 National League Rookie of the Year, Dwight Gooden. The Doc followed up that campaign by going 24-4 with a 1.53 ERA, and a Cy Young Award, in 1985.

Is Gooden the exception, or is McCovey? Or neither? To try to find the answer, we looked at all players who were active in 1993, and examined their stats for their rookie season (if they had a minimum of 250 plate appearances), their sophomore season, and then for the rest of their careers. Here's how they fared; "RC/27" is runs created per 27 outs, a standard Bill James measurement of offensive production:

Searching for the Hitter's Sophomore Jinx

Year	Avg	OBP	Slg	RC/27
1st	.265	.326	.393	4.43
2nd	.265	.329	.397	4.53
3rd+	.275	.343	.420	5.09

(1993 active players; minimum 250 PA in the 1st year)

Looking at this data, there's little reason to think that the average rookie will slump in his sophomore year; the players actually improved a little during their second season, and then improved still more after that. This is, of course, perfectly reasonable when you think about it. Most players are fairly young when they begin their careers, and the tendency is to improve until they reach their peak at around age 27. Improvement is no surprise; it's to be expected.

How do pitchers fare in their sophomore years? Here's the same comparison, for pitchers active in 1993:

Searching for the Pitcher's Sophomore Jinx

Year	G	IP	W	L	Pct	Sv	ERA
1st	6,498	21,086.1	1,257	1,153	.522	470	3.71
2nd	6,292	21,143.2	1,273	1,145	.526	638	3.68
3rd+	36,401	128,555.1	7,820	6,921	.530	4,584	3.63

(1993 active pitchers; minimum 100 IP or 40 games pitched in rookie year)

The results are similar to what happened to the hitters: pitchers also improve in their sophomore years, and then keep improving after that. Again this is logical, as younger players tend to progress toward their peak seasons.

Of course, this data is for players overall, and doesn't address the question of whether there's been a Sophomore Jinx—or at least a falloff—for the ones who were named Rookie of the Year. Since we want to follow the players' careers for at least two seasons following their rookie campaign, we'll stop with the 1991 winners. Here is how the hitters who won the award have fared in their sophomore year and afterward:

Rookies of the Year, 1947-91 (Hitters)

Year	Avg	OBP	SLG	RC/27
1st	.285	.348	.443	5.51
2nd	.275	.339	.416	5.00
3rd+	.278	.350	.437	5.48

There is a definite second-year falloff here, though the performances remained quite good. In actuality, a dropoff in the year after an exceptional performance is to be expected; it's hard to maintain such a high level. As a group, the players came back to perform at about their rookie levels over the rest of their careers, but no better, which suggests how good the rookie seasons were. You could call what happened in their second season a "Sophomore Jinx," but it would be a stretch. Most players would love to have seasons like this.

Only 23 pitchers have won the Rookie of the Year award, and what happened to them is quite interesting:

Rookies of the Year, 1947-91 (Pitchers)

Year	G	IP	W	L	Pct	Sv	ERA
1st	937	4597.2	337	192	.637	115	2.77
2nd	910	4236.2	263	229	.535	106	3.46
3rd+	5646	25583.1	1549	1324	.539	556	3.51

Like the hitters, the pitchers were unable to maintain their rookie magic, though like the hitters, their level of performance remained good. As a group, however, their rookie seasons were far better than the rest of their careers. A number of them turned out to be flukes: Joe Black, Harry Byrd, Bob Grim, Butch Metzger, Don Schwall, to name five. Only one pitcher who won a Rookie of the Year award has made the Hall of Fame: Tom Seaver. A great rookie season from a pitcher, we have to conclude, is a much less reliable indicator of future stardom than one from a hitter.

In summary, there *is* no "sophomore jinx" for most players; the average player tends to do better, not worse, in his second season. Rookies of the Year do tend to experience a dropoff, though they continue to play well overall. The expectation would be that Mike Piazza and Tim Salmon won't be as good in 1994 as they were in 1993, and that people will call it the "sophomore jinx"—even though they're likely to remain high-quality players.

A complete listing of this category can be found on page 273.

ARE THESE THE GOOD OLD DAYS?

What was baseball like in 1910? Or 1935? Or 1953? We have books and newsreel footage, but one of our best sources is the record of what happened: the stuff in the encyclopedias. We thought we'd go down the decades, starting in 1901, and discuss what made each one unique. Beam me down to where I can find Nap Lajoie and Honus Wagner, Scottie:

Decade	Avg	OBP	Slg	R/G	HR/G	SB/G	W/9	K/9	ERA
1901-09	.252	.310	.326	7.86	0.3	2.4	2.5	3.6	2.79

This is usually called the "Dead Ball Era," and though the game was pretty lively on the field, that's a fair enough assessment. With anemic home run rates and low ERAs, teams had to scramble for runs with the bunt, the hit-and-run, and the stolen base, which was at the highest rate for this century. Player and pitcher of the decade: Honus Wagner (.348) and Christy Mathewson (236 wins).

Decade	Avg	OBP	Slg	R/G	HR/G	SB/G	W/9	K/9	ERA
1910-19	.255	.322	.338	7.84	0.3	2.3	3.0	3.7	2.96

Still the Dead Ball Era, but more depressing: this one ended with the White Sox throwing the World Series. There were signs that offense was beginning to pick up, and Babe Ruth made his debut. Player and pitcher of the decade: Ty Cobb (.387) and Walter Johnson (265 wins).

Decade	Avg	OBP	Slg	R/G	HR/G	SB/G	W/9	K/9	ERA
1920-29	.285	.347	.397	9.61	0.8	1.2	3.0	2.8	4.03

"The Ruth is mighty and shall prevail," as Heywood Broun put it in 1923. Offense picked up enormously, with the best batting average for any decade. But vestiges of the old game were still around: in the '20s, there were still more triples hit than home runs. Player and pitcher of the decade: Babe Ruth (.355, 467 homers) and Grover Cleveland Alexander (165 wins).

Decade	Avg	OBP	Slg	R/G	HR/G	SB/G	W/9	K/9	ERA
1930-39	.279	.342	.399	9.87	1.1	0.8	3.3	3.4	4.28

The best decade for scoring, and the home run rate went over one a game for the first time. Ruth and Gehrig went out, but Joe DiMaggio, Ted Williams and Bob Feller came in. Player and pitcher of the decade: Jimmie

Foxx (.336, 415 homers) and Lefty Grove (199 wins).

Decade	Avg	OBP	Slg	R/G	HR/G	SB/G	W/9	K/9	ERA
1940-49	.260	.332	.368	8.61	1.0	0.7	3.6	3.6	3.75

The decade was dominated by World War II, but while no one was looking, batting averages dropped almost 20 points. Jackie Robinson debuted in 1947, and began a revolution. Player and pitcher of the decade: Ted Williams (.356, 234 homers) and Bob Feller (137 wins), each of whom lost at least three seasons to the war.

Decade	Avg	OBP	Slg	R/G	HR/G	SB/G	W/9	K/9	ERA
1950-59	.259	.331	.391	8.89	1.7	0.6	3.6	4.4	3.97

The best decade for home runs, and the worst for stolen bases: a bunch of big galoots like Ralph Kiner slamming the ball over the fence. The Dodgers and Giants moved west in 1958, and began another revolution. Player and pitcher of the decade: Stan Musial (.330, 266 homers) and Warren Spahn (202 wins).

Decade	Avg	OBP	Slg	R/G	HR/G	SB/G	W/9	K/9	ERA
1960-69	.249	.314	.374	8.08	1.6	0.8	3.1	5.7	3.56

Baseball expanded in 1961, and Roger Maris hit 61 homers. The owners put an end to that fun by expanding the strike zone in 1963, and the decade was dominated by pitching; for the only decade in the century, the batting average dropped below .250, which helped revive the stolen base. Player and pitcher of the decade: Hank Aaron (.308, 375 homers) and Sandy Koufax (137 wins).

Decade	Avg	OBP	Slg	R/G	HR/G	SB/G	W/9	K/9	ERA
1970-79	.256	.323	.377	8.31	1.5	1.2	3.3	5.2	3.70

Offense picked up again after the strike zone was reduced, but this was another great decade for pitchers, with Jim Palmer, Steve Carlton, Tom Seaver, Ferguson Jenkins, and many others. The free agent era began after the 1976 season, beginning yet another revolution. Player and pitcher of the decade: Joe Morgan (.282, 173 homers) and Jim Palmer (186 wins).

Decade	Avg	OBP	Slg	R/G	HR/G	SB/G	W/9	K/9	ERA
1980-89	.259	.324	.388	8.60	1.6	1.5	3.2	5.4	3.87

The game revives: offense on the upswing, young players coming in, attendance rising. The stolen base rate was the highest since the teens, and the complete game became a thing of the past. Player and pitcher of the decade: Mike Schmidt (313 home runs) and Jack Morris (162 wins).

Decade	Avg	OBP	Slg	R/G	HR/G	SB/G	W/9	K/9	ERA
1990-93	.259	.326	.388	8.65	1.6	1.5	3.3	5.7	3.93

Still going on at a ballpark near you. Barry Bonds, Frank Thomas, Mile High Stadium, the Braves pitching staff. We like it already. Players of the (four-tenths of a) decade: Barry Bonds (.310, 138 homers) and Greg Maddux (70 wins).

A complete listing for this category can be found on page 274.

III. QUESTIONS ON OFFENSE

WHO OUGHT TO BE A LEADOFF MAN?

Every club has a leadoff man, but the leadoff man isn't the only player who leads off innings. Got that? What we mean is that, over the course of a season, every player in the batting order is going to lead off an inning a number of times. If the man performing that role does things that help produce runs, the club's offense will be better.

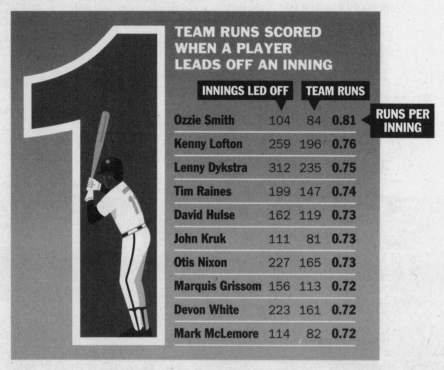

TEAM RUNS SCORED WHEN A PLAYER LEADS OFF AN INNING

	INNINGS LED OFF	TEAM RUNS	RUNS PER INNING
Ozzie Smith	104	84	0.81
Kenny Lofton	259	196	0.76
Lenny Dykstra	312	235	0.75
Tim Raines	199	147	0.74
David Hulse	162	119	0.73
John Kruk	111	81	0.73
Otis Nixon	227	165	0.73
Marquis Grissom	156	113	0.72
Devon White	223	161	0.72
Mark McLemore	114	82	0.72

The chart shows the most effective "leadoff men" of 1993—whether or not they were batting number one in the lineup. It shows the number of times the player led off an inning, the number of runs his club scored in those innings, and the average number of runs scored per inning. On that basis, the most productive leadoff man was the Wizard himself, Ozzie Smith of the Cardinals. Oddly enough, Smith didn't bat leadoff at all last year, as he spent most of the season in his familiar number-two spot. But the numbers suggest he was being mis-used, which is not really a far-fetched idea. Even at his advanced age, Smith still possesses discipline, speed and the ability to steal an occasional base—the qualities clubs look for in a leadoff man.

Most of the other players on the list, though, *were* number-one hitters, like Kenny Lofton, Lenny Dykstra and Tim Raines. Many of the others, like Smith, batted second. The only exceptions were Marquis Grissom, a sometimes-number one hitter who usually hit third last year, and that speedy leadoff-type hitter, John Kruk of the Phillies. Kruk's presence points up the fact that any "leadoff man" looks better if he has some potent hitters in the lineup behind him to move him around and drive him in.

Another way to look at this category is to rate the hitters on how consistently their clubs scored at least one run in the innings they led off. For example, Grissom of the Expos led off 156 innings last year, and the Expos scored at least one run in 64 of them, for a "run-scoring percentage" of .410. That was the best performance in baseball last year:

Player, Team	Innings Led Off	1+Runs Scored	RunSc%
Marquis Grissom, Mon	156	64	.410
Ozzie Smith, StL	104	42	.404
Devon White, Tor	223	90	.404
Kenny Lofton, Cle	259	103	.398
Matt Williams, SF	149	59	.396
Orlando Merced, Pit	101	40	.396
Ron Gant, Atl	132	52	.394
Derrick May, Cubs	121	47	.388
Tim Raines, WSox	199	77	.387
Ken Griffey Jr, Sea	131	50	.382

This list is somewhat different from the first. While there are some real leadoff men like Lofton and Raines, and some others like Grissom and Smith who could (or should) be, there are also a lot of unlikely characters like Matt Williams and Ron Gant. Why were the Giants so consistently good at scoring runs in innings led off by the slow-footed Williams? Well, for one thing, he often took care of that chore himself, leading off 14 innings with home runs last year. He also had a trusty "number-two" hitter—the man who hit behind him in the lineup, Barry Bonds.

On the other hand, there was Jody Reed of the Dodgers, a guy who's often batted leadoff in his career. Last year Reed was a frequent number-two hitter, and his on-base percentage was a serviceable .333. Yet his club averaged only 0.36 runs per inning in the frames he led off, and scored at least one run in only 16.8 percent of them. Part of that was due to the fact that when Reed wasn't hitting second, he was usually batting eighth. Most of the problem, though, was due to lack of punch in the Dodger lineup. You can't be an effective "leadoff man" without some good people following you.

A complete listing for this category can be found on page 275.

WILL THE AMERICAN LEAGUE DOMINATE THE FUTURE?

Thirty years ago, the National League appeared to be the dominant league. The NL won the All-Star game every year from 1963 to 1970, and four of the five World Series from 1963 through 1967. A key to that dominance was all the young talent in the league. For example, Roberto Clemente was only 28 years old in 1963. Frank Robinson was 27. Vada Pinson was 26. Orlando Cepeda, Willie McCovey and Billy Williams were 25. Lou Brock was 24. Ron Santo and Willie Stargell were 23, and Pete Rose, that season's Rookie of the Year, was only 22. That's a very impressive array of talent, most of it consisting of African- and Latin-American players. In fact, much of the National League's edge back then was due to the fact that it was quicker to integrate than the American League.

Such an edge no longer exists, and these days, people are starting to say that the American League is the dominant one. The AL has now won five straight All-Star games, and the last three World Series. And as was the case 30 years ago, young talent is the key. Last year Rafael Palmeiro was only 28 years old. Albert Belle and Kenny Lofton were 26. Roberto Alomar and Frank Thomas were 25. Carlos Baerga, Travis Fryman, John Olerud and Tim Salmon were 24. Juan Gonzalez and Ken Griffey Jr. were 23, and Ivan Rodriguez just 21. That's impressive as well.

One of our readers is an American League booster, and he suggested that we compare last year's American League All-Star team to the National League squad 30 years before that, with an eye on the younger talent. It sounded like a good idea, but we immediately encountered some problems. For one thing, All-Star teams always include some players who look a little less than immortal in retrospect. And the league's selectors always leave off some very worthy players. So we'll alter the idea by choosing squads of the best young players in each league for the years in question. Since we know the complete career accomplishments of the '63 team but not the '93 one, we'll even things out a little by showing the career stats for the earlier generation only through 1963. Here are each league's best position players who were 28 or younger (age as of July 1), with their career records to that point:

1963 National League Stars (Age 28 or Under)

Name	Age	Avg	OBP	Slg	G	HR	RBI	SB
Lou Brock	24	.258	.310	.392	275	18	72	40
Orlando Cepeda	25	.310	.352	.537	920	191	650	83
Roberto Clemente	28	.303	.337	.439	1,213	92	570	44
Tommy Davis	24	.313	.346	.467	552	69	343	49
Willie McCovey	25	.282	.362	.549	502	108	295	8
Vada Pinson	26	.309	.357	.492	806	102	446	131

Frank Robinson	27	.303	.392	.557	1,190	262	800	125
Pete Rose	22	.273	.337	.371	157	6	41	13
Ron Santo	23	.266	.330	.434	573	74	309	12
Willie Stargell	23	.248	.298	.430	118	11	51	0
Joe Torre	22	.286	.344	.422	337	29	139	5
Billy Williams	25	.285	.355	.477	496	74	281	22

1993 American League Stars (Age 28 or Under)

Name	Age	Avg	OBP	Slg	G	HR	RBI	SB
Roberto Alomar	25	.297	.364	.416	914	56	395	247
Carlos Baerga	24	.301	.344	.440	581	59	335	28
Albert Belle	26	.270	.330	.505	506	108	376	36
Travis Fryman	24	.277	.337	.451	527	72	311	32
Juan Gonzalez	23	.274	.326	.535	486	121	348	8
Ken Griffey	23	.303	.375	.520	734	132	453	77
Kenny Lofton	26	.299	.377	.376	316	6	84	138
John Olerud	24	.297	.398	.488	552	71	289	1
Rafael Palmeiro	28	.296	.360	.472	1,046	132	526	50
Ivan Rodriguez	21	.266	.301	.379	348	21	130	8
Tim Salmon	24	.269	.369	.500	165	33	101	6
Frank Thomas	25	.321	.441	.561	531	104	383	11

You can see why people are impressed with the level of young talent in the American League today. While none of the current AL stars have the career totals compiled by Orlando Cepeda or Frank Robinson through '63, the current players tend to be younger. And they've already accomplished a lot. We can't say that Juan Gonzalez will grow up to be Frank Robinson, or that Frank Thomas' numbers will eventually surpass Willie McCovey's. But they're off to a very good start, and there's good reason to be excited.

We haven't discussed pitchers in this article, mostly because the careers of young pitchers are notoriously unpredictable. But the 1963 National League included Sandy Koufax (age 27), Don Drysdale (26) and Juan Marichal (25), to name three. We'll have to wait and see whether the likes of Jack McDowell (27 last year), Kevin Appier (25), Mike Mussina (24) and Alex Fernandez (23) can measure up to those immortals, but the American League doesn't embarrass itself in *that* comparison, either. Will they dominate? We'll have to wait and see.

HOW GOOD IS AVERAGE?

If you were an American League manager, would you like this lineup? Behind the plate, you've got a good defensive catcher with a respectable bat, Dave Valle. At first base, there's a great veteran, Don Mattingly. At second, another scrappy vet, Scott Fletcher. At short and third, two well-regarded young players in Mike Bordick and Ed Sprague. Your outfield seems solid with Brady Anderson, Bernie Williams and Ellis Burks. Your designated hitter—we're assuming he didn't retire—is that great old warhorse, George Brett.

Would you like that lineup? Well, if you had a team full of those players, you'd have a team of players who performed at just about the average level for each of their positions in 1993. We do this exercise every year, and it fools even us. A lot of these guys seem like stars—some because they have been in the past, others because they give promise of being stars in the future. But at this point in their career, they're not stars, they're average.

Here is the average level at each American League position last year, along with the player whose stats came closest to the norm. It was a great year for offense, so average looks pretty good:

Average Performance—1993 American League (per 600 PA)

Pos	Avg	OBP	Slg	HR	RBI	Most Typical Performer
C	.255	.324	.396	15	70	Dave Valle
1B	.282	.368	.469	21	83	Don Mattingly
2B	.270	.339	.370	7	58	Scott Fletcher
3B	.266	.335	.400	13	66	Ed Sprague
SS	.261	.318	.358	7	58	Mike Bordick
LF	.269	.344	.429	16	69	Brady Anderson
CF	.275	.339	.410	12	60	Bernie Williams
RF	.263	.335	.417	17	73	Ellis Burks
DH	.262	.332	.426	19	81	George Brett

Now we'll do the National League. Behind the plate there's Scott Servais, who showed some promise last year. At first, you've got Will Clark. Will Clark! Your double play combination consists of two promising young players in Carlos Garcia and Royce Clayton, and at third you've got the 1991 National League MVP, Terry Pendleton. Your outfield has you excited about the future: Al Martin, Steve Finley and Reggie Sanders. Again, who wouldn't want these guys? And again, if you had them, you'd have a group of players who performed at an average level in 1993.

Here are the NL figures:

Average Performance—1993 National League (per 600 PA)

Pos	Avg	OBP	Slg	HR	RBI	Most Typical Performer
C	.255	.317	.400	16	71	Scott Servais
1B	.287	.353	.449	18	79	Will Clark
2B	.268	.334	.386	9	52	Carlos Garcia
3B	.273	.335	.431	17	79	Terry Pendleton
SS	.272	.338	.366	6	52	Royce Clayton
LF	.277	.343	.451	19	79	Al Martin
CF	.275	.341	.408	12	59	Steve Finley
RF	.274	.339	.441	19	77	Reggie Sanders

As with the American League, the NL "all-average" team points up the fact that players who perform at an average level are often far from "mediocre." If you had a good pitching staff and a lineup like the National League group, you'd feel pretty good heading into this season. But to go all the way, you'd probably need Clark or Pendleton to make a big comeback, or have one or two of the young players suddenly blossom—to be something more than average, in other words.

As we've pointed out in the past, a lot of clubs fail to win pennants precisely because they fail to receive average performance at one or more positions. But clubs need stars, as well, and the mistake a lot of them make is thinking that someone like the 1993-level Terry Pendleton is still one of them. Both the Mets and the Royals made this kind of mistake with the man we used to call "Mr. Average," Kevin McReynolds; they kept trying to build a lineup around him, and found they couldn't. Average is okay—it's fine, decent, respectable. You just have to avoid thinking that it's more than that.

A complete listing for this category can be found on page 276.

HOW IMPORTANT IS THE GO-AHEAD RBI?

The "Go-Ahead RBI" is the logical, and better successor, to the "game winning RBI," an official stat from a few seasons back. The problem with the game-winning RBI, people never tired of saying, was that it was supposed to be a clutch statistic, but a guy could get one for driving in a run in the first inning. We could say something smart-alecky (who, us?), like, "Don't those runs, count, too?" But the stat had its faults.

No, the problem with that particular stat was that, while it's neat to give a guy credit for driving in the run which put his club ahead for good, if his club blew the lead, there went the game-winner. So being the modern and clever guys that we are, we now measure "go-ahead RBI"—ones that put the player's club ahead, whether the team holds the lead or not. And if you think that giving a club the lead isn't important, whatever the inning, go to the back of the class. It's *very* important, and a valid clutch stat.

These are the 1993 leaders in go-ahead RBI:

GO-AHEAD RBI LEADERS   1993

GO-AHEAD RBI	
Albert Belle	36
Ron Gant	32
Frank Thomas	31
Todd Zeile	30
Travis Fryman	30
Paul Molitor	30
Larry Walker	28
Mark Whiten	28
Jay Buhner	28
Eddie Murray	28
George Brett	28

Some pretty fair hitters here, led by Albert Belle, who drove in more runs than anyone else in the majors last year, and including guys like Frank Thomas and Larry Walker, who have a reputation for producing in the clutch. Todd Zeile, who ranked second in the category, used to have a reputation as a terrible clutch hitter, and justifiably so. This stat shows how much he's improved. It's nice to see George Brett, who had a reputation as one of the best clutch hitters ever, still doing it in his final season.

However, one name is conspicuously missing from this list: National League MVP Barry Bonds. Bonds had 25 go-ahead ribbies last year, not far from the top 10 but not what you'd expect from a man of his stature. It was nothing new for Bonds: in the years we've been measuring this stat, his go-ahead RBI totals have been 8, 18, 23, 19 and 25 . . . not good until 1993, and somewhat disappointing even then. We won't say that Bonds isn't a great player; it's obvious that he is. One problem for Bonds, which we point out in another essay, is that pitchers often don't give him much to hit in important situations, and he ends up drawing a walk. Give Bonds some credit: his 1993 figures, despite the fact that teams were pitching around him more than ever, represent a considerable improvement over past seasons.

We also like to look at this stat on a percentage basis, eliminating the bias created by the fact that some players have more RBI opportunities than others. Since you can get only one go-ahead RBI per plate appearance no matter how many runs you drive in, we compare plate appearances in which a player had a go-ahead RBI with all the plate appearances in which he drove in one or more runs. Got that? Here are the leaders for 1993 (minimum 50 total RBI):

1993 Leaders—Go-Ahead RBI Percentage

Player, Team	Go-Ahead RBI	PA with 1+ RBI	Pct
Barry Larkin, Cin	22	46	47.8
George Brett, KC	28	63	44.4
Will Clark, SF	27	61	44.3
Larry Walker, Mon	28	64	43.8
Andre Dawson, Bos	23	54	42.6
Andy Van Slyke, Pit	17	40	42.5
Todd Zeile, StL	30	72	41.7
Travis Fryman, Det	30	73	41.1
Mark Whiten, StL	28	69	40.6
Gregg Jefferies, StL	27	67	40.3
Orestes Destrade, Fla	27	67	40.3

This list is a little different from the first one, with Barry Larkin, who missed considerable time due to injuries last year, stepping to the front. As he should.

Here are the trailers in go-ahead RBI percentage for 1993:

1993 Trailers—Go-Ahead RBI Percentage

Player, Team	Go Ahead RBI	PA with 1+ RBI	Pct
Ed Sprague, Tor	6	58	10.3
Todd Hundley, Mets	5	43	11.6
Dean Palmer, Tex	9	65	13.8
Wil Cordero, Mon	6	42	14.3
Chad Kreuter, Det	6	41	14.6

Mostly young players here, and ones who have shown some problems in other measurements of clutch hitting. For example, Dean Palmer of the Rangers has made the bottom five in each of the last two years. Can you drive in 96 runs, and yet be a poor clutch hitter? Yes, you can; there's this stat, and Palmer's .200 average with men in scoring position last year.

A complete listing for this category can be found on page 277.

WHY WERE JOHN ORELUD'S 107 RBI LAST YEAR BETTER THAN ALBERT BELLE'S 129?

There are any number of stats to measure offensive performance, but there's always been a mystique about the guys who lead the league in RBI. Many people will tell you this is the only "clutch" stat worth knowing; after all, a hitter's most important task is to produce runs.

We'll buy the part about the importance of producing runs, but the RBI, like any "counting" stat, has one real problem: it doesn't tell you how many opportunities the player was given. Over the course of a season, the cleanup man for a club like the high-scoring Detroit Tigers, Cecil Fielder, will come up with lot more runners on base than the cleanup man for the weak-hitting California Angels, Chili Davis. The difference can be close to 100 runners a year, and sometimes even more.

So over the last few years, we've presented a leaders list which listed the best and worst performers in "RBI percentage": runners driven in as a percentage of the total number of runners on base. That helped identify some of the hidden run producers, but several people thought there might be a problem with our approach. As one reader, Michael S. Deckert, pointed out, patient hitters like Barry Bonds and Frank Thomas wound up being penalized because they would often draw a walk with runners on base; those walks would be considered failed opportunities to drive in runs. Why should that be labeled a negative, Deckert thought, when the end result—one more man on the bases—was positive?

This is a very persuasive argument, and with a grateful nod to Michael, we've decided to revise the way we compute our RBI percentage. The change is this: if a plate appearance ends in a walk, hit by pitch or an advance to first due to catchers' interference, any runners on base would not count as "RBI opportunities" for the hitter. The one exception would be if the BB, HBP or CI occurred with the bases full and forced in a run. In that case, the batter would be charged with one opportunity, to balance the run which was forced in.

There is, of course, a counter-argument to this system, one which was made by Steve Garvey in the 1970s. Asked why he seldom drew a walk, Garvey would say, "I'm not paid to walk. I'm paid to drive in runs." Fair enough, but to buy that argument is to join forces with the idiots in the Chicago press who used to say that Frank Thomas should "swing the bat more." Doesn't every intelligent study of offensive performance wind up concluding that the greatest hitters were the ones who best combined power and discipline, most notably Babe Ruth and Ted Williams? Are we supposed to say, "Yeah, the Babe, he was okay, but he could have been a

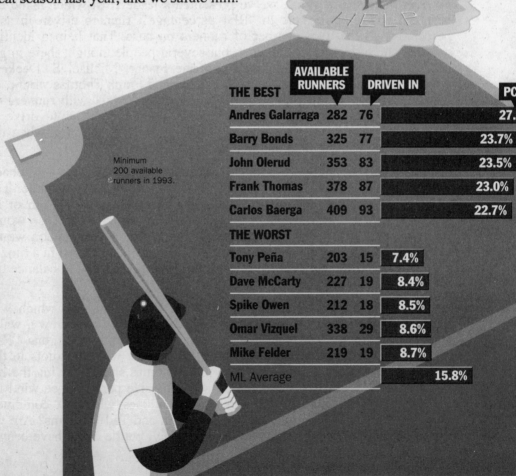

really good hitter, another Steve Garvey, if only he hadn't been so darned picky"? Sorry, Garv; it's a nice selling job, but we ain't buying.

The chart shows the 1993 leaders list in RBI percentage, using our revised formula. And naturally, the leader is a man who draws a walk about as often as the Chicago Cubs win a pennant, Andres Galarraga. His approach may not be the one recommended in Theodore S. Williams' *The Science of Hitting*, but there's no knocking The Big Cat's results. While Galarraga's numbers were helped mightily by Mile High Stadium—he had 64 RBI at home, 34 on the road—he had a great season last year, and we salute him.

Minimum 200 available runners in 1993.

THE BEST	AVAILABLE RUNNERS	DRIVEN IN	PC
Andres Galarraga	282	76	27.0
Barry Bonds	325	77	23.7%
John Olerud	353	83	23.5%
Frank Thomas	378	87	23.0%
Carlos Baerga	409	93	22.7%
THE WORST			
Tony Peña	203	15	7.4%
Dave McCarty	227	19	8.4%
Spike Owen	212	18	8.5%
Omar Vizquel	338	29	8.6%
Mike Felder	219	19	8.7%
ML Average			15.8%

But you'll notice that the second, third and fourth spots are occupied by the three hitters who were generally conceded to be the best offensive players in the game last year: Barry Bonds, John Olerud and Frank Thomas. This is just another indication of how good they really are. The presence of Cleveland's Carlos Baerga—who drew only 34 walks last year—in the top five shows that the revised formula doesn't really give an advantage to the patient hitters; it just doesn't penalize them the way the old one did. Rounding out the top 10 were Mike Piazza (22.7 percent), Albert Belle (22.4), Roberto Alomar (22.1), Chili Davis (22.0) and B.J. Surhoff (21.8). While Belle led the majors in RBI last year, the RBI percentage says that Olerud was a better run producer . . . along with a few others.

Cecil Fielder, if you're wondering, was well down the leaders list, driving home only 18.4 percent of his available runners. So why did he have so many RBI? Opportunity had a lot to do with it. Fielder had 472 available runners to drive in last year, most in the majors. Joe Carter of the Blue Jays was next with 456 runners, and Fielder's teammate Travis Fryman was third with 453. Fryman drove in only 16.6 percent of those runners, not much above the major league average of 15.8, but had 97 RBI because he had so many opportunities. It must be great to be young and a Tiger.

The trailers list was led by Boston's Tony Peña, who has become such a poor hitter that all the "clubhouse leadership" in the world couldn't guarantee his job with the Red Sox. We will say this: nobody ever had to tell Peña to "swing the bat more."

A complete listing for this category can be found on page 278.

WHICH HITTERS CAN HANDLE THE TOUGHEST PITCHERS?

One measure of a really superior hitter, one would think, would be an ability to handle the toughest pitchers—the Randy Johnsons, the Duane Wards, the Greg Madduxes. After all, a lot of guys can handle the easy pitchers; who can handle the tough ones?

We decided to find out, using data from the last five seasons. What we did was to pick a list of the 25 toughest pitchers in each league, with a minimum of 400 innings pitched in that league over the period. As our criterion, we used opponents on-base plus slugging average, one of the most useful indicators of offensive production (or the ability to stifle offensive production, from a pitcher's standpoint). The list includes the pitchers you'd expect to see, like Johnson, Ward, Maddux and Jose Rijo, along with an occasional surprise like Bud Black or Zane Smith. Overall, it's an extremely tough group of pitchers, with a .239 opponents batting average for the American Leaguers, and a .238 mark for the National League pitchers.

To choose the best hitters against this group, we used the same criterion—the hitters' on-base plus slugging average, or OPS. Here are the top 10 for the 1989-93 period, with a minimum of 100 plate appearances against the top pitchers:

Best Hitters vs Top Pitchers: 1989-1993

Hitter	AB	H	HR	RBI	Avg	OBP+Slg
Frank Thomas	385	118	21	68	.306	.969
Kevin Mitchell	546	158	42	111	.289	.925
Barry Bonds	692	204	35	120	.295	.919
Rickey Henderson	519	160	17	45	.308	.905
Fred McGriff	617	179	32	95	.290	.900
Dave Hollins	360	103	16	47	.286	.873
Mike Piazza	132	39	8	25	.295	.859
Mark Grace	783	251	20	102	.321	.857
Paul Molitor	614	201	18	76	.327	.850
Harold Baines	440	129	19	70	.293	.844

(Minimum 100 PA)

Ask a baseball fan to pick the two best offensive performers over the last five years, and the answer would probably be Frank Thomas in the American League and Barry Bonds in the National. So it's no shock to find Thomas and Bonds in the top three on this list. The surprise is the man who ranks between the two: Kevin Mitchell. Maybe it shouldn't be such a shock, however. This period includes Mitchell's National League MVP season of 1989, when he had 47 homers and a .635 slugging average, and he's been a fearsome hitter in the years since then—when he's been healthy enough to play. In fact, in overall OPS against all pitchers for the 1989-93 period, Mitchell's .920 mark ranks fourth behind Thomas (1.007), Bonds (.978) and Fred McGriff (.927).

Almost the entire top 10, in fact, consists of players who are great performers against *all* pitchers, not just these. There are a couple of notable overachievers, however. Dave Hollins of the Phillies has an overall OPS of .813 for his career, which began in 1990; that ranks a lowly 44th among players who have logged 500 at-bats during the 1989-93 period. Yet against the top pitchers, Hollins actually does better, ranking sixth overall with an OPS of .873. Harold Baines is another: an .835 OPS overall, but an .844 mark against the toughest American League pitchers.

Probably the biggest surprise is the way some of these hitters were able to tear into some very tough pitching. Look at Mitchell's batting line against the top pitchers: 546 at-bats 42 homers, 111 RBI. His slugging average against these guys is .571! Simply awesome. Other players have some very superior power numbers as well, like Thomas (21 homers in only 385 at-bats) and Bonds (35 homers in 692 AB). But nobody's quite like Mitchell.

In terms of best batting average against the top pitchers, the leaders are two you'd expect: Tony Gwynn (.335) and Paul Molitor (.327). But ranking third is a surprise, the Japan-bound Dion James (.325). Some talented pitchers are glad to say, "Sayonara, Dion."

The "Hall of Shame" for this category would include John Orton of the Angels, who managed only nine hits in 94 at-bats against the top pitchers, for an .096 batting average and a .318 OPS; Ed Sprague of the world champion Blue Jays, who has only 16 hits in 124 at-bats for a .129 average and a .449 OPS; and Ron Karkovice of the AL West champion White Sox (.167 average, .503 OPS). These fellows would like to testify that this is a group of *very* tough pitchers. Frank Thomas might disagree.

A complete listing for this category can be found on page 280.

WHO'S THE KING WHEN IT COMES TO CAUSING PITCHING SWITCHES?

Ask a baseball fan which hitter induced the most pitching changes by the opposition last year, and he'd probably guess Barry Bonds. Or Frank Thomas. Or Juan Gonzalez. But none of those players was the scheduled hitter when the most pitching changes were made last year. Who, then? Fred McGriff? Albert Belle? Ken Griffey, Jr.? Not even close. It was Jeff King of the Pirates, a fine player but a man at the top of no one's list of the most feared hitters in baseball. Here are the players who induced the most changes last season:

Scheduled Hitter During the Most Pitching Changes—1993

Player, Team	Pitching Changes
Jeff King, Pit	62
Jay Buhner, Sea	61
Albert Belle, Cle	60
Fred McGriff, SD-Atl	59
John Olerud, Tor	58
Barry Bonds, SF	56
Travis Fryman, Det	53
Juan Gonzalez, Tex	53
Lenny Dykstra, Phi	52
Pete Incaviglia, Phi	52
Danny Tartabull, Yanks	52

There's plenty of great hitters on the list: Belle, McGriff, John Olerud, Bonds, Gonzalez, Lenny Dykstra. But why would King be in their company, much less at the top of the list? And why would Jay Buhner, another good-but-not-great hitter, rank second? Well, let's see if we can find some common characteristics among the group:

1. They're all dangerous hitters, though some are obviously more dangerous than others. Nine of the 11 drove in at least 95 runs last year; the ones who didn't were Dykstra, a leadoff man who finished second in the MVP voting, and Pete Incaviglia, who drove in 89 runs in only 368 at-bats.

2. As would befit a dangerous hitter, most of them batted in one of the power spots in the batting order—third, fourth or fifth. The only exceptions were Dykstra and Incaviglia, who usually batted sixth.

3. In every case except two, the player who usually batted in front of this hitter was one who hit from the opposite side. Here's a list of the players

and the man or men who usually hit in front of them:

Hitter	Bats	Preceding Hitter(s)	Bats
Jeff King	R	Al Martin, Andy Van Slyke	L
Jay Buhner	R	Ken Griffey, Jr.	L
Albert Belle	R	Carlos Baerga	S
Fred McGriff	L	Gary Sheffield (SD), Ron Gant (Atl)	R
John Olerud	L	Joe Carter	R
Barry Bonds	L	Matt Williams	R
Travis Fryman	R	Lou Whitaker	L
Juan Gonzalez	R	Rafael Palmeiro	L
Lenny Dykstra	L	Pitcher	-
Pete Incaviglia	R	Darren Daulton	L
Danny Tartabull	R	Don Mattingly	L

We'll get to Dykstra, one of the two exceptions, in a minute. The other, Carlos Baerga, is a switch-hitter who bats lefty about two-thirds of the time. So like most of the group, Belle was usually batting behind a man who hit from the opposite side.

4. The preceding hitter, in every case but one, was a dangerous hitter in his own right.

When you have two excellent hitters coming up back to back but hitting from opposite sides of the plate, there are going to be many situations in which the opposing manager will change pitchers when the second hitter comes to bat, in order to gain a platoon advantage. (Often the opponents will make *two* switches in a row in order to gain two advantages. That was the case in Seattle, where Ken Griffey induced 44 pitching changes and Buhner 61.) These players induce pitching changes in part because they're good hitters; in part because the players hitting in front of them are also good hitters; and, more than anything, because they swing from the opposite side of the hitter in front of them. As for King, the reason he leads the list is that he was easily the biggest RBI threat in the Pirate lineup.

The odd case in this scenario is Dykstra, who was usually hitting behind the pitcher. Why did so many teams change pitchers when Dykstra came to the plate? Because the top of the Phillie lineup was top-heavy with lefty swingers: often the top five included Dykstra, Mickey Morandini, John Kruk and Darren Daulton, four lefty swingers. This is a case where the good hitters coming up *behind* this good one dictated the pitching switch. Usually, however, it's the preceding hitter who makes the difference.

A complete listing for this category can be found on page 282.

HOW IMPORTANT IS "PROTECTION"?

The notion that a good hitter needs "protection"—another good hitter coming up behind him—seems to be widely accepted. According to the theory, someone like Matt Williams had a bad year in 1992, and a great one in 1993, because last year he had Barry Bonds to "protect" him and guarantee that he'd get good pitches to hit. With weaker hitters coming up behind him in 1992, pitchers could nibble the corners and even walk him without much damage. That's the theory, anyway.

This sounds fairly logical, but you never see any numbers to support it. So we decided to look at the evidence. Our method was, first, to pick a group of hitters who had established themselves as stars: they had at least 75 runs created in 1993, and at least 150 RC over the period from 1991 to 1993. There were a total of 80 of those players in 1993, an average of about three per team. It's a good group: on average, the players had a .293 batting average, a .374 on-base average and a .479 slugging average.

We then compared the hitters' figures in two situations: when they were batting with another star as the next scheduled hitter, and when they weren't. If "protection" is important, the hitters would figure to perform better with a star in the on-deck circle. In particular, they'd figure to draw fewer walks and hit more home runs. Here's how the hitters performed:

1993 Stars with and without "Protection"

	PA	HR/PA	BB/PA	Avg	OBP	Slg
Overall	50259	.034	.110	.293	.374	.479
Star Batting Next	19995	.035	.104	.296	.371	.484
Star Not Batting Next	30264	.033	.115	.291	.375	.475

(Minimum 75 runs created in 1993 and 150 RC in 1991-93)

As a group, the hitters *did* benefit from having another star coming up behind them. They hit for better batting and slugging averages, and they homered at a rate about six percent higher. They also drew 10 percent fewer walks, suggesting that the pitchers were reluctant to put them on base with a free pass. However, the overall improvement was very slight. Using on-base plus slugging average (OPS) as a measure of overall production, the players had a .855 OPS with a star coming up next, and a .850 mark with a lesser player. A hitter who had 30 home runs without "protection" could be expected to hit 32 homers with it. No big deal, in others words—certainly not enough to justify the talk about how "important" this is to a hitter.

How about if we raised the standards a little, to players who had at least 100 runs created in 1993, and 200 total in 1991-93? There were only 30 of those players in 1993, whom we'll call "superstars"; as a group they batted .303, slugged .509, and had an on-base percentage of .392. Here's how they fared with and without a similar player coming up behind them:

1993 Superstars with and without "Protection"

	PA	HR/PA	BB/PA	Avg	OBP	Slg
Overall	21987	.039	.125	.303	.392	.509
Superstar Batting Next	4125	.048	.097	.303	.374	.536
Superstar Not Batting Next	17862	.036	.131	.303	.396	.502

(Minimum 100 runs created in 1993 and 200 RC 1991-93)

These differences are more substantial. When a superstar was in the on-deck circle, the players improved their slugging averages by 34 points, homered at a rate 33 percent higher, and drew 26 percent fewer walks. They "got more good pitches to hit," in other words, and they hit them. But the reduction in walks lessens the overall increase in production: the players' on-base plus slugging average was .898 without a superstar coming up next, .910 with one. So while the players performed better with a great hitter coming up next, they were still very good even without the "protection."

Our conclusion is that it *does* help a player to have another dangerous hitter coming up behind him; it would be surprising if it didn't help at least a little. However, the benefit wouldn't seem to be enough to explain an unusually good or bad season. Having Barry Bonds in the on-deck circle undoubtedly did help improve Matt Williams' figures last year compared to 1993. But the person who deserved most of the credit wasn't Barry Bonds; it was Matt Williams.

DO ROOKIES COOL OFF THE SECOND TIME AROUND THE LEAGUE?

There's an old baseball axiom which says that every rookie goes through a period of adjustment "the second time around the league," when the pitchers have figured out his weaknesses. Sometimes those weaknesses will be so serious that a guy who looked like a star will turn out to be a flash in the pan, like Bob Speake in 1955 (the original "Mr. May") or Dave Hostetler in 1982 (he was going to make us forget about Babe Ruth). But even if the rookie is the real thing, there's general agreement that he'll have to deal with *some* sort of adjustment once the league learns which pitches he can handle easily, and which ones he can't.

Truth or fiction? Let's look at all the rookies who came into the major leagues from 1989 to 1993 and had a minimum of 225 plate appearances in their first season; sometimes they had briefly appeared in the major leagues in the past, but they still qualified as rookies, and this was their first extended action in the majors. These days nobody makes "trips around the league" any more, as clubs will often go months without playing each other. So we divided their seasons in three segments: the games which included their first 75 plate appearances, the ones which included the next 75, and those afterward. That's around 20 games per segment, and enough time for opposing pitchers and scouts to have noticed the player's strengths and weaknesses. If the theory is valid, we ought to see some sort of dropoff after the first 75 appearances. Here are the results:

Rookies the "Second Time Around the League"

	Avg	OBP	Slg
1st 75 plate app	.270	.334	.403
2nd 75 plate app	.254	.318	.367
Rest of year	.257	.320	.378
(1989-93 rookies)			

This is one old axiom which appears to be true. As a group, the rookies performed very well during their first 75 plate appearances. But then there was a sharp falloff, with their batting average dropping 16 points and their slugging percentage more than twice that. Finally there appeared to be a slight recovery, as the hitters seemed to readjust a little; that recovery was very small, however, and probably not significant.

We found plenty of cases where hitters started out like crazy, then cooled off and never really recovered. Here are three:

	Vinnie Castilla 1993		Alex Cole 1990		Mark Lewis 1991	
	Avg	Slg	Avg	Slg	Avg	Slg
1st 75 plate app	.362	.536	.397	.429	.400	.477
2nd 75 plate app	.264	.431	.275	.362	.282	.324
Rest of Year	.214	.347	.253	.305	.208	.258

These three stars had a painful dip in the middle, but then fought back:

	Albert Belle 1989		Delino DeShields 1990		John Olerud 1990	
	Avg	Slg	Avg	Slg	Avg	Slg
1st 75 plate app	.262	.508	.333	.424	.266	.484
2nd 75 plate app	.169	.282	.250	.467	.230	.279
Rest of Year	.244	.402	.287	.375	.275	.455

But these players actually got better as the rookie season rolled on:

	Scott Cooper 1992		Mark Lemke 1990		Robin Ventura 1990	
	Avg	Slg	Avg	Slg	Avg	Slg
1st 75 plate app	.231	.262	.153	.203	.123	.228
2nd 75 plate app	.250	.353	.231	.277	.224	.328
Rest of Year	.299	.431	.261	.322	.274	.331

Clearly, there are no hard-and-fast rules about rookies. Some start off hot, cool off, and never recover. Others start out slowly, then come on. Still others are able to readjust after the pitchers change their pattern. The most common tendency, however, is to cool off a little once the pitchers have figured out a few of their weaknesses. Almost everyone seems to go through *some* adjustment period as they learn the pitchers and the pitchers learn them. The good ones, you can say, are the ones who make the best adjustment.

A complete listing for this category can be found on page 283.

WHO ARE THE "HUMAN AIR CONDITIONERS"?

We keep track of how often each hitter swings and misses, and face it, a big reason is that it's a fun stat—we love to talk about the prowess of such "human air conditioners" as Dean Palmer, Rob Deer and the legendary Cecil Fielder. But the stat has a useful side, as well. We've discovered that some hitters fan the breeze on a regular basis, yet don't provide all that much payoff in the form of home run power. Other hitters make contact much more frequently, but still have the ability to hit the ball a long way.

The chart below will show you what we mean. None of the five swing-and-miss leaders from 1993 is a surprising name. All five are home run hitters, and all five are known for their tendency to strike out. Yet this is hardly a list of baseball's premier sluggers. The top home run total among the five was Sammy Sosa's 33, and Rob Deer managed only 21—about one for every 18 missed swings. While no one expects Deer to turn into a contact hitter at this stage of his career, that's unsatisfactory even by his standards. In 1992, for instance, Deer swung and missed 284 times, but produced 32 dingers, one home run for every 8.9 misses. No wonder his career is in trouble.

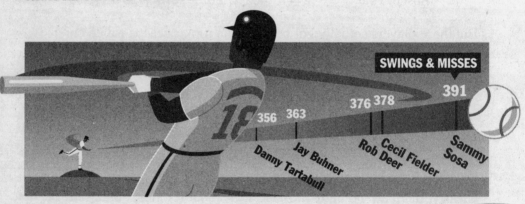

Now compare the swing-and-miss kings, who averaged one home run for every 13 missed swings last year, with the five hitters who belted at least 40 home runs in 1993. Juan Gonzalez swung-and-missed 276 times, yet produced 46 homers. Dave Justice had 241 misses, 40 home runs. Ken Griffey Jr. had 218 misses, 45 homers. Most remarkable were the two league MVPs. Barry Bonds swung and missed only 154 times in 1993, yet still tied for the major league lead with 46 home runs. The White Sox' Frank Thomas was even more amazing: he swung and missed only 121 times all season, yet still drove 41 balls out of the park. He's a contact home run hitter! Among the many impressive Thomas stats in this book, that one ranks near the top of the list.

The purest way to measure swing-and-miss leaders is to do to it on a percentage basis: missed swings as a percentage of total swings. On that basis, the 1993 leader was a familiar name to everyone, and especially to veteran followers of this category. It was that star of screen, television commercials and swinging-and-missing, Bo Jackson:

Highest % of Swings that Missed—1993

Batter, Team	Swung	Missed	Pct
Bo Jackson, WSox	648	248	38.3
Phil Hiatt, KC	517	190	36.8
Rob Deer, Det-Bos	1,047	376	35.9
Danny Tartabull, NYA	1,038	356	34.3
Gary Gaetti, Cal-KC	737	239	32.4
Pedro Munoz, Min	735	237	32.2
Ron Karkovice, WSox	871	278	31.9
Cory Snyder, LA	1,095	347	31.7
Ryan Thompson, NYN	591	187	31.6
Jay Buhner, Sea	1,151	363	31.5
Al Martin, Pit	961	303	31.5

(Minimum 400 pitches swung at)

With the possible exceptions of Tartabull and the promising Al Martin, this is a group of one-dimensional sluggers who produce an occasional home run, but little else. The overall scouting report would be "easy to pitch to," because they'll swing at just about anything. The king of them is Jackson, who last year had 16 homers in 294 at-bats, but also 106 strikeouts and only 23 walks. Some blame his hip injury, saying it made it harder for him to hold up his swing. But heck, when did Bo *ever* want to hold up his swing?

In the opposite camp are the extreme contact hitters who seldom miss when they swing. Wade Boggs and Tony Gwynn usually top this list, but last year they lost out to another smart hitter, Ozzie Smith:

Lowest % of Swings that Missed—1993

Batter, Team	Swung	Missed	Pct
Ozzie Smith, StL	959	54	5.6
Wade Boggs, NYA	1,003	58	5.8
Tony Gwynn, SD	778	46	5.9
Chuck Knoblauch, Min	1,037	70	6.8
Felix Fermin, Cle	770	53	6.9
Gregg Jefferies, StL	870	65	7.5
Scott Fletcher, Bos	793	61	7.7

Lowest % of Swings that Missed—1993

Batter, Team	Swung	Missed	Pct
Joey Cora, WSox	1,027	80	7.8
Brett Butler, LA	1,082	86	8.0
Lance Johnson, WSox	853	68	8.0

(Minimum 400 pitches swung at)

Most of the players in this group are smart singles hitters who hit for a good average. The king of these is Boggs, who over the last three seasons has swung and missed only 137 times in over 1,850 plate appearances—about half the total Bo had in 308 plate appearances in 1993. But lest you think this group is strictly "singles city," look at Gregg Jefferies: a .342 batting average and 16 homers, with only 65 missed swings all year.

Frank Thomas produced his .317 average and 77 extra-base hits while failing to make contact on only 12.2 percent of his swings last year. Remarkable.

A complete listing for this category can be found on page 285.

DID FRANK THOMAS DESERVE THE MVP?

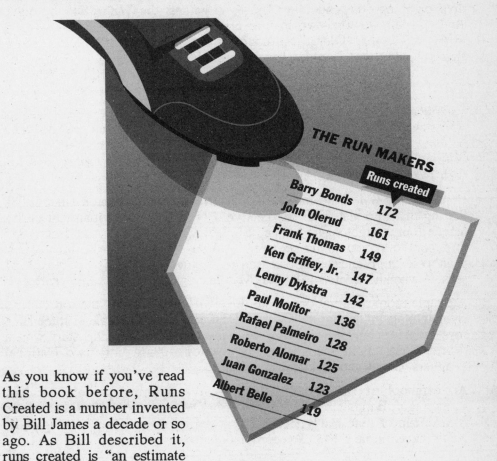

THE RUN MAKERS

	Runs created
Barry Bonds	172
John Olerud	161
Frank Thomas	149
Ken Griffey, Jr.	147
Lenny Dykstra	142
Paul Molitor	136
Rafael Palmeiro	128
Roberto Alomar	125
Juan Gonzalez	123
Albert Belle	119

As you know if you've read this book before, Runs Created is a number invented by Bill James a decade or so ago. As Bill described it, runs created is "an estimate of the number of team runs that would result from a player's offensive statistics." Like runs scored or RBI, anything over 100 is excellent.

"Did Frank Thomas Deserve the MVP?" may seem like a strange question, because many of us felt that Thomas should have picked up the award in 1991 or 1992; after all, he led the American League in runs created both seasons (and had he played a full season in 1990, he would probably have led then, too). In fact, in last year's *Scoreboard*, we titled the runs created essay, "Is Frank Thomas Underrated?" Seeing as how he had just finished eighth in the 1992 MVP vote after leading the A.L. by a wide margin with 142 runs created, our answer was "Yes."

So what happened in 1993? Thomas *didn't* lead the league in runs created, and yep, he finally won an MVP. Who *did* create the most runs in the A.L.? John Olerud. The two make for a perfect comparison. Both play first base—Olerud is a pretty good fielder, Thomas is terrible. Both clubs won division titles—the Blue Jays by seven games, the White Sox by eight. And the pair was one-two in runs created. So why did Thomas win the award rather than Olerud? A couple things stick out: (1) There was a strong feeling that Thomas has been slighted in the past, and (2) more importantly, Thomas drove in 128 runs (as opposed to 107 for Olerud), and MVP voters have traditionally focused on RBI.

Inexplicably, the question people were asking last September was not "Who should be A.L. MVP, Thomas or Olerud?" but rather, "Who should be N.L. MVP, Bonds or Dykstra?" Barry Bonds, of course, led the National League (and the majors) with 172 runs created. Lenny Dykstra, with 142, was a distant second.

Bonds has now led the majors in runs created every season since 1990. Putting that into historical perspective, Bonds is the first man to lead his league four straight seasons since Mickey Mantle led the A.L. from 1955 through 1960, an amazing six straight. Also, Bonds' 172 runs created last year were the highest single-season total since Norm Cash's freak 1961 season, when he created 178 runs (Mantle created 174 that same year).

A couple more observations about the chart, which shows the top 10 runs created totals in the majors last year. First of all, the presence of three Blue Jays helps explain how a team with just a decent pitching staff won a World Series. And second, among the top 10 are only two National Leaguers, Bonds and Dykstra.

An offshoot of runs created is offensive winning percentage. Not surprisingly, Bonds also led the majors in OWP, at .877. What that means is, a lineup of nine Barry Bondses, backed by an average pitching staff, would have run up a 143-19 record. Not bad.

1993 Leaders—Offensive Winning Percentage

Player, Team	Off Win%
Barry Bonds, SF	.877
John Olerud, Tor	.861
Frank Thomas, WSox	.821
Andres Galarraga, Col	.816
Chris Hoiles, Bal	.795
Ken Griffey, Sea	.792
John Kruk, Phi	.774
Juan Gonzalez, Tex	.771
Lenny Dykstra, Phi	.770
Gregg Jefferies, StL	.755

The above list includes only batting-title qualifiers (at least 502 plate appearances), so Cubs catcher Rick Wilkins, who had a .762 OWP but only 500 plate appearances, just missed making the list. For more on him and the #5 man, Chris Hoiles, see the Orioles essay202.

Offensive winning percentage highlights guys like Andres Galarraga and Gregg Jefferies, who missed time with injuries but were devastating when able to play.

So did Thomas deserve the MVP? We say yes, though it's close. While Olerud created more runs, he had lots of help in the Blue Jay attack, while Thomas *was* the White Sox attack for much of the season. It seemed like every time the Sox needed a big hit, he produced it. So we give Thomas the nod (while admitting some pro-Chicago prejudice).

A complete listing for this category can be found on page 287.

IS BARRY STILL BEST IN THE SECONDARY?

Welcome to Chapter 29 in "The Life and Legend of Barry Bonds." In this episode, Barry takes on those "two-sport stars." He runs. He walks. He slugs. He steals. He intercepts passes. He makes slam dunks. He kills penalties and works the power play. He reaches the 625-yard par five in two. He demonstrates his wicked slice serve. He dominates the "Punch Stat" figures, and wins every round on all three cards. He . . . well, you get the picture.

Forget Deion Sanders and Bo Jackson; Barry Bonds is *our* idea of an "all-around athlete," one who doesn't need another sport to show off all his skills. Bill James has a stat called "secondary average," which is meant to give a player credit for the skills that don't show up in batting average: drawing walks, hitting for power and stealing bases. The formula is:

$$\text{Secondary Average} = (2B + 3Bx2 + HRx3 + BB + SB - CS)/AB$$

Bonds, who is superb in all these areas—and a .336 hitter to boot—dominates this category. Here are the 1993 leaders in secondary average:

1993 Leaders—Secondary Average

Player, Team	Secondary Avg
Barry Bonds, SF	.607
Rickey Henderson, Oak-Tor	.528
Frank Thomas, WSox	.497
Ken Griffey Jr, Sea	.486
Darren Daulton, Phi	.465
Mickey Tettleton, Det	.448
John Olerud, Tor	.439
Chris Hoiles, Bal	.439
Danny Tartabull, Yanks	.433
Lonnie Smith, Pit-Bal	.422

(Minimum 250 plate appearances)

For Bonds, it's the third straight year he's finished first in secondary average; in 1990, he was third. With 88 extra-base hits—including 46 homers—126 walks and 29 stolen bases, he showed skills in every offensive area. As usual.

Bonds has no real challengers when it comes to supremacy in secondary average, but there are a few other players who make the leaders list every year. Rickey Henderson, who has everything but Bonds' home run power, has finished second, fourth, second and second in this category the last four years. Frank Thomas, who has everything but Bonds' speed, has finished second, ninth and third in his three full major league seasons. Danny Tartabull and Mickey Tettleton, who also lack speed and who hit for much lower averages than the others, have both made the top 10 in each of the last three seasons. But none of these players can match Bonds' all-around skills—and remember, this stat completely ignores his Gold Glove defense.

Secondary average, of course, measures the skills that batting average neglects. Every year, some of the worst performers in this category have very respectable batting averages; this stat exposes how empty their averages really were:

1993 Trailers—Secondary Average

Player, Team	Secondary Avg
Jose Lind, KC	.072
Pat Meares, Min	.075
Rey Sanchez, Cubs	.087
Junior Ortiz, Cle	.100
Felix Fermin, Cle	.102
Gary DiSarcina, Cal	.106
Dave McCarty, Min	.114
Ozzie Guillen, WSox	.118
Scott Livingstone, Det	.122
Jeff Branson, Cin	.126

When a guy like Rey Sanchez or Ozzie Guillen has a season in the .280 range, the less-enlightened members of the press will write about what "good hitters" they are. But while a .280 average has some value, a .280 average without walks, power or steals simply doesn't have a lot of value, and doesn't make for a good hitter . . . much as we admire those Chicago shortstops. As for Jose "Chico" Lind, he had 15 extra-base hits in 431 at-bats last year, drew 13 walks, and was tossed out twice in five steal attempts. And his batting average was .248. As an offensive player, he's a hell of a fielder.

A complete listing for this category can be found on page 289.

ARE GALARRAGA AND OLERUD FOR REAL?

"You know what the difference between hitting .250 and .300 is? It's 25 hits. Twenty-five hits in 500 at-bats is 50 points, OK? There's six months in a season, that's about 25 weeks. That means if you get just one extra flare a week, just one, a gork, you get a ground ball, you get a *ground ball with eyes*, you get a dying quail, just one more dying quail a week. . . you're in Yankee Stadium."   — Crash Davis in *Bull Durham*

When you write about baseball, you're expected to come up with *explanations*, reasons for why things happen. But as Crash Davis/Kevin Costner stated so eloquently, sometimes there isn't a reason for why things happen, other than just plain dumb luck.

In the chart below, we offer the biggest gainers and losers in batting average last season. And we'll offer some explanations and predictions, too—just don't underestimate the power of the gork.

BIGGEST BATTING AVERAGE CHANGES 1992–93

UP	1992	1993	CHANGE
Andres Galarraga	.243	.370	+127
John Olerud	.284	.363	+79
Matt Williams	.227	.294	+67
Orlando Merced	.247	.313	+66
Paul O'Neill	.246	.311	+65
DOWN			
Bip Roberts	.323	.240	−83
Tom Brunansky	.266	.183	−83
Mike Felder	.286	.211	−75
Leo Gomez	.265	.197	−68
Tony Peña	.241	.181	−60

The Gainers:

Andres Galarraga's 127-point increase was the largest since we started keeping track of this in 1989. True, he hit .402 in the friendly confines of Mile High, but Galarraga's .328 on the road wasn't too shabby, either. We think he'll be a decent hitter in 1994, but another batting title is unlikely, to say the least.

Number two in improvement was the other batting champ, John Olerud. Olerud is a different story, in that he was always thought to be a future star, even if his numbers didn't show it. Again, we don't think he'll make a run at .400 every year, but he should continue to be one of the league's better hitters.

Williams, Merced, and O'Neill are similar in that they all played slightly over their heads after seasons well below their norms. Expect all three to drop slightly, back to their established performance levels.

The Losers:

Bip Roberts was a huge disappointment last season. After establishing himself as one of the top leadoff men in the game in 1992, Roberts crashed in 1993. When a career .299 hitter hits .240, there's often an injury involved. Sure enough, Roberts had a jammed thumb for most of the season, and mercifully went out for good in July. There is little reason to think he won't be back this spring.

Leo Gomez was another big disappointment, but he also had an extenuating injury, in his case a bad wrist. In addition, he seemed to be trying to uppercut everything. With the Orioles signing Chris Sabo, Gomez might not get much a chance to rebound.

Tom Brunansky and Tony Peña are another story. Both are veterans who have been steadily declining, though Brunansky did have some lower back problems last season. Unfortunately, back problems are often chronic, and we won't be listing him very high on our fantasy baseball draft forms.

Mike Felder's .286 average in 1992 was 35 points higher than his previous career average, so it wasn't surprising that "Tiny" saw his average get tinier in 1993. But .211? Here's where the gorks come in. Felder reportedly wasn't hurt last year, and looked fine at the plate. Give him 15 gorks, and his average is up to .254, right at his career norm. We think Felder will be fine.

A complete listing for this category can be found on page 290.

WHAT ARE THE BEST COUNTS TO STEAL ON?

What's the best count to steal on? Some basestealers like to go on the first pitch. Others prefer to wait until the hitter is ahead in the count, when there's little danger of a pitchout. Still others like the element of surprise, stealing on any count, even unorthodox ones, if they think they can get a good jump.

But while there's great variation from player to player, some counts are much more popular than others when the runner is deciding when to take off. And some counts yield superior results, as well. Here's a chart of all stolen base attempts for the last three seasons, broken down by the ball-and-strike count:

Best and Worst Counts to Steal On, 1991-93

Count	SB	CS	Pct
0-0	2,565	1,166	.687
0-1	1,080	498	.684
0-2	465	166	.737
1-0	1,284	664	.659
1-1	1,048	590	.640
1-2	802	345	.699
2-0	330	132	.714
2-1	611	383	.615
2-2	777	322	.707
3-0	29	6	.828
3-1	213	136	.610
3-2	443	420	.513

And the best count to steal on is . . . 3-and-0! Over the last three years, runners have been successful on 83 percent of their steal attempts on this count. But there were only 35 steal attempts in three years (that's over 6,000 games), and anyway, why would anyone *want* to risk stealing on this count? In the first place, the odds are very good that the hitter will draw a walk before the at-bat is up. In addition, the hitter will seldom be swinging 3-and-0, so the pitcher can usually afford to throw one right down the middle—the sort of pitch which gives the catcher his best chance to throw the runner out. The end result is that the potential reward—getting to second, which is where the runner would be anyway after a walk—simply doesn't justify the risk.

The reason for the good success rate on 3-and-0 is the element of surprise (or maybe shock). It's not a recommended move, though one baserunner, Roberto Alomar, was 6-for-6 on 3-0 counts the last three years. Roberto also does things like trying to steal third with two out, as he did in the World Series—with disastrous results. Unorthodox is not always smart.

Next to 3-and-0, the next best success rate (.737) was on another unusual count for stealing, 0-and-2. This is seemingly a risky count, as the defense can easily call a pitchout if it senses a steal attempt coming. But it works as a surprise move, and if there's no pitchout, the runner has an advantage: the 0-2 offering is frequently a "waste" pitch out of the strike zone, which puts the catcher at a disadvantage.

The most popular pitch to steal on is the first one, but that's mostly because there are more 0-0 counts than any other. Roughly 27 percent of all counts over the last three years were 0-0; roughly 26 percent of all steal attempts came on that count, meaning that runners attempted to steal on the first pitch no more often, proportionally, than they did on any other pitch.

The worst success rates come on 3-and-2 (.513), 3-and-1 (.610) and 2-and-1 (.615). One reason for this is that these are popular hit-and-run counts, on which even slow baserunners will be sent. But the following chart, which is limited to the most prolific basestealers—ones who had a total of at least 100 steal attempts over the last three years—shows that these are tough counts for even the good runners:

The Elite Basestealers, 1991-93

Count	SB	CS	Pct
0-0	999	274	.785
0-1	345	116	.748
0-2	129	35	.787
1-0	497	187	.727
1-1	344	141	.709
1-2	231	72	.762
2-0	140	45	.757
2-1	209	87	.706
2-2	212	64	.768
3-0	13	2	.866
3-1	48	24	.666
3-2	72	39	.649

(Minimum 100 SBA)

Apart from the small number of attempts on 3-and-0 and 0-and-2, the elite runners have their best success on the first pitch. These runners know their business, and don't need extra pitches to "read" the pitcher's move.

A complete listing for this category can be found on page 291.

WILL THE GIANTS STILL HAVE THE BEST "HEART OF THE ORDER" IN '94?

The 1993 season was a big one for offense, so it's not surprising that a lot of clubs were loaded in the "heart of the order"—the key 3-4-5 spots in the lineup. In 1992, only six clubs received more than 300 RBI from their 3-4-5 hitters; only one of them, the Phillies, was in the National League. But in 1993, over half the clubs in the majors—15—received that kind of production.

The chart shows the best hearts of the order in three offensive categories, but it's just the tip of the iceberg. There were so many good combinations that the National League champion Phillies, with John Kruk, Dave Hollins and Darren Daulton manning the 3-4-5 slots, couldn't crack the leaders list. Rating the top five 1993 combinations isn't easy, but here goes:

MOST EFFECTIVE "HEARTS OF THE ORDER"

HOME RUNS		RBI		SLUGGING PCT.	
Giants	107	Blue Jays	350	Giants	.548
Rangers	104	Giants	344	Rangers	.526
Braves	96	Yankees	344	Rockies	.523
Mariners	94	Rockies	336	Blue Jays	.519
Yankees	91	Indians	335	Yankees	.499

1. Toronto. Cito Gaston is often thought of as a "push-button manager," but the Blue Jay skipper has made some surprisingly gutsy moves. Last year Gaston made free-agent pickup Paul Molitor his number-three hitter, even though Molitor hadn't provided much power when the Brewers batted him third in '92. Molitor came through brilliantly for Gaston, hitting .332 and reaching 20 homers and 100 RBI for the first time in his career. Along with cleanup man Joe Carter, number-five hitter John Olerud, and the great Roberto Alomar, who batted .420 in 100 at-bats in the third slot, the Jays received devastating production from their power slots all season long.

2. San Francisco. Will Clark may have had a sub-par year in 1993 (.283-14-73), but Giant cleanup man Matt Williams and National League MVP Barry Bonds, the number-five hitter, were so outstanding that the

Giants had the best heart of the order in the National League, and arguably the best in baseball. The only problem we have was with Bonds hitting fifth. While doing that may have helped Williams, it was also an invitation for NL managers to give the best hitter in baseball an intentional walk. . . which they did 43 times, the most for any batter since 1969. Batting third or fourth, Bonds would have received more opportunities to swing the bat.

3. Atlanta. The Braves' heart of the order ranked in the top three only in home runs, but don't forget that Fred McGriff, the key to the Atlanta offense, didn't join the club until after the All-Star break. From that point on, the Braves trio of Ron Gant, McGriff and Justice was the best in baseball, producing 55 homers and 179 RBI in only 73 games. They could be the best threesome in 1994.

4. Texas. People thought the Rangers were finished last year when Jose Canseco went out for the season in June. Instead, led by number-three hitter Rafael Palmeiro, who batted .426 with 34 RBI in July, the Texas attack was better than ever. Julio Franco, the primary number-five hitter after Canseco went out, also had a great second half, and the Ranger cleanup man was Juan Gonzalez. 'Nuf said. Palmeiro is gone for 1994, but the Rangers shouldn't miss him much; his replacement is Will Clark.

5. New York Yankees. Though not exactly DiMaggio, Gehrig and Dickey, the Yankee heart of the order—primarily Don Mattingly, Danny Tartabull and Paul O'Neill—gave the club the best heart of the order it's had in several years. Mike Stanley often took the fifth spot against lefties, and batted .324 with 14 homers and 41 RBI in only 170 at-bats while hitting in that slot. Mike Stanley?

Based on the raw stats, the Colorado Rockies trio of Dante Bichette, Andres Galarraga and Charlie Hayes merited a spot in the top five. We didn't give it to them because their figures were padded enormously by playing at Mile High stadium. We probably would have put the Cleveland Indians ahead of the Rockies; with Carlos Baerga and Albert Belle, the Tribe's three- and four-hitters were are good as anyone's, but the club didn't get top-grade production from its number-five hitters. The Phillies' trio of Kruk, Hollins and Daulton also rates well ahead of Colorado.

The worst heart of the order last year probably belonged to the Florida Marlins, who received only 46 homers and 242 RBI from their 3-4-5 hitters. In power-crazy 1993, that was pretty darn bad. The Montreal Expos were another club that lacked "heart." The Expos' low total of 286 RBI from their power slots probably cost them a chance to challenge the Phillies.

A complete listing for this category can be found on page 293.

WHO GETS THE "SLIDIN' BILLY TROPHY"?

Welcome to the annual STATS award banquet, held at that exclusive Chicago-area eatery, Rikki's fast-food restaurant in Skokie, Illinois. Since it's a special night, all the candidates will be receiving complimentary cheese fries. (We at STATS spare no expense.) The next award will be the "Slidin' Billy Hamilton Trophy," given to the best leadoff man of 1993.

You probably want to know the credentials of the candidates. We begin by ranking the leadoff hitters according to their on-base percentage when batting first. Here's the top 10:

1993 Leaders—Leadoff On-Base Percentage

Player, Team	OBP	AB	R	H	BB	SB
Tony Phillips, Det	.443	559	111	174	131	16
Rickey Henderson, Oak-Tor	.432	466	111	137	112	50
Lenny Dykstra, Phi	.420	637	143	194	129	37
Marquis Grissom, Mon	.411	138	30	51	11	20
Rich Amaral, Sea	.408	158	23	56	15	5
Kenny Lofton, Cle	.408	566	114	184	81	69
Tim Raines, WSox	.400	413	75	127	62	21
Wade Boggs, Yanks	.397	253	44	80	35	0
Delino DeShields, Mon	.388	423	66	127	59	34
Darryl Hamilton, Mil	.387	304	42	99	30	15

(Minimum 150 plate appearances while batting leadoff)

A rundown on the finalists:

Tony Phillips. One of the very best, Phillips led all leadoff men in on-base percentage and walks, and tied for third in runs scored. His only negative was his low stolen base total (16).

Rickey Henderson. No, they didn't name the restaurant after him. Though he's considered the best leadoff man of all time, Henderson is still looking for his first Slidin' Billy trophy (Paul Molitor and Brady Anderson were the first two winners). Despite having a "bad season" in 1993 by some accounts, Rickey ranked second among leadoff men in OBP, tied Phillips for third in runs scored, was third in walks, and ranked fourth in stolen bases. He also hit 21 home runs, tied with Craig Biggio for most among leadoff hitters. This is a bad season?

Lenny Dykstra. He's the one with the barbecue sauce stains on his tuxedo. He may be uncouth, but Dykstra led all leadoff men in runs scored, with the highest total by a National League player in 61 years. He was third in leadoff OBP, first in hits, second in walks, and among the leaders in stolen bases. Obviously, he's the favorite.

Kenny Lofton. No sophomore jinx here. Lofton was tied for fifth in leadoff OBP, ranked second in runs scored, and was first in stolen bases with 69. How much better can he get?

The envelope, please, Rikki. Phillips, Lofton and Dykstra are all worthy candidates, but how can we pick against Dykstra, who led all National League players in hits *and* walks *and* runs scored? The Slidin' Billy Hamilton Trophy for 1993 goes to Lenny Dykstra. Handshakes—and chocolate shakes—all around.

The booby prizes go to the leadoff men who had the worst leadoff on-base percentages in 1993. Or should we give it to the managers who insisted on batting these guys first? Anyway, here's the bottom 10 for 1993:

1993 Trailers—Leadoff On-Base Percentage

Player, Team	OBP	AB	R	H	BB	SB
Willie Wilson, Cubs	.273	145	17	36	4	5
Al Martin, Pit	.281	162	29	41	7	0
Ryan Thompson, Mets	.293	186	22	47	8	1
Darren Lewis, SF	.299	429	68	108	23	34
Deion Sanders, Atl	.303	228	32	60	13	17
Bernie Williams, Mets	.306	289	36	69	27	1
Felix Jose, KC	.307	347	48	91	22	18
Luis Alicea, StL	.308	143	16	37	10	3
Carlos Garcia, Pit	.314	377	55	104	16	17
Vince Coleman, Mets	.316	369	63	103	21	38

In his prime, Willie Wilson was an American League batting champion, with as many as 230 hits, 83 stolen bases and 133 runs scored in a season. But hey, Cubbies, that was a long time ago! Now Wilson is ancient, and can't even steal bases anymore. He should never be hitting first.

Wilson, at least, was given a limited amount of opportunities in the leadoff role. But the San Francisco Giants gave over 400 plate appearances in the leadoff spot to Darren Lewis, who neither hits for average nor draw walks. He does have a little speed. Couldn't the Giants, who had some big boppers in the middle of their lineup, have found someone to get on base for Barry Bonds and company?

A complete listing for this category can be found on page 294.

WHO'S THE BEST BUNTER?

After being dethroned in 1991 by Steve Finley, Brett Butler came back in 1992 to reclaim his title, "King of the Bunters." So the question in 1993 was, could the 36-year-old fight off the challengers for his title? Sorry, if we told you now, you'd probably just skip to the next essay.

When you talk about bunting, you're really talking about two related, but separate skills: bunting for the sacrifice, and bunting for the base hit. The chart below ranks the top nine sacrifice bunters by percentage, with a minimum of 10 successful sacrifices:

Top Sacrifice Bunters, 1993

Bunter, Team	Sac	Att	Pct
John Valentin, Bos	16	16	100
Andy Benes, SD	14	14	100
Jose Lind, KC	13	13	100
Greg Swindell, Hou	10	10	100
Jody Reed, LA	17	18	94
Jose Offerman, LA	25	27	93
Jay Bell, Pit	13	14	93
Darren Lewis, SF	12	13	92
Joe Girardi, Col	12	13	92

A year ago, Pirate shortstop Jay Bell topped the list with 19 sacs, but seeing as how he was the best hitter in the Pirates lineup last year, it didn't make a lot of sense for him to be bunting. On the other hand, the leader this year is another hard-hitting shortstop, the Red Sox' John Valentin. Valentin had a fine season, with 54 extra-base hits and a .447 slugging percentage, and we expect that, like Bell, he'll be asked to sacrifice a bit less in 1994.

Jose Offerman might not have been the most successful sacrificer, at "only" 93 percent, but with 25 he was certainly the most prolific. What's more, his Dodger teammate Jody Reed picked up 17, and Brett Butler had 14. Not surprisingly, the Dodgers led the majors with 107 sacrifice hits.

Mr. Butler doesn't make the above list because along with his 14 sac hits, he failed to move the runner three times, so his percentage puts him behind the other guys. But Butler is famous for bunting for *singles*, not outs. And in 1994, he once again led the majors with 26 bunt hits, despite the fact that third basemen routinely play so close that Butler can tell which ones don't use mouthwash. Here are the top 10 base-hit bunters, ranked by sheer quantity:

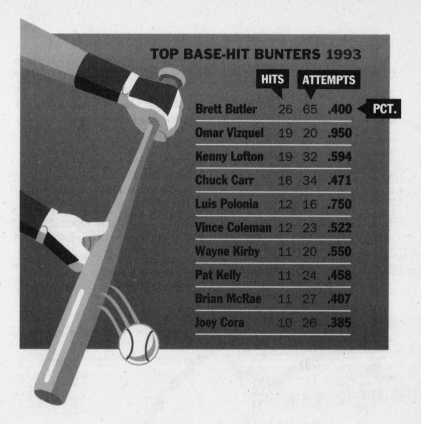

TOP BASE-HIT BUNTERS 1993

	HITS	ATTEMPTS	PCT.
Brett Butler	26	65	.400
Omar Vizquel	19	20	.950
Kenny Lofton	19	32	.594
Chuck Carr	16	34	.471
Luis Polonia	12	16	.750
Vince Coleman	12	23	.522
Wayne Kirby	11	20	.550
Pat Kelly	11	24	.458
Brian McRae	11	27	.407
Joey Cora	10	26	.385

First of all, back to Butler's 26 bunt hits. Yes, he did lead the majors again, but his total was way down from 1992, when he had 42 bunt hits in 70 attempts. We suspect that the dropoff is due in large part to those fearless third basemen. But you certainly can't say it's hurt Butler, seeing as how he hit .298 overall last year.

The numbers that really jump out at you here are Omar Vizquel's. Vizquel put the ball in play 20 times while bunting for a hit, and he made it to first an amazing 19 of them, *for a .950 average.* In addition to those hits, Vizquel had 13 sacrifices (in 15 tries). Unlike most, if not all of the leaders, Vizquel doesn't depend on his speed to get him to first after his bunts. He is not regarded as a particularly fast runner—though he did steal 12 bases last year, Vizquel was also thrown out 14 times. It looks to us like most of his bunt hits were due simply to excellent placement. So Omar, next to your 1993 Gold Glove on the mantel, you can place the "STATS FlatBat," our award for the best bunter in the game.

A complete listing for this category can be found on page 295.

WHY WAS 1993 THE "YEAR OF THE MOON SHOT"?

Any time there's a substantial boost in offense from one season to the next, a certain element of the population—most of whom seem to be sportswriters—will say, "The ball's juiced." Or "Expansion is ruining baseball." Or something. There's no question that 1993 was a very unusual season, and we know that people will be searching for an explanation . . . whether there is one or not.

First, the data. Last year was the best season for offense since 1987, which was, not coincidentally, the last time the lively ball theory was sweeping the nation. But we have an unusual bit of data to add to the conventional numbers. As you probably know, STATS reporters keep track of the direction and distance of every batted ball, which enables us to measure how far every home run ball travels. We present an annual chart of the longest home runs hit during each season, which you can see below.

460 FEET
Andres Galarraga (2)
Mark Whiten (2)
George Brett
Rob Deer
Cecil Fielder
Juan Gonzalez
Kent Hrbek
Kevin Mitchell
Matt Nokes
Sammy Sosa
Danny Tartabull

470 FEET
Cecil Fielder
Kent Hrbek
Bo Jackson
Chad Kreuter
Danny Tartabull

480 FEET
Cecil Fielder

THE LONGEST HOMERS

What's different about the 1993 chart is the sheer number of long home runs which were hit. Ordinarily it celebrates all the players who hit a home run of 450 feet or more, but last year there were so many "moon shots" that we had to limit the leaders list to the players who hit a home run 460 feet or greater. Here's a chart showing season-by-season offensive figures starting with 1987, along with the total number of 450 foot-plus home runs:

Year	Avg	R/G	HR/G	450-ft. HRs
1987	.263	9.5	2.1	32
1988	.254	8.3	1.5	32
1989	.254	8.3	1.5	19
1990	.258	8.5	1.6	32
1991	.256	8.6	1.6	19
1992	.256	8.2	1.4	16
1993	.265	9.2	1.8	47

Last season was huge in a lot of ways, but the jump in the number of long home runs is almost off the map. Even granted the fact that there were 162 additional games on the schedule due to National League expansion, it's still a quantum leap—after adjusting for the extra games, there would have been 44 long-distance homers, 12 more than in any other year, including 1987.

How can one explain this? Here are several theories:

1. **The "Denver Factor."** We examine the effects of the Denver altitude in another essay, but an obvious question is whether there was a disproportionate number of long home runs at Mile High Stadium. There were five, which is more than random chance would give them, but fewer than the number of 450-foot home runs hit at the Metrodome, Tiger Stadium and Yankee Stadium (seven each). Even eliminating Denver, there were still more long home runs hit last year than in any other season.

2. **The weather.** Our studies have shown that warm weather generally helps the ball travel farther, and the question is whether 1993 was an exceptionally warm summer. It *was* a warm summer, with the second-highest number of 80-degree games in the seven seasons we've measured the temperature. However, this is only a partial explanation; among other things, 10 of the 47 home runs were hit in the domed stadiums at Minnesota and Seattle, where the climate is controlled.

3. **Expansion-diluted pitching.** This one is appealing, but hard to measure. Fourteen of the 47 long home runs last year were hit off pitchers who either didn't pitch in the majors in 1992, or who worked 10 games or fewer that year. However, there are many new players even in non-expansion seasons; in addition, this list includes pitchers like Jose Bautista, Angel Miranda, Blas Minor and Armando Reynoso, who were clearly qualified to pitch in the majors, and who very likely would have made a major league roster even without expansion. Dilution-by-expansion was certainly a factor, but not enough by itself to explain such a huge jump in long-distance home runs.

4. **Measurement differences.** Our scorers generally rely on the home run distance announced in the press box, but face it, it's hardly scientific. Was the ball really jumping in Minnesota last year, or was there some enthusiastic measurement going on by P.R. people who like to see their players listed on the "IBM Tale of the Tape" leaders list? Your guess is as good as ours, but it could have made a little difference in the credited number of long home runs.

5. **The lively ball.** Sort of the "grassy knoll" of baseball; conspiracy theories are always popular, aren't they? We've always had our doubts about this particular theory, for a logical reason: since it's generally been proven that fans love offense, why wouldn't they juice up the ball *every* year? But we can't really debunk it completely. There have been subtle changes in the manufacture of the ball from time to time, leading to slumps and surges in the scoring rate. You can't prove it, but you can't disprove it either.

6. **Other theories**. How about sunspots, the ozone layer, nuclear testing, the Hubble telescope, the end of the cold war, NAFTA, the Brady Bill, or some kind of "giant sucking sound" which caused more balls to jump out of the stadiums? We at STATS believe that all these theories have equal validity. Watch for our info-mercial.

7. **Some great sluggers in their prime.** An unpopular theory among sour-grapes sportswriters, who just *know* the players were better back when *they*—the writers—were younger. But for the record, check the players who blasted 450-foot home runs last year, and you'll see names like Cecil Fielder, Danny Tartabull, Bo Jackson, Juan Gonzalez, Andres Galarraga, Mark Whiten, Sammy Sosa, Frank Thomas, Ken Griffey Jr. Pretty impressive.

Whatever happened last year, there's little denying it was a lot of fun. As the chart shows, Fielder had the longest home run of the year, a 480-foot blast. Cecil also had one 470-foot blast, one of 460, and one of 450. We worry about him on other pages, but Fielder was clearly the "long distance king" of 1993. Why not just enjoy it?

A complete listing for this category can be found on page 296.

IV. QUESTIONS ON
PITCHING

DOES A BIG INNING BY YOUR OFFENSE MEAN BIG TROUBLE FOR YOUR PITCHER?

Surely you've seen this one happen. Your club has a big inning, scoring four runs, maybe more. The rally takes awhile, and your starting pitcher spends a long time sitting in the dugout. When the inning ends and it's his turn to pitch, the other club starts knocking *him* around. The announcers get into a long discussion about how, when a pitcher has to sit for a long time, his arm stiffens up.

National League fans are familiar with that situation, and another one unique to their league. It occurs when their pitcher reaches base. He has to run the bases, at least a little and sometimes a lot. If he has a few problems when he finally takes the mound again, the announcers will be sure to say, "Jones got winded running the bases."

Fact, or fiction? Are pitchers' arms so fragile that going 20 minutes or so without pitching will cause them problems? Are they in such poor shape that doing a little baserunning will destroy their effectiveness on the mound? First, let's examine the "big-inning" situation. We looked at 1993 starting pitchers who took the mound after their offense had scored four or more runs—meaning that, at a minimum, seven hitters came to bat. That should be a long enough rally to cause arm-stiffening, and presumably, problems. Here's how the pitchers performed in the next inning, compared with the inning before the big-inning uprising:

Pitcher Performance Following a Big Inning — 1993

Big innings	Opp. scored next inning	Scoring pct	ERA following inning	ERA previous innings
641	179	27.9	3.83	3.21

The "big innings" total here only includes ones in which the starter actually took the mound for the next frame. As you can see, the moundsmen did pitch worse in the inning following a scoring uprising; they had a 3.21 ERA in the inning before the uprising, a 3.83 mark in the inning afterward. A 3.83 ERA is still better than average—major league starters had a 4.26 overall ERA last year—but it *is* a dropoff. This is probably due only in part to "arm stiffening." One thing that happens after a big inning is that the pitcher usually has a cushion to work with; he's likely to relax a little, and thus his ERA would likely be higher. But for whatever reason, pitchers are less effective after having to sit in the dugout for a while due to an offensive uprising.

Now let's look at the other situation, the one in which National League starting pitchers have to run the bases. There were 883 situations last year in which a pitcher was on base, then had to take the mound the next inning (the starter was lifted on eight occasions). Here are the results:

NL Pitcher Performance After Running the Bases — 1993

Pitcher ran bases	Opp. scored next inning	Scoring pct	ERA following inning	ERA previous inning
883	241	27.3	4.30	2.79

Again, there's evidence to indicate that this is a problem for pitchers. Overall, the moundsmen had a very fine 2.79 ERA in the inning before they ran the bases; they would figure to have a fine ERA, since someone pitching badly probably wouldn't be allowed to hit. But after they had run the sacks, their ERA was nearly a run and a half higher at 4.30, and also higher than the overall 4.08 ERA for National League starters. The ERA rise was more than twice as high as in the first situation, indicating that fatigue probably was a factor. We'll avoid saying that National League pitchers are wimps, but . . .

The evidence seems pretty clear: pitchers *do* pitch worse after having to sit in the dugout for a while due to a big inning, and National League pitchers have even more of a negative reaction to having to run the bases. This is one bit of "conventional wisdom" which turned out to be true.

IS JACK McDOWELL A QUALITY STARTER?

The definition of a "quality start"—at least six innings pitched, no more than three earned runs allowed—still stirs such controversy that we usually begin our essay on the subject with some sort of apology. So let's get it out of the way: we're heartily sorry if you think the standards for "quality" (in this game, country, universe, whatever) are too low. We see the point (so, shut up already!), but we keep using the stat for a simple reason—it works. A pitcher who makes a quality start is giving his team an excellent chance to win the game, and year after year, the relationship between the QS and the W is very high. That's enough reason for us to keep using it.

The chart lists the 1993 leaders in quality starts. It includes most of the names you'd expect to see, like two-time Cy Young Award winner Greg Maddux, who has led the National League in quality starts (and many other things) in each of the last two seasons. But conspicuous by his absence was American League Cy Young Award winner Jack McDowell, who worked a quality start only 21 times in 34 outings, or 61.8 percent of the time. McDowell, who has a reputation for coasting when he gets a lead,

THE QUALITY STARTERS

	GAMES STARTED	QUALITY STARTS	PCT.
Kevin Appier	34	29	85.3%
Greg Maddux	36	29	80.6%
Jose Rijo	36	28	77.8%
Tom Glavine	36	28	77.8%
Jimmy Key	34	25	73.5%
Erik Hanson	30	22	73.3%
Pete Harnisch	33	24	72.7%
Steve Avery	35	25	71.4%
Chuck Finley	35	25	71.4%
John Burkett	34	24	70.6%
David Cone	34	24	70.6%

Minimum 20 starts.

gave up four earned runs or more in *13* of his 22 wins last year. Black Jack also had six starts in which he gave up five earned runs or more; his record in those games was 4-2. Was that "coasting," or just the good fortune to be pitching for a team which was averaging 5.4 runs per game for him?

Compare McDowell's season with that posted by the 1993 quality start leader, Kevin Appier. The Royals righthander, who received nearly one run less per game in support (4.5) than Black Jack did, gave four earned runs or more in only one of his 18 victories last year. In addition, Appier yielded five earned runs or more (exactly five each time) on only three occasions; his record in those contests was 1-2. Was the difference that McDowell knows how to coast with a lead, or just that Appier was the better pitcher? Probably we won't know the answer until McDowell goes through a season with poor run support, and Appier has one in which the Royals score like crazy for him. (Dream on, Kev.) In the meantime, we feel that Jack McDowell is a very fine pitcher, but if we'd been given a Cy Young ballot last year (dream on, John and Don), the top spot would have been marked, "Appier."

Speaking of run support, these pitchers needed plenty. They had the lowest percentage of quality starts among regular major league starters last year:

Lowest Percentage of Quality Starts—1993

Pitcher	Games Started	Quality Starts	Pct
Doug Brocail, SD	24	7	29.2
Jack Morris, Tor	27	8	29.6
Bob Walk, Pit	32	10	31.3
Melido Perez, Yanks	25	8	32.0
Hipolito Pichardo, KC	25	8	32.0
John Dopson, Bos	28	9	32.1
Todd Stottlemyre, Tor	28	9	32.1
Andy Ashby, Col-SD	21	7	33.3
Chris Haney, KC	23	8	34.8
Scott Erickson, Min	34	12	35.3

Somehow Bob "Whirlybird" Walk had a record close to .500 (13-14), despite his high ERA (5.68) and low percentage of quality starts. Yeah, we know; "he just knows how to win." That's what they used to say about Jack Morris, who went 7-12 for the world champions last year. Where were all Morris' defenders in 1993?

A complete listing for this category can be found on page 297.

WHO GETS THE EASY SAVES?

As we've noted before, not all saves are created equal. There's a big difference between coming in with a three-run lead and the bases empty, and entering the game with men on second and third and a one-run lead with nobody out. The reliever in Game A can allow two runs and pick up a save, while the reliever in Game B could strike out two hitters, then get charged with a blown save when the shortstop throws a ball into the stands.

So for the purposes of comparison, we at STATS have come up with different categories of saves: Easy, Regular, and Tough. The definitions are as follows:

Easy Save: first batter faced is not the tying run *and* reliever pitches one inning or less. Example: Randy Myers comes in with a 4-1 lead and no one on base to start the ninth. Under the current rules, this is a Save Opportunity. We call it an Easy Save Opportunity.

Tough Save: reliever comes in with the tying run anywhere on base. Example: Tom Henke comes in with a 4-1 lead, two outs and the bases loaded in the ninth. This is a Tough Save Opportunity.

Regular Save: All other saves fall into the "Regular" category.

We used to have a different name for Easy Saves—"Cheap Saves"—but we changed it after some highly-paid major league pitchers wrote us some highly-threatening letters. Well, not really. We just thought "Easy" matched up better with "Tough." Anyway, our categories match up pretty well with actual conversion percentages. As was the case in 1991 and '92, relievers converted better than 90 percent of their Easy Save Opportunities last year, but only around 40 percent of their Tough Save Opportunities. Here are the 1993 figures:

	Easy			Regular			Tough			Total		
League	Sv	Op	%	Sv	Op	%	Sv	Op	%	Sv	Op	%
AL	234	258	91	273	379	72	86	231	37	593	868	68
NL	256	271	94	269	399	67	74	190	39	599	860	70
MLB Total	490	529	93	542	778	70	160	421	38	1,192	1,728	69

The most interesting things here are the Easy Save numbers. In the past, the National League generally recorded fewer Easy Save opportunities than the American, even allowing for the fact that until last year there were two fewer teams in the senior circuit. But last season, National League firemen actually had *more* Easy Save Opportunities than their A.L. brethren. We suspect this is simply a case of strategy catching up. Tony La

Russa and Dennis Eckersley really pioneered the one-inning closer, and it naturally became popular faster in the American League than the National. But if last season is any indication, there is no difference between the leagues any more.

Let's look at how the top American League closers were used last year:

Reliever, Team	Easy			Regular			Tough			Total		
	Sv	Op	%	Sv	Op	%	Sv	Op	%	Sv	Op	%
Montgomery, KC	13	14	93	27	30	90	5	7	71	45	51	88
Ward, Tor	29	29	100	14	14	100	2	8	25	45	51	88
Henke, Tex	15	15	100	16	23	70	9	9	100	40	47	85
Hernandez, WSox	16	17	94	16	19	84	6	8	75	38	44	86
Eckersley, Oak	21	23	91	9	14	64	6	9	67	36	46	78
Aguilera, Min	19	20	95	12	16	75	3	4	75	34	40	85
Russell, Bos	19	21	90	12	13	92	2	3	67	33	37	89
Olson, Bal	20	20	100	8	11	73	1	4	25	29	35	83
Farr, Yanks	14	14	100	10	12	83	1	5	20	25	31	81
Henneman, Det	9	9	100	14	17	82	1	3	33	24	29	83

A few things here jump out at you. First of all, though Jeff Montgomery and Duane Ward each converted 45 of 51 save opportunities, Montgomery's campaign looks quite a bit more impressive. Montgomery had fewer than half as many Easy Save Opportunities than did Ward. What's more, he was much more successful in converting Tough Saves. Montgomery picked up the Rolaids Relief Award, and he deserved it.

Tom Henke had a weird season. He was perfect on the easy ones, but had trouble converting Regular opportunities. Put him in a tough spot, however, and he was a perfect nine for nine.

The trend away from putting closers in the game in a Tough Save situation continued last year. In 1992, Jeff Russell had 16 such opportunities, and the late Steve Olin had 10. Last season, no A.L. reliever saw double figures in that category.

Let's look at the National League figures for 1993:

Reliever, Team	Easy			Regular			Tough			Total		
	Sv	Op	%	Sv	Op	%	Sv	Op	%	Sv	Op	%
Myers, Cubs	31	33	94	18	20	90	4	6	67	53	59	90
Beck, SF	22	22	100	18	21	86	8	9	89	48	52	92
Smith, StL-Yanks	30	31	97	13	18	72	3	4	75	46	53	87
Harvey, Fla	18	18	100	25	28	89	2	3	67	45	49	92

Reliever, Team	Easy			Regular			Tough			Total		
	Sv	Op	%	Sv	Op	%	Sv	Op	%	Sv	Op	%
Wetteland, Mon	15	15	100	18	24	75	10	10	100	43	49	88
Williams, Phi	31	32	97	12	17	71	0	0	--	43	49	88
Stanton, Atl	17	18	94	8	11	73	2	4	50	27	33	82
Jones, Hou	11	12	92	11	16	69	4	6	67	26	34	76
Holmes, Col	10	10	100	12	15	80	3	4	75	25	29	86
Ge.Harris, SD	9	9	100	12	15	80	2	7	29	23	31	74

Randy Myers set a National League saves record with 53, and he obviously had a little help from his manager, picking up 31 Easy saves. The number-two man, Rod Beck, actually converted four more "regular plus tough" saves than did Myers. What's more, Beck's 2.16 ERA was nearly a full run better than Myers' 3.07.

John Wetteland was the Tom Henke of the National League—perfect on the easy ones, had problems with the Regular chances, but blew away the opposition when he was called upon for a Tough Save. Wetteland's 10 tough saves led the majors.

Speaking of tough saves, did you notice those goose eggs for Mitch Williams? Phillies manager Jim Fregosi had so little faith in his closer that he didn't bring him in once during the regular season with the tying run on base. Fregosi didn't put him in one of those spots in the World Series, either. But of course, Mitch proved perfectly capable of doing that himself.

A complete listing for this category can be found on page 298.

WHICH STARTING STAFFS STAR, AND WHICH STARTING STAFFS REEK?

Those subversive foreigners, the Toronto Blue Jays, appear intent on destroying the old notions on the importance of starting pitching. In 1992, the Jays won the world title despite a starting staff which ranked eighth in the American League in team ERA. In 1993, the Jays repeated as champions, but once again seemed to win despite—not because of—their starting staff.

While winning the American League East for the third straight season, the Jays relied primarily on their offense, which was second in the league in runs scored, and on a bullpen which had the league's best ERA. Starting pitching? Forget it. Jays starters had a 4.63 ERA, a mark which tied the Milwaukee Brewers for 21st-best in the majors. In the League Championship Series, the Jays took on the Chicago White Sox, a club which had the best overall ERA in the league, and a starting staff with the most wins, the most innings per start and the best ERA in the league. Despite the supposed edge to the club with better pitching, the Jays won the series in six games.

Here's how the American League starting and relief staffs stacked up in 1993:

American League Starters					American League Relievers				
Staff	W	L	IP	ERA	Staff	W	L	IP	ERA
White Sox	76	55	1,067.1	3.72	Blue Jays	25	17	442.0	3.30
Red Sox	55	56	1,001.0	3.81	Indians	34	32	561.1	3.51
Mariners	62	54	1,043.2	3.99	White Sox	18	13	386.2	3.72
Royals	59	55	1,040.0	4.03	Red Sox	25	26	451.1	3.79
Yankees	60	55	1,011.2	4.26	Orioles	23	21	465.1	3.81
Angels	57	71	1,039.1	4.32	Brewers	19	23	411.0	4.05

American League Starters				American League Relievers				
Staff	W	L	IP	ERA	Staff	W	L	IP	ERA
Rangers	63	59	968.2	4.39	Rangers	23	17	469.2	4.06
Orioles	62	56	977.1	4.57	Royals	25	23	405.1	4.06
Brewers	50	70	1,036.0	4.63	Twins	21	13	478.1	4.35
Blue Jays	70	50	999.1	4.63	Athletics	27	31	548.1	4.43
Tigers	64	51	940.1	4.78	Angels	14	20	391.0	4.47
Twins	50	78	966.0	4.92	Tigers	21	26	496.1	4.57
Athletics	41	63	904.0	5.19	Yankees	28	19	426.2	4.62
Indians	42	54	884.1	5.25	Mariners	20	26	410.0	4.74
League Avg.	58	59	991.1	4.40	League Avg.	23	22	453.0	4.10

Often a weakness in one area or the other can keep a club from contending for a title. The Yankees, for example, might have mounted a more serious challenge to the Blue Jays in the East if they'd had a more reliable bullpen. The same goes for the Mariners in the West. The Cleveland Indians, with a horrible starting staff but a surprisingly good bullpen despite the death of Steve Olin, undoubtedly would have been over .500 with better starting pitching. The Tribe began addressing the problem in the offseason with the signing of free agent Dennis Martinez, and figure they can contend in the proposed AL Central if they pick up another quality starter.

Sometimes the numbers don't tell the whole story about the strength of a club's starting or relief staff. The California Angels ranked a respectable sixth in starters ERA, but they were far from respectable if Mark Langston or Chuck Finley wasn't on the mound:

Angels Starters, 1993					
	GS	IP	W	L	ERA
Langston and Finley	70	507.2	32	25	3.17
Other starters	92	531.2	25	46	5.42

In the National League, the Atlanta Braves were the opposite of the Blue Jays. The Braves had the best starting staff in baseball, and the best relief ERA as well. As expected, the Braves won the West, but the old saw about good pitching beating good hitting took another jolt when the Braves lost to the Philadelphia Phillies in the playoffs. Here are the National League starting and relief figures:

National League Starters					National League Relievers				
Staff	W	L	IP	ERA	Staff	W	L	IP	ERA
Braves	79	42	1,083.0	3.13	Braves	25	16	372.0	3.15
Astros	72	53	1,049.1	3.48	Dodgers	24	22	439.0	3.38
Dodgers	57	59	1,033.2	3.55	Expos	30	24	512.1	3.43
Expos	64	44	944.1	3.61	Giants	21	16	476.0	3.44
Giants	82	43	980.2	3.72	Astros	13	24	392.0	3.51
Mets	45	76	1,064.1	3.88	Cubs	26	16	468.1	3.61
Phillies	69	42	1,040.2	3.95	Padres	19	29	498.2	3.65
Cardinals	61	49	973.1	4.03	Marlins	17	26	480.2	3.78
Marlins	47	72	959.2	4.33	Phillies	28	23	432.0	4.00
Cubs	58	62	981.1	4.45	Cardinals	26	26	479.2	4.24
Reds	49	62	969.0	4.50	Mets	14	27	373.2	4.53
Padres	42	72	939.0	4.53	Reds	24	27	465.0	4.55
Pirates	46	64	954.0	4.78	Pirates	29	23	491.2	4.74
Rockies	37	73	878.2	5.49	Rockies	30	22	552.2	5.36
League Avg.	58	58	989.1	4.08	League Avg.	23	23	459.2	3.98

The Phillies, like the Blue Jays, seemed to win despite—not because of—their pitching staff. In the LCS against the Braves, Atlanta pitchers had a 3.15 ERA, the Phils a 4.75 mark, but the Phillies won anyway. The World Series, as would be expected from a match-up of two clubs with less-than-topflight pitching, was a slugfest. Jays pitchers had a 5.77 ERA in the Series, but the Phillies were even worse with a 7.57 mark. Both clubs' starting and relief staffs were inept:

	Starters	Relievers	Overall
Blue Jays	5.91	5.57	5.77
Phillies	6.75	9.00	7.57

It made for some entertaining games, anyway.

A complete listing for this category can be found on page 299.

DO HIT-BY-PITCHES INTIMIDATE HITTERS . . . OR PITCHERS?

Our fan in the stands, Joe "These Are the Bad Old Days" Livinthepast, would like to say a few words about the current state of the game: "These modern pitchers! Wimps! Afraid to pitch inside! Give the hitter the whole plate! One millionaire afraid to hit another! Union wouldn't like it! Wimps! Sal Maglie would hit Jackie Robinson 30 times a year! Jackie wouldn't even flinch! Not like these modern ballplayers! Wimps! Give me Don Drysdale! Give me Bob Gibson! Give me Jim Bunning! Give me Don Drysdale! Give me Bob Gibson . . ."

Sorry, old Joe starts repeating himself when he gets excited, and anyway, it's time for his nap. But Joe was simply repeating a lament we seem to hear every time two old ballplayers gather around a microphone: modern pitchers are afraid to pitch inside. In fact, the evidence directly contradicts that theory. Last year, for example, National League pitchers averaged 0.50 hit batters per league game. In 1965, when Drysdale, Gibson and Bunning were in their heyday, the league average was 0.50 hit batters a game—exactly the same. And last year's American League hit-batter rate of 0.56 per game was higher than in any season during the hair-on-your-chest 1960s.

So today's pitchers *do* pitch inside . . . or at least, a good many do. But with what effect? One thing we wondered was what happens in the plate appearance after a hit batsmen. Are the hitters a little intimidated, and less effective as a result? Or is it the pitchers who get flustered, worrying about warnings from umpires, hitters charging the mound, and the like? The following chart, which is based on data from the last three seasons, gives a batting line for the hitters who come up after one of their teammates has been plunked. So that you can get a better feel for the data, we've pro-rated it per 600 plate appearances, which is about a season's worth for a regular hitter. We also show the pro-rated results for other plate appearances which did *not* follow an HBP:

PA After HBP and Other Events

Situation	AB	H	2B	3B	HR	BB	K	HBP	Avg	OBP	Slg
PA after HBP	524	145	29	5	14	47	85	3	.276	.334	.432
PA after Hit	515	139	24	3	12	52	83	4	.270	.336	.403
PA after BB	524	140	24	3	14	45	90	4	.267	.324	.404
PA after K	537	131	23	3	11	56	103	4	.244	.319	.363
PA after Out	536	135	24	3	12	56	95	4	.251	.325	.375

(1991-93 data, pro-rated per 600 plate appearances)

Any time a pitcher allows a baserunner via a hit, walk or hit-by-pitch, it's a sign that he's lost a little bit of effectiveness; as a result, he tends to perform a little worse against the next batter than if he'd recorded an out. But pitchers perform worse after hitting the previous hitter than when they allow a walk or even give up a hit. The next batter hits for a better average, and with a lot more power.

So the hitters aren't intimidated by the hit by pitch, but the pitchers seem to be. Why would that be? Well, old Joe is still taking his nap, but if he were awake, he'd be moaning about umpires issuing warnings and hitters charging the mound and dugouts emptying—the whole scene which seems to be played out nightly on ESPN, all of which are supposed to be taking the pitchers' weapons away. Is there some merit to this thinking? We couldn't say for sure, unless we had similar data for the "good old days," which we don't. However, we could make some reasonable speculations:

1. In most cases, the pitcher wasn't trying to hit the batter, and the HBP was a sign of both lack of control *and* effectiveness. The next batter is facing a pitcher who's probably well off his game.

2. If the hit batsman was indeed an accident, the pitcher is probably going to be more conscious than before about throwing strikes. He'll probably take a little off his pitches to make sure they're going to be in the strike zone. He won't simply cut loose and fire as much, and the hitters will take advantage.

3. The danger of an umpire warning probably *is* a factor. If he hits a second player in a row, he might well be tossed out the game. Consciously or not, he's probably not going to be pitching inside as much as he usually does. Again, the hitters will take advantage.

Does that make sense? It may not be that the pitcher is consciously trying to do anything different, but it's reasonable to suppose he'd be affected by what happened. While "pitching inside" may be a good philosophy (and not everyone's in agreement on that), a pitcher's knocked a little off balance by hitting a batter—something which doesn't happen all that often. Most pitchers will probably regain that balance shortly, and return to their normal pitching rhythm. But in the short term, the next at-bat, the advantage belongs to the hitter. And it has nothing to do with pitchers being "wimps."

A complete listing for this category can be found on page 300.

WHO ARE THE HIDDEN RELIEF STARS?

When a middle reliever performs his job successfully by protecting a lead in a close game, we credit him with a hold. When a closer performs his job successfully by finishing a close game with the lead intact, we credit him with a save. But to properly evaluate a relief pitcher's effectiveness, we need to factor in how often he failed, as well as how often he succeeded.

The blown save has become the commonly accepted stat for measuring closers' failures. But since a chance to record a hold is by definition a save opportunity, middle relievers' failed opportunities are also recorded as "blown saves"—even though they seldom get a chance to actually nail down the save. As a result, middle men often wind up with poor save percentages, and look worse than they really are. A perfect example is Bob Scanlan of last year's Cubs. The save percentages will tell you that Scanlan had three save opportunities last year, and failed all of them. But we all know that Scanlan succeeded numerous times by protecting a lead; it's just that when the ninth inning came around, the Cubbies would bring in Randy Myers.

So to get a better perspective on relief pitchers, we've come up with the "hold-plus-save percentage." It's pretty simple, really; you just add the two kinds of successes together (holds plus saves), and measure them against the failures (blown saves). Here are the 1993 leaders in hold-plus-save percentage:

1993 Leaders—Hold-Plus-Save Percentage

Pitcher, Team	Holds	Saves	H+S Opp	H+S Pct
Greg McMichael, Atl	12	19	33	94.0
Rod Beck, SF	0	48	52	92.3
Bryan Harvey, Fla	0	45	49	91.8
Rick Honeycutt, Oak	20	1	23	91.3
Eric Plunk, Cle	16	15	34	91.2
Randy Myers, Cubs	0	53	59	89.8
Jeff Russell, Bos	1	33	38	89.5
Bob Scanlan, Cubs	25	0	28	89.3
Rob Murphy, StL	24	1	28	89.3
Jim Gott, LA	7	25	36	88.9

(Minimum 20 opportunities)

By this standard, Greg McMichael of the Braves was the most effective reliever of 1993. McMichael spent the first half of the year as a set-up man, and recorded 12 holds. After the All-Star break, he became the

Braves' closer and notched 19 saves. All season long, he failed to hold the lead only twice, for a superior success rate of 94 percent.

Since middle men and closers have such different roles, it's hard to argue that a set-up man like Rick Honeycutt was a more effective pitcher than a closer like Randy Myers, even though he had a higher percentage. It's better to measure set-up men against each other, and closers against closers. We would separate the two kinds of pitchers on the leader board, except for the fact that so many pitchers are asked to perform in both roles. What the leaders board does most effectively is identify the hidden stars like Honeycutt, whose solid work might otherwise go unrecognized.

This stat is also useful in the negative sense, in identifying the relievers who were *not* effective last year. Here are the 1993 trailers in hold-plus-save percentage:

1993 Trailers—Hold-Plus-Save Percentage

Pitcher, Team	Holds	Saves	H+S Opp	H+S Pct
Jeff Nelson, Sea	17	1	28	64.3
Rob Dibble, Cin	0	19	28	67.9
Doug Henry, Mil	0	17	24	70.8
Greg Harris, Bos	17	8	35	71.4
Mel Rojas, Mon	14	10	33	72.7
Jerry DiPoto, Cle	6	11	23	73.9
Gene Harris, SD	1	23	32	75.0
Doug Jones, Hou	1	26	35	77.1
Paul Assenmacher, Cubs-Yanks	17	0	22	77.3
Jeremy Hernandez, SD-Cle	9	8	22	77.3

Primarily a middle man, Jeff Nelson of the Mariners was given a brief shot at closing some games after Norm Charlton went on the shelf last year. Obviously, it didn't work. Including the games he was working as a middle man, Nelson blew 10 hold or save opportunities last year, while notching only one save. Even adding in his 17 holds, he still had the worst save-plus-hold percentage among regular relievers for the second straight year. This is not a man who can be trusted in a close game.

The trailers list includes some closers, some middle men, and some who worked in both roles last year. The common thread was unreliability; no club feels safe with a relief pitcher, whether middle-man or closer, who blows leads this often.

A complete listing for this category can be found on page 301.

DID STEVE FARR INHERIT A TICKET OUT OF TOWN?

Relief pitching can be a savage business, and relief pitching in New York—where the tabloids and the talk shows jump on the slightest mistake—must be doubly tough. Steve Farr, late of the Yankees, can give testament to that.

In 1992, Farr saved 30 games and posted a 1.56 ERA as Yankees closer. But even then, there was a sign of trouble. Farr inherited 18 runners from preceding pitchers in '92, and allowed eight of them to score—runs that did not count against his ERA, but runs which scored all the same. In 1993, none of Farr's stats were satisfactory: not his save total (25), not his ERA (4.21), and especially not his inherited runners percentage. As the chart shows, Farr permitted 17 of 28 inherited runners to score, the worst ratio for any pitcher who inherited 25 or more. The Yankees didn't worry about his feelings; they brought in Lee Smith for the September stretch run, and bade Farr adios when the season ended.

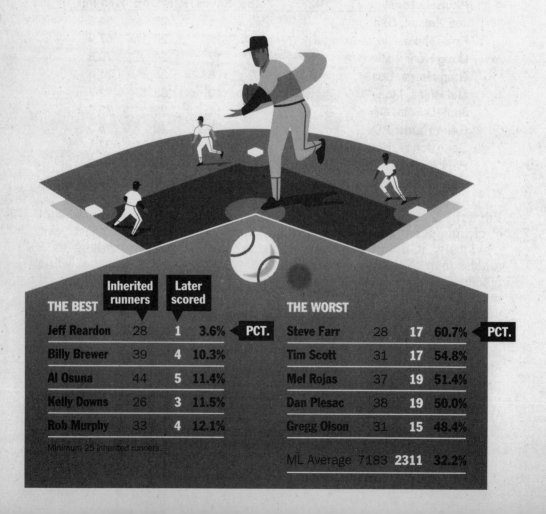

THE BEST	Inherited runners	Later scored			THE WORST	Inherited runners	Later scored		
Jeff Reardon	28	1	3.6%	PCT.	Steve Farr	28	17	60.7%	PCT.
Billy Brewer	39	4	10.3%		Tim Scott	31	17	54.8%	
Al Osuna	44	5	11.4%		Mel Rojas	37	19	51.4%	
Kelly Downs	26	3	11.5%		Dan Plesac	38	19	50.0%	
Rob Murphy	33	4	12.1%		Gregg Olson	31	15	48.4%	
Minimum 25 inherited runners.					ML Average	7183	2311	32.2%	

Though still somewhat underpublicized, the inherited runner stat is one of the most useful for evaluating relief men. Jeff Reardon is a good example. In 1992, Reardon posted a seemingly respectable 3.41 ERA, but we were among the observers who weren't fooled. Not only did Reardon fail the Atlanta Braves late in the year, but his inherited runner figures—30 inherited, 15 scored—indicated how shaky his work really was. In 1993, though, Reardon had the opposite kind of season. Pitching for the Reds, his ERA was a lofty 4.09, but this time he pitched a whole lot better than that figure indicated. The best indicator of Reardon's solid work was his inherited runner percentage: he allowed only one of 28 to score, the best figure in either league.

Reardon wasn't the only reliever whose ERA belied some very good work last year. Lefty specialist Tony Fossas of the Red Sox had a 5.18 ERA last year, but permitted only 11 of his 60 inherited runners to score (18.3 percent), a superior ratio. Highly regarded rookie Trevor Hoffman had a 3.90 ERA for the Marlins and Padres, but his inherited runner figures (45 inherited, only six scored) were a much better indicator of his talent. Another well-regarded rookie, Steve Reed of the Rockies, had a 4.48 ERA, but permitted only nine of his 44 inherited runners to score.

As we've often noted in the past, today's closers will come in at the start of an inning whenever possible. As a result, the relief pitchers who inherit the most runners—and the most troublesome situations—are the middle men. That was more true in 1993 than ever. Set-up man Jeff Nelson of the Mariners inherited a staggering 95 runners last year; he permitted 32 of them to score (33.7 percent), which is about average. Todd Frohwirth of the Orioles inherited 79 runners (20 scored), and Greg Harris of the Red Sox inherited 75 (18 scored). Frohwirth was a middle man, and so was Harris, though the latter did assume some closer duties late in the year.

The 1993 save leaders, though, came in far less frequently with men on base. Randy Myers of the Cubs, with 53 saves, inherited only 24 runners all year (just four scored). Lee Smith of the Cardinals and Red Sox, with 46 saves, inherited 25 (five scored). Duane Ward of the Blue Jays and Jeff Montgomery of the Royals, who tied for the American League save lead with 45, inherited just 26 and 30 runners, respectively. So while a good closer is important, it's the middle men who face the most heat.

You'd think that preventing inherited runners from scoring would be crucial to a club's success, but that's not necessarily true. The worst teams in the American League at permitting inherited runners to score last year were the two division champions, the White Sox (37.8 percent) and Blue Jays (35.1). The Atlanta Braves, who won the NL West, had the National

League's second-worst mark (37.4 percent). Meanwhile, the best club in baseball at preventing inherited runners from scoring was the lackluster Cincinnati Reds, who permitted only 26.9 of their inherited runners to score. It's a sign that this stat, while important, isn't *all*-important if your club has other assets. The team figures:

Runners Inherited and Scored Percentages

American League				National League			
Team	Inherited	Scored	Percent	Team	Inherited	Scored	Percent
Rangers	310	90	29.0	Reds	219	59	26.9
Angels	265	78	29.4	Astros	194	53	27.3
Orioles	339	100	29.5	Dodgers	230	64	27.8
Red Sox	331	100	30.2	Marlins	286	86	30.1
Athletics	297	91	30.6	Giants	234	74	31.6
Yankees	292	91	31.2	Expos	222	72	32.4
Mariners	335	106	31.6	Cardinals	252	82	32.5
Tigers	298	95	31.9	Phillies	192	63	32.8
Royals	192	63	32.8	Cubs	273	90	33.0
Twins	291	97	33.3	Padres	265	89	33.6
Indians	349	120	34.4	Pirates	215	73	33.0
Brewers	285	99	34.7	Rockies	279	99	35.5
Blue Jays	231	81	35.1	Braves	163	61	37.4
White Sox	198	75	37.9	Mets	146	60	41.1

A complete listing for this category can be found on page 302.

WHO HOLDS THE FORT?

The Michael Jackson who entertains fans the world over has become a very controversial figure. There's little controversy, though, about the Michael Jackson who pitches for the San Francisco Giants. One of the best set-up men in baseball, Mike Jackson, keeps the Giants' closer, Rod Beck, looking beautiful—and that ain't easy. One of the stats we use to measure middle relief pitchers, the "hold," indicates that Jackson is more than good: he's one of the best who's ever handled the set-up role.

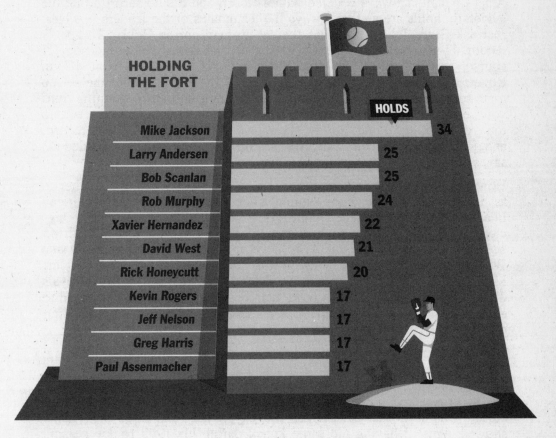

HOLDING THE FORT

	HOLDS
Mike Jackson	34
Larry Andersen	25
Bob Scanlan	25
Rob Murphy	24
Xavier Hernandez	22
David West	21
Rick Honeycutt	20
Kevin Rogers	17
Jeff Nelson	17
Greg Harris	17
Paul Assenmacher	17

The chart lists the 1993 leaders in holds. That's what a relief pitcher earns when he enters a game in a save situation, preserves the lead while retiring at least one batter, and then passes on the save situation to a subsequent reliever. It's an important job, and as you can see, Jackson had more holds last year than any pitcher in baseball. In fact, he had over 25 percent more holds than any other relief pitcher in either league.

Jackson's margin over the Phillies' Larry Andersen and the Cubs' Bob Scanlan gives you some idea of how good he was at his job. But we have even more evidence of that. We've been recording the leaders in holds for five seasons now, and Jackson's 34 is the highest anyone has recorded over that span. Only one other pitcher amassed at least 30 holds during the period—Barry Jones of the White Sox, who had exactly 30 in 1990. Given that the set-up role is fairly new to baseball, there's a very good chance that Jackson's total was the best ever.

A set-up man is always coupled with a closer, and it's no surprise that the leaders in holds are almost always the teammates of the leaders in saves. Just ask Barry Jones, who was the set-up man during Bobby Thigpen's record 57-save season in 1990. It was true again in 1993. Jackson, of course, was the set-up man for Beck, and got some help from Kevin Rogers; Larry Andersen and David West of the Phillies were the set-up men for Mitch Williams, who saved 43 games before running into post-season disaster; Bob Scanlan of the Cubs was the primary set-up reliever for 53-save man Randy Myers, who set a National league record; and Rob Murphy of the Cardinals set up Lee Smith, who recorded 43 saves before moving to the Yankees for the final month.

However, every year some clubs will have problems finding a pitcher to assume the set-up role. For example, after years as one of the American League's best set-up men, Duane Ward became the Toronto Blue Jays closer last year. Ward was brilliant, tying for the league lead with 45 saves, but the Jays were unable to develop a reliable set-up man to take Ward's place. Their leader in holds was Tony Castillo, with only 13. Jeff Montgomery of the Royals tied Ward for the saves lead, but the Royals didn't have any pitchers with more than eight holds. Kansas City tried to solve the problem by acquiring Stan Belinda at the July 31 trading deadline, but Belinda was a disappointment.

Some skippers, though, seem to have the knack for developing a strong, deep bullpen, and as a result their pitching staffs always record a lot of holds. The established master is Tony La Russa of the A's, whose club led the American League in holds last year despite a sub-par year from his closer, Dennis Eckersley. Across the bay, Dusty Baker of the Giants showed signs of having the same knack during his 1993 rookie season. Baker's Giants recorded 84 holds last year, by far the highest total in baseball. The team totals:

American League		National League	
Team	Holds	Team	Holds
Athletics	62	Giants	84
Mariners	60	Cubs	71
Indians	57	Cardinals	61
Twins	54	Phillies	59
Rangers	53	Astros	47
Tigers	48	Braves	45
Orioles	47	Dodgers	40
Blue Jays	46	Marlins	38
Red Sox	44	Expos	32
White Sox	37	Reds	32
Angels	34	Pirates	31
Brewers	34	Padres	30
Yankees	33	Rockies	29
Royals	31	Mets	19

Remember when the New York Mets had the best pitching staff in baseball, with a strong, deep bullpen? It seems like forever.

A complete listing for this category can be found on page 303.

IS RANDY JOHNSON THE "LEADING SCORER" AMONG PITCHERS?

What was the most dominating pitching performance of 1993? Let's pick three finalists:

1. On September 25, Jose Rijo pitched a one-hit shutout against the Rockies in which he struck out eight and walked nobody.

2. On May 16, Randy Johnson pitched a one-hit shutout against the A's in which he struck out 14 batters while walking three.

3. On September 8, Darryl Kile pitched a no-hitter against the Mets, fanning nine and walking one. However, he did give up an unearned run.

Three great games, but which one was the best? A few years ago, Bill James came up with a yardstick for pitching performances which he called a "game score." It's simple, and fun. Here's how game scores are figured:

(1) Start with 50. (2) Add 1 point for every hitter the pitcher retires. (3) Add 2 points for each inning the pitcher completes after the fourth inning (that is, 4 points for six innings, 10 points for a nine-inning complete game, etc.) (4) Add 1 point for each strikeout. (5) Subtract 1 point for each walk. (6) Subtract 2 points for each hit. (7) Subtract 4 points for each earned run he gives up. (8) Subtract 2 points for each unearned run.

As Bill put it back in 1988, "this is my annual fun stat, a kind of garbage stat that I present not because it helps us understand anything in particular, but because it's fun to play around with." So it ain't rocket science; it's just fun. According to the formula, here are the top game scores of 1993:

Top Game Scores of 1993

Pitcher, Team	Opp	Date	IP	H	R	ER	BB	K	Game Score
Randy Johnson, Sea	Oak	5/16	9.0	1	0	0	3	14	96
Darryl Kile, Hou	Met	9/08	9.0	0	1	0	1	9	93
Jose Rijo, Cin	Col	9/25	9.0	1	0	0	0	8	93
Tim Belcher, Cin	Atl	5/26	9.0	1	0	0	3	10	92
Pete Harnisch, Hou	Cub	7/10	9.0	1	0	0	3	10	92
Jimmy Key, Yanks	Cal	4/27	9.0	1	0	0	1	8	92
Wilson Alvarez, WSox	Oak	6/15	9.0	3	0	0	1	11	91
Kevin Appier, KC	Tex	7/27	9.0	1	1	1	1	11	91
Jason Bere, WSox	Bos	9/08	8.0	2	0	0	0	13	91
Chuck Finley, Cal	Cle	4/22	9.0	2	0	0	2	10	91
Pete Harnisch, Hou	Col	8/14	9.0	3	0	0	2	12	91
Pete Harnisch, Hou	SD	9/17	9.0	1	0	0	1	7	91
Randy Johnson, Sea	Tex	9/21	9.0	3	0	0	1	11	91
Ben McDonald, Bal	KC	7/20	9.0	1	0	0	3	9	91

And the winner is . . . Randy Johnson! It might seem strange that Johnson's game would rank ahead of a no-hitter, but in terms of sheer dominance, it *was* a more awesome performance. Kile lost two points because he gave up a run, but he still would have been a point short of Randy. (No, Kile didn't lose any points because his game came against the Mets . . . though maybe he should have.) Jim Abbott's no-hitter, in which he issued five walks while striking out only three, had a game score of 85.

Johnson and Pete Harnisch were the kings of the dominant pitching performances last year. Harnisch appears three times, but Johnson's games were slightly more impressive. The White Sox have to feel pretty good about having both Wilson Alvarez *and* Jason Bere on their pitching staff; they also had Tim Belcher for the stretch run. Not bad.

Does Johnson's performance rank among the top game scores of recent years? Nope, not even close. Here are the top game scores of the last four years:

Top Game Scores, 1989-93

Pitcher, Team	Opp	Date	IP	H	R	ER	BB	K	Game Score
Jose DeLeon, StL	Cin	8/30/89	11.0	1	0	0	0	8	103
Nolan Ryan, Tex	WSox	8/17/90	10.0	3	0	0	0	15	101
Nolan Ryan, Tex	Tor	5/01/91	9.0	0	0	0	2	16	101
Nolan Ryan, Tex	WSox	4/26/90	9.0	1	0	0	2	16	99
Nolan Ryan, Tex	Oak	6/11/90	9.0	0	0	0	2	14	99
Eric Hanson, Sea	Oak	8/01/90	10.0	2	0	0	0	11	99
David Cone, Mets	Phi	10/06/91	9.0	3	0	0	1	19	99

Jose DeLeon has had enormous problems winning, despite one of the great arms in the game. His awesome 11-inning one-hitter in 1989 was typical of his luck: all he got for it was a no-decision. The Cardinals won in the 12th, 1-0. Eric Hanson also went unrewarded in his gem. Hanson was lifted after 10 with the score still 0-0. His mound opponent, Dave Stewart, ended up winning with an 11-inning five-hitter (game score: 89).

Nolan Ryan, at least, won *his* games. Back in 1990, when Ryan was just a kid of 43 and could still throw hard, he turned in three of the greatest performances a pitcher could have. We saw that 10-inning, 15-strikeout three-hitter against the White Sox, and *that* was domination. But a year later, he topped that performance with his 16-strikeout no-hitter against the Blue Jays. The big showoff.

A complete listing for this category can be found on page 304.

HOW MANY PITCHES SHOULD YOU THROW?

There's been a lot of discussion the last few years of pitch counts. It got so heated in New York a couple years ago that the Mets wouldn't release David Cone's pitch counts to the press, as if anyone who cared couldn't keep track themselves. We think this recent attention is good for baseball, because we don't like to see promising young pitchers blow their arms out. As we note in the Braves essay, perhaps the best example of intelligent concern is in Atlanta, where the starters throw a lot of innings but not a lot of pitches.

Below are the 10 highest-pitch outings of last season:

Most Pitches in a Game—1993

Pitcher, Team	Date	Opp	Fin	W/L	IP	H	ER	BB	K	Pit
Tim Wakefield, Pit	4/27	Atl	6-2	W	10	6	2	10	1	172
Chuck Finley, Cal	9/02	Bal	3-4	L	9	13	4	3	8	158
Randy Johnson, Sea	6/24	Oak	2-3	L	9	4	2	8	14	157
Cal Eldred, Mil	8/30	KC	2-1	W	9	4	1	2	7	156
Armando Reynoso, Col	6/26	SF	5-1	W	9	7	1	2	8	152
Willie Banks, Min	8/14	Oak	5-1	ND	8	6	1	4	13	151
Randy Johnson, Sea	10/01	Min	8-2	W	9	9	2	2	7	150
Bobby Witt, Oak	10/03	Cal	3-7	L	9	11	7	6	7	150
Dwight Gooden, Mets	5/28	Cin	2-5	ND	9	8	2	5	4	149
Cal Eldred, Mil	8/20	Cal	7-2	W	10	6	1	2	9	149

It's not readily apparent, but Randy Johnson is the champion of this category. He only occupies third and seventh place on this chart, but if we carried it down a few spots, he'd be 11th, 12th, 13th, 14th and 15th. As we noted last year, Johnson generally seems unaffected by throwing that many pitches. This is just a guess, but we think it might have something do with the fact that he's larger than a human should be.

Cal Eldred is "good" at this, too. In addition to his two spots above, Eldred ranks just behind The Big Unit at 16th and 17th. So you have two pitchers accounting for 11 of the top 18 (Swindell is tied for 17th) high-pitch outings of the season. It remains to be seen whether Eldred will be able to handle such a heavy workload.

Anyway, back to the original list. . . One of the issues we've looked at in the past is whether or not throwing a lot of pitches in one game can have a negative effect on future starts. In 1992, a bunch of pitchers struggled in their first start after a high-pitch outing. So for 1993, we checked the start following eight of the top 10 high-pitch outings (the other two came at the end of the season). This time, we didn't find anything dramatic—the eight pitchers combined for a 3.79 ERA for the season, and a 4.21 ERA in the first start after their long games. So there was a blip, but it was within the range of random chance. We also checked their next *three* starts, and in those games they had a 3.46 ERA, even better than the season as a whole.

So though we remain convinced that young pitchers shouldn't throw a ton of innings in one season (see Charles Nagy), the evidence doesn't conclusively show that throwing a ton of *pitches* in a particular game does any damage. As the data in the Braves essay shows, however, most teams are careful not to give their young pitchers too many high-pitch outings over the course of the season.

The opposite side of the pitch coin is, of course, the low-pitch outing. The champion last year was Tom Glavine, who beat the Mets with 79 pitches on June 15. Glavine's gem was the most efficient outing since Bob Tewksbury got by with only 76 pitches in 1990, and it was a strange one. He allowed six hits, *but didn't walk or strike out a single batter*. On the strength of that game, Glavine was the winner of our 1993 "Red Barrett Trophy," named in honor of the Braves pitcher who supposedly tossed a 58-pitch complete game in 1944.

Fewest Pitches in a 9-Inning Complete Game—1993

Pitcher, Team	Date	Opp	Fin	W/L	IP	H	ER	BB	K	Pit
Tom Glavine, Atl	6/15	Mets	2-1	W	9	6	1	0	0	79
Jim Abbott, Yanks	4/12	KC	4-1	W	9	8	1	0	4	85
Orel Hershiser, LA	7/26	SF	15-1	W	9	5	1	0	2	85
Bill Swift, SF	9/17	Cin	13-0	W	9	7	0	0	4	85
Darryl Kile, Hou	9/08	Mets	7-1	W	9	0	0	1	9	88
Bill Wegman, Mil	5/07	Bos	0-1	L	9	4	0	3	2	90
Bob Walk, Pit	6/22	Cubs	7-2	W	9	3	2	0	4	90
Steve Avery, Atl	8/28	Cubs	5-1	W	9	6	0	0	3	91
Tom Glavine, Atl	7/01	Col	4-0	W	9	4	0	0	2	93
John Doherty, Det	9/24	Bal	2-0	W	9	7	0	0	4	93

We find the "Opp" column sort of interesting. You'll note that the Mets and the Cubs were victimized twice, not surprising given that both clubs were among the league's worst at drawing walks. Darryl Kile's low-pitch game, a no-hitter, was especially embarrassing from the Mets' standpoint, because Kile doesn't fit the low-pitch profile. He generally walks and strikes out a lot of hitters, and in fact, he turned in 140- and 136-pitch outings when facing teams that didn't swing at everything that moved.

A complete listing for this category can be found on page 305.

WHOSE HEATER IS HOTTEST?

In every edition of the *Baseball Scoreboard*, we've presented a list of the leaders in strikeouts per nine innings (minimum 50 innings). After four seasons, we were ready to begin calling it the "Rob Dibble Award." Here's how the Reds reliever fared from 1989 to 1992:

Rob Dibble, 1989-92

Year	K/9 IP	Rank
1989	12.8	1st
1990	12.5	1st
1991	13.6	1st
1992	14.1	1st

Nothing lasts forever, and we're sad to announce that the Dibble Dynasty is history. Bothered by injuries and "control problems" which had to do with more than just getting the ball over the plate, Dibble didn't qualify for the list last year—he worked just 41.2 innings. But he wouldn't have led the category even if he'd been eligible. Last year Dibble averaged a feeble, pathetic 10.6 K's per nine innings, which wouldn't have even made the top five. There's a new "King of the K's," Duane Ward. Long live the King!

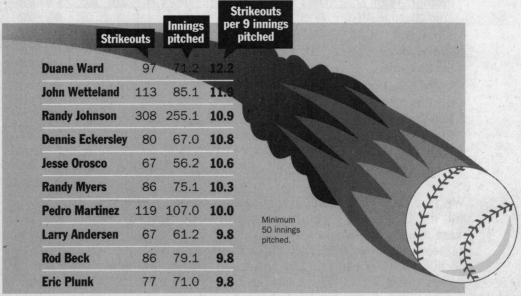

	Strikeouts	Innings pitched	Strikeouts per 9 innings pitched
Duane Ward	97	71.2	12.2
John Wetteland	113	85.1	11.9
Randy Johnson	308	255.1	10.9
Dennis Eckersley	80	67.0	10.8
Jesse Orosco	67	56.2	10.6
Randy Myers	86	75.1	10.3
Pedro Martinez	119	107.0	10.0
Larry Andersen	67	61.2	9.8
Rod Beck	86	79.1	9.8
Eric Plunk	77	71.0	9.8

Minimum 50 innings pitched.

Ward's ascendance to the throne, and Dibble's dominance in years past, points up the fact that this category continues to do be dominated by late relief men. Last year there was only one starting pitcher on the leaders list, fireballer Randy Johnson of Seattle. This isn't too surprising; late relievers only average an inning or so per appearance, and they're able to go all out on every pitch. Starters have to pace themselves over six innings or more, so their strikeout rates tend to be lower. But there's more to it than that. As we've pointed out in the past, there's been a trend in recent years to put the hardest throwers in the bullpen. That trend shows no signs of abating: among the 25 top pitchers in this category last year, Johnson was the only full-time starter.

Of course, a lot of pitchers can record high strikeout totals without a great fastball. Guys like Jesse Orosco and Larry Andersen won't break any speed gun records, but a wicked slider or curveball will get them plenty of K's. A deceptive delivery, like Dennis Eckersley's, can help also.

Can a pitcher succeed without striking out a lot of hitters? Well, yes, but it's a struggle. Despite all the romantic talk you hear about "smart pitchers" who rely on finesse, the trailers in the strikeout category usually have trouble winning. The 1993 list was no exception:

Fewest Strikeouts Per Nine Innings—1993

Pitcher, Team	IP	K	K/9 IP	ERA
Hilly Hathaway, Cal	57.1	11	1.7	5.02
Jeff Ballard, Pit	53.2	16	2.7	4.86
Rafael Novoa, Mil	56.0	17	2.7	4.50
Ricky Bones, Mil	203.2	63	2.8	4.86
John Doherty, Det	184.2	63	3.1	4.44
Jeff Mutis, Cle	81.0	29	3.2	5.78
Kirk Rueter, Mon	85.2	31	3.3	2.73
Steve Howe, Yanks	50.2	19	3.4	4.97
Bob Welch, Oak	166.2	63	3.4	5.29
Joe Magrane, StL-Cal	164.0	62	3.4	4.66

(Minimum 50 Innings Pitched)

As you can see, of all the pitchers on this list, there was only one really successful pitcher last year, rookie Kirk Rueter of the Expos. Rueter came up in mid-season and dazzled the opposition with an 8-0 record. He has some talent, but that sort of domination isn't likely to continue, and for a simple reason: he just doesn't throw hard enough.

While Rueter will undoubtedly stick around, past history has shown that the trailers in this category often disappear from the majors within a year or so. That's hardly a comforting thought for, say, Steve Howe, Bob Welch or Joe Magrane.

A Rob Dibble comeback is a much better bet. Come back, King!

A complete listing for this category can be found on page 306.

WHO'S AFRAID OF THE DARK?

When Dwight Gooden was in his heyday back in the mid-1980s, he was virtually unhittable at night, but merely mortal in the daytime. Over the first five years of his career, under the lights he was an amazing 63-20 with a 2.20 ERA; but when it *was* light, he was merely mortal, 28-15, 3.52. The most popular explanation was this: "Gooden is a power pitcher, and power pitchers are generally better at night, because it's simply harder for the batter to see the ball." This theory was supported by a study Bill James published in the 1984 *Baseball Abstract*.

But as far as we know, no one has really looked at the issue since then, and we thought it was worth a second look. Below are the 11 active pitchers who have seemingly been helped most by pitching at night (minimum 100 innings in both day and night games over the last five seasons):

Better in Night Games

Pitcher	Day ERA	Night ERA	Diff
John Wetteland	4.44	2.23	2.21
Bob Scanlan	4.65	2.96	1.69
Willie Blair	5.72	4.05	1.67
Curt Schilling	4.42	2.85	1.57
David Wells	4.92	3.36	1.56
Ben McDonald	5.02	3.49	1.53
Storm Davis	5.40	4.04	1.36
Dave Fleming	4.95	3.59	1.36
Kevin Brown	4.69	3.36	1.32
Wally Whitehurst	4.75	3.46	1.29
Omar Olivares	4.75	3.47	1.28
Tim Leary	5.59	4.31	1.28

Bill's original study was quite a bit more involved than our relatively simple chart, but we have to say that the results match up pretty well. At the top of the list is John Wetteland, who throws about as hard as anyone in the game. Then you have Bob Scanlan, who throws in the low 90s and could be primed for a big season now that he won't be playing all those day games in Wrigley any more. Willie Blair certainly won't break any radar guns, but Schilling, Wells and McDonald are all very hard throwers.

To go at it another way: Let's look at the top strikeout pitchers, per nine innings. They're discussed in "Whose Heater is Hottest?", which appears elsewhere in this book; the group includes Duane Ward, Wetteland, Randy Johnson, Dennis Eckersley, Jesse Orosco, Randy Myers, Pedro J. Martinez, Larry Andersen, Rod Beck and Eric Plunk. Last season, those 10 pitchers had a 2.75 ERA in the daytime, but a 2.85 ERA at night. "But," you're saying, "all those guys don't throw real hard, do they?" You're right, they don't. Eckersley relies on a deceptive motion, while Andersen and Orosco throw more sliders than fastballs. If we throw those three out of the study, we're left with seven acknowledged fastballers. And it turns out that those seven *did* have a slight advantage at night last year: 2.69 day ERA, 2.64 night. However, that difference isn't far from the major league norm. In 1993, all pitchers combined had a 4.17 ERA in the daytime, 4.20 at night.

Though the evidence certainly isn't overwhelming, we're pretty sure that power pitchers have an advantage under the artificial lights. But are there any pitchers who seem to be helped by the sunlight? Here are the 10 hurlers who have gained the most advantage by pitching in the daytime:

Better in Day Games

Pitcher	Day ERA	Night ERA	Diff
Doug Jones	1.79	3.72	1.93
Mark Guthrie	2.73	4.46	1.73
Kirk McCaskill	2.50	4.17	1.67
Dave Johnson	3.91	5.58	1.67
Joe Hesketh	3.36	4.88	1.52
Mike Witt	3.64	5.16	1.52
Eric Plunk	2.51	3.96	1.45
Luis Aquino	2.50	3.90	1.40
Charlie Hough	3.09	4.49	1.39
Anthony Young	3.02	4.40	1.38

Obviously, this is quite a different group. Only Plunk (who had the 10th-highest strikeout rate last year) and Young throw particularly hard. The rest of the group includes a master of the change-up (Doug Jones) and a master of the knuckleball (Charlie Hough), along with a number of other finesse pitchers. Why do junkballers fare poorly in the evening? You got us, but the simple truth is that if you take a large enough group of pitchers, random chance dictates that some of them will have big day/night splits. So maybe there's no explanation.

By the way, you might be wondering about Dwight Gooden. As his strikeout rates have gone down steadily, so has his effectiveness under the lights. In fact, over the last five seasons he's had a 3.52 ERA at night, 3.60 in day games.

A complete listing for this category can be found on page 308.

ARE PITCHERS LEARNING TO HIT AGAIN?

One of the remarkable hitting feats of the 1993 season came from a very unlikely source: a pitcher. For much of the season, Dodgers pitcher Orel Hershiser batted well over .400, threatening the record for National League pitchers set by the Giants' Jack Bentley in 1923 when he hit .427 (historians cringed when Bentley was referred to numerous times as "John"). Hershiser cooled off toward the end of the year, but still wound up hitting a very nifty .356.

Hershiser wasn't the only National League pitcher to enjoy a good season with the bat. The Reds' Jose Rijo (.268) and the Giants' Bill Swift (.263) joined Hershiser as pitchers who had more than 20 hits—a milestone no NL pitcher had been able to reach in 1992. The Phillies' Tommy Greene hit two home runs and drove in 10 runs, and the Mets' Dwight Gooden, the Marlins' Chris Hammond, and the Rockies' Armando Reynoso also belted two homers. Even the Giants' John Burkett, a legendarily bad-hitting pitcher, had his moments. Burkett, who entered the season with nine hits in 174 lifetime at-bats, had nine hits in 1993 alone. He even drew five walks. Were they pitching around him?

If you thought National League pitchers were having a good year with the bat last year, you were right. The league average jumped considerably from the level established during the previous four seasons:

National League Pitchers' Hitting

Year	Avg
1989	.139
1990	.138
1991	.138
1992	.137
1993	.150

Is this just another example of the effects of "expansion-diluted pitching"? That was probably one factor, as was the extreme hitters' park in Denver. But it also seems true that NL pitchers—and clubs—are beginning to realize how much they can help themselves with the bat. Cincinnati Reds pitchers, for example, batted an extremely respectable .217 last year. Dodger pitchers hit .199, and Cardinal pitchers batted .186. By pitcher-hitting standards, those are very fine figures.

The chart below lists the best-hitting pitchers, lifetime, among active pitchers. We run this list every year, and in the past it's been dominated by old-timers like Don Robinson and Dan Schatzeder. Those two have retired, and there's now some younger names on the list, like Omar Olivares, Bill

Swift and Tommy Greene. Other pitchers who help themselves with the bat include Hammond (.208 lifetime), Gooden (.198), Rijo (.196), and the Braves trio of Tom Glavine (.183), Greg Maddux (.181) and Steve Avery (.177).

PITCHERS WHO CAN HIT

	HR	AVG.
Omar Olivares	2	.232
Bill Swift	0	.221
Tim Leary	1	.221
Tommy Greene	4	.217
Orel Hershiser	0	.215

Active pitchers with a minimum of 150 plate appearances lifetime.

Of course, none of these guys can rival the great-hitting pitchers of the past like Wes Ferrell and Red Ruffing, and the old axiom is still true: most pitchers can't hit. To put things into perspective, we offer the list of pitchers with the *worst* lifetime averages:

Worst Hitting Pitchers—Active Career Leaders

Pitcher	Avg	AB	H	HR	RBI
John Burkett	.072	250	18	0	10
Terry Mulholland	.079	356	28	0	6
Bruce Ruffin	.080	288	23	0	6
Ted Power	.089	157	14	1	7
Jim Deshaies	.089	372	33	0	12

(Minimum 150 plate appearances lifetime)

Don't tell the Padres' Tim Worrell about "expansion-diluted" pitching: he came to bat 31 times last year, and produced one hit. And the Marlins' Charlie Hough, who began his minor league career as a third baseman back in 1966, didn't exactly enjoy his return to the National League last year. Swinging the bat for the first time since 1980, "The Chuckster" batted a mighty .032 (2-for-63).

A complete listing for this category can be found on page 310.

IS THAT LEFTY YOU'RE BRINGING IN JUST GOING TO PITCH TO A RIGHTY?

Tony Fossas is the ultimate symbol of just how specialized baseball has become. Pitching for the Boston Red Sox last year, Fossas got into 71 games, which seems like a heavy workload. Yet in those 71 appearances, Fossas worked only 40 innings and pitched to just 175 hitters—barely over two per game. Why was he in and out of contests so quickly? It's simple. Fossas is a left-handed reliever, and his specialty is to come into a game and work to one or two lefty swingers. When he can do that, he's extremely effective: last year he held lefties to a meager .129 batting average. Yet when Fossas had to work to a righty, his magic disappeared: his opponents' average was .333. No wonder he was in and out of games so quickly.

The only problem was that, even with a usage pattern clearly designed to have him avoid facing righthanders, Fossas actually wound up pitching to more righties than lefties: righthanders had 87 at-bats against him, lefthanders only 70. One reason for this is that the opposition knows how tough Fossas is against lefties; they'll counter his effectiveness with a right-handed pinch hitter.

So if even a Fossas winds up facing more righties than lefties, is the whole lefty-vs.-lefty strategy overrated? To find the answer, we looked at all situations last year in which a left-handed reliever came into a game. The first set of a numbers below shows the percentage of time that the scheduled hitter was a lefty swinger. The second set shows how often the pitcher actually wound up facing a lefty:

Pitcher	G	Due Up			Batted		
		LHB	RHB	LHB%	LHB	RHB	LHB%
Lefthander	3,335	1,932	1,403	57.9	1,609	1,726	48.2

As you can see, the southpaw relievers wound up facing a lefty far less often than their managers intended. The scheduled batter was a lefty 58 percent of the time, while the actual hitter was a lefty only 48 percent of the time. The reason is that opposing managers often counter with a righty pinch hitter. This is definitely a left-handed phenomenon; last year righty relievers were brought in to face a righty 68 percent of the time, and actually pitched to one on 64 percent of the occasions, a far less significant drop.

Of course, this is data for all relievers; what about the true specialists like Fossas, the ones who come to the mound most often? Here's the same data for the lefties who made the most relief appearances last year:

Pitcher	G	Due Up			Batted		
		LHB	RHB	LHB%	LHB	RHB	LHB%
David West, Phi	76	39	37	51.3	30	46	39.5
Rob Murphy, StL	73	41	32	56.2	34	39	46.6
Randy Myers, Cubs	73	27	46	37.0	18	55	24.7
Scott Radinsky, WSox	73	49	24	67.1	42	31	57.5
Paul Assenmacher, Cubs-Yanks	72	53	19	73.6	43	29	59.7
Tony Fossas, Bos	71	54	17	76.1	47	24	66.2
Rich Rodriguez, SD-Fla	70	41	29	58.6	32	38	45.7
Bob MacDonald, Det	68	36	32	52.9	31	37	45.6
Mitch Williams, Phi	65	16	49	24.6	9	56	13.8
Gary Wayne, Col	65	54	11	83.1	48	17	73.8

A couple of these pitchers, we should point out, aren't "lefty specialists" at all; Randy Myers and Mitch Williams are closers, and their managers will bring them in to face any kind of hitter, righty or lefty. But it turns out that even the true specialists like Fossas are brought in to face a righty a fair percentage of the time. Of the top 10, only Paul Assenmacher, Fossas and Gary Wayne had a lefty as the first scheduled hitter more than 70 percent of the time. How often do the opposing managers counter with a righty pinch swinger? It varies from pitcher to pitcher, but generally it's around 10 percent of the time. In Fossas' case, he wound up facing a lefty 66 percent of the time, instead of 76 percent. Only one reliever, Gary Wayne, wound up facing a lefty more than 70 percent of the time.

It's obvious that most of the situations in which specialists like Fossas or Wayne came in to pitch to righties were less crucial ones; given his problems with righties, you'd never want to bring in Fossas to face a righty with a game on the line. In the important situations, the managers will usually get the desired lefty-vs.-lefty match-up. But since most hitters are right-handed, even these specialists are going to wind up facing a lot of righties, some of them when the game is on the line. In order to survive, they need to have a least a minimal amount of effectiveness against righties.

A complete listing for this category can be found on page 311.

WHICH PITCHERS CAN REST IN PEACE?

Melido Perez, New York Yankees: can't you see him fidgeting on the mound, picking up the baseball, looking it over warily, thinking, "They want me to *pitch* this thing? The seams are too high! It weighs too much! And anyway, Frank Thomas is up. I think I'll just stand here and fidget for awhile." And why shouldn't he feel that way? Like his brother Pascual, Melido always seems to have a dark cloud hanging over his head. This is a fellow with a world of stuff—and a career record of 64-76.

Derek Lilliquist, Cleveland Indians: can't you see him standing on the mound, smiling, thinking, "The Braves gave up on me when they were the worst team in baseball. Then the Padres gave up on me. I work cheap, and the *Padres* gave up on me! Gee, it's great to just *be* here." You can almost see the sunbeam shining over his left shoulder. And why shouldn't he feel that way? One of those guys who was given a thousand chances and failed them all, Lilliquist kept at it and finally found success.

Perez and Lilliquist are pitchers whose careers seem headed in opposite directions, and in 1993—of course!—they were pitchers with very different luck when it came to bullpen support. In another essay we examine the relief pitchers who are best at preventing inherited runners from scoring. From the point of view of the preceding pitcher, those are "bequeathed runners," and if they score, they'll be charged against the first pitcher's ERA. A pitcher can't control how his relievers perform, but those performances will have a major effect on his ERA. As it turns out, Perez was the pitcher most victimized by his relievers last year, while Lilliquist was the one who received the most help. The chart lists the leaders in each category among pitchers who had at least 20 bequeathed runners last year.

Imagine that Perez had been the one who benefitted from the solid bullpen support, and Lilliquist as the one whose bullpen mates had deserted him. Perez would have been charged with 11 fewer earned runs, and his ERA would have been 4.58 instead of 5.19—still bad, but a big improvement. Lilliquist, though, would have been charged with 17 *more* earned runs, and his ERA would have more than doubled, from 2.25 to 4.64. He wouldn't be feeling so lucky in that case!

We should point out that, as a relief pitcher, Lilliquist would be unlikely to be victimized by his bullpen mates as much as a starting pitcher like Perez. The reason is that a starter won't ordinarily be lifted in mid-inning unless he gets into major trouble, with at least one runner in scoring position. A relief pitcher, though, works shorter stints, often coming in only to pitch to a hitter or two. He might give up a walk or a single, and then depart. Those runners will be less likely to score, so the relief pitcher has a bit of an advantage in this category.

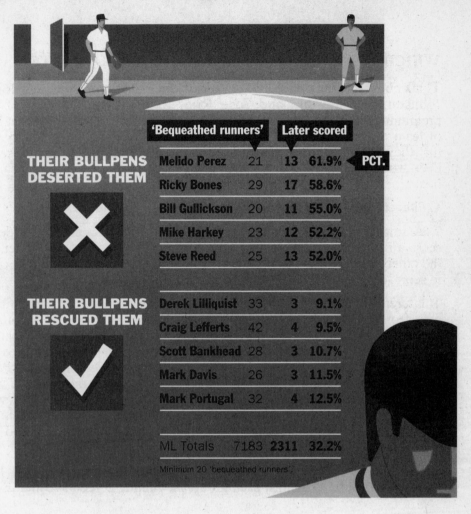

'Bequeathed runners'		Later scored	
THEIR BULLPENS DESERTED THEM			
Melido Perez	21	13	61.9%
Ricky Bones	29	17	58.6%
Bill Gullickson	20	11	55.0%
Mike Harkey	23	12	52.2%
Steve Reed	25	13	52.0%
THEIR BULLPENS RESCUED THEM			
Derek Lilliquist	33	3	9.1%
Craig Lefferts	42	4	9.5%
Scott Bankhead	28	3	10.7%
Mark Davis	26	3	11.5%
Mark Portugal	32	4	12.5%
ML Totals	7183	**2311**	32.2%

Minimum 20 'bequeathed runners'.

You can get a sense of this by looking at the leaders list. Only one of the pitchers whose "bullpens deserted them" was a reliever, Steve Reed of the Rockies. On the other hand, only one of the pitchers whose "bullpen rescued them" was a fulltime starter, Mark Portugal of the Astros.

However, even if we restrict the study to starting pitchers, it's obvious that some of them get a lot more help from their bullpens than others do. For example, if Portugal had been victimized the way Perez was, he would have allowed 16 more earned runs last year. His ERA would have gone up from 2.77 to a much-less-impressive 3.46, and he probably would have received a far less lucrative free-agent contract. Thank the Lord for a good bullpen, Mark!

A complete listing for this category can be found on page 312.

WHICH TEAMS DO DOMINANT PITCHERS DOMINATE?

Think about the great pitchers in baseball, the really dominant ones: Randy Johnson, David Cone and Jose Rijo, to name three. Two of our programmers, David Pinto and Rob McQuown, were wondering what kind of team a pitcher like this would perform best against. Their theory was that they would have their best success against singles-hitting clubs, and their worst problems against home-run hitting clubs. The logic goes like this:

1. Pitchers like this are, by definition, extremely difficult to hit.

2. A singles-hitting club needs to string several hits together in order to score a run. That's difficult to accomplish against this sort of pitcher. On the other hand, a home-run hitting club doesn't need a lot of hits in order to score; all it needs to do is jerk one out of the yard.

This premise made sense to us, and we decided to test the theory, using data from the last five years. Our qualification for being a "dominant pitcher" during an individual season was to have an opponents' batting average under .240, with at least 100 innings pitched. We defined the "home run teams" for those years as ones which exceeded the league home run average by at least 10 percent; "singles teams" were those which were under the league average by 10 percent or more. All other clubs were categorized as "neutral." Over the five-year period, 45 of the 132 teams fell into the "singles" category, 44 into the "neutral" category, and 43 into the "home run" category, a very even split.

Here's how the dominant pitchers fared against each group, vs. how pitchers overall fared against each group, in winning percentage and ERA:

	Dominant Pitchers		All Pitchers	
Opponent	Pct	ERA	Pct	ERA
Singles Teams	.594	2.91	.516	4.10
Neutral Teams	.590	3.01	.495	4.29
Home Run Teams	.585	3.15	.489	4.47

Looking at the first column, one thinks the premise has been proven; the dominant pitchers had better ERAs and higher winning percentages against the singles-hitting teams than they did against either neutral or home run-hitting teams. However, the second column shows that as a group, *all* pitchers perform better against the singles-hitting teams, and have their biggest problems with the home run clubs. When you think about it, this is perfectly logical. "Home run clubs" from 1993 included the Toronto Blue Jays, Texas Rangers and San Francisco Giants: clubs that score a lot of runs and are tough for any pitcher. The "singles" group from 1993 included a lot of lower-scoring teams like the Boston Red Sox and Florida Marlins. While there are always exceptions, the home run clubs tend to offer a pitcher more of a challenge.

If the premise is true, you'd expect the single most dominant pitchers to show consistent ERA advantages against singles-hitting clubs. How did the most dominant pitchers of the last five years to perform against the different groups? Here are the pitchers with the 10 lowest opponents' averages over the period, with a minimum of 500 innings pitched:

The Most-Dominant Pitchers, 1989-93

Pitcher	Opp Avg	ERA vs. Singles	ERA vs. Neutral	ERA vs. Home Run
Nolan Ryan	.197	3.69	3.54	2.97
Sid Fernandez	.202	3.15	2.76	3.04
Duane Ward	.214	2.13	4.44	2.57
Randy Johnson	.215	3.56	3.37	4.76
Juan Guzman	.224	2.55	3.21	4.03
David Cone	.225	3.17	3.26	3.28
Jose DeLeon	.228	3.18	3.77	3.46
Jose Rijo	.228	2.13	2.69	2.82
Roger Clemens	.229	1.92	3.43	3.08
John Smoltz	.230	3.34	3.25	3.79

(Minimum 500 IP, 1989-93)

This data is not quite what we'd expect. Eight of the 10 pitchers did have better ERAs against the singles-hitting clubs, and some significantly better. But in some cases the differences were pretty small, and there were two big exceptions: Nolan Ryan and Sid Fernandez, the two toughest pitchers to hit. Ryan's ERA was 0.72 runs higher against the single-hitting clubs, and his won-lost record over the period was 19-10 against the home run clubs, 18-16 against the singles-hitting clubs. Exactly the opposite of what you'd expect.

In addition, only three of the 10 pitchers had the expected progression of rising ERAs as they moved from singles to neutral to home run teams. So while there is some reason to think that, as a group, dominating pitchers might have relatively better success against singles-hitting clubs than most pitchers do, the difference isn't all that great, and there are numerous exceptions. It varies greatly, depending upon the pitcher and the individual opponent; it's not the sort of thing you could make a confident prediction about, heading into a particular game.

A complete listing for this category can be found on page 313.

HOW IMPORTANT IS RUN SUPPORT?

When Jack McDowell was voted the American League Cy Young Award winner for 1993, most people applauded, but a few cried "Foul!" While McDowell led the league with 22 victories, a lot of his other numbers weren't all that impressive. Black Jack's 3.37 ERA was one of the highest ever for a Cy Young winner, and he permitted 261 hits, second-most in the American League. Cy who?

McDowell's defenders are fond of repeating that old saw, "Forget the stats. He just knows how to win." We unabashedly agree that Jack's a terrific pitcher, but we also have to point out that McDowell had an edge last year: a White Sox offense which averaged 5.40 runs a game for him. Our annual investigation into the effects of run support pairs up McDowell with a guy who was considered a big disappointment in 1993, Kansas City's David Cone. Here's a comparison of the two, without their won-lost records:

	GS	IP	H	HR	BB	SO	ERA
McDowell	34	256.2	261	20	69	158	3.37
Cone	34	254.0	205	20	114	191	3.33

Looking at these figures, one would be hard-pressed to find much difference in quality. The games started and home run totals are identical, the innings pitched and ERAs nearly so. Cone, who permitted more walks but far fewer hits, allowed 329 baserunner last year (including hit batsmen); McDowell allowed 333.

So why was McDowell 22-10 last year, and Cone only 11-14? Because Jack McDowell's a real man, while David Cone's a wimp. Sorry, wrong answer; the biggest difference was that while McDowell was enjoying the benefits of the White Sox offense, Cone was saddled with a Royals attack which produced only 2.94 runs per nine innings for him. The Bill James formula which measures "tough losses"—games in which a starter pitched well enough to win, but still wound up with a loss—had Cone saddled with 10 tough losses last year, the most of any pitcher in baseball.

The chart on the next page shows the McDowell/Cone figures, and two more comparisons between pitchers who posted similar ERAs over a like number of innings, while posting very different won-lost records. There were other interesting matches. For instance, Doug Drabek of the Astros, considered one of 1993's major "free agent flops," made 34 starts last year, worked 237.2 innings, and had a 3.79 ERA. The man we paired him with, the Giants' John Burkett, made 34 starts, worked 231.2 innings and had a 3.65 ERA. Yet Burkett, whose offense averaged 5.52 runs per nine ninnings, was a hero with a 22-7 record. Drabek, whose offense managed only 3.64 runs a contest, was a "bum" with a 9-18 record.

Some people will contend, "That's tough." They'll say that someone like McDowell will coast with a lead, turn it on when he needs an out, and that

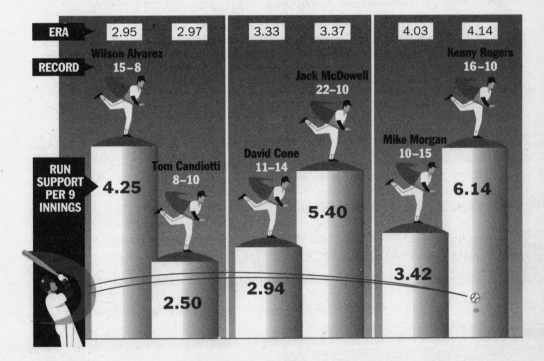

the real winners make the best of the support they receive. There's some merit to the argument. For example, last August 22, the White Sox pushed across a run for McDowell in the top of the first, then failed to score the rest of the day. Though Black Jack was in trouble throughout the game, he held the Twins scoreless for a brilliant 1-0 victory. It wasn't the first time McDowell had pitched a game like that, and it probably won't be the last.

But let's not get overly romantic on the subject. Doug Drabek is a former Cy Young Award winner also, and Cone, who went 20-3 in 1988, has been a contender for the award on several occasions. Did they forget how to win last year? We don't think so. We think it's more logical that *any* pitcher will have trouble winning if he gets poor support.

But don't get us wrong: we also think Jack McDowell is one heckuva pitcher.

A complete listing for this category can be found on page 314.

CAN ANYONE WIN 300 AGAIN?

Back in the early 1960s, when Warren Spahn beat out Early Wynn in their race to 300 wins, Wynn was quoted as saying that maybe this wasn't such a bad thing. Why? With the decline in complete games and the increased use of relief pitchers, Wynn thought he might be the *last* to win 300.

As it turned out, Wynn couldn't have been more wrong; in the 30 years since Old Gus finally reached the goal himself, six more pitchers—Steve Carlton, Phil Niekro, Gaylord Perry, Nolan Ryan, Tom Seaver and Don Sutton—reached 300 victories. However, Wynn's story sticks in our mind, because 30 years later, people are saying the exact same thing—that the changing nature of pitching usage will make it impossible for anyone to win that many games again.

Can anyone win 300 again? Unless the game changes more than it has, there's no reason why not. Last year 12 pitchers won 18 or more games, including five with 20 or more. That's enough of a seed to eventually reap a 300-win harvest. Don Sutton, who won 324 games, had only one 20-win season in his career. Nolan Ryan had only two 20-win seasons in all the years he pitched. Phil Niekro wasn't much different: three 20-win seasons, with a high of 23. You don't need to win 20 games every year to win 300; you just need to win consistently.

Probably the best way to show that winning 300 isn't impossible is to look at the pace set by the six to reach the mark since Spahn and Wynn. This chart shows the number of career victories that each compiled from age 27 to age 39, with ages figured as of July 1:

The Path to 300—Career Victories by Age

Age	Steve Carlton	Phil Niekro	Gaylord Perry	Nolan Ryan	Tom Seaver	Don Sutton
27	104	6	45	91	116	102
28	117	17	60	105	135	120
29	133	31	76	122	146	139
30	148	54	95	141	168	155
31	168	66	118	151	182	176
32	191	81	134	167	203	190
33	207	97	158	178	219	205
34	225	110	177	189	235	217
35	249	130	198	205	245	230
36	262	145	216	219	259	241
37	285	162	231	231	264	258
38	300	178	246	241	273	266
39	313	197	267	253	288	280

People tend to think of winning 300 in impossible terms—you have to average 20 wins a year for 15 years! But as you can see from the chart, nobody does it like that, and there are all sorts of career paths to winning 300, from the "hare," Tom Seaver, to the "tortoise," Phil Niekro.

To put the chart into a little perspective, Steve Avery, who was 23 last year and who has 50 career victories, could take the next four years off and still be ahead of the 300-win pace of Phil Niekro and Gaylord Perry . . . and also Warren Spahn, who had only 44 career wins by age 27. Knuckleballer Tim Wakefield, 26 last year with exactly 14 career victories, is still well ahead of Niekro's pace.

Niekro, Perry and Spahn were late developers who kept winning past the ages of 40. There are lots of pitchers ahead of their pace. But several active pitchers are at or ahead of the pace set by the likes of Seaver, Carlton or Sutton. Roger Clemens, as we point out in the Red Sox article, has stats very similar to Seaver's at the same age; he has 163 victories, only five fewer than Seaver at the same age, and Seaver set the *fastest* early pace among the recent 300-game winners. Clemens has more wins through age 30 than any of the others, and many more than Spahn (108) or Wynn (101) as well. Despite his slump last year, he's still a strong candidate to win 300.

With 154 victories through age 28, Dwight Gooden is far ahead of the pace set by any of the recent 300-game winners; in fact, he's more than a year ahead of Seaver's pace. But slowed by arm problems and pitching for a lousy team, Gooden has averaged only 12 wins a year over the last three seasons. A more logical candidate would be Greg Maddux, with 115 wins through age 27—like Clemens, a pace almost identical with Seaver's. Tom Glavine and Jack McDowell, both 27 last year, have shown the consistent winning pattern that a 300-game winner needs, but Glavine has only 95 career victories and McDowell 81 . . . a long way to go.

Studying the chart, it's obvious that anyone who wins 300 will have to keep winning consistently past the age of 35. The problem is that over the last few years, pitchers who looked the type, like Jack Morris or Frank Viola (174 wins through age 33) have come down with injuries and fallen off the pace. But then, almost every 300-game winner has experienced injuries or a career slump which set them back. The ones who made it were able to come back and resume winning. Despite the tendency to ridicule the work ethic of "these modern athletes," we think there are plenty of pitchers around who have that ability to overcome adversity. We think that at least one active pitcher will win 300 before he's through, and maybe more than one.

WHICH FIREMEN AREN'T THE SAME WITHOUT A GREAT BIG BLAZE?

Doesn't it seem like some relief pitchers sort of . . . lose interest . . . unless they're in an especially difficult situation? When Bobby Thigpen was in his heyday with the White Sox, he always seemed like the worst pitcher in the world unless the game was on the line. And there's the legendary Mitch Williams, whose "specialty" seems to be walking the bases full, then going 3-and-0 on the next hitter before he finally gets down to business.

But is this perception true of some relievers, most relievers, or just something we imagined in a bad dream? To find the answer, we looked at all relief pitchers with at least 30 save opportunities over the last three years—basically the top closers, plus the best set-up men. We then defined their "close games" as follows: the reliever comes in either with the score tied, his club trailing by no more than one run, or in a "tough" or "regular" save situation (the definitions are in the essay, "Who Gets the Easy Saves?"). We then compared the relievers' ERAs in those games with their ERAs in their other, lower-pressure situations.

If we look at the group as a whole, the answer is easy: they performed almost identically in both pressure and non-pressure situations. Their ERA in close games was 3.01; their ERA the rest of the time was 3.07. No significant difference. But that's just the forest which obscures the individual trees. There were enormous differences among individuals; some pitched much better under pressure, and some pitched much worse. The chart on the next page shows the top five in each category.

It turns out that our perceptions about Bobby Thigpen were right. In important situations over the last three years, Thigpen was a reasonably competent reliever, but when the game wasn't close, he was a disaster. The same was true for another former relief great, Dave Righetti—the man who held the single-season save record before Thigpen broke it. While it might seem that neither pitcher was given many opportunities in close games over the last couple of years, well over half of Thigpen's innings, and 46 percent of Righetti's, came in close games. They might not have been as good as they were in their prime, but they did handle pressure roles a whole lot better than non-pressure ones.

More interesting than Thigpen and Righetti—because he's still in his prime—is Jeff Russell of the Red Sox. Russell, who led the American League in save percentage last year, has had an ERA almost half as low in pressure situations as he did in his other appearances. His overall ERA of 2.70 last year didn't indicate how good he really was.

The opposite extreme from Russell was represented by Gregg Olson of the Orioles. Olson had a 3.61 ERA in close games over the last three years—about the same as Bobby

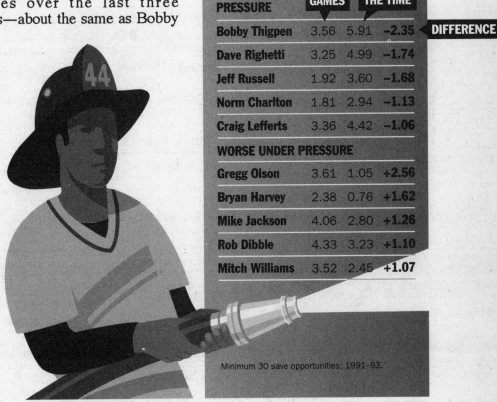

BETTER UNDER PRESSURE	ERA		DIFFERENCE
	CLOSE GAMES	REST OF THE TIME	
Bobby Thigpen	3.56	5.91	−2.35
Dave Righetti	3.25	4.99	−1.74
Jeff Russell	1.92	3.60	−1.68
Norm Charlton	1.81	2.94	−1.13
Craig Lefferts	3.36	4.42	−1.06
WORSE UNDER PRESSURE			
Gregg Olson	3.61	1.05	+2.56
Bryan Harvey	2.38	0.76	+1.62
Mike Jackson	4.06	2.80	+1.26
Rob Dibble	4.33	3.23	+1.10
Mitch Williams	3.52	2.45	+1.07

Minimum 30 save opportunities; 1991–93.

Thigpen's—but an airtight 1.05 ERA when the pressure was off. That may have been almost as big a factor in the Orioles' decision to let Olson test the free-agent market as his arm problems.

Bryan Harvey had the next biggest pressure/non-pressure difference next to Olson, but that can pretty much be discounted, as his 2.38 ERA in close games was so good. But Mike Jackson, Rob Dibble and Mitch Williams—yes, him—have no such excuses. All were fine when the pressure was low, not nearly so fine when it was high. Sometimes that "walk the bases loaded" stuff doesn't work out in the end.

The opposite extreme from the those two groups is represented by this group of five, who pitched virtually identical ball, whatever the situation:

The Steady Relievers

Pitcher	ERA Close Games	ERA Rest of the Time	Difference
Rick Aguilera	2.78	2.76	0.02
Dennis Eckersley	2.91	3.01	−0.10
Stan Belinda	3.53	3.42	0.11
Jim Gott	2.64	2.51	0.13
Mel Rojas	2.38	2.54	−0.16

(1991-93; minimum 30 save opportunities)

One thing you can say about Dennis Eckersley: he doesn't need pressure to hold his concentration.

A complete listing for this category can be found on page 315.

V. QUESTIONS ON DEFENSE

ARE GOLD GLOVE AWARDS HOPELESSLY BIASED?

The Gold Glove awards are kind of like the Hall of Fame voting. Everyone says the selections are biased, and everyone (including us) thinks they can do a better job than the voters. The voting, which is conducted through a poll of major league managers and coaches, has been criticized for several reasons:

1. Players seem to get the award on the basis of their "reputation," rather than on their performance in a particular year. As a result, young players get shut out; old players live off their past.

2. Players who are good hitters seem to have an advantage over players who are not.

3. Outfield awards are all lumped together, even though left, center and right field are distinct positions, with very distinct responsibilities.

All of the criticisms seem to have some validity. Number three, in particular, has always bugged us, which is why we give our outfield awards to people who actually played left, center or right. What we'd like to do in this essay is focus on numbers one and two. How often do players really get by on the basis of their past reputation, and how often does a guy get the nod because he's a good hitter? It's a big subject, going back to 1957, when the award began. So we'll limit our study to three positions where stats are plentiful—second base, third base and shortstop—and to a few years where we felt an injustice was clearly done. We'll show the pertinent stats; games are at that position only, and "range" is putouts plus assists per game (since we didn't have a count of defensive innings until the late 1980s):

1959 National League—SS

Player	Gm	PO	A	E	DP	FPct	Range
Roy McMillan	73	163	205	10	50	.974	5.04
Ernie Banks	154	271	519	12	95	.985	5.13

Good hitters don't *always* have an advantage in the Gold Glove voting—especially at shortstop, where there's often a prejudice against power hitters. Ernie Banks had a great season at short in '59, leading the league in assists and setting a National League record, since broken, for fielding percentage. However, the voters gave the award to Roy McMillan, the 1957 and '58 winner, even though McMillan got into only 73 games because of a broken collarbone. Banks would win the Gold Glove in 1960, but he deserved it for 1959 as well. Certainly McMillan had no business winning in '59, given his limited playing time.

1963 American League—SS

Player	Gm	PO	A	E	DP	FPct	Range
Zoilo Versalles	159	301	448	30	87	.962	4.71
Ron Hansen	144	247	483	13	95	.983	5.07

1965 American League—SS

Player	Gm	PO	A	E	DP	FPct	Range
Zoilo Versalles	160	248	487	39	105	.950	4.59
Ron Hansen	161	287	527	26	97	.969	5.06

Zoilo Versalles of the Twins was an exciting, but erratic, defensive player who committed 30 or more errors six times. Ron Hansen of the White Sox was mostly known for his steadiness. Yet as the numbers indicate, Hansen actually had better range figures than Versalles. These numbers were no fluke, as Hansen led American League shortstops in putouts twice, assists four times, and double plays three times; Versalles, a contemporary, led in putouts twice, assists once and double plays twice, not as good a record. (Versalles' best year defensively was 1962, when he *didn't* get the award. Of course.) The only real edge Versalles had over Hansen in 1963 and '65 was on offense; he outhit Hansen, a .234 career hitter, by 35 points in 1963, and was the American League's Most Valuable Player in 1965, a year in which Hansen batted .235. Hansen clearly deserved both these Gold Gloves, which were awarded to Versalles.

1971 American League—3B

Player	Gm	PO	A	E	DP	FPct	Range
Brooks Robinson	156	131	354	16	35	.968	3.11
Graig Nettles	158	159	412	16	54	.973	3.61

Brooks Robinson was one of the greatest defensive third baseman of all time, maybe *the* greatest. He won 16 consecutive Gold Gloves, and deserved most of them. Graig Nettles, who came up when Robinson was in his 30s, was also a great fielder and, eventually, a two-time Gold Glove winner. In 1971, Nettles had one of the greatest defensive seasons a third baseman ever had, maybe *the* greatest. His 54 double plays that year—an extraordinary total—were the most ever for a third baseman, and he dominated Robinson in every statistical area. Yet Robinson got the award. Nettles, like Robinson, was an outstanding hitter (28 homers that year), but in 1971, he had two problems: it was early in his career, and he played for the Cleveland Indians. Denying Nettles that award was highway robbery.

1975 National League—3B

Player	Gm	PO	A	E	DP	FPct	Range
Ken Reitz	160	124	279	23	21	.946	2.52
Mike Schmidt	151	132	368	24	30	.965	3.29

Don't tell Mike Schmidt that the Gold Glove always goes to a good hitter. The 1975 award went to Ken Reitz of the Cardinals, a so-so batsman with one defensive attribute: he was usually a sure-handed fielder. In 1975 he didn't even have *that* going for him, but with the "incumbent" Gold Glove third baseman, five-time winner Doug Rader, wearing down, they gave the award to Reitz, partly due to an aggressive campaign by people in St. Louis. A year later the voters realized their mistake and gave Schmidt the first of his nine straight Gold Gloves. That doesn't make up for the 1975 outrage, however.

1986 National League—3B

Player	Gm	PO	A	E	DP	FPct	Range
Mike Schmidt	124	78	220	6	27	.980	2.40
Terry Pendleton	156	133	371	20	36	.962	3.23

Like Brooks Robinson, Schmidt deserved most of the Gold Gloves he received, and as we just saw, he should have received at least one more. But by 1985, Schmidt was 35 and seemed to be slipping, and the voters gave the Gold Glove award to Tim Wallach, breaking Schmidt's nine-year run. In 1986, Schmidt posted some of the weakest defensive numbers of his career, and was even moved to first base for 35 games. But when the Gold Glove voting came out after the season, Schmidt was the Gold Glove winner. Why? Three reasons. One was that Wallach had a poor year in 1986—especially at bat, where he hit only .233. Another was that Terry Pendleton, who clearly deserved the award off his superior stats, was only in his second full year and thus "unproven"; just as importantly, Pendleton had batted .239 with one homer. So the award went to Schmidt, who, ahem, happened to be having an MVP year at bat. The next year, the voters "corrected the oversight" and gave the award to Pendleton, who would go on to receive several more.

What we've shown you here is just the tip of the iceberg; there are many other cases where bewildering, illogical choices were made. Here's what we conclude:

1. Good hitting isn't a prerequisite for a Gold Glove, as weak batsmen like Bobby Knoop and Roy McMillan have taken the award. But it's generally tough for a weak hitter to win unless he has some pretty overwhelming

qualifications. For instance, there were years in the early 1960s when Clete Boyer appeared to be just as good as Robinson, and Boyer probably deserved at least one American League award. (He would finally win one in 1969, in the National League.) But Robinson, a much better hitter, always got the nod.

2. Past performance is crucial; the voters seem to have the attitude, "Prove yourself over several seasons; then we'll give you the award." As a result, choices are made which seem impossible to defend.

3. The voters seem susceptible to publicity campaigns on behalf of one candidate or another. For years, the Pirates whined about how Chico Lind deserved the second base award over Ryne Sandberg, even though the numbers always supported Sandberg. In 1992, Lind finally got his award—undeservedly, we thought. In 1993, the same trick seemed to work for Jay Bell, who beat out Ozzie Smith for the shortstop award. We felt Smith still deserved it. There have been other cases like this, such as Reitz in 1975.

The awards aren't hopeless. Great fielders *do* get recognized, and win their share. The problem is that players often receive them for work that has little to do with performance in a particular season. That needlessly tarnishes the whole process.

HOW IMPORTANT IS A GOOD-THROWING CATCHER?

As we point out in our Orioles essay, the 1993 season was a great one for catchers. Mike Piazza, Rick Wilkins and Chris Hoiles led a group of receivers who posted some of the best batting figures ever at the position.

However, that's only part of a catcher's job. Consider the case of Mickey Tettleton. For several seasons, the Tiger receiver has been one of the best-hitting catchers in the game, and 1993 was no exception. Last year, Tettleton reached the 30-home run mark for the third straight time, drew 100-plus walks for the fourth straight year, and drove in more than 100 runs for the first time in his 10-year career.

The only thing was, Tettleton compiled most of those figures while playing positions like right field, left field and first base. The Tigers wound up giving most of the playing time behind the plate to Chad Kreuter, a much stronger defensive catcher. Look at how Tettleton and Kreuter compared in two key areas—throwing out baserunners and handling pitchers:

Catcher	Innings Caught	SB	CS	Pct	ERA when C
Kreuter	897.0	57	35	38.0	4.51
Tettleton	430.0	36	5	12.2	5.09

Though they were working with the same pitching staff, Kreuter was three times more successful when it came to tossing out runners. In addition, Tigers pitchers had a better ERA when Kreuter was behind the plate.

Kreuter has long been known as a solid defensive catcher, and Tettleton has been known as a catcher who can hit. But the Tigers didn't switch to Kreuter until last year, and the main reason was this: Kreuter's hitting improved dramatically. It's an old story. The graphic on the next page, which lists the catchers with the best and worst success rates against basestealers last year, indicates that given a choice between a catcher with defensive skills and a guy who can hit, most managers will choose the hitter.

For example, the leader, Steve Lake, has long been known as one of the best throwers around, but he's spent most of his career on the bench due to a weak bat. Junior Ortiz is another career backup. Ron Karkovice of the White Sox and Kirt Manwaring of the Giants have always had the defensive goods, but didn't become regulars until they were able to improve their hitting. On the other hand, catchers like Darrin Fletcher and Don Slaught are able to stay in the lineup despite suspect defensive skills. Slaught is a good example of a catcher whose throwing figures rise and fall from year to year, depending on how effective his pitchers are at helping

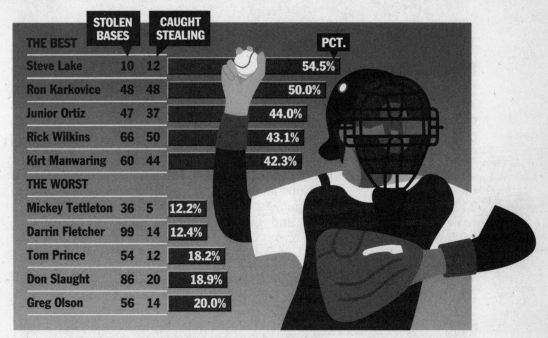

THE BEST	STOLEN BASES	CAUGHT STEALING	PCT.
Steve Lake	10	12	54.5%
Ron Karkovice	48	48	50.0%
Junior Ortiz	47	37	44.0%
Rick Wilkins	66	50	43.1%
Kirt Manwaring	60	44	42.3%
THE WORST			
Mickey Tettleton	36	5	12.2%
Darrin Fletcher	99	14	12.4%
Tom Prince	54	12	18.2%
Don Slaught	86	20	18.9%
Greg Olson	56	14	20.0%

him control the running game. In 1991, for example, he tossed out 35 percent of opposing baserunners, a rate almost twice as high as his 1993 figure. It points up the fact that all catchers can be helped or hurt considerably by their pitching staffs. But a good thrower behind the plate *does* make a difference. Look at the figures for the three catchers who did most of the receiving for the White Sox:

Catcher	Innings Caught	SB	CS	Pct
Karkovice	1,038.2	48	48	50.0
LaValliere	259.2	8	21	72.4
Fisk	125.2	22	1	4.3

Working with basically the same group of pitchers, Ron Karkovice and Mike LaValliere had outstanding throw-out rates, while future Hall-of-Famer Fisk was so inept that the Sox released him in midseason.

Who was the best all-around catcher last year? The Dodgers' Mike Piazza had a fabulous rookie season at bat, and threw out 34.9 percent of opposing runners, which ain't bad. But for all-around brilliance, it would be hard to pick anyone but the Cubs' Rick Wilkins. Playing regularly for the first time in his career, Wilkins batted .303, had a mighty .561 slugging average, belted 30 homers in only 446 at-bats . . . and tossed out 43.1 percent of opposing basestealers, one of the best figures in the majors.

A complete listing for this category can be found on page 316.

WHICH PARKS PRODUCE THE MOST ERRORS?

Most fans realize that each stadium is unique, and has an effect on how the game is played. Some parks are great for sluggers; some are great for guys who can drive a ball into the gaps. Some are good for power pitchers; others give an advantage to groundballers.

A lesser-known park effect—and one which few people consider—is the way a field contributes to defensive errors. We discovered that ourselves in the very first issue of the *Scoreboard*, when we studied errors by parks for the seasons 1987-89. The Cubs and their opponents, we found, committed 33 percent more errors in games at Wrigley Field than they did in Cub road games. The Phillies and their opponents, on the other hand, committed 12 percent fewer errors in games at Veterans Stadium than they did when the Phils were on the road.

We thought it was time to update the study, especially since there have been so many park changes in the last few years. Our method, as usual, is to compute the number of errors committed by both teams (home and road) in a club's home games, and compare that figure with the error total in the club's road games. We divide the home figure by the road figure and multiply by 100 to produce an index. An index of 100 indicates a neutral park; one with an index over 100 means that an above-average number of errors are being committed at the park. Here is the index for the American League, which is based on the last three seasons unless the park was new or changed configuration:

Park Errors Indexes—American League

Team	Home Errors	Road Errors	Index	Team	Home Errors	Road Errors	Index
Orioles 92-93	193	214	90	Brewers	396	367	109
Red Sox	415	329	126	Twins	320	366	87
Angels	426	368	116	Yankees	349	367	95
White Sox	366	386	94	Athletics	378	364	104
Indians 92-93	283	280	101	Mariners 92-93	215	251	86
Tigers	372	397	94	Rangers	404	414	98
Royals	390	336	116	Blue Jays	331	394	84

(1991-93 unless noted)

A high error index is often the result of a rough infield surface which creates a lot of bad hops. Fenway Park and Anaheim Stadium might be in that category, but Kauffman Stadium in Kansas City is an artificial turf field, and turf stadiums are supposed to have "true hops" and *fewer* errors; that is indeed the case for the turf fields in Minnesota, Seattle and Toronto, which have the three lowest error indexes in the league. Theories abound as to why there were so many errors at Kauffman Stadium—from old, worn-out turf to old, worn-out official scorers who like to call errors. It's a mystery we can try to unravel for one more year; after that, Kansas City will rip out the turf and go back to natural grass, as God intended.

Here are the indexes for the National League:

Park Errors Indexes—National League

Team	Home Errors	Road Errors	Index	Team	Home Errors	Road Errors	Index
Braves	473	378	125	Expos	371	480	86
Cubs	423	365	113	Mets	392	389	100
Reds	360	426	85	Phillies	400	422	93
Rockies 93	240	130	185	Pirates	365	354	101
Marlins 93	165	147	112	Padres	405	408	99
Astros 92-93	221	275	80	Giants 93	135	157	86
Dodgers	447	412	108	Cardinals 92-93	245	271	90

(1991-93 unless noted)

We discuss some of the unique characteristics of Denver's Mile High Stadium in other essays, but one of the *most* unique is the extraordinarily high number of errors committed there. Just look at the raw totals; there were more errors committed at Mile High in 1993 than in the last *two* seasons combined at the Astrodome! The altitude is said to contribute to the dry, "rocky" infield, but who knows? Maybe it's just hard to catch the ball when you can't breathe.

Wrigley Field continues to be a difficult park for defensive players, and so does Atlanta's Fulton County Stadium; however, the Wrigley error index decreased from 133 in the 1987-89 period to 113 for 1991-93, indicating an improved playing surface. Dodger Stadium is also a tough place for fielders, and so is Joe Robbie Stadium in Miami. As in the American League, most of the NL turf stadiums have very low error indexes; the only one higher than 93 was Pittsburgh at 101.

WHO LED THE LEAGUE IN FUMBLES?

Almost everyone knows that error rates are only part of a fielder's profile. There's also range, throwing, and for infielders, the ability to turn the double play. But it *is* important to avoid errors; commit too many of them, and you're liable to be shifted to a new position, or even to the bench.

We annually compare players with "soft hands" (the sure-handed ones) to those with "stone hands" (the fumble-fingered guys). The 1992 stone-handers included third baseman Gregg Jefferies, who's now a first sacker; center fielder Juan Gonzalez, who's now in left field; and second baseman Steve Sax, who spent 1993 as a little-used bench player. See what we mean about the hazards of committing too many errors?

STONE HANDS		Games per error*	SOFT HANDS		
P	Willie Banks	3.2	P	Jose Rijo	0 in 28.6
C	Pat Borders	10.1	C	Kirt Manwaring	60.6
1B	Orestes Destrade	7.5	1B	Don Mattingly	41.4
2B	Jeff Kent	6.6	2B	Jose Lind	32.0
3B	Gary Sheffield	3.7	3B	Steve Buechele	15.0
SS	Wil Cordero	3.8	SS	Greg Gagne	14.8
LF	Ron Gant	14.0	LF	Jeff Conine	67.4
CF	Derek Bell	14.0	CF	Darren Lewis	0 in 120.1
RF	Dante Bichette	13.9	RF	Dave Justice	31.0

*A 'game' is equivalent to 9 defensive innings played; minimum 1,000 defensive innings (162 for pitchers).

The chart lists the 1993 leaders in each category, based on the most and fewest errors per nine innings. For example, Steve Buechele averaged one error for every 15 games at third base last year; Gary Sheffield averaged a miscue about every four contests, roughly four times as often. Sheffield, whose fielding average was an 1890-ish .899 last year, will be tried as a right fielder in 1994, an idea he—and the fans behind first base who had to duck every time he wound up to throw—has heartily endorsed.

The Sheffield position-switch, not to mention the Sheffield error-rate, underscores an old axiom: if you can swing the bat, they'll find a place for you. Another member of the "Stone Hands" team, Derek Bell, probably won't be back in center field this year, but he'll be playing regularly somewhere—the dude can hit. Middle infielders Jeff Kent and Wil Cordero also pack some offensive punch along with their shaky gloves, and there's already talk of switching them to third, a (presumably) less demanding defensive position.

To err is human, but:

1. Rookie pitcher Scott Ruffcorn of the White Sox got into three games last year, and had a perfect fielding record: three chances, three errors. It's got to get better, doesn't it, Scott?

2. Ruffcorn will have to prove his butterfingers over the long haul to earn the title of "worst-fielding pitcher in baseball." For instance, consider the legendary Mitch Williams, whose lifetime fielding average is .835. We know exactly what Mitch was thinking when Carter hit the home run: "Well, at least that one didn't hit me in the head!"

3. Veteran readers of this essay will recall how we've raved over the error-making exploits of Matt Young. Sad to say, Young, whose 1992 fielding average was a "typically Matt" .625 (16 chances, six errors), committed only one miscue in 1993—a sure sign that he's nearing the end.

3. Pardon us for being unsentimental, but has anyone but us noted that Nolan Ryan was one of the worst-fielding pitchers ever to stand on the mound? Ryan committed three errors in eight chances last year, reducing his lifetime fielding average to .894. Makes a fellow want to reach for that jar of "Ad-vil." ("If I had to do it all over again," Robin Ventura was heard to moan last summer, "I'd pretend I was a grounder.")

4. As a third basemen with the Pirates, Bobby Bonilla was a charter member of our first "Stone Hands" team. Naturally, those clever New York Mets returned Bonilla to third for 52 games last year. He made 11 errors and fielded .928. No wonder the Mets win the pennant every year.

The "Soft Hands" team doesn't completely match up with the list of Gold Glove winners—much less with the "Stone Hands" team when it comes to pure fun. But most of the players on the list do more than avoid errors. Both Kirt Manwaring and Don Mattingly won the award last year, and many people thought Greg Gagne and Darren Lewis—who has great range, and who has never committed an error—were equally deserving. The only players on this list who wouldn't be considered well above-average on defense are Jeff Conine and Dave Justice.

But give us Scott Ruffcorn every time.

A complete listing for this category can be found on page 317.

WHO ARE THE PRIME PIVOT MEN?

If you want to be a top second baseman, there are two things you *have* to be able to do. Field everything hit in your area, sure, which is something we measure in a variety of ways. But almost as important is the ability to turn double plays. Unfortunately, the traditional fielding stats don't know what to do with double plays. Sure, you can just count them, but there's a huge influence in the raw number—the propensity of the pitching staff for inducing ground balls.

We've come up with something better, the "pivot percentage." Quite simply, what we do is record all the situations where a double-play pivot is possible—man on first, less than two outs, ball hit to another infielder and the second baseman takes the throw. Then we record the actual number of double plays turned by that second baseman. Divide the double plays by the opportunities, and you've got pivot percentage.

When we check out the data, we have to split it up by leagues, because there are far fewer double plays turned in the National League than the American. This is because the senior circuit features a lot more one-run strategies—bunts, steals, hit-and-runs—and consequently, there are fewer double-play chances. Here's how the leagues differed in 1993:

1993 Second Base DP Opportunities

League	Opp	DP	Pct
American	853	1,402	60.8
National	745	1,294	57.6

That 3.2 percent difference may not seem like much, but it is. Anyway, here are the top five American League second basemen on the double-play pivot for 1993 (minimum 50 opportunities):

Best Pivot Men — 1993 American League

Player, Team	Opp	DP	Pct
Chuck Knoblauch, Min	92	63	68.5
Joey Cora, WSox	81	54	66.7
Rich Amaral, Sea	51	34	66.7
Brent Gates, Oak	72	47	65.3
Carlos Baerga, Cle	89	58	65.2

Knoblauch, who has always been about average at turning the twin killing, was excellent last year. He was a shortstop in the minors, and perhaps he's just now getting the hang of hanging in there. Two rookies did well, too, Amaral and Gates (though at 31 years old, perhaps they should have invented a new category for Amaral—"senior rookie" or something). Baerga is very good, too, as we'll see later on.

Here are the National League leaders:

Best Pivot Men — 1993 National League

Player, Team	Opp	DP	Pct
Robby Thompson, SF	73	49	67.1
Jeff Kent, Mets	53	35	66.0
Mark Lemke, Atl	99	64	64.6
Delino DeShields, Mon	72	45	62.5
Jody Reed, LA	64	38	59.4

Robby Thompson has consistently been among the top double-play men in the National League since we began keeping track back in 1989, and with the retirement of Willie Randolph, he probably has no peer. Jeff Kent is not a particularly good second baseman, but, as is often the case with power-hitting middle infielders, he has a strong arm and can turn the DP. One more note: the worst National Leaguer was Padre Jeff Gardner, of whom Joe McIlvaine once said, "He turns the double play like Bill Mazeroski." Of course, Mazeroski is 57 years old.

Gardner was a rookie last year, so that's all the data we have to work with to evaluate him. However, it's instructive to look at the active leaders over the last four years (minimum 150 opportunities):

Best Pivot Men — 1990-1993

Player, Team	Opp	DP	Pct
Carlos Baerga	261	181	69.3
Billy Ripken	216	142	65.7
Scott Fletcher	270	177	65.6
Chuck Knoblauch	269	172	63.9
Robby Thompson	315	199	63.2

Baerga on top; the guy can hit a little, too. By the way, the major league average for those four seasons was 58.6 percent. As we mentioned earlier, National Leaguers are at a disadvantage here; aside from Thompson, the best over the four years in the senior circuit were Delino DeShields and Mark Lemke. The worst in the majors was Juan Samuel, at just 43.3 percent, though he did improve somewhat with the Reds last year. Maybe he should have shaved years ago.

A complete listing for this category can be found on page 319.

WHICH OUTFIELDERS HAVE THE CANNONS?

Few things are more impressive in baseball than a perfect throw from right field to retire a runner; consider Dave Parker's amazing throw in the 1979 All-Star game to nail Brian Downing at the plate. There's no doubt about it; assists—or "baserunner kills," as Bill James prefers we call them—are a good way to evaluate the arms of right fielders.

However, when you get to center and left fields, assists are not a particularly good yardstick. This is because weak-armed center and left fielders will frequently be tested, and consequently have more chances for assists. Below are the assist leaders at each outfield position for last season:

1993 Outfield Assist Leaders

Right Field		Center Field		Left Field	
Dante Bichette, Col	14	Chad Curtis, Cal	13	Bernard Gilkey, StL	19
Larry Walker, Mon	13	Steve Finley, Hou	11	Albert Belle, Cle	16
Wayne Kirby, Cle	13	Kenny Lofton, Cle	11	Phil Plantier, SD	14
Mark McLemore, Bal	13				

In right, Bichette and Walker are well known for their strong arms; Walker has even been known to throw out batters on "routine" groundball singles to right field. But in center, though Chad Curtis' arm isn't well-regarded, he has recorded 29 assists over the last two seasons. In left, Albert Belle and Phil Plantier both are thought to have below-average arms.

The question is, are guys like Curtis and Plantier getting all those baserunner kills because they have great arms, or because opposing runners don't fear them, and thus present lots of assist opportunities?

We here at STATS can tell you, because we calculate a "hold percentage" for each outfielder. Hold percentage is simply extra bases taken on the outfielder divided by the number of opportunities. For example, if a single is lined to center field with men on first and second, and one man scores but the other stops at second, that is one extra base taken on two opportunities, a 50.0 hold percentage.

We've been keeping this data for five years now, and we think it's been proven by the test of time. Let's look at last year's numbers:

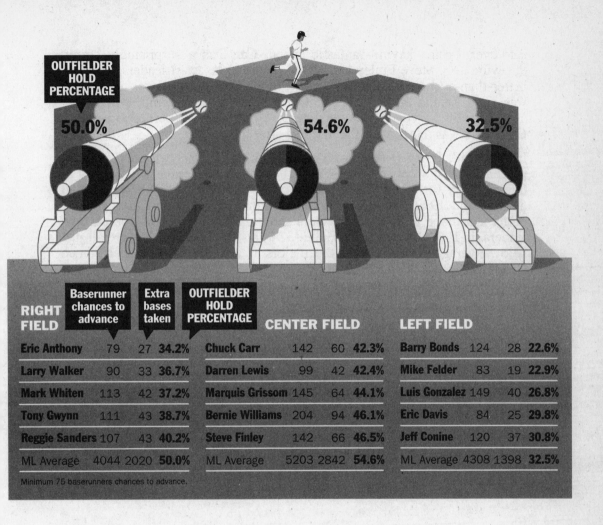

	OUTFIELDER HOLD PERCENTAGE		
	50.0%	54.6%	32.5%

RIGHT FIELD	Baserunner chances to advance	Extra bases taken	OUTFIELDER HOLD PERCENTAGE
Eric Anthony	79	27	34.2%
Larry Walker	90	33	36.7%
Mark Whiten	113	42	37.2%
Tony Gwynn	111	43	38.7%
Reggie Sanders	107	43	40.2%
ML Average	4044	2020	50.0%

Minimum 75 baserunners chances to advance.

CENTER FIELD			
Chuck Carr	142	60	42.3%
Darren Lewis	99	42	42.4%
Marquis Grissom	145	64	44.1%
Bernie Williams	204	94	46.1%
Steve Finley	142	66	46.5%
ML Average	5203	2842	54.6%

LEFT FIELD			
Barry Bonds	124	28	22.6%
Mike Felder	83	19	22.9%
Luis Gonzalez	149	40	26.8%
Eric Davis	84	25	29.8%
Jeff Conine	120	37	30.8%
ML Average	4308	1398	32.5%

In right field, there aren't any shockers. Walker and Gwynn have a batch of Gold Gloves to their credit, and Whiten has perhaps the most feared arm in the game. Likewise, Eric Anthony has a fine arm, though his reputation hasn't really caught up, and so too with Reggie Sanders. Which regular right fielder had the worst hold percentage? Mark McLemore, who was third among major league right fielders with 13 assists. However, his 63.0 hold percentage is not surprising, given that he used to be a second baseman. McLemore's hold percentage suggests strongly that he picked up those assists because runners took a lot of liberties.

In center field, Chuck Carr is certainly a surprise, at least to casual observers. Physique-wise, Carr is a dead ringer for Vince Coleman, and Coleman has trouble breaking a pane of thin glass with his throws.

However, beside having fantastic speed, Carr has a surprisingly strong throwing arm. Steve Finley and Kenny Lofton, the assist leaders, also had better-than-average hold percentages (Finley made the top five, and Lofton was right behind at 48.4). Chad Curtis, on the other hand, was below average at 56.2 percent. The worst center fielder, at 63.8 percent, was Alex Cole, who was released by the Rockies after the season.

In left field, Barry Bonds (who else?) led all regulars with a 22.6 hold percentage. No surprise here—Bonds has led major league left fielders in this category for four straight years now, which makes Sid Bream's mad dash in the 1992 playoffs seem even more unlikely than ever. You'll notice that none of the assist leaders show up among the hold percentage leaders. In fact, Gilkey (33.1), Belle (32.9) and Plantier (34.2) were all just below average. The worst in the majors was the aforementioned Vince Coleman, whose hold percentage was just 38.6. If only he could have short-armed that big firecracker . . .

A complete listing for this category can be found on page 320.

CAN THEY "ZONE IN" BETTER ON TURF?

Zone Ratings, a STATS invention, measure the percentage of outs each fielder records per batted ball hit into his "fielding zone." That's the area about 50 feet wide, around where a player normally positions himself. Among other things, zone ratings eliminate the bias created by a flyball or groundball pitching staff, a high-strikeout staff, or pure luck—factors which often result in one fielder getting a chance to handle many more balls than does another. We've been using them for several years, and we're firm believers that they do a lot to help identify the best fielders.

However, several readers have wondered whether there might not be a hidden bias in the ratings—one which favors players who perform on grass fields. They noted that, especially among infielders, most of the yearly leaders seemed to come from clubs which played on grass. We thought there might be some validity to the argument; turf fields are said to play "faster," meaning that a fielder might have more trouble turning a batted ball into an out.

Were the readers correct? The chart shows the zone ratings, on both grass and turf, for all major league games over the

ZONE RATINGS— GRASS AND TURF 1991-93

POSITION	GRASS	TURF
First base	.842	.846
Second base	.895	.887
Third base	.848	.837
Shortstop	.888	.880

last three seasons. As you can see, there *is* a difference, but the differences are very small. First basemen actually had better zone ratings on turf. However, the other infielders had slightly better ratings on grass fields.

Does this have any impact on evaluating individual fielders? Let's look at the zone ratings leaders for each of the infield positions over the last three seasons, in three ways: overall, on grass, and on turf (minimum 1,000 innings overall).

First Base—Zone Rating Leaders, 1991-93

Overall		Grass		Turf	
John Olerud	.896	John Olerud	.915	Rafael Palmeiro	.906
Wally Joyner	.895	Don Mattingly	.906	Mark Grace	.899
Don Mattingly	.890	Kent Hrbek	.905	Wally Joyner	.894
Mark Grace	.882	Wally Joyner	.897	Jeff Bagwell	.885
Kent Hrbek	.880	Mark Grace	.875	John Olerud	.883

(Minimum 150 balls in zone on grass and 100 on turf)

John Olerud and Mark Grace both ranked highly on grass and turf. Olerud, good on turf and a star on grass, deserved his number-one overall ranking.

Second Base—Zone Rating Leaders, 1991-93

Overall		Grass		Turf	
Ryne Sandberg	.945	Ryne Sandberg	.949	Carlos Baerga	.938
Bret Barberie	.927	Jody Reed	.925	Bret Barberie	.936
Jody Reed	.913	Bret Barberie	.921	Ryne Sandberg	.935
Carlos Baerga	.910	Bip Roberts	.914	Jeff Kent	.919
Mark Lemke	.908	Mark Lemke	.912	Chuck Knoblauch	.909

(Minimum 200 balls in zone on grass and 135 on turf)

Ryne Sandberg is sometimes said to be overrated, a player who looks better than he is because of Wrigley Field's slow grass. But Sandberg's excellent rating on turf fields shows that he deserves his great reputation. Bret Barberie also fared well on both surfaces.

Third Base—Zone Rating Leaders, 1991-93

Overall		Grass		Turf	
Wade Boggs	.898	Mike Pagliarulo	.923	Matt Williams	.909
Gary Gaetti	.887	Wade Boggs	.899	Robin Ventura	.890
Matt Williams	.885	Ken Caminiti	.893	Gary Gaetti	.890
Robin Ventura	.883	Gary Gaetti	.887	Wade Boggs	.889
Mike Pagliarulo	.880	Robin Ventura	.881	Kelly Gruber	.864

(Minimum 175 balls in zone on grass and 125 on turf)

Wade Boggs has always prided himself on his defensive work, and the figures here say he has a right to be proud: he ranks highly on both grass and turf. Gary Gaetti and Robin Ventura also performed well on both surfaces.

Shortstop—Zone Rating Leaders, 1991-93

Overall		Grass		Turf	
Rey Sanchez	.950	Rey Sanchez	.948	Gary DiSarcina	.981
Cal Ripken	.937	Ozzie Smith	.943	Rafael Belliard	.978
Gary DiSarcina	.934	Dick Schofield	.934	Cal Ripken	.976
Ozzie Guillen	.933	Ozzie Guillen	.933	Alan Trammell	.964
Dick Schofield	.927	Cal Ripken	.930	Rey Sanchez	.956

(Minimum 200 balls in zone on grass and 125 on turf)

The best shortstops in the overall rankings—Rey Sanchez, Cal Ripken, and Gary DiSarcina—all played well on both kinds of surfaces . . . which was generally the case for infielders overall.

All in all, the overall ratings seemed to hold up pretty well; while there appears to be a slight advantage for second basemen, third baseman and shortstops who play on grass, the advantage isn't great enough to destroy the validity of the overall rankings.

A complete listing for this category can be found on page 321.

WHO'S BEST IN THE INFIELD ZONE?

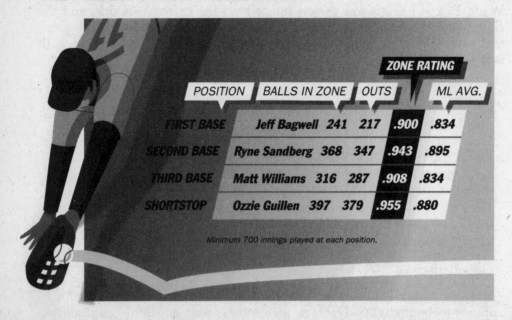

POSITION	BALLS IN ZONE	OUTS	ZONE RATING	ML AVG.
FIRST BASE	Jeff Bagwell 241	217	.900	.834
SECOND BASE	Ryne Sandberg 368	347	.943	.895
THIRD BASE	Matt Williams 316	287	.908	.834
SHORTSTOP	Ozzie Guillen 397	379	.955	.880

Minimum 700 innings played at each position.

"Fielding Stats DO Make Sense," Bill James once wrote, and we're inclined to agree with him. Sure, there are biases in fielding stats, but there are biases in batting average and ERA, also, and you don't hear anyone complaining about those numbers.

Fielding stats started out by measuring percentages of clean plays handled. We don't know exactly when they started doing it that way, but we think it was sometime during the Grant administration (and we don't mean "Mudcat"). That's where they stayed for around a century. Then in the 1970s, Bill came up with "range factor," which in its refined form is simply plays made per nine innings. But range factors have one big problem, which is this: if you're a second baseman behind a flyball pitching staff, you're not going to make as many plays as your colleague who plays behind a staff of sinkerballers.

So a few years ago, we took fielding stats one step further with "zone ratings." Our scorers note the direction of every batted ball, so we can figure out roughly how many balls fall into an individual fielder's "zone," and how many of them he turned into outs. To get a player's zone rating, we simply divide successful plays into the number of balls in his zone.

Let's look at the five zone rating leaders, plus the trailer, at each infield position for 1992 (minimum 700 innings played):

First Basemen—1993 Zone Ratings

Jeff Bagwell, Hou	.900
Don Mattingly, Yanks	.892
Kevin Young, Pit	.887
John Olerud, Tor	.875
Wally Joyner, KC	.873
Worst	
Frank Thomas, WSox	.748

Zone ratings are the only measure which can objectively evaluate first basemen's range. Mattingly and Joyner have always been regarded as excellent fielders. Bagwell and Young are young converted third basemen, so we would expect them to have some range. The surprise is Olerud, who is not regarded as a good fielder. However, he ranked second on the list in both 1991 and '92, and indications are strong that he is actually a fine defensive player. Unfortunately for White Sox fans, the signing of Julio Franco means another brutal season of Frank Thomas at first.

Second Basemen—1993 Zone Ratings

Ryne Sandberg, Cubs	.943
Jeff Gardner, SD	.935
Craig Biggio, Hou	.927
Torey Lovullo, Cal	.927
Pat Kelly, Yanks	.927
Robby Thompson, SF	.927
Worst	
Carlos Garcia, Pit	.821

Robby Thompson may have supplanted Ryno as the NL Gold Glove winner, but Sandberg can obviously still pick it. A big surprise here is Lovullo, a utility man who played every infield position for the Angels last year. After all these years, maybe Sparky was right. . . At the bottom of the list is Garcia, a converted shortstop. Take heart, Carlos—a year ago, converted catcher Biggio was at the bottom, and look where he is now.

Third Basemen—1993 Zone Ratings

Matt Williams, SF	.908
Wade Boggs, Yanks	.881
Robin Ventura, WSox	.878
B.J. Surhoff, Mil	.877
Steve Buechele, Cubs	.871
Worst	
Gary Sheffield, SD-Fla	.720

The Gold Glove winners finished number one and number three, so we certainly can't quibble with the voters. Surhoff, another converted catcher, is quite a surprise (now if he could just *hit* like a third baseman). Not only was Sheffield's fielding percentage just .899, the worst in 15 years, but his .720 zone rating was easily the worst in the majors. That switch to right field is looking better all the time (at least, until we see him play right field).

Shortstops—1993 Zone Ratings	
Ozzie Guillen, WSox	.955
Rey Sanchez, Cubs	.945
Ozzie Smith, StL	.940
Omar Vizquel, Sea	.930
Jose Vizcaino, Cubs	.925
Worst	
Andujar Cedeno, Hou	.809

How about those Chicago shortstops? Guillen, Sanchez and Vizcaino are all well thought of, and their zone ratings suggest they deserve the accolades. The other two? Vizquel won his first Gold Glove, and Ozzie Smith just missed his 14th. Nobody was worse than Cedeno, who will have to hit more than 11 homers to make up for his defense.

And now, the annual STATS infield Gold Gloves, which rely on zone ratings, pivot numbers, fielding averages, other stats, and careful observation:

First Base: Don Mattingly, AL, and Mark Grace, NL. We were tempted by Bagwell, but in our opinion a right-handed throwing first baseman, whose glove is on the wrong side for most of the duties of his position, needs to be *exceptionally* good to overcome that handicap and merit the award. Grace, who throws lefty, just missed making the top five with an .866 zone rating, and we think he merits the award. By the way, our awards match up with the official ones, which is both a testament to zone ratings and the good judgment of major league managers and coaches.

Second Base: Harold Reynolds, AL, and Robby Thompson, NL. Really, it's a toss-up between Thompson and perennial winner Ryne Sandberg. Thompson is much better at the double play than Ryno, who has more range than Thompson. We'll give it to Thompson—he's been underrated for a long time, and he played 13 more games. In the American League, nobody stands out. The guys who are good at the double play don't have much range, and vice versa. Reynolds was above-average at both, and he did win three Gold Gloves in the '80s. Roberto Alomar, whom coaches and announcers rave about, still hasn't proven to us that he deserves his reputation. Season after season, both his zone ratings and pivot percentages are sub-par. He does look good, though.

Third Base: Robin Ventura, AL, and Matt Williams, NL. Again, our picks match up with the official ones. Ventura's zone rating was marginally lower than Boggs', but Robin played 21 more games and he's 10 years younger, so we give him the nod.

Shortstop: Ozzie Guillen, AL, and Ozzie Smith, NL. A clean sweep for the Ozzies. . . The Wizard may have lost out to Jay Bell for the "real" Gold Glove, but around STATS he's still the best. We thought about the two Cubbies, but neither Sanchez nor Vizcaino played full-time, and we don't think there's room in the Glove for two hands. By the way, Bell's zone rating was .856, well below average.

A complete listing for this category can be found on page 323.

WHO'S BEST IN THE OUTFIELD ZONE?

The zone rating, as we explained in a previous article, measures the number of outs recorded by each fielder in relation to the number of balls hit into his fielding area. Thorough fellows that we are, we figure zone ratings for outfielders, too. So with no further delay, here are the 1993 zone rating leaders at each of the outfield positions (minimum 600 innings):

Left Field—1993 Zone Ratings	
Phil Plantier, SD	.881
Greg Vaughn, Mil	.873
Rickey Henderson, Oak-Tor	.866
Eric Davis, LA-Det	.865
Kevin Mitchell, Cin	.848
Worst	
Jeff Conine, Fla	.721

Greg Vaughn is up there every year, Rickey Henderson is one of the greatest players ever, and Eric Davis used to be an excellent center fielder. But Phil Plantier? And Kevin Mitchell?! Actually, Mitchell has always been a lot better than you would think (and nobody's better at the barehand snag). At the bottom of the list is Jeff Conine, who plays left field like the first baseman he used to be.

Center Field—1993 Zone Ratings	
Darren Lewis, SF	.887
Chad Curtis, Cal	.875
Milt Cuyler, Det	.873
Kenny Lofton, Cle	.872
Lance Johnson, WSox	.871
Worst	
Andy Van Slyke, Pit	.757

Darren Lewis isn't much of a hitter, but boy, can he play some center field. He goes back as well as anyone, and as you can see, he led the majors in zone rating by a wide margin. The other four guys are all highly regarded. As for Andy Van Slyke, no, he didn't rank low because he was hobbled by injuries. Van Slyke, though a perennial Gold Glover, has never had good zone ratings.

Right Field—1993 Zone Ratings

Tony Gwynn, SD	.886
Wayne Kirby, Cle	.880
Jim Eisenreich, Phi	.880
Tim Salmon, Cal	.867
Rob Deer, Det-Bos	.867
Worst	
Jay Buhner, Sea	.762

Gwynn and Eisenreich are always near the top of this list; in fact, over the last three seasons combined, Eisenreich is number one. Kirby and Salmon were both playing regularly for the first time, so we'll wait another year or two to pass judgment on them. Rob Deer played the best right field of his life, and was promptly signed by the Hanshin Tigers as a defensive specialist. Buhner gets the booby prize for the second year in a row. Throwing isn't everything, Jay.

Here are the STATS outfield Gold Glove winners, based on zone ratings, throwing arms, and observation:

Left Field: Greg Vaughn, AL and Barry Bonds, NL. Repeat winners from last year. . . True, Bonds doesn't make the top five in zone ratings, but he is number six, and he has the best throwing arm.

Center Field: Kenny Lofton, AL and Darren Lewis, NL. Lofton picked up a "real" Gold Glove, but Lewis was inexplicably overlooked. Not only did he have a great zone rating, but *he has never made an error in the majors*. That's good enough for us.

Right Field: Paul O'Neill, AL and Tony Gwynn, NL. O'Neill wins by default; Kirby and Salmon still have to win their spurs. O'Neill's got a good arm, and his .842 zone rating was better than average. Larry Walker is the popular choice over Gwynn, but Gwynn has more range and his arm is nearly as good.

A complete listing for this category can be found on page 325.

DO THE BRAVES HAVE THE MOST EFFICIENT DEFENSE?

Many baseball people still evaluate team defense the easy way: they think the clubs which make the fewest errors are the best. By that measure, the Seattle Mariners (fielding average .985) were the best defensive club in the majors last year, and the Colorado Rockies (fielding average .973) were the worst.

But there's more to defense—both individual and team—than the simple ability to avoid errors. That's why Bill James invented the "Defensive Efficiency Record." This simple measuring system begins by counting the number of balls put into play against each team. Then you count the number of times the team turned those balls into outs, and divide the second figure by the first. We all know that DER is hardly perfect, as a lot of batted balls simply *can't* be turned into outs. But most can, and there's another reason we like the stat: in the past, we've found that clubs which have a good DER are usually winners.

Here are the 1993 American League rankings in Defensive Efficiency Record:

American League	Balls in Play	Plays Made	DER
Kansas City Royals	4,545	3,114	.685
Chicago White Sox	4,593	3,126	.681
Boston Red Sox	4,606	3,132	.680
Baltimore Orioles	4,668	3,169	.679
Milwaukee Brewers	4,895	3,303	.675
New York Yankees	4,721	3,179	.673
California Angels	4,759	3,201	.673
Toronto Blue Jays	4,596	3,088	.672
Seattle Mariners	4,503	3,016	.670
Oakland Athletics	4,864	3,248	.668
Detroit Tigers	4,890	3,259	.666
Texas Rangers	4,669	3,110	.666
Minnesota Twins	4,828	3,165	.656
Cleveland Indians	4,868	3,184	.654

After struggling through a 72-90 season in 1992, the Kansas City Royals decided that they needed to improve their defense. So they traded for second baseman Chico Lind, and signed shortstop Greg Gagne as a free agent. Since Kaycee already had a slick center fielder in Brian McRae and a solid-enough catcher in Mike Macfarlane, they instantly had the "strength up the middle" which clubs prize. It seemed to work; the Royals moved from seventh to first in DER—and perhaps not coincidentally, won 12 more games than they did in 1992.

The Chicago White Sox, with a fast outfield and solid defensive players almost everywhere, was another club which ranked highly both in DER and won-lost record. The main exception to this rule was the world champion Blue Jays, who were mediocre in DER. While Toronto has some glittering fielders like Devon White and Roberto Alomar, they also had some problem positions last year, particularly third base. The '93 Jays depended more heavily on offense than in the past; in 1992, the world champion Jays ranked second in DER.

We should mention something here. While it's true that a good defense will help a pitching staff, it's also true, probably to a larger degree, that a good pitching staff will help a defense, at least with regard to DER. Simply put, a good pitching staff will induce more soft grounders, pop-ups, lazy flies, etc., and those plays are easier for the defense to make.

While the Jays proved you can win with a so-so DER, it's very hard to win with a poor one. Clubs like the Rangers and Indians, who have ranked near the bottom in DER the last few years, will have to improve their defenses if they want to win a division crown in 1994.

Here are the National League rankings:

National League	Balls in Play	Plays Made	DER
Atlanta Braves	4,474	3,116	.696
Montreal Expos	4,689	3,207	.684
San Francisco Giants	4,603	3,139	.682
Houston Astros	4,505	3,057	.679
Los Angeles Dodgers	4,626	3,133	.677
Florida Marlins	4,689	3,168	.676
Philadelphia Phillies	4,633	3,113	.672
Pittsburgh Pirates	4,884	3,267	.669
St. Louis Cardinals	4,998	3,342	.669
New York Mets	4,801	3,208	.668
Chicago Cubs	4,761	3,179	.668
San Diego Padres	4,717	3,132	.664
Cincinnati Reds	4,675	3,093	.662
Colorado Rockies	4,909	3,134	.638

The Atlanta Braves are known for their great pitching staff and their solid offense, but don't underestimate the importance of a good defense to Atlanta's success. In 1991, the Braves ranked third in DER; in 1992 and

1993, they ranked first in DER, while winning the West all three times. Atlanta's DER was the best in the majors last year, so it's about time we gave the Braves credit for their sound defensive work.

When the San Francisco Giants signed free agent Barry Bonds before the 1993 season, they were thinking primarily about his bat. But Bonds is also a Gold Glove fielder, and the Giants moved from eighth in DER in 1992 to third in 1993. Give Matt Williams, Robby Thompson, Will Clark and Darren Lewis some credit also.

The Philadelphia Phillies were like the Blue Jays: mediocre in DER, but winners on the field. Like the Jays, they weren't really horrible on defense, just not outstanding . . . but like the Jays, they had an outstanding offense.

Easily the worst club in DER, and fielding average as well, was the expansion Colorado Rockies, who had the Denver altitude and a "rocky" home field to deal with . . . along with some really bad defensive players. They almost have to be better in '94, don't they?

A complete listing for this category can be found on page 327.

WHO ARE THE "ALL-AMERICAN FIELDERS"?

In our fielding section, we present a number of statistics which are useful in identifying the best defensive players at each position. Among the stats we use are zone ratings, pivot ratings for second basemen, outfield arm ratings, and even the old stand-by, fielding percentage (which we use indirectly in "Who Led the League in Fumbles?"). Now we'd like to combine those figures into one number, to identify the best overall defensive players (statistically) at each infield and outfield position.

The method we've chosen produces a number akin to batting average, so that you can get a mental image of a second baseman who's a ".320 pivot man" or a first sacker who has a ".220 zone rating." The formula's too complex to print here, but basically it uses standard deviations to establish the spread from best to worst. We don't use all the stats for every position, and their importance varies from position to position, so we've weighted the ratings as follows:

Pos	Weighting
1B	Zone Rating 75%, Fielding Pct 25%
2B	Zone Rating 60%, Fielding Pct 15%, Pivot Rating 25%
3B	Zone Rating 60%, Fielding Pct 40%
SS	Zone Rating 80%, Fielding Pct 20%
LF	Zone Rating 65%, Fielding Pct 15%, OF Arm 20%
CF	Zone Rating 55%, Fielding Pct 15%, OF Arm 30%
RF	Zone Rating 50%, Fielding Pct 15%, OF Arm 35%

Without further ado, here is the 1993 STATS "All-American Fielding Team" for infielders and outfielders, with the leaders and trailer at each position (minimum 600 innings):

First Base	Zone	FPct	Rating
Don Mattingly, Yanks	.319	.318	.319
Kevin Young, Pit	.315	.316	.315
Jeff Bagwell, Hou	.325	.281	.314
Mark Grace, Cubs	.301	.310	.303
Wally Joyner, KC	.306	.291	.302
Worst			
Frank Thomas, WSox	.219	.244	.225

Don Mattingly may not be quite the hitter he once was, but he's still "over .300" when it comes to his defensive value. Pirate rookie Kevin Young's high rating was a bit of a surprise, but he appears to have the defensive goods. At the other end of the spectrum, Frank Thomas *does* seem like a .225 fielder if you watch him play; Frank beat out Cecil Fielder (.230) for the booby prize on this list. We could still find a place for them on our team.

Second Base	Zone	FPct	Pivot	Rating
Robby Thompson, SF	.308	.305	.310	.308
Ryne Sandberg, Cubs	.323	.303	.246	.301
Pat Kelly, Yanks	.309	.263	.288	.297
Delino DeShields, Mon	.297	.283	.291	.293
Craig Biggio, Hou	.309	.279	.262	.293
Torey Lovullo, Cal	.309	.275	.265	.293
Mark Lemke, Atl	.293	.281	.300	.293
Harold Reynolds, Bal	.288	.296	.301	.293
Worst				
Carlos Garcia, Pit	.210	.285	.269	.236

Robby Thompson's number-one ranking at second base is a credit to his all-around outstanding play, particularly on the double-play pivot. That was the major difference between him and Ryne Sandberg last year. The Yankees' Pat Kelly was the top man in the American League; he finished ahead of a bunch of fellows from both leagues with .293 marks. Pittsburgh's Carlos Garcia, a former shortstop who's still learning the second base position, clearly has a lot to learn.

Third Base	Zone	FPct	Rating
Matt Williams, SF	.327	.307	.319
Gary Gaetti, Cal-KC	.310	.307	.309
Wade Boggs, Yanks	.309	.308	.308
Steve Buechele, Cubs	.302	.315	.307
Robin Ventura, WSox	.307	.301	.304
Worst			
Gary Sheffield, SD-Fla	.198	.204	.200

As these figures show, Matt Williams' Gold Glove is *not* due to his offensive prowess; he deserves it. Gary Gaetti and Wade Boggs ranking ahead of Robin Ventura is something of a surprise, but Ventura is very close to the top. As for Gary Sheffield, it's no wonder he's happy that the Marlins are shifting him to right field.

Shortstop	Zone	FPct	Rating
Ozzie Guillen, WSox	.335	.285	.325
Rey Sanchez, Cubs	.327	.279	.317
Ozzie Smith, StL	.323	.290	.316
Omar Vizquel, Sea	.316	.305	.314
Greg Gagne, KC	.301	.322	.305
Worst			
Andujar Cedeno, Hou	.221	.241	.225

No Chicago prejudice here . . . honest. We see Ozzie Guillen and Rey Sanchez a lot of over the course of a season, and we think they deserve their high ratings—especially Guillen. The Cubs' Jose Vizcaino (no Chicago prejudice, of course) and the Angels' Gary DiSarcina were also ".300-fielding shortstops." The Astros' Andujar Cedeno has proven he can hit, but his defense still needs a lot of work. Maybe he should change his name to "Aparicio Belanger," or something.

Left Field	Zone	FPct	OF Arm	Rating
Greg Vaughn, Mil	.320	.290	.343	.320
Phil Plantier, SD	.326	.298	.267	.310
Eric Davis, LA-Det	.313	.301	.293	.307
Barry Bonds, SF	.298	.285	.333	.303
Rickey Henderson, Oak-Tor	.314	.261	.257	.295
Worst				
Jeff Conine, Fla	.204	.304	.287	.236

Greg Vaughn has always ranked high in our ratings, and his number-one mark here seems well-deserved. We were surprised to see Phil Plantier rank ahead of Barry Bonds; though Plantier did have good numbers last year, Bonds has proven himself over the longer haul. The trailer at the position, Jeff Conine, is a first baseman playing out of position, and it shows.

Center Field	Zone	FPct	OF Arm	Rating
Darren Lewis, SF	.322	.326	.329	.325
Kenny Lofton, Cle	.311	.248	.303	.299
Brett Butler, LA	.293	.326	.292	.298
Bernie Williams, Yanks	.284	.287	.313	.293
Marquis Grissom, Mon	.283	.267	.322	.292
Worst				
Alex Cole, Col	.248	.262	.234	.246

Even before looking at these stats, we couldn't understand why Darren Lewis—a player with great range and a great arm who has also never committed an error in the majors—didn't win a Gold Glove. Now it's even more bewildering, as Lewis ranked miles ahead of some very stiff center field competition. Maybe next year. The Indians' Kenny Lofton also deserved a Gold Glove last year, and got one.

Right Field	Zone	FPct	OF Arm	Rating
Tony Gwynn, SD	.320	.284	.314	.313
Larry Walker, Mon	.303	.281	.321	.306
Eric Anthony, Hou	.274	.323	.330	.301
Jim Eisenreich, Phi	.315	.343	.263	.301
Wayne Kirby, Cle	.315	.281	.278	.297
Worst				
Jay Buhner, Sea	.217	.276	.273	.245

Lots of good National Leaguers here, with perennial favorite Tony Gwynn leading the way. There were no .300 performers in the American League; rookie Wayne Kirby was the best of the bunch, edging out the league's Rookie of the Year, California's Tim Salmon (.294). Seattle's Jay Buhner is noted for his strong arm, but the figures here indicate that he was having lots of defensive problems last year.

A complete listing for this category can be found on page 328.

VI. QUESTIONS ON MANAGERS

WAS LA RUSSA'S "50-PITCH STRATEGY" A GOOD IDEA?

When the Oakland pitching staff was floundering last summer, Tony La Russa came up with an idea: why not use his pitchers for shorter stints—say, 50 pitches—about every other day, with the hope that the frequent work would keep them sharp? La Russa tried the plan for a few games without notable success, but then, the A's staff hadn't been notably successful the conventional way, either. He quickly abandoned the idea, not sticking with it long enough to prove anything one way or the other.

Was this a good idea—working pitchers in what amounts to three-inning shifts about every other day? La Russa certainly wasn't the first to consider it. We seem to recall Chuck Tanner discussing the same system around 15 years ago, though Tanner never went beyond the talking phase. And back in 1961, *Los Angeles Herald* and *Express* writer Sam Balter wrote a column advocating the very same plan, stating, "I want to see a pitcher go only three innings every other day. I claim it would save these worn-out arms and beat-up pitchers, and provide better pitching, too." Other people probably had the idea before Balter.

Does the notion make sense? Let's look at some evidence. For several years, we've collected pitching data based on 15-pitch segments, 15 pitches being roughly what a hurler will work in an average inning. Using that data, we looked at how 1993 starting pitchers performed over their first 45 pitches, how they fared from pitch 46 to 75, and then how they performed from pitch 76 on, using opponents' on-base plus slugging average as a measure of effectiveness (minimum 100 batters faced at pitch 1-45 and 75 batters faced at pitch 46-75). The chart shows the results. As you can see, pitchers tended to lose effectiveness as the game went on. They were at their best for the first 45 pitches.

PITCHES	OBP+SLG*
1 to 45	.730
46 to 75	.740
76 and up	.748

* OBP+SLG is on-base avg. plus slugging average. 1993 major league games.

This supports the notion that La Russa, Tanner and Balter knew what they were talking about. It doesn't really "prove" three-innings-every-two-days would work, since it's based on pitchers who were working in a conventional rotation. But one problem is that the data is for all pitchers added together, and there were enormous pitcher-to-pitcher variations. For example, these pitchers fit the model, losing effectiveness as the game went on:

On-Base Average + Slugging Average

Pitcher, Team	Pitch 1-45	Pitch 46-75	Pitch 76+
Andy Benes, SD	.505	.723	.844
Jimmy Key, Yanks	.597	.693	.714
Greg Maddux, Atl	.555	.592	.645

But these pitchers tended to get better as the game went on:

On-Base Average + Slugging Average

Pitcher, Team	Pitch 1-45	Pitch 46-75	Pitch 76+
Kevin Brown, Tex	.769	.626	.594
Chuck Finley, Cal	.711	.699	.628
Jack McDowell, WSox	.813	.650	.602

Many pitchers like McDowell have reputations as "slow starters"; they tend to have problems early in the game, particularly in the first inning, then settle down. If you yanked them after 45-50 pitches, people argue, you'd be pulling them just when they were getting into a groove. And that's the objection most people raise to the whole idea: why pull a guy who's pitching well?

But of course, that's what they used to say about removing a middle reliever who was going well in order to bring in a set-up man or closer. La Russa did as much as anyone to buck that notion, giving his firemen sharply defined roles. And though taking out an effective reliever sometimes backfires, most people feel that this system does a lot to keep the set-up man and closer sharp, making *them* more effective.

It's possible that if you used starters in this way, bringing them back every couple of days, guys like McDowell would get enough work to be sharp from the start of the game. It's also possible that nothing would change, and that you'd be wasting their talents by taking them out just as they were beginning to pitch their best ball. We won't know the answer until someone tries this plan for a lot longer than La Russa tried it last year. Until then, it'll continue to intrigue people.

A complete listing for this category can be found on page 330.

DO SOME MANAGERS PLAY FOR ONE RUN TOO OFTEN?

What's a "one-run strategy"? On offense, it's a strategy designed to advance baserunners, while either giving up an out or risking doing so. The stolen base, the sacrifice bunt and the hit-and-run are all good examples of this type of strategy, in which the chances to score one run increase, but the chances for a big inning go down. When a club is on defense, one-run strategies would include the pitchout and the intentional walk, both of which risk the big inning, at least to an extent, in order to get an out.

Do major league managers differ in how often they employ these strategies? They sure do. Let's look at the 1993 managers by leagues, separating their offensive one-run strategies (stolen base, sacrifice bunt, hit-and-run) from their defensive ones (pitchout, intentional walk). We'll start with the American League.

American League

Offensive One-Run Strategies

Manager, Team	SB Att	Sac Att	H&R Att	Total
Buck Rodgers, Cal	269	65	174	508
Phil Garner, Mil	231	74	153	458
Tony La Russa, Oak	190	59	186	435
Kevin Kennedy, Tex	180	95	140	415
Mike Hargrove, Cle	214	56	138	408
Hal McRae, KC	175	76	153	404
Lou Piniella, Sea	159	86	152	397
Gene Lamont, WSox	163	93	110	366
Cito Gaston, Tor	219	61	84	364
Sparky Anderson, Det	167	47	118	332
Butch Hobson, Bos	111	97	88	296
Tom Kelly, Min	142	39	115	296
Johnny Oates, Bal	127	65	90	282
Buck Showalter, Yanks	74	35	51	160

What a contrast between Buck Rodgers of the Angels—a man who plays it strictly one run at a time—and Showalter of the Yankees, the ultimate big-inning skipper. Why the difference? Personnel was a big reason; Showalter had a slow-footed, power-laden lineup, while Rodgers had a speedy but underpowered team, and felt he had to grind it out one run at a time. But as we point out in the Angels essay, Rodgers has always had his teams trying to steal, even when they're not particularly good at it. Somehow we doubt that he'll ever change much.

Defensive One-Run Strategies

Manager, Team	Pitchout	IW	Total
Butch Hobson, Bos	99	87	186
Sparky Anderson, Det	78	92	170
Lou Piniella, Sea	83	56	139
Mike Hargrove, Cle	77	53	130
Tony La Russa, Oak	61	59	120
Hal McRae, KC	82	36	118
Gene Lamont, WSox	82	36	118
Cito Gaston, Tor	67	38	105
Buck Rodgers, Cal	68	35	103
Phil Garner, Mil	30	58	88
Buck Showalter, Yanks	24	58	82
Johnny Oates, Bal	30	50	80
Tom Kelly, Min	37	34	71
Kevin Kennedy, Tex	26	42	68

The defensive one-run strategies are a version of the old Merv Griffin game show, "Play Your Hunch": I think he'll be stealing here, so I'll pitch out. Butch Hobson of the Red Sox is the American League's premier hunch-player, while Kevin Kennedy of the Rangers is the sober-faced guy who prefers to play it straight. Again, personnel makes a difference: with Pudge Rodriguez behind the plate, Kennedy probably feels he doesn't *need* to pitch out.

National League

In the National League last year, both Davey Johnson of the Reds and Dallas Green of the Mets took over their clubs early in the year. We used only the games managed by Johnson and Green for these charts, with the numbers projected to 162 games for comparative purposes.

Offensive One-Run Strategies

Manager, Team	SB Att	Sac Att	H&R Att	Total
Felipe Alou, Mon	284	120	156	560
Don Baylor, Col	236	88	166	490
Tommy Lasorda, LA	187	137	161	485
Dusty Baker, SF	185	128	155	468
Joe Torre, StL	225	81	162	468
Davey Johnson, Cin*	199	86	114	399
Jim Lefebvre, Cubs	143	85	160	388
Bobby Cox, Atl	173	103	101	377
Art Howe, Hou	163	107	106	376
Jim Leyland, Pit	147	100	126	373

Offensive One-Run Strategies

Manager, Team	SB Att	Sac Att	H&R Att	Total
Rene Lachemann, Mon	173	77	105	355
Jim Riggleman, SD	133	110	104	347
Dallas Green, Mets*	108	119	112	339
Jim Fregosi, Phi	123	116	56	295

*Numbers based on manager's 1993 totals projected to 162 games

You might recall that Felipe Alou, Don Baylor and Dusty Baker, all fairly new managers, are fond of walking a player with two out in order to get to the pitcher (see essay, "Who Issues the 'Automatic' Intentional Walk?"). That's a definite one-run strategy, so it's not surprising to find them near the top of this list as well. But while the "little-ball" strategy makes some sense for Alou, who has a very speedy club, or for Tommy Lasorda, who was struggling for runs last year, what are Baylor and Baker doing near the top of this list? Baker had a powerful lineup led by Barry Bonds, while Baylor managed in the ultimate hitters' park, Mile High Stadium—a place where using one-run strategies makes no sense whatsoever.

Defensive One-Run Strategies

Manager, Team	Pitchout	IW	Total
Jim Lefebvre, Cubs	96	61	157
Don Baylor, Col	75	66	141
Jim Riggleman, SD	67	72	139
Dusty Baker, SF	79	46	125
Bobby Cox, Atl	66	59	125
Dallas Green, Mets*	50	63	113
Davey Johnson, Cin*	73	37	110
Art Howe, Hou	57	52	109
Tommy Lasorda, LA	39	68	107
Joe Torre, StL	52	50	102
Rene Lachemann, Fla	35	58	93
Felipe Alou, Mon	44	38	82
Jim Leyland, Pit	39	43	82
Jim Fregosi, Phi	30	33	63

* Projected to 162 games

Baylor's near the top of *this* list, also, just below Jim LeFebvre of the Cubs, who was managing in Wrigley Field, another hitters' park. That's stupid; no wonder LeFebvre got fired. The National League's "big-inning manager" is clearly Jim Fregosi of the Phillies, who apparently likes these one-run strategies about as much as he likes Joe Carter. Judging from the results, it looks like he knew what he was doing.

WHICH MANAGERS HAVE THE "QUICK HOOK"?

When Sparky Anderson managed the Reds in the 1970s, he was known as "Captain Hook"—a skipper who would lift his starting pitcher at the first sign of trouble. The opposite extreme, or so it seemed, was personified by Tommy Lasorda of the Dodgers. Lasorda would keep Fernando Valenzuela and company in the game until their arms fell off (which often happened).

Were those reputations justified? Are Sparky and Tommy still the same? And how do other managers compare in the way they handle a starting pitcher? To find the answer, we'll used a couple of terms first defined by Bill James—"quick hooks" and "slow hooks":

Quick Hook: The manager relieves a starting pitcher who has pitched less than six innings, while giving up three runs or less.

Slow Hook: The manager leaves a starter in the game who has either pitched more than nine innings, given up seven or more runs, or whose combined innings pitched and runs allowed totals 13 or more.

Those are reasonable definitions; a manager employing a slow hook, especially, is going a *long way* with his starter. Here's how American League managers compared in the two categories last year:

Quick and Slow Hooks—American League, 1993

Quick Hooks		Slow Hooks	
Indians	35	Blue Jays	25
Athletics	31	Brewers	21
Twins	22	Angels	20
Rangers	20	Athletics	17
Orioles	18	Orioles	16
Red Sox	15	Mariners	14
Tigers	15	Twins	13
Royals	15	Indians	12
Brewers	14	Tigers	11
Yankees	14	Royals	10
Mariners	14	Yankees	10
Angels	12	Rangers	10
Blue Jays	11	White Sox	6
White Sox	8	Red Sox	4

You can see some real differences in managerial philosophy here. For instance, there's Cito Gaston of the Blue Jays, who has a unique managing style, as we discuss in another essay. In 1993, it was obvious that Gaston didn't have a lot of confidence in his middle relief corps. So he tended to stay with his starting pitchers even when they weren't pitching effectively. Given the way the Jays' middle relievers performed in the World Series, it was easy to understand Cito's lack of confidence.

Unlike Gaston, Mike Hargrove of the Indians had lots of confidence in his relief pitchers. Hargrove wasn't reluctant to take out a starter early in the game, even if wasn't always obvious that the pitcher had lost his stuff. Hargrove had the most quick hooks in the league, more even than Tony La Russa of the A's, who's known for going to his bullpen fairly quickly.

Managerial philosophy is a big factor in how quick or slow a hook a skipper has. But the makeup of the staff is probably just as important. For instance, Gene Lamont of the White Sox had a very young and talented starting corps last year. Lamont felt that his pitchers could recover from early-inning problems, so he didn't have many quick hooks. However, he didn't want those talented arms staying in the game and absorbing a *lot* of punishment, so he didn't have many slow hooks, either.

As for Anderson, he's no longer "Captain Hook," as he ranked around the middle of the pack when it came to quick hooks. Again, makeup of the staff was a big reason. In his Reds days, Anderson had a so-so corps of starters, but a world-class bullpen with Clay Carroll, Pedro Borbon and all those guys. These days, Sparky doesn't have that kind of talent in his pen, so he'll let his starters go a little longer.

Here are the National League rankings in quick and slow hooks:

Quick and Slow Hooks—National League, 1993

Quick Hooks		Slow Hooks	
Expos	34	Mets	14
Rockies	29	Rockies	14
Giants	27	Pirates	11
Padres	26	Reds	10
Pirates	20	Cubs	9
Reds	14	Phillies	9
Phillies	14	Padres	9
Braves	13	Astros	8
Cubs	13	Expos	6
Astros	13	Dodgers	6
Dodgers	13	Cardinals	5
Cardinals	13	Marlins	4
Marlins	13	Braves	3
Mets	12	Giants	3

In the National League, there's more uniformity among managers. While American League teams ranged from four to 25 in the number of slow hooks they had, no N.L. skipper had more than 14. And eight of the 14 N.L. clubs had either 13 or 14 quick hooks. The reason for the uniformity is simple: National League pitchers have to hit. If their pitchers are giving up a lot of runs, N.L. skippers are usually going to have to use a pinch hitter to keep their clubs in the game. They'll also tend to have fewer quick hooks, because when they bring in a reliever, it usually means using two players (the new pitcher, plus someone to hit for him) instead of just one, as is the case in American League.

Still, there are some interesting differences here. We've noted similarities in other categories between Felipe Alou of the Expos, Don Baylor of the Rockies and Dusty Baker of the Giants. And sure enough, those three had more quick hooks than anyone else in the league last year. Do they all read the same book or something? Baker, at least, separated himself from the others by having only three slow hooks all year, a category where Baylor was tied for the league lead with 14. Baylor's high total of slow hooks made sense for a skipper managing in Mile High Stadium. There were numerous high-scoring games in Denver last year, and when a starter gave up a lot of runs, it didn't necessarily mean he'd lost his stuff . . . or that his club was out of the game. But then, why did Baylor have so many quick hooks? It's hard to figure.

In other essays, we've expressed our admiration for the way manager Bobby Cox and pitching coach Leo Mazzone of the Braves have protected their talented young starting corps from too much abuse. The Braves' extremely low total of slow hooks is another indication of this, but there's another reason why Atlanta had such a small number: their pitchers seldom gave up enough runs to be in "slow hook" territory!

As for Tommy Lasorda, is it possible that he's learned something from the trail of dead arms around Dodger Stadium over the years? Back in 1990, Lasorda had 15 slow hooks, a figure which tied him for the league lead. But since then, he's been in single digits every year, and last year he had only six all season. His pitchers should be grateful.

HOW IS CITO DIFFERENT?

Blue Jay manager Cito Gaston, in case you haven't noticed, has his own unique style. To some people, he's a fellow who "doesn't know strategy"; to others, he's someone who "lets his players play." Whatever the truth, we can say two things about Gaston: he does things differently from most managers, and he's been very successful doing it. Let's look at a few of Gaston's characteristics, and see what makes him different:

He doesn't use many pinch hitters. The Blue Jays used only 30 pinch hitters all last season. Think about that: it's less than one pinch swinger *every five games*. American League managers generally don't use a pinch hitter as much as their National League counterparts, because the most logical use of a pinch hitter is to bat for a pitcher. But even among AL skippers, Gaston is in a class by himself. Johnny Oates of Baltimore, the American League manager who ranked second to Gaston in his reluctance to use a pinch hitter, used 70 last year, more than twice as many.

Is there justification for this? Well, one has to ask whom Gaston would be pinch hitting for. The most likely candidates would be the weaker hitters in the lineup: Ed Sprague, Pat Borders, the left (or right) fielders before the Jays got Rickey Henderson. One problem is that the Jays didn't have many effective players to sub for those guys, but that reflects on the manager as well. Some skippers—Buck Showalter comes to mind—would *never* be without players who could come off the bench and give him a little edge. Gaston isn't like that; he'll take his chances with Ed Sprague.

He sticks with his starting pitchers. We cover this in another essay, but "quick hooks" measure how often managers remove a starter at an early sign of ineffectiveness, and "slow hooks" how often they stick with a starter who's absorbed a lot of punishment. Gaston had the second-fewest quick hooks, and the most slow hooks, in the American League last year. Personnel makes a difference here—as we saw in the postseason, the Jays had a pretty bad middle relief corps, and Gaston couldn't be faulted for his reluctance to go to them. But this is also right in line with his personality: you're my man, and I'm staying with you.

He doesn't hit-and-run much. According to our compilation in the *STATS 1994 Major League Handbook* (where most of these numbers can be found), Gaston called only 84 hit-and-run plays last year, second-fewest in the American League; only Showalter, with 51, called fewer. Does this make sense? The Blue Jays had a very fast club, with the most stolen bases and the best success rate in the American League. They made excellent contact, with only 861 strikeouts, third-fewest in the league. They hit a below-average number of ground balls (1.16 for each fly ball, vs. the league average of 1.25), but given their speed and ability to make contact, the hit-and-run total seems abnormally low. But again, this is Cito through and through: don't make a lot of moves.

He doesn't change his lineup much. The Blue Jays used 72 different lineup combinations last year, which seems like a lot, but isn't—at all. It was the lowest total in the American League, by plenty; Gene Lamont of the White Sox ranked second with 92. Tony La Russa of the Athletics, a man who could be considered the antithesis of Gaston in a lot of ways, used 149 different lineups in 162 games.

Gaston, we should point out, is more conventional in some other areas. He called 67 pitchouts last year, a figure which ranked in the middle of the pack among American League managers (La Russa called only 61); he called for the sacrifice bunt 61 times, which was below average but not exceptionally so; and his club attempted 219 steals, third-most in the league but not an exceptional number given the club's number-one ranking in stolen-base success rate. In those areas, he's not unique.

But Gaston's basic managerial profile is pretty well established: he's not a guy who makes a lot of moves. People criticize him for this, and say he's just "lucky" to be winning; anyone could win with that talent.

To which we say: bunk. Think of all the teams which are supposed to have "great talent," but never win it all; it's no snap to win, even with the talent. Despite all you hear about the importance of managerial strategy, it's only one part of a manager's job. The most important part of the job is the same as any manager's, in any occupation: get the most out of your workers. In a big way, the key questions about a manager are: Do his people respect him? Will they go to the wall for him? Will they play their best for him, and battle back from adversity? In all *those* areas, we defy you to find a better manager than Cito Gaston. He's one of the best in the business.

WHO ISSUES THE "AUTOMATIC" INTENTIONAL WALK?

You've seen this one about a million times. It's a National League game, and the number-eight hitter strolls to the plate. There are two outs, and first base is open. The manager of the team in the field signals toward first base, and the hitter strolls to first with an intentional walk. "And they'll put Smeddly on, to get to the pitcher," the announcer says. He doesn't question the strategy.

Maybe *he* doesn't question it, but *we* certainly do. Why would you walk a hitter in order to get to the pitcher? "Because the pitcher's a weak hitter," is the usual answer. The counter-argument is that the walk is usually issued to the number-eight hitter, the weakest hitter in the lineup apart from the pitcher. If you get him out—and the odds are strongly in favor of it—then the pitcher will be leading off the next inning, which puts his club at a disadvantage. Most statistical studies wind up concluding that the intentional walk is bad strategy in most situations, but especially this one. But that doesn't stop managers from doing it anyway.

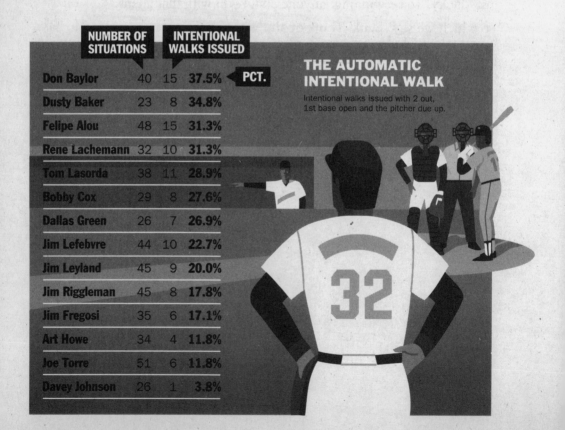

THE AUTOMATIC INTENTIONAL WALK

Intentional walks issued with 2 out, 1st base open and the pitcher due up.

	NUMBER OF SITUATIONS	INTENTIONAL WALKS ISSUED	PCT.
Don Baylor	40	15	37.5%
Dusty Baker	23	8	34.8%
Felipe Alou	48	15	31.3%
Rene Lachemann	32	10	31.3%
Tom Lasorda	38	11	28.9%
Bobby Cox	29	8	27.6%
Dallas Green	26	7	26.9%
Jim Lefebvre	44	10	22.7%
Jim Leyland	45	9	20.0%
Jim Riggleman	45	8	17.8%
Jim Fregosi	35	6	17.1%
Art Howe	34	4	11.8%
Joe Torre	51	6	11.8%
Davey Johnson	26	1	3.8%

However, some managers employ it much more often than others do. We suspected that there would be significant differences in how often National League managers called for the "automatic intentional walk," and that turned out to be exactly right. The chart shows how often each NL skipper issued the two-out intentional walk with first base open and the pitcher due up last year. Ordinarily it's the number-eight hitter who receives the walk, but since a pitcher can wind up anywhere in the batting order due to pinch hitting, double switches, etc., we counted all cases where the pitcher was due up, whatever place in the batting order.

What a difference! Davey Johnson of the Reds is from the Earl Weaver school, and Weaver liked intentional walks about as much as he liked the 1969 Mets. So it's not surprising that Johnson walked a man to get to the pitcher only once in nearly a full season of managing the Reds. On the other hand, Don Baylor of the Rockies, who also played for Weaver, employed the strategy 15 times. They must have been sitting on opposite ends of the bench back in their Baltimore days, absorbing different lessons ("Earl's platooning me," thought Baylor. "Platooning's *dumb* . . .").

Interestingly, Baylor and Dusty Baker, two first-year skippers who had never managed before, even in the minor leagues (Baker did have a stint in the Arizona Fall League), issued the intentional walk to get to the pitcher more than anyone else. This may be an indication of inexperience, though veteran skippers like Tommy Lasorda and Bobby Cox seem to like it well enough, also.

We're more in the Davey Johnson camp, though there are admittedly times when this move would make some sense. Sometimes an intentional walk to the number eight hitter will "force" the opposing manager to pinch-hit for his pitcher; if the opposing pitcher is the club's closer or ace starter, that would seem like a reasonable move. And hardly anybody would question walking Barry Bonds if the opposing pitcher was the next player up because of a double-switch. But those are unusual circumstances. Our general feeling is that this move is made way too much, and our hunch is that Baylor, Baker and Alou will be issuing fewer walks to get to the pitcher in future years.

WILL PHILADELPHIA'S SUCCESS INSPIRE MORE PLATOONING?

Will platooning, which has been very much out of fashion in recent years, make a comeback thanks to the Philadelphia Phillies? Every season we make an annual survey of the best platoons of the previous year, and every season we lament how seldom the strategy is used. But that was before 1993, and the success of Jim Fregosi's Phillies. The Phils platooned in left field, right field and usually second base, receiving excellent production from all three positions. Though the club's regulars deserve most of the credit, the platooners helped the Phillies produce the NL's best offense in a number of seasons. The result was a trip to the World Series.

In baseball, success breeds imitation, so it's logical to think that more teams may try platooning this year. Only trouble is, other clubs have had success with platooning in recent times—notably the Braves and Pirates—and *that* didn't inspire much imitation. But Philadelphia's success may help revive the idea. We hope so; as we've often pointed out, platooning can help make a weak position strong.

These were our choices for the best platoons of 1993. The figures quoted are the players' totals when playing that position only:

Philadelphia Phillies—RF	AB	H	HR	RBI	Avg
Jim Eisenreich	337	109	7	51	.323
Wes Chamberlain	264	76	12	44	.288

This was a classic platoon, featuring two players who had struggled recently, but who found success as a combination. Eisenreich and Chamberlain combined for a .308 average, 19 homers and 95 RBI, figures an Earl Weaver or Casey Stengel platoon used to post every year.

Philadelphia Phillies—LF	AB	H	HR	RBI	Avg
Milt Thompson	311	81	4	41	.260
Pete Incaviglia	317	88	23	78	.278

This Phillies combination was even more effective than Eisenreich/Chamberlain, amassing 27 homers and 119 RBI. It was not a strict platoon, however, as Incaviglia often started against righties. But as with the right field combo, it got the most out of two talents which were considered marginal heading into the 1993 season.

Detroit Tigers—2B	AB	H	HR	RBI	Avg
Lou Whitaker	367	106	9	62	.289
Tony Phillips	182	64	1	20	.352

Phillips is an everyday player, but as one of the most versatile players around, he can switch between several positions without losing effectiveness. His ability to handle second base—probably his best position—allows Sparky Anderson to platoon him with the great veteran Lou Whitaker. Sweet Lou is still a very effective hitter, but has problems hitting lefties, so Phillips has been a godsend.

Houston Astros—C	AB	H	HR	RBI	Avg
Eddie Taubensee	281	70	9	42	.249
Scott Servais	253	63	11	32	.249

Catching platoons are among the few which have remained common in recent years. Last year marked the demise of the Mike LaValliere/Don Slaught combo with the Pirates, and the Matt Nokes/Mike Stanley platoon with the Yankees ended because Stanley was hitting so well that he earned an everyday job. So the best platoon behind the plate was the young Houston combination of Eddie Taubensee and Scott Servais. Each has his weaknesses, but they combined to provide 20 homers and 74 RBI, which is very good production. This one should continue in 1994.

Milwaukee Brewers—DH	AB	H	HR	RBI	Avg
Kevin Reimer	307	80	9	36	.261
Greg Vaughn	219	55	11	38	.251

Vaughn, like Tony Phillips, is an everyday player, and ordinarily the Brewer left fielder. But the Brewers needed someone to platoon with Kevin Reimer at DH, and Vaughn got that job when he wasn't playing left. The platoon was effective, though it's unlikely to last. Vaughn is simply too good a left fielder to keep on the bench.

New York Yankees—RF	AB	H	HR	RBI	Avg
Paul O'Neill	332	103	16	52	.310
Danny Tartabull	186	43	11	32	.231

A curious sort of platoon, since both O'Neill and Tartabull were basically regulars. O'Neill also saw frequent action in left field, and Tartabull was the Yankees' primary designated hitter. But when they were sharing right field—a sensible move for O'Neill, since he's weak against lefties—the combination was very effective. Also very expensive.

APPENDIX

For the last five years, I've done the same old damn thing on this book: write about 100 computer programs in a month to produce the data the writers use for the essays, write another 75 programs in a week to produce the charts you see on the following pages, fight with some cockamamie desktop publishing software until three or four in the morning, every morning, for another week, straining my already bloodshot eyes to make sure I can squeeze the name "Galarraga" or "Henderson R" into a column, construct a 400-entry Index from scratch, with only the vaguest memory about what each essay actually was about, then, when I really wouldn't mind just going home and watching an episode or two of *The Bob Newhart Show* (the one where he's a psychologist in Chicago) and falling asleep, Don Zminda comes over and asks me, "Are you workin' on the intro to the Appendix?"

I wouldn't miss it for the world.

'Cause, you see, even though the *Scoreboard* looks the same every year—it's the same number of pages, it's the same size, and we even repeat some of the questions from the previous year—it is completely new and different on the inside. First, it gets better every year. Second, I learn more about baseball and baseball history working on this book than in the other 10 months of the year combined.

This Appendix contains the great scenes that were left on the cutting room floor. In the essay on Barry Bonds (page 65), we could only show you a partial list of the highest runs created, secondary averages, and offensive winning percentages in baseball history; in the Appendix, we show you the top 55. One of my favorite essays, "Who are the Prime Pivot Men?" has room to list only a handful of second basemen: the Appendix gives you every active player over the last five years. Anal retentive, and just have to know every single reliever who registered a "hold" in 1993? Well, the Appendix has 'em all for you. We also crammed every pennant winner since 1901—including those Federal League standout teams Indianapolis and Chicago (what *are* their nicknames?)—onto two pages for you.

Like always, we tried to give you all the data we worked with for each essay so that you can do a little investigating yourself. Feel free to write us with your comments and suggestions. If they're good, you just might wind up with your name in next year's edition of this book. For some of the essays, most or all of the figures used for that particular study appear in the essay itself. In such cases, there is no additional data back here. Last year, we added a Teams section; this year, we've added a Managers section. (Next year, "Team Mascots" section.)

Each Appendix is keyed twice. The "Title" key serves as a reminder as to what topic is being covered, and corresponds to the title in the Table of Contents. The "Page" key refers to the page where you'll find the appropriate essay. In addition, each Appendix is accompanied by a label describing how the list has been ordered (most alphabetically), a "minimum requirement" telling how much of what a player needed to make the list, and a key for deciphering any obscure abbreviations.

The team abbreviation following a player's name refers to the team with which he finished the season. Here are the abbreviations:

American League Teams		National League Teams	
Bal	Baltimore Orioles	Atl	Atlanta Braves
Bos	Boston Red Sox	ChN	Chicago Cubs
Cal	California Angels	Cin	Cincinnati Reds
ChA	Chicago White Sox	Col	Colorado Rockies
Cle	Cleveland Indians	Fla	Florida Marlins
Det	Detroit Tigers	Hou	Houston Astros
KC	Kansas City Royals	LA	Los Angelese Dodgers
Mil	Milwaukee Brewers	Mon	Montreal Expos
Min	Minnesota Twins	NYN	New York Mets
NYA	New York Yankees	Phi	Philadelphia Phillies
Oak	Oakland Athletics	Pit	Pittsburgh Pirates
Sea	Seattle Mariners	StL	St. Louis Cardinals
Tex	Texas Rangers	SD	San Diego Padres
Tor	Toronto Blue Jays	SF	San Francisco Giants

Enjoy!

Bob Mecca
Owner and General Manager, *New England Anarchists*
Ozark Mountain League
(currently second place, and dropping like a rock)

BALTIMORE ORIOLES: IS THIS THE "GOLDEN AGE" FOR CATCHERS? (p. 6)

Listed below are the top 21 offensive seasons for catchers since 1876. The 6 catchers included in each group are those with the highest On-Base plus Slugging Percentage (**OPS**) with 400+ AB.

Major Leagues — Listed by Season
(Minimum 6 Catchers with 400 AB)

Year	OPS	Avg	OBP	Slg	AB	H	2B	3B	HR	RBI	BB	K
1993	.919	.296	.384	.535	2719	806	150	11	159	507	388	567
	Stanley, Kreuter, Hoiles, Wilkins, Piazza, Daulton											
1938	.876	.310	.390	.486	2629	816	148	22	90	498	341	182
	Dickey, Ferrell, Lombardi, Pytlak, Danning, York											
1977	.876	.283	.384	.492	2926	827	159	17	140	512	480	518
	Bench, Simmons, Fisk, Tenace, Ferguson, Carter											
1950	.875	.288	.374	.501	2644	762	121	21	133	481	364	242
	Cooper, Seminick, Berra, Lollar, Westrum, Campanella											
1970	.871	.309	.378	.493	3111	961	159	29	119	530	346	455
	Torre, Dietz, Bench, Fosse, Sanguillen, Munson											
1979	.865	.285	.394	.471	2780	793	121	17	120	490	501	403
	Bench, Simmons, Tenace, Ferguson, Porter, Downing											
1932	.859	.304	.383	.476	2600	791	155	30	77	451	332	170
	Hartnett, Cochrane, Davis, Dickey, Ferrell, Lombardi											
1956	.850	.277	.361	.489	2729	756	122	15	142	511	359	340
	Berra, Lollar, Campanella, Lopata, Bailey, Triandos											
1937	.847	.308	.369	.478	2637	813	144	30	81	485	253	171
	Sewell, Dickey, Phelps, Pytlak, Todd, York											
1931	.842	.316	.383	.459	2491	788	159	23	50	410	268	158
	Hartnett, Cochrane, Hogan, Davis, Dickey, Ferrell											
1975	.842	.295	.378	.464	3096	913	148	16	114	517	416	430
	Bench, Sanguillen, Simmons, Munson, Tenace, Porter											
1980	.835	.277	.356	.479	2663	737	133	18	123	464	330	410
	Bench, Simmons, Tenace, Carter, Parrish, Hassey											
1936	.833	.312	.370	.463	2668	833	147	26	68	424	245	171
	Hartnett, Dickey, Mancuso, Ferrell, Lombardi, Hayes											
1935	.828	.305	.385	.443	2609	796	175	37	37	383	337	141
	Hartnett, Cochrane, Dickey, Hemsley, Ferrell, Bolton											
1961	.828	.289	.359	.469	2591	749	124	17	103	371	281	387
	Battey, Howard, Pagliaroni, Roseboro, Romano, Torre											
1972	.826	.278	.354	.472	2892	803	143	22	125	468	342	443
	Freehan, Kirkpatrick, Bench, Simmons, Fisk, Williams											
1922	.825	.315	.387	.438	2518	792	132	34	37	379	297	183
	Ainsmith, O'Neill, Severeid, Schang, O'Farrell, Henline											
1978	.819	.274	.360	.459	2912	799	165	22	110	454	389	374
	Bench, Simmons, Fisk, Porter, Boone, Stearns											
1933	.816	.303	.377	.439	2859	866	154	27	60	448	340	158
	Sewell, Hartnett, Cochrane, Davis, Dickey, Ferrell											
1934	.815	.308	.373	.442	2555	788	156	21	48	400	264	169
	Hartnett, Cochrane, Dickey, Hemsley, Ferrell, Lombardi											
1985	.815	.271	.345	.470	2986	810	144	13	141	502	336	376
	Fisk, Carter, Whitt, Parrish, Gedman, Scioscia											

CALIFORNIA ANGELS: WOULD A BETTER RUNNING GAME GIVE THEM A BETTER CHANCE? (p. 10)

The chart below list the number of plate appearances with a runner or runners in scoring position for each teams' #3, #4, and #5 hitters. The second half of the chart lists each teams' Stolen Bases (**SB**), Caught Stealings (**CS**) and Stolen Base Percentage (**SB%**) for 1993.

American League

Team	#3	#4	#5	Tot	SB	CS	SB%
Orioles	223	191	177	591	73	54	57
Red Sox	199	222	188	609	73	38	66
Angels	201	215	182	598	169	100	63
White Sox	232	233	201	666	106	57	65
Indians	217	216	198	631	159	55	74
Tigers	236	266	227	729	104	63	62
Royals	199	216	201	616	100	75	57
Brewers	198	199	197	594	138	93	60
Twins	210	242	215	667	83	59	58
Yankees	192	215	209	616	39	35	53
Athletics	229	217	185	631	131	59	69
Mariners	208	223	218	649	91	68	57
Rangers	197	216	183	596	113	67	63
Blue Jays	240	243	211	694	170	49	78
AL Average	**213**	**222**	**199**	**634**	**1549**	**872**	**64**

National League

Team	#3	#4	#5	Tot	SB	CS	SB%
Braves	215	222	204	641	125	48	72
Cubs	201	218	208	627	100	43	70
Reds	215	214	199	628	142	59	71
Astros	188	215	211	614	103	60	63
Dodgers	231	229	196	656	126	61	67
Expos	232	257	236	726	228	56	80
Mets	176	170	152	498	79	50	61
Phillies	249	255	245	749	91	32	74
Pirates	218	238	218	674	92	55	63
Cardinals	205	262	234	701	153	72	68
Padres	175	207	195	577	92	41	69
Giants	210	214	209	633	120	65	65
Rockies	209	205	196	610	146	90	62
Marlins	198	201	191	590	117	56	68
NL Average	**209**	**222**	**207**	**638**	**1714**	**788**	**69**

CLEVELAND INDIANS: WILL THEIR NEW PARK BE THE GATEWAY TO SUCCESS? (p. 15)

The chart below lists each team that has moved into a new park, and their record and finish in their last season they spent in their old park (**Last Year**) and the first season they spent in their new park (**First Year**).

		Last Year			First Year	
TEAM	**Year**	**W-L**	**Fin(GB)**	**Year**	**W-L**	**Fin(GB)**
Giants	1959	83-71	3(4)	1960	79-75	5(16)
Dodgers	1961	89-65	2(4)	1962	102-63	2(1)
Mets	1963	51-111	10(48)	1964	53-109	10(40)
Astros	1964	66-96	9(27)	1965	65-97	9(32)
Angels	1965	75-87	9(27)	1966	80-82	6(18)
Cardinals-a	1965	80-81	7(16.5)	1966	83-79	6(12)
Reds-c	1969	89-73	3(4)	1970	102-60	1
Pirates-b	1969	88-74	3(12)	1970	89-73	1
Phillies	1970	73-88	5(15.5)	1971	67-95	6(30)
Royals	1972	76-78	4(16.5)	1973	88-74	2(6)
Yankees	1975	83-77	3(12)	1976	97-62	1
Expos	1976	55-107	6(46)	1977	75-87	5(26)
Twins	1981	41-68	7(23)	1982	60-102	7(33)
Blue Jays-d	1988	87-75	3(2)	1989	89-73	1
White Sox	1990	94-68	2(9)	1991	87-75	2(8)
Baltimore	1991	67-95	6(24)	1992	89-73	3(7)
Total		**1197-1314**			**1305-1279**	
		(.477)			(.505)	
162-Game Record		**77-85**			**82-80**	

Notes on mid-season moves:

a-St. Louis began play in Busch II on 5/12/66

b-Pittsburgh moved into Three Rivers 7/16/70

c-Cincinnati began play at Riverfront on 6/30/70

d-Toronto moved into Skydome 6/5/89

KANSAS CITY ROYALS: WHAT ARE TURF FIELDS REALLY LIKE? (p. 20)

The chart below lists the Park Indeces in various statistical categories for artificial turf parks. The Indeces cover the 1991-1993 seasons, except for Seattle, which covers only 1992-93.

A Index for a specific stat is simply the rate of that statistic in a team's home games divided by the rate of that stat in a team's road games, multiplied by 100. Thus, an Index over 100 means a park "favors" that stat.

Chart 1: Turf Field Error Index

Park	Home Games			Road Games			Index
	G	E	E/G	G	E	E/G	
Cin	243	260	1.07	243	325	1.34	80
Hou	162	164	1.01	162	220	1.36	75
KC	243	299	1.23	243	260	1.07	115
Min	243	249	1.02	243	282	1.16	88
Mon	230	312	1.36	256	391	1.53	89
Phi	245	318	1.30	241	339	1.41	92
Pit	246	279	1.13	240	256	1.07	106
Sea	162	184	1.14	162	187	1.15	98
StL	162	175	1.08	162	209	1.29	84
Tor	243	263	1.08	243	312	1.28	84
TOT	2179	2503	1.15	2195	2781	1.27	91

Chart 2: Turf Field Double Index

Park	Home Games			Road Games			Index
	AB	DB	DB/AB	AB	DB	DB/AB	
Cin	16296	777	0.0477	16570	734	0.0443	108
Hou	10952	503	0.0459	10934	521	0.0476	96
KC	16813	930	0.0553	16372	766	0.0468	118
Min	16802	914	0.0544	16518	786	0.0476	114
Mon	15353	771	0.0502	17327	770	0.0444	113
Phi	16809	809	0.0481	16420	762	0.0464	104
Pit	16670	834	0.0500	16493	781	0.0474	106
Sea	11132	630	0.0566	10928	499	0.0457	124
StL	11138	521	0.0468	11224	537	0.0478	98
Tor	16519	848	0.0513	16514	746	0.0452	114
TOT	148484	7537	0.0508	149300	6902	0.0462	110

Chart 3: Turf Field Triple Index

Park	Home Games			Road Games			Index
	AB	TP	TP/AB	AB	TP	TP/AB	
Cin	16296	103	0.0063	16570	133	0.0080	79
Hou	10952	73	0.0067	10934	76	0.0070	96
KC	16813	142	0.0084	16372	74	0.0045	187
Min	16802	120	0.0071	16518	79	0.0048	149
Mon	15353	102	0.0066	17327	116	0.0067	99

Chart 3: Turf Field Triple Index

	Home Games			Road Games			
Park	AB	TP	TP/AB	AB	TP	TP/AB	Index
Phi	16809	121	0.0072	16420	116	0.0071	102
Pit	16670	147	0.0088	16493	123	0.0075	118
Sea	11132	47	0.0042	10928	57	0.0052	81
StL	11138	78	0.0070	11224	78	0.0069	101
Tor	16519	118	0.0071	16514	80	0.0048	147
TOT	148484	1051	0.0071	149300	932	0.0062	113

Chart 4: Turf Field Home Run Index

	Home Games			Road Games			
Park	AB	HR	HR/AB	AB	HR	HR/AB	Index
Cin	16296	451	0.0277	16570	343	0.0207	134
Hou	10952	208	0.0190	10934	257	0.0235	81
KC	16813	251	0.0149	16372	382	0.0233	64
Min	16802	375	0.0223	16518	398	0.0241	93
Mon	15353	278	0.0181	17327	363	0.0209	86
Phi	16809	367	0.0218	16420	371	0.0226	97
Pit	16670	335	0.0201	16493	378	0.0229	88
Sea	11132	281	0.0252	10928	293	0.0268	94
StL	11138	225	0.0202	11224	257	0.0229	88
Tor	16519	457	0.0277	16514	377	0.0228	121
TOT	148484	3228	0.0217	149300	3419	0.0229	95

Groundball Pitchers 1989-1993 on Grass/Turf

On Grass

Yr	W	L	WIN%	IP	H	ER	ERA	Avg
89	285	313	.477	5400.0	5107	2279	3.80	.250
90	296	287	.508	5119.2	4762	2177	3.83	.247
91	235	253	.482	4599.2	4379	2109	4.13	.251
92	255	247	.508	4573.1	4311	1941	3.82	.251
93	260	264	.496	4851.0	4666	2251	4.18	.254
	1331	1364	.494	24543.2	23225	10757	3.94	.250

On Turf

Yr	W	L	WIN%	IP	H	ER	ERA	Avg
89	190	190	.500	3272.0	2985	1389	3.82	.243
90	165	193	.461	3112.0	2988	1414	4.09	.254
91	159	171	.482	2996.2	2768	1337	4.02	.247
92	154	165	.483	2843.1	2731	1236	3.91	.254
93	175	165	.515	2865.1	2744	1370	4.30	.252
	843	884	.488	15089.1	14216	6746	4.02	.250

MILWAUKEE BREWERS: IS A GOOD SECOND HALF A GOOD SIGN FOR A ROOKIE? (p. 22)

Slow Starts/Fast Finishes for Rookies: 1988-1993

Slow Start = OBP+SLG .675 Before All-Star Break

Fast Finish = Minimum 15% Increase in OBP+SLG After All-Star Break

Both Leagues — Listed Alphabetically
(Minimum 100 PA in the Rookie Season; 50 in each Half)

PLAYER	Year	1ST HALF SLOW START					2ND HALF SURGE				
		AVG	OBP	SLG	HR	RBI	AVG	OBP	SLG	HR	RBI
Roberto ALOMAR	1988	.237	.279	.342	6	19	.296	.375	.423	3	22
Kent ANDERSON	1989	.212	.265	.231	0	7	.244	.302	.294	0	10
Carlos BAERGA	1990	.207	.248	.320	3	19	.309	.347	.463	4	28
Derek BELL	1992	.189	.282	.289	2	8	.310	.380	.437	0	7
Juan BELL	1991	.131	.159	.164	0	4	.189	.218	.284	1	11
Jay BUHNER	1988	.188	.250	.319	3	13	.224	.320	.458	10	25
Scott COOPER	1992	.253	.321	.313	0	18	.294	.365	.439	5	15
Steve FINLEY	1989	.210	.270	.306	2	18	.301	.337	.333	0	7
Joe GIRARDI	1989	.211	.243	.254	1	5	.279	.351	.395	0	9
Craig GREBECK	1990	.125	.153	.143	0	2	.206	.288	.317	1	7
Juan GUERRERO	1992	.167	.231	.267	0	7	.231	.288	.308	1	7
Scott HEMOND	1993	.197	.293	.258	0	4	.282	.379	.483	6	22
Carlos HERNANDEZ	1992	.248	.316	.267	0	6	.278	.316	.431	3	11
Darrin JACKSON	1988	.248	.259	.389	2	9	.293	.329	.547	4	11
Gregg JEFFERIES	1989	.230	.284	.318	1	27	.287	.345	.470	11	29
Terry JORGENSEN	1993	.203	.250	.250	0	4	.239	.284	.318	1	8
Felix JOSE	1990	.243	.278	.349	4	19	.283	.337	.414	7	33
Chad KREUTER	1989	.118	.200	.184	1	4	.183	.337	.341	4	5
Ray LANKFORD	1991	.241	.285	.331	1	27	.260	.315	.447	8	42
Mark LEMKE	1990	.171	.286	.224	0	6	.252	.287	.307	0	15
Kenny LOFTON	1992	.261	.326	.329	2	20	.312	.400	.405	3	22
Carlos MARTINEZ	1989	.248	.296	.347	1	13	.321	.358	.430	4	19
Derrick MAY	1992	.243	.280	.329	3	18	.296	.327	.407	5	27
Joey MEYER	1988	.234	.261	.380	4	13	.284	.348	.447	7	32
Dave NILSSON	1992	.200	.238	.320	3	15	.281	.395	.406	1	10
Tom PAGNOZZI	1988	.244	.287	.305	0	6	.310	.342	.345	0	9
Mark PARENT	1988	.182	.224	.218	0	2	.206	.239	.508	6	13
Geronimo PENA	1991	.222	.297	.333	1	6	.263	.345	.463	4	11
Alonzo POWELL	1991	.164	.230	.273	1	6	.268	.344	.464	2	6
Jody REED	1988	.237	.333	.333	1	8	.314	.399	.392	0	20
Jeff SCHAEFER	1990	.196	.208	.216	0	3	.214	.267	.250	0	3
Scott SERVAIS	1992	.200	.262	.242	0	7	.294	.341	.341	0	8
Luis SOJO	1991	.228	.263	.287	0	11	.285	.324	.363	3	9
Sammy SOSA	1989	.264	.264	.333	1	3	.252	.325	.387	3	10
Eddie TAUBENSEE	1992	.173	.260	.218	0	11	.262	.331	.409	5	17
Lenny WEBSTER	1992	.206	.260	.279	0	5	.380	.426	.580	1	8
Walt WEISS	1988	.232	.291	.299	3	26	.273	.339	.348	0	13

IS YANKEE STADIUM STILL THE "HOUSE THAT FORD BUILT"? (p. 26)

The charts below lists the Park Indices in Earned Run Average for right- and left-handed pitchers. The Indeces cover the 1991-1993 seasons, except for Baltimore, Cleveland, Seattle, and St. Louis, which covers only 1992-93, San Francisco, Colorado, and Florida, which covers only 1993.

The Index for each ERA is simply the ERA in a team's home games divided by the ERA in a team's road games, multiplied by 100. Thus, an Index of 110 means a park increases ERA by 10%.

Left-Handed Pitchers ERA Index

Team	Home IP	ER	ERA	Road IP	ER	ERA	Index
Baltimore Orioles	759.2	379	4.49	758.1	379	4.50	100
Boston Red Sox	1199.0	543	4.08	1284.2	566	3.97	103
California Angels	1819.2	713	3.53	1649.2	657	3.58	98
Chicago White Sox	1161.1	472	3.66	1196.0	536	4.03	91
Cleveland Indians	786.2	405	4.63	842.1	417	4.46	104
Detroit Tigers	1268.0	670	4.76	1318.2	687	4.69	101
Kansas City Royals	1023.2	494	4.34	1002.0	442	3.97	109
Milwaukee Brewers	1034.2	517	4.50	973.0	458	4.24	106
Minnesota Twins	1181.2	606	4.62	1238.2	570	4.14	111
New York Yankees	1484.2	708	4.29	1352.2	645	4.29	100
Oakland Athletics	760.0	344	4.07	782.0	398	4.58	89
Seattle Mariners	1038.0	503	4.36	1031.0	493	4.30	101
Texas Rangers	1057.1	554	4.72	1178.2	598	4.57	103
Toronto Blue Jays	1132.0	507	4.03	1150.1	527	4.12	98
Atlanta Braves	1742.1	710	3.67	1736.2	683	3.54	104
Chicago Cubs	1219.1	530	3.91	1256.1	523	3.75	104
Cincinnati Reds	1450.0	649	4.03	1517.1	696	4.13	98
Houston Astros	793.0	377	4.28	774.1	345	4.01	107
Los Angeles Dodgers	1025.2	393	3.45	1126.1	439	3.51	98
Montreal Expos	1440.1	568	3.55	1507.1	637	3.80	93
New York Mets	1622.0	645	3.58	1555.1	670	3.88	92
Philadelphia Phillies	1739.1	767	3.97	1596.1	705	3.97	100
Pittsburgh Pirates	1824.0	809	3.99	1821.0	776	3.84	104
St. Louis Cardinals	1008.0	457	4.08	1065.0	512	4.33	94
San Diego Padres	1410.2	648	4.13	1378.0	561	3.66	113
San Francisco Giants	471.2	212	4.05	468.2	245	4.70	86
Colorado Rockies	353.0	236	6.02	338.1	147	3.91	154
Florida Marlins	328.0	132	3.62	367.0	162	3.97	91

Right-Handed Pitchers ERA Index

Team	Home IP	Home ER	Home ERA	Road IP	Road ER	Road ERA	Index
Baltimore Orioles	2158.0	995	4.15	2127.2	934	3.95	105
Boston Red Sox	3159.1	1386	3.95	3044.2	1196	3.54	112
California Angels	2538.1	1101	3.90	2644.2	1144	3.89	100
Chicago White Sox	3207.2	1468	4.12	3195.2	1447	4.08	101
Cleveland Indians	2122.0	950	4.03	2088.1	964	4.15	97
Detroit Tigers	3032.1	1619	4.81	3028.0	1522	4.52	106
Kansas City Royals	3363.2	1408	3.77	3337.1	1390	3.75	101
Milwaukee Brewers	3292.0	1410	3.85	3437.2	1631	4.27	90
Minnesota Twins	3179.0	1466	4.15	3085.0	1335	3.89	107
New York Yankees	2837.0	1351	4.29	3003.1	1440	4.32	99
Oakland Athletics	3582.1	1588	3.99	3560.2	1811	4.58	87
Seattle Mariners	1886.2	868	4.14	1854.2	841	4.08	101
Texas Rangers	3294.1	1465	4.00	3216.0	1593	4.46	90
Toronto Blue Jays	3174.1	1564	4.43	3194.1	1385	3.90	114
Atlanta Braves	2568.1	1110	3.89	2638.0	1010	3.45	113
Chicago Cubs	3235.2	1394	3.88	3038.0	1280	3.79	102
Cincinnati Reds	2844.1	1305	4.13	2836.1	1097	3.48	119
Houston Astros	2129.0	758	3.20	2103.1	901	3.86	83
Los Angeles Dodgers	3325.1	1206	3.26	3264.1	1266	3.49	94
Montreal Expos	2697.0	1032	3.44	3087.2	1184	3.45	100
New York Mets	2750.2	1122	3.67	2747.2	1108	3.63	101
Philadelphia Phillies	2659.1	1205	4.08	2728.1	1189	3.92	104
Pittsburgh Pirates	2581.1	1099	3.83	2514.0	1172	4.20	91
St. Louis Cardinals	1912.0	752	3.54	1878.0	789	3.78	94
San Diego Padres	2961.2	1161	3.53	2962.2	1185	3.60	98
San Francisco Giants	978.1	384	3.53	974.0	465	4.30	82
Colorado Rockies	1077.2	672	5.61	1108.0	489	3.97	141
Florida Marlins	1139.1	480	3.79	1060.1	410	3.48	109

SEATTLE MARINERS: HOW IMPORTANT IS A GREAT CLOSER? (p. 31)

1993 Seattle Relief Pitchers — Listed by Innings Pitched in Relief

Seattle Relievers — 1993

Reliever	W	L	Sv	Op	Sv%	Hd	IP	ER	ERA
Nelson J	5	3	1	11	9.1	17	60.0	29	4.35
Henry Dw	2	1	2	2	100.0	0	49.2	34	6.16
DeLucia	3	5	0	4	0.0	6	40.2	19	4.21
Powell D	0	0	0	0	0.0	11	37.2	17	4.06
Holman	1	3	3	3	100.0	2	36.1	15	3.72
Charlton	1	3	18	21	85.7	1	34.2	9	2.34
Power	2	2	13	15	86.7	4	25.1	11	3.91
Swan	3	3	0	0	0.0	5	19.2	20	9.15
Ayrault	1	1	0	1	0.0	1	19.2	7	3.20
Ontiveros	0	2	0	0	0.0	0	18.0	2	1.00
King	0	1	0	1	0.0	4	11.2	8	6.17
Hampton	1	0	1	1	100.0	2	10.0	5	4.50
Leary	0	1	0	1	0.0	0	9.2	8	7.45
Plantenberg	0	0	1	1	100.0	6	9.2	7	6.52
Bosio	1	0	1	2	50.0	1	8.0	4	4.50
Hanson	0	1	0	0	0.0	0	6.0	6	9.00
Cummings	0	0	0	0	0.0	0	3.2	6	14.73
Salkeld	0	0	0	0	0.0	0	3.1	1	2.70
Shinall	0	0	0	0	0.0	0	2.2	1	3.37
Wainhouse	0	0	0	0	0.0	0	2.1	7	27.00
Johnson R	0	0	1	1	100.0	0	1.1	0	0.00
Totals	20	26	41	64	64.1	60	410.0	216	4.74
w/o Charlton	19	23	23	43	53.5	59	375.1	207	4.96

TEXAS RANGERS: CAN GONZALEZ (AND GRIFFEY) THREATEN AARON'S HOME RUN RECORD? (p. 33)

120+ Home Runs by Age 24

Player	Age 24 HR	Career HR
Hank Aaron	140	755
Johnny Bench	154	389
Jose Canseco	128	245
Orlando Cepeda	157	379
Tony Conigliaro	124	166
Joe DiMaggio	137	361
Jimmie Foxx	174	534
Juan Gonzalez	121	121
Ken Griffey Jr	132	132
Bob Horner	138	218
Al Kaline	125	399
Mickey Mantle	173	536
Eddie Mathews	190	512
Mel Ott	176	511
Boog Powell	130	339
Frank Robinson	165	586
Hal Trosky	136	228
Ted Williams	127	521

300+ Career Home Runs

Player	Age 24 HR	Career HR
Hank Aaron	140	755
Joe Adcock	31	336
Dick Allen	89	351
Ernie Banks	65	512
Don Baylor	22	338
Johnny Bench	154	389
Yogi Berra	47	358
Bobby Bonds	67	332
George Brett	42	317
Gary Carter	75	324
Norm Cash	4	377
Orlando Cepeda	157	379
Ron Cey	1	316
Jack Clark	88	340
Rocky Colavito	87	374
Andre Dawson	69	412
Joe DiMaggio	137	361
Darrell Evans	12	414
Dwight Evans	51	385
Carlton Fisk	24	376
George Foster	20	348
Jimmie Foxx	174	534

300+ Career Home Runs

Player	Age 24 HR	Career HR
Lou Gehrig	84	493
Hank Greenberg	74	331
Gil Hodges	12	370
Rogers Hornsby	36	301
Willie Horton	77	325
Frank Howard	40	382
Reggie Jackson	100	563
Al Kaline	125	399
Harmon Kill'br'w	84	573
Ralph Kiner	74	369
Dave Kingman	59	442
Chuck Klein	54	300
Greg Luzinski	91	307
Fred Lynn	33	306
Mickey Mantle	173	536
Eddie Mathews	190	512
Lee May	14	354
Willie Mays	116	660
Willie McCovey	64	521
Johnny Mize	44	359
Dale Murphy	79	398
Eddie Murray	111	441
Stan Musial	36	475
Graig Nettles	12	390
Mel Ott	176	511
Dave Parker	33	339
Lance Parrish	60	317
Tony Perez	16	379
Boog Powell	130	339
Jim Rice	87	382
Frank Robinson	165	586
Babe Ruth	49	714
Ron Santo	104	342
Mike Schmidt	55	548
Roy Sievers	27	318
Al Simmons	51	307
Reggie Smith	55	314
Duke Snider	88	407
Willie Stargell	32	475
Billy Williams	49	426
Ted Williams	127	521
Dave Winfield	51	453
Carl Yastrzemski	59	452

1% chance for 500 HR

Player	%
Juan Gonzalez	53%
Ken Griffey Jr	40
Barry Bonds	36
Dave Winfield	26
Fred McGriff	25
Frank Thomas	23
Albert Belle	16
Matt Williams	14
Cecil Fielder	12
Dean Palmer	7
Dave Justice	7
Eddie Murray	6
Ron Gant	4
Joe Carter	3
Rafael Palmeiro	2
Danny Tartabull	1
Jose Canseco	1
Phil Plantier	1

1% chance for 600 HR

Player	%
Juan Gonzalez	31
Ken Griffey Jr	20
Barry Bonds	13
Frank Thomas	8
Fred McGriff	5
Albert Belle	3

1% chance for 700 HR

Player	%
Juan Gonzalez	17
Ken Griffey Jr	8

1% chance for 756 HR

Player	%
Juan Gonzalez	11
Ken Griffey Jr	3

1% chance for 800 HR

Player	%
Juan Gonzalez	7

ATLANTA BRAVES: HAVE THEY STARTED A PITCHING REVOLUTION? (p. 38)

Both Leagues — Listed Alphabetically
(1993 Active Pitchers with 100+ starts since 1989)

# of Games Started with 130+ Pitches									# of Games Started with 130+ Pitches								
Pitcher	'87	'88	'89	'90	'91	'92	'93	Tot	Pitcher	'87	'88	'89	'90	'91	'92	'93	Tot
Abbott J	-	-	0	1	1	3	0	5	Jones J	0	0	0	0	0	0	0	0
Appier	-	-	0	2	1	1	3	7	Key	3	0	1	0	0	0	0	4
Armstrong	-	0	0	1	0	2	0	3	Krueger	-	0	0	0	0	0	0	0
Avery	-	-	-	0	2	1	0	3	Langston	9	9	11	5	4	3	3	44
Ballard	1	2	0	0	0	-	0	3	Leary	0	5	0	3	0	1	0	9
Bankhead	0	0	0	0	0	-	-	0	Leibrandt	8	3	1	2	0	2	0	16
Belcher	0	1	8	1	3	1	1	15	Maddux G	0	4	2	2	0	3	0	11
Benes	-	-	0	1	2	3	0	6	Magrane	3	0	1	2	-	0	0	6
Bielecki	0	0	2	2	0	0	0	4	Martinez D	1	3	1	2	4	0	1	12
Black	0	0	1	5	1	0	0	7	Martinez R	-	1	3	8	3	2	3	20
Boddicker	5	2	3	3	1	0	0	14	McCaskill	0	3	2	0	1	0	0	6
Bosio	0	2	1	1	0	0	1	5	McDonald	-	-	-	1	0	2	0	3
Brown	-	1	2	0	1	2	4	10	McDowell J	0	0	-	3	3	6	1	13
Browning	0	0	0	0	0	0	0	0	Milacki	-	0	4	0	1	0	0	5
Burkett	-	-	-	3	1	0	0	4	Moore Mike	8	1	4	1	5	3	2	24
Candelaria	0	1	0	0	-	-	-	1	Morgan	2	0	1	0	0	2	0	5
Candiotti	7	6	2	4	4	7	4	34	Morris	8	4	1	3	2	1	1	20
Clemens	10	13	12	3	7	9	4	58	Moyer	3	1	0	0	0	-	1	5
Cone	0	4	7	6	7	11	9	44	Mulholland	-	0	0	0	2	2	0	4
Cox	0	0	-	-	0	0	0	0	Navarro	-	-	0	0	3	2	0	5
Darling	1	2	0	0	1	1	2	7	Ojeda	0	1	0	0	1	2	0	4
Darwin	1	1	-	1	0	1	0	4	Perez Mld	0	0	3	2	0	4	2	11
Davis S	0	0	1	0	0	0	1	2	Portugal	0	-	0	1	0	0	0	1
DeLeon	3	2	2	0	1	0	0	8	Rasmussen	5	3	0	1	0	0	0	9
Deshaies	0	3	1	2	1	0	0	7	Rijo	2	2	0	5	0	0	5	14
Dopson	-	0	1	0	-	0	0	1	Ruffin B	0	0	1	0	1	0	1	3
Downs	0	1	0	0	0	0	0	1	Ryan N	3	3	16	6	3	2	0	33
Drabek	0	1	0	1	0	5	1	8	Saberhagen	8	2	3	2	0	0	0	15
Eckersley	0	-	-	-	-	-	-	0	Sanderson	0	-	0	2	0	1	0	3
Erickson	-	-	-	0	1	1	2	4	Smiley	-	0	0	0	0	1	0	1
Farrell	1	2	3	1	-	-	0	7	Smith B	0	0	0	0	0	0	0	0
Fernandez A	-	-	-	3	2	1	2	8	Smith P	0	1	0	0	0	0	0	1
Fernandez S	1	1	1	2	0	4	1	10	Smith Z	3	2	0	0	0	0	1	6
Finley	0	3	3	9	8	6	6	35	Smoltz	-	0	3	6	0	4	2	15
Gardner	-	-	0	1	0	1	1	3	Stewart	7	9	3	4	6	1	0	30
Glavine	0	0	0	0	2	0	2	4	Stieb	2	1	0	0	0	0	0	3
Gooden	3	2	3	1	1	0	2	12	Stottlemyre	-	0	0	0	0	0	0	0
Gross Kev	0	4	3	1	0	2	0	10	Sutcliffe	4	4	2	0	0	4	2	16
Gubicza	6	8	3	1	0	0	0	18	Swift	-	0	0	0	0	0	0	0
Gullickson	0	-	-	2	0	0	0	2	Swindell	2	3	1	1	0	0	1	8
Guzman Jose	5	2	-	-	4	0	1	12	Tanana	2	2	7	2	3	0	0	16
Hanson	-	1	0	6	4	1	5	17	Tapani	-	-	0	0	0	1	0	1
Harnisch	-	0	4	4	3	0	2	13	Tewksbury	0	0	0	0	0	0	0	0
Heaton	1	0	0	0	0	-	-	1	Valenzuela	15	4	3	4	0	-	0	26
Hershiser	4	1	5	0	0	0	1	11	Viola	3	0	3	6	3	3	2	20
Hibbard	-	-	1	0	0	0	0	1	Walk	0	0	1	0	0	0	0	1
Higuera	8	2	0	1	0	-	0	11	Wegman	2	1	0	0	0	5	1	9
Hill K	-	0	0	1	1	0	0	2	Welch	10	5	1	0	2	1	0	19
Honeycutt	0	-	-	-	-	-	-	0	Witt B	3	8	10	8	2	0	3	34
Hough	14	12	6	4	4	3	0	43	Witt M	4	4	2	1	0	-	0	11
Hurst	6	3	3	0	1	2	0	15	Young Curt	1	0	0	0	0	0	0	1
Jackson D	4	3	0	0	0	0	0	7	Young M	-	-	0	6	1	0	0	7
Johnson R	-	1	4	9	4	11	13	42									

CINCINNATI REDS: WHY DOESN'T RIJO WIN MORE? (p. 42)

Both Leagues — Listed Alphabetically
(Active Pitchers with a Minimum 800 IP as a Starter from 1989-1993)

Pitcher	GS	W-L	ERA	Sup/9	Team W-L	ND	7+	LwL	LL
Abbott J	128	46-54	3.61	4.13	55-73	28	78	48	13
Appier	119	58-33	2.74	4.48	71-48	28	71	54	11
Benes	132	53-51	3.41	3.61	61-71	28	70	55	11
Brown	128	57-45	3.70	4.78	74-54	26	88	43	10
Burkett	132	61-34	3.88	5.06	79-53	37	62	55	12
Candiotti	125	46-49	3.05	3.58	63-62	30	82	42	9
Clemens	127	68-41	2.77	4.24	78-49	18	94	52	10
Cone	132	56-48	3.17	4.03	71-61	28	94	32	6
Drabek	136	61-49	3.09	4.55	76-60	26	89	46	13
Finley	132	59-44	3.30	4.52	78-54	29	81	52	13
Glavine	136	72-37	3.17	5.02	83-53	27	80	56	6
Gooden	121	54-42	3.64	5.06	62-59	25	83	47	8
Gullickson	129	57-45	4.29	5.38	72-57	27	58	54	9
Hanson	120	44-45	3.75	4.49	53-67	31	71	46	14
Harnisch	131	48-39	3.40	4.64	69-62	44	61	51	19
Johnson R	131	58-43	3.64	4.87	71-60	30	76	50	13
Key	127	60-38	3.39	5.38	77-50	29	61	60	13
Langston	134	58-50	3.54	4.05	69-65	26	94	53	12
Maddux G	143	70-47	2.82	4.16	80-63	26	100	48	10
Martinez D	129	55-42	2.91	4.09	71-58	32	84	45	14
Martinez R	123	55-42	3.35	4.44	68-55	26	70	35	6
McDowell J	136	73-39	3.42	5.41	82-54	24	94	55	12
Moore Mike	138	60-44	4.23	4.98	75-63	34	59	63	14
Morgan	132	51-48	3.25	3.81	67-65	33	76	38	10
Morris	132	61-48	4.37	5.33	72-60	23	81	48	10
Mulholland	120	50-43	3.57	4.62	60-60	27	66	32	12
Navarro	124	51-42	4.27	5.04	65-59	31	68	48	17
Rijo	128	58-33	2.56	4.58	72-56	37	78	54	11
Smoltz	140	58-47	3.52	4.79	72-68	35	83	53	16
Stewart	128	57-40	3.87	5.37	78-50	31	73	58	13
Swindell	127	45-46	3.68	4.30	60-67	36	65	45	13
Tapani	131	56-43	3.84	5.13	68-63	32	70	55	14
Viola	134	57-47	3.30	4.20	70-64	30	77	58	14

Sup/9 = Pitcher Run Support per 9 IP

Team W-L = Team's record when this pitcher started

ND = # of "No Decisions" (neither Win nor Loss) for this pitcher

7+ = # of times this pitcher pitched 7 innings or more

LwL = # of times this pitcher left the game with the lead

LL = # of times this pitcher left the game with the lead and did not get a win.

HOUSTON ASTROS: HOW IMPORTANT IS MANAGERIAL EXPERIENCE? (p. 48)

Inexperienced Managers who won pennants in their 1st year with a new club

Manager	Year	Team	W-L	Year Before W-L	Fin
Dyer, Eddie	1946	StL	98-58	95-59	2
Houk, Ralph	1961	NYA	109-53	97-57	1
Berra, Yogi	1964	NYA	99-63	104-57	1
Williams, Dick	1967	Bos	92-70	72-90	9
Martin, Billy	1969	Min	97-65	79-83	7
Anderson, Sparky	1970	Cin	102-60	89-73	3
Virdon, Bill	1972	Pit	96-59	97-65	1
Lasorda, Tom	1977	LA	98-64	92-70	2
Frey, Jim	1980	KC	97-65	85-77	2
Howser, Dick	1980	NYA	103-59	89-71	4
Lanier, Hal	1986	Hou	96-66	83-79	3
Kelly, Tom	1987	Min	85-77	71-91	6
All Inexperienced Mgr			7872-8043 (.495)	7960-8694 (.478)	

Experienced Managers who won pennants in their 1st year with a new club

Manager	Year	Team	W-L	Year Before W-L	Fin
Harris, Bucky	1947	NYA	97-57	87-67	3
Shotton, Burt	1947	Bkn	92-60	96-60	2
Stengel, Casey	1949	NYA	97-57	94-60	3
Bauer, Hank	1966	Bal	97-65	94-68	3
Rigney, Bill	1970	Min	98-64	97-65	1
Williams, Dick	1971	Oak	101-60	89-73	2
Dark, Alvin	1974	Oak	90-72	94-68	1
McNamara, John	1979	Cin	90-71	92-69	2
Torre, Joe	1982	Atl	89-73	50-56	5
Altobelli, Joe	1983	Bal	98-64	94-68	2
Frey, Jim	1984	ChN	96-65	71-91	5
Piniella, Lou	1990	Cin	91-71	75-87	5
All Experienced Mgrs			7176-7316 (.495)	7040-7732 (.477)	

LOS ANGELES DODGERS: CAN AN OLDER MANAGER RELATE? (p. 50)

All Seasons since 1946 — Listed Alphabetically
(Minimum 60 years old and 1/2 games of season managed)

Manager	Year	Tm	Age	W-L	Fin	Manager	Year	Tm	Age	W-L	Fin
Alston, Walter	1972	LA	60	85-70	3		1936	PhA	73	53-100	8
	1973	LA	61	95-66	2		1937	PhA	74	39-80	7
	1974	LA	62	92-60	1		1938	PhA	75	53-99	8
	1975	LA	63	88-74	2		1940	PhA	77	54-100	8
	1976	LA	64	90-68	2		1941	PhA	78	64-90	8
Bamberger, G.	1986	Mil	60	71-81	6		1942	PhA	79	55-99	8
Corriden, Red	1950	ChA	62	52-72	6		1943	PhA	80	49-105	8
Craig, Roger	1990	SF	60	85-77	3		1944	PhA	81	72-82	5
	1991	SF	61	75-87	4		1945	PhA	82	52-98	8
	1992	SF	62	72-90	5		1946	PhA	83	49-105	8
Dressen, Chuck	1960	Mil	61	88-66	2		1947	PhA	84	78-76	5
	1961	Mil	62	71-58	3		1948	PhA	85	84-70	4
	1963	Det	63	55-47	5		1949	PhA	86	81-73	5
	1964	Det	64	85-77	4		1950	PhA	87	52-102	8
	1965	Det	65	65-55	4	Mattick, Bobby	1980	Tor	64	67-95	7
Durocher, Leo	1966	ChN	60	59-103	10		1981	Tor	65	37-69	7
	1967	ChN	61	87-74	3	Mauch, Gene	1986	Cal	60	92-70	1
	1968	ChN	62	84-78	3		1987	Cal	61	75-87	6
	1969	ChN	63	92-70	2	McCarthy, Joe	1948	Bos	61	96-59	2
	1970	ChN	64	84-78	2		1949	Bos	62	96-58	2
	1971	ChN	65	83-79	3	Meyer, Bill	1962	Pit	60	42-112	8
	1972	ChN	66	46-44	4	Morgan, Joe	1991	Bos	60	84-78	2
	1972	Hou	66	16-15	2	O'Neill, Steve	1952	PhN	60	59-32	4
	1973	Hou	67	82-80	4		1953	PhN	61	83-71	3
Dykes, Jimmy	1959	Det	62	74-63	4		1954	PhN	62	40-37	3
	1960	Det	63	44-52	6	Onslow, Jack	1949	ChA	60	63-91	6
	1961	Cle	64	77-83	5	Owens, Paul	1984	PhN	60	81-81	4
Franks, Herman	1977	ChN	63	81-81	4	Richards, Paul	1976	ChA	67	64-97	6
	1978	ChN	64	79-83	3	Robinson, Wilb't	1923	Bkn	60	76-78	6
	1979	ChN	65	78-77	5		1924	Bkn	61	92-62	2
Garcia, Dave	1981	Cle	60	52-51	6		1925	Bkn	62	68-85	6
	1982	Cle	61	78-84	6		1926	Bkn	63	71-82	6
Gleason, Kid	1923	ChA	60	69-85	7		1927	Bkn	64	65-88	6
Haney, Fred	1958	Mil	60	92-62	1		1928	Bkn	65	77-76	6
	1959	Mil	61	86-70	2		1929	Bkn	66	70-83	6
Houk, Ralph	1981	Bos	61	59-49	5		1930	Bkn	67	86-68	4
	1982	Bos	62	89-73	3		1931	Bkn	68	79-73	4
	1983	Bos	63	78-84	6	Sheehan, Tom	1960	SF	66	46-50	5
	1984	Bos	64	86-76	4	Shotton, Burt	1947	Bkn	62	92-60	1
Lasorda, Tom	1988	LA	60	94-67	1		1948	Bkn	63	48-33	3
	1989	LA	61	77-83	4		1949	Bkn	64	97-57	1
	1990	LA	62	86-76	2		1950	Bkn	65	89-65	2
	1991	LA	63	93-69	2	Stengel, Casey	1951	NYA	60	98-56	1
	1992	LA	64	63-99	6		1952	NYA	61	95-59	1
	1993	LA	65	81-81	4		1953	NYA	62	99-52	1
Lobert, Hans	1942	PhN	60	42-109	8		1954	NYA	63	103-51	2
Mack, Connie	1923	PhA	60	69-83	6		1955	NYA	64	96-58	1
	1924	PhA	61	71-81	5		1956	NYA	65	97-57	1
	1925	PhA	62	88-64	2		1957	NYA	66	98-56	1
	1926	PhA	63	83-67	3		1958	NYA	67	92-62	1
	1927	PhA	64	91-63	2		1959	NYA	68	79-75	3
	1928	PhA	65	98-55	2		1960	NYA	69	97-57	1
	1929	PhA	66	104-46	1		1962	NYN	70	40-120	10
	1930	PhA	67	102-52	1		1963	NYN	71	51-111	10
	1931	PhA	68	107-45	1		1964	NYN	72	53-109	10
	1932	PhA	69	94-60	2		1965	NYN	73	31-64	10
	1933	PhA	70	79-72	3						
	1934	PhA	71	68-82	5						
	1935	PhA	72	58-91	8						

SAN FRANCISCO GIANTS: HOW GOOD IS BARRY BONDS? (p. 65)

Secondary Average .540+			Offensive Winning Pct .877+			172+ Runs Created		
Player	Year	SA	Player	Year	OW%	Player	Year	RC
RUTH, Babe	1920	.825	WILLIAMS, Ted	1941	.942	RUTH, Babe	1921	238.1
RUTH, Babe	1921	.767	WILLIAMS, Ted	1957	.939	RUTH, Babe	1923	223.4
RUTH, Babe	1923	.730	RUTH, Babe	1920	.935	DUFFY, Hugh	1894	217.2
RUTH, Babe	1927	.685	MANTLE, Mickey	1957	.930	RUTH, Babe	1920	211.1
RUTH, Babe	1926	.679	WILLIAMS, Ted	1946	.928	GEHRIG, Lou	1927	207.9
BONDS, Barry	**1992**	**.664**	RUTH, Babe	1923	.927	FOXX, Jimmie	1932	207.1
RUTH, Babe	1930	.654	RUTH, Babe	1921	.922	HAMILTON, Billy	1894	206.9
WILLIAMS, Ted	1941	.651	WILLIAMS, Ted	1947	.920	COBB, Ty	1911	206.9
RUTH, Babe	1924	.647	WILLIAMS, Ted	1942	.918	RUTH, Babe	1924	205.0
RUTH, Babe	1928	.646	COBB, Ty	1910	.916	RUTH, Babe	1927	203.7
MANTLE, Mickey	1957	.641	RUTH, Babe	1926	.914	WILLIAMS, Ted	1941	202.2
MANTLE, Mickey	1961	.638	COBB, Ty	1911	.913	HORNSBY, Rogers	1922	200.4
CLARK, Jack	1987	.637	HORNSBY, Rogers	1924	.911	GEHRIG, Lou	1936	199.4
BONDS, Barry	**1993**	**.629**	COBB, Ty	1917	.906	RUTH, Babe	1926	196.2
WILLIAMS, Ted	1946	.628	RUTH, Babe	1924	.905	GEHRIG, Lou	1930	195.3
WILLIAMS, Ted	1957	.626	COBB, Ty	1909	.905	GEHRIG, Lou	1934	194.6
MORGAN, Joe	1976	.625	MANTLE, Mickey	1956	.904	O'NEILL, Tip	1887	194.2
RUTH, Babe	1932	.608	HORNSBY, Rogers	1925	.900	WILLIAMS, Ted	1949	192.9
DAVIS, Eric	1986	.602	COBB, Ty	1912	.900	RUTH, Babe	1931	192.0
McCOVEY, Willie	1970	.600	COBB, Ty	1915	.899	RUTH, Babe	1930	191.3
WILLIAMS, Ted	1947	.598	RUTH, Babe	1927	.898	BROWNING, Pete	1887	191.2
GEHRIG, Lou	1927	.596	COBB, Ty	1913	.898	MUSIAL, Stan	1948	191.0
WILLIAMS, Ted	1949	.595	WILLIAMS, Ted	1948	.898	WILSON, Hack	1930	189.0
GREENBERG, Hank	1938	.595	WAGNER, Honus	1908	.897	FOXX, Jimmie	1938	188.9
FOXX, Jimmie	1932	.588	**BONDS, Barry**	**1992**	**.896**	WILLIAMS, Ted	1946	188.1
RUTH, Babe	1919	.586	VAUGHAN, Arky	1935	.895	MANTLE, Mickey	1956	187.6
WYNN, Jimmy	1969	.584	MUSIAL, Stan	1948	.895	HORNSBY, Rogers	1925	187.1
KILLEB'W, Harmon	1969	.584	WAGNER, Honus	1907	.893	WILLIAMS, Ted	1947	186.3
HENDERS'N, Rickey	1990	.583	KAUFF, Benny	1914	.893	HORNSBY, Rogers	1924	186.3
McCOVEY, Willie	1969	.582	CASH, Norm	1961	.893	KLEIN, Chuck	1930	185.7
DAVIS, Eric	1987	.582	MANTLE, Mickey	1961	.892	GEHRIG, Lou	1931	185.1
MANTLE, Mickey	1956	.582	RUTH, Babe	1931	.891	WILLIAMS, Ted	1942	185.0
MORGAN, Joe	1975	.580	McCOVEY, Willie	1969	.890	FOXX, Jimmie	1933	183.9
KINER, Ralph	1951	.580	COBB, Ty	1916	.890	HORNSBY, Rogers	1929	183.0
RUTH, Babe	1931	.577	GEHRIG, Lou	1927	.890	HERMAN, Babe	1930	182.5
FOXX, Jimmie	1938	.575	KLEIN, Chuck	1933	.889	KELLEY, Joe	1894	182.3
WILLIAMS, Ted	1942	.575	MORGAN, Joe	1976	.889	RUTH, Babe	1928	181.8
HENDERS'N, Rickey	1982	.575	LAJOIE, Nap	1904	.889	GEHRIG, Lou	1937	180.9
KINER, Ralph	1949	.572	SPEAKER, Tris	1916	.889	O'DOUL, Lefty	1929	180.1
GEHRIG, Lou	1936	.572	JACKSON, Joe	1911	.888	LAJOIE, Nap	1901	178.2
MATHEWS, Eddie	1954	.571	WILLIAMS, Ted	1949	.888	MANTLE, Mickey	1957	178.1
MANTLE, Mickey	1958	.570	KAUFF, Benny	1915	.888	HAMILTON, Billy	1895	178.1
RUTH, Babe	1922	.569	COBB, Ty	1918	.886	KELLEY, Joe	1896	177.9
JACKSON, Reggie	1969	.565	YASTR'MSKI, Carl	1967	.885	CASH, Norm	1961	177.7
CASH, Norm	1961	.553	SPEAKER, Tris	1912	.884	GREENB'G, Hank	1937	177.6
WILSON, Hack	1930	.552	MUSIAL, Stan	1946	.884	DELAHANTY, Ed	1895	175.7
SCHMIDT, Mike	1979	.549	RUTH, Babe	1919	.882	SISLER, George	1920	175.6
STRAWB'RY, Darryl	1987	.549	FOXX, Jimmie	1932	.881	KEELER, Willie	1897	175.6
MORGAN, Joe	1974	.549	ALLEN, Dick	1972	.881	DELAHANTY, Ed	1899	175.4
GEHRIG, Lou	1934	.547	BRETT, George	1980	.881	KAUFF, Benny	1914	175.2
FOXX, Jimmie	1934	.545	AARON, Hank	1971	.880	SPEAKER, Tris	1912	175.0
KINER, Ralph	1950	.545	LAJOIE, Nap	1901	.880	JACKSON, Joe	1911	174.6
HENDERS'N, Rickey	1993	.545	MORGAN, Joe	1975	.878	MANTLE, Mickey	1961	173.9
BONDS, Barry	**1990**	**.543**	**BONDS, Barry**	**1993**	**.877**	COBB, Ty	1912	173.6
GENTILE, Jim	1961	.543	JACKSON, Joe	1913	.877	MUSIAL, Stan	1949	173.0
STOVEY, Harry	1890	.543	WAGNER, Honus	1904	.877	DiMAGGIO, Joe	1937	172.8
						BONDS, Barry	**1993**	**172.2**

WHO DO YOU WANT BEHIND THE PLATE WHEN YOU'VE GOT A PLANE TO CATCH? (p. 70)

Separated by League — Listed Alphabetically
1989-93 Nine-Inning Games at Home Plate
(Minimum 100 Games)

American League			National League		
Umpire	G	Avg. Time	Umpire	G	Avg. Time
Barnett, Larry	147	2:50:33	Bonin, Greg	154	2:42:12
Brinkman, Joe	172	2:50:49	Crawford, Jerry	167	2:47:26
Clark, Al	160	2:49:14	Darling, Gary	162	2:44:44
Coble, Drew	147	2:50:33	Davidson, Bob	166	2:43:11
Cooney, Terry	111	2:50:23	Davis, Gerry	161	2:46:26
Cousins, Derryl	155	2:54:23	DeMuth, Dana	159	2:47:56
Denkinger, Don	151	2:49:51	Froemming, Bruce	159	2:45:54
Evans, Jim	162	2:53:25	Gregg, Eric	118	2:44:37
Ford, Dale	170	2:50:00	Hallion, Tom	131	2:45:50
Garcia, Rich	163	2:49:57	Harvey, Doug	121	2:43:16
Hendry, Ted	153	2:50:39	Hirschbeck, Mark	119	2:42:08
Hirschbeck, John	145	2:49:47	Hohn, Bill	140	2:46:12
Johnson, Mark	148	2:51:06	Layne, Jerry	136	2:45:07
Joyce, Jim	135	2:51:47	Marsh, Randy	166	2:46:07
Kaiser, Ken	139	2:48:57	McSherry, John	141	2:44:00
Kosc, Greg	163	2:50:46	Montague, Ed	141	2:43:14
McClelland, Tim	158	2:51:14	Pulli, Frank	156	2:40:28
McCoy, Larry	155	2:48:44	Quick, Jim	147	2:43:37
McKean, Jim	152	2:50:46	Rapuano, Ed	106	2:44:30
Meriwether, Chuck	109	2:55:06	Reliford, Charlie	105	2:47:40
Merrill, Durwood	166	2:50:04	Rennert, Dutch	107	2:46:38
Morrison, Dan	159	2:54:30	Rippley, Steve	164	2:42:38
Phillips, Dave	157	2:54:03	Runge, Paul	132	2:44:25
Reed, Rick	158	2:54:50	Tata, Terry	163	2:42:50
Reilly, Mike	158	2:49:40	Wendelstedt, Harry	146	2:44:50
Roe, Rocky	163	2:54:56	West, Joe	155	2:41:49
Scott, Dale	138	2:49:18	Williams, Charlie	155	2:43:25
Shulock, John	158	2:52:01	Winters, Mike	128	2:45:41
Tschida, Tim	141	2:51:47	**NL Average**		**2:44:23**
Voltaggio, Vic	134	2:52:27			
Welke, Tim	159	2:48:03			
Young, Larry	150	2:53:14			
AL Average		**2:51:22**			

IF YOU HIT .450 FOR A MONTH, CAN YOU HIT .450 FOR A YEAR? (p. 72)

The Top Batting and Pitching Months of 1993

Batting (75 or more Plate Appearances)

Player	Month	AVG	SLG	OBP	AB	R	H	2B	3B	HR	RBI	SB	BB
Olerud, Tor	April	.450	.650	.527	80	15	36	7	0	3	18	0	13
Gwynn T, SD	August	.448	.600	.487	105	23	47	10	0	2	14	2	10
Jefferies, StL	June	.444	.685	.465	108	18	48	10	2	4	16	10	5
Bonds, SF	April	.431	.889	.553	72	23	31	8	2	7	25	5	21
Olerud, Tor	June	.427	.760	.525	96	17	41	17	0	5	30	0	22
Palmeiro, Tex	July	.426	.852	.484	108	28	46	13	0	11	34	4	14
Mitchell, Cin	June	.421	.737	.457	76	17	32	7	1	5	16	0	5
Galarraga, Col	June	.420	.720	.458	100	20	42	8	2	6	21	0	6
Wilkins, ChN	June	.414	.793	.485	87	19	36	7	1	8	20	0	11
Galarraga, Col	April	.412	.647	.435	85	11	35	8	0	4	25	1	5
Bagwell, Hou	May	.412	.676	.467	102	22	42	6	0	7	25	2	14
McGriff F, Atl	July	.412	.863	.430	80	22	33	7	1	9	22	0	4
Vaughn M, Bos	April	.412	.735	.474	68	12	28	10	0	4	16	2	9
Gibson, Det	April	.407	.661	.520	59	14	24	6	0	3	15	3	14
Trammell, Det	August	.405	.631	.457	84	18	34	6	2	3	18	1	9
Alomar Jr, Cle	August	.405	.619	.409	84	13	34	4	1	4	24	1	0
Segui, Bal	June	.403	.558	.444	77	8	31	6	0	2	16	0	9
Thompson R, SF	June	.398	.612	.443	98	22	39	6	0	5	15	4	8
Sanchez, ChN	June	.395	.500	.419	86	9	34	5	2	0	10	0	4
Thompson R, SF	August	.394	.727	.464	99	23	39	7	1	8	18	0	11
Whitaker, Det	June	.394	.690	.506	71	18	28	9	0	4	13	0	17
DeShields, Mon	July	.393	.479	.432	117	16	46	4	3	0	10	11	8
Mack, Min	July	.392	.578	.447	102	18	40	10	0	3	14	5	11
Baines, Bal	July	.392	.689	.448	74	12	29	4	0	6	22	0	10
Velarde, NYA	Sep-Oct	.390	.597	.402	77	9	30	6	2	2	11	0	2
Olerud, Tor	July	.389	.700	.491	90	17	35	10	0	6	19	0	18
Greenwell, Bos	Sep-Oct	.387	.595	.443	111	19	43	7	2	4	13	3	11
Bell Jay, Pit	August	.386	.526	.453	114	23	44	8	1	2	13	2	13
Kruk, Phi	May	.385	.462	.517	91	26	35	7	0	0	16	2	27
Henderson R, Tor	July	.385	.736	.477	91	27	35	8	0	8	15	5	18

Pitching (25 or more Innings Pitched)

Pitcher	Month	ERA	W	L	S	IP	H	R	ER	BB	K
Fassero, Mon	July	0.72	1	0	0	25.0	20	3	2	8	27
Key, NYA	April	0.93	3	0	0	38.2	22	4	4	5	24
Appier, KC	Sep-Oct	1.02	4	2	0	44.0	25	6	5	17	36
Alvarez, ChA	Sep-Oct	1.03	5	0	0	43.2	23	5	5	20	32
Hernandez J, Cle	June	1.08	1	1	4	25.0	13	3	3	5	12
Brown, Tex	April	1.14	2	1	0	31.2	28	9	4	7	23
Kile, Hou	June	1.16	5	0	0	31.0	26	4	4	11	23
Harnisch, Hou	Sep-Oct	1.16	4	1	0	38.2	23	5	5	13	32
Astacio, LA	Sep-Oct	1.33	4	2	0	47.1	30	9	7	12	41
Darwin, Bos	May	1.33	5	0	0	40.2	24	7	6	6	26
Jackson D, Phi	August	1.35	2	1	0	26.2	25	7	4	7	16
Black, SF	June	1.36	4	0	0	33.0	28	6	5	12	20
Maddux G, Atl	Sep-Oct	1.39	4	1	0	45.1	36	9	7	11	39
Greene, Phi	May	1.45	5	0	0	43.1	27	8	7	8	35
Candiotti, LA	August	1.46	2	0	0	37.0	33	8	6	7	26
Wells, Det	April	1.47	4	0	0	30.2	20	6	5	5	16
Viola, Bos	April	1.47	4	1	0	36.2	31	7	6	7	15
Candiotti, LA	July	1.49	3	0	0	42.1	26	8	7	13	29
Rijo, Cin	August	1.50	3	2	0	42.0	37	8	7	13	40
Leiter M, Det	May	1.88	3	0	0	38.1	33	10	8	15	24

WILL THINGS BE BACK TO NORMAL IN "EXPANSION YEAR PLUS ONE"? (p. 77)

The table below shows each expansion league (denoted by an *) and the number of players reaching certain levels of Batting Average, Home Runs, Runs Batted In, Wins, and Pitcher Strikeouts in that season, and in the seasons surrounding the expansion season.

Both the American League and National League numbers are shown in any year in which either league expanded.

Year	Lg	.300+ Avg	HR 20-29	30-39	40+	RBI 80-89	90-99	100-109	110+	WINS 15-17	18-19	20+	SO 200+
1960	AL	6	8	4	1	6	4	3	1	4	2	0	1
1961	AL*	11	16	0	6	9	4	1	6	8	1	2	2
1962	AL	11	13	6	1	8	6	5	3	4	2	4	1
1960	NL	5	8	3	2	3	4	1	3	5	4	3	1
1961	NL	13	12	5	2	8	4	1	5	3	4	2	2
1962	NL*	17	18	5	2	7	5	4	6	7	5	4	4
1961	AL*	11	16	0	6	9	4	1	6	8	1	2	2
1962	AL	11	13	6	1	8	6	5	3	4	2	4	1
1963	AL	4	19	2	2	8	4	1	1	6	1	5	1
1961	NL	13	12	5	2	8	4	1	5	3	4	2	2
1962	NL*	17	18	5	2	7	5	4	6	7	5	4	4
1963	NL	12	12	2	2	5	4	4	2	6	3	5	5
1968	AL	1	9	2	1	3	1	2	0	8	1	4	5
1969	AL*	7	14	5	5	7	5	2	6	6	2	6	3
1970	AL	15	18	4	3	7	4	3	4	7	1	7	3
1968	NL	5	7	4	0	5	4	1	0	5	4	3	7
1969	NL*	15	14	5	2	8	8	2	4	9	2	9	12
1970	NL	24	17	9	3	12	7	4	9	6	4	4	6
1976	AL	11	9	1	0	8	8	3	0	12	4	3	4
1977	AL*	23	24	9	0	10	8	8	6	11	3	3	3
1978	AL	7	17	6	1	12	10	1	3	9	5	6	2
1976	NL	21	9	3	0	8	4	2	2	9	1	5	3
1977	NL	17	12	8	2	9	5	3	6	4	2	6	3
1978	NL	12	18	2	1	4	5	1	3	7	4	2	3
1992	AL	9	17	5	2	9	2	6	6	12	2	3	3
1993	AL	25	22	9	3	6	8	6	9	7	5	1	1
1992	NL	18	10	3	0	6	5	5	0	9	0	2	2
1993	NL*	28	17	8	2	14	8	5	5	9	2	4	2

DO THROWS TO FIRST THROW OFF THE HITTER? (p. 80)

The chart below shows a player's Batting Average based on the number of pickoff throws made.

Both Leagues — Listed Alphabetically
(Minimum 115 PA in 1993 with a man on first)

Batter, Team	All	0	1	2+	Batter, Team	All	0	1	2+
Alomar, Tor	.297	.328	.129	.435	Lemke, Atl	.278	.284	.250	.250
Anthony, Hou	.298	.304	.259	.333	Magadan, Sea	.264	.246	.148	.455
Baerga, Cle	.327	.337	.355	.278	Mattingly, NYA	.342	.358	.235	.333
Bagwell, Hou	.380	.319	.429	.469	May, ChN	.341	.365	.286	.222
Bell D, SD	.333	.346	.385	.000	McGriff F, Atl	.314	.292	.387	.308
Bell Jay, Pit	.339	.407	.304	.256	McLemore, Bal	.259	.176	.400	.278
Belle, Cle	.325	.345	.267	.286	Merced, Pit	.331	.329	.250	.467
Bichette, Col	.351	.418	.250	.250	Molitor, Tor	.263	.280	.200	.267
Blauser, Atl	.402	.364	.531	.353	Murray, NYN	.277	.278	.258	.300
Boggs, NYA	.398	.397	.421	.381	O'Neill, NYA	.297	.318	.077	.400
Bonds, SF	.431	.431	.462	.000	Offerman, LA	.231	.180	.250	.306
Bonilla, NYN	.282	.316	.154	.111	Olerud, Tor	.385	.424	.333	.214
Bordick, Oak	.226	.176	.310	.333	Palmeiro, Tex	.331	.326	.333	.353
Brett, KC	.292	.333	.194	.269	Palmer, Tex	.347	.360	.300	.333
Buhner, Sea	.266	.323	.273	.000	Pendleton, Atl	.302	.330	.231	.313
Burks, ChA	.261	.232	.400	.500	Piazza, LA	.324	.343	.348	.200
Caminiti, Hou	.227	.197	.226	.308	Puckett, Min	.299	.367	.200	.143
Carter, Tor	.220	.227	.269	.167	Reimer, Mil	.270	.278	.227	.294
Cedeno A, Hou	.235	.261	.294	.000	Reynolds, Bal	.223	.213	.222	.286
Clark W, SF	.358	.397	.217	.385	Ripken C, Bal	.357	.369	.433	.190
Conine, Fla	.322	.284	.407	.500	Rodriguez I, Tex	.259	.324	.174	.071
Cooper, Bos	.293	.291	.261	.357	Sabo, Cin	.291	.322	.258	.188
Cora, ChA	.311	.323	.250	.344	Salmon, Cal	.336	.355	.320	.313
Curtis, Cal	.261	.276	.136	.323	Sandberg, ChN	.289	.306	.095	.393
Daulton, Phi	.286	.295	.364	.100	Sanders R, Cin	.225	.190	.350	.250
Davis C, Cal	.286	.301	.235	.214	Segui, Bal	.274	.295	.250	.000
Davis E, Det	.269	.261	.375	.211	Sheffield, Fla	.289	.237	.500	.333
Dawson, Bos	.256	.226	.412	.286	Sierra, Oak	.273	.281	.304	.158
Deer, Bos	.284	.284	.421	.125	Smith O, StL	.297	.338	.226	.281
Destrade, Fla	.234	.248	.273	.067	Snyder, LA	.306	.337	.227	.167
Devereaux, Bal	.236	.267	.222	.174	Sorrento, Cle	.265	.286	.214	.267
Fernandez, Tor	.320	.315	.333	.333	Sosa, ChN	.288	.313	.174	.308
Fielder, Det	.237	.259	.231	.000	Sprague, Tor	.246	.273	.125	.214
Finley, Hou	.286	.269	.222	.400	Strange, Tex	.231	.272	.056	.222
Fryman, Det	.312	.388	.108	.294	Surhoff, Mil	.250	.240	.304	.222
Gagne, KC	.252	.205	.333	.350	Tartabull, NYA	.252	.250	.273	.250
Gant, Atl	.324	.349	.278	.300	Tettleton, Det	.276	.283	.154	.364
Gates, Oak	.305	.338	.300	.226	Thomas, ChA	.330	.338	.280	.375
Gonzalez J, Tex	.346	.369	.267	.250	Valle, Sea	.240	.247	.182	.250
Gonzalez L, Hou	.280	.271	.310	.263	Vaughn G, Mil	.304	.326	.300	.227
Grace, ChN	.327	.323	.314	.353	Vaughn M, Bos	.287	.295	.357	.000
Greenwell, Bos	.336	.250	.531	.500	Ventura, ChA	.296	.300	.267	.300
Griffey Jr, Sea	.371	.414	.316	.222	Vizcaino, ChN	.350	.329	.412	.375
Grissom, Mon	.263	.221	.261	.370	Vizquel, Sea	.281	.286	.286	.250
Gwynn T, SD	.403	.370	.455	.462	Walker L, Mon	.300	.255	.417	.290
Hayes, Col	.315	.300	.344	.400	Weiss, Fla	.311	.333	.333	.222
Hollins, Phi	.293	.330	.160	.200	Whitaker, Det	.306	.286	.385	.263
Jefferies, StL	.309	.400	.200	.278	White Dev, Tor	.257	.234	.250	.350
Johnson L, ChA	.331	.330	.375	.286	Whiten, StL	.296	.313	.324	.176
Joyner, KC	.323	.289	.308	.600	Williams B, NYA	.322	.321	.350	.273
Justice, Atl	.323	.337	.300	.250	Williams M, SF	.265	.279	.167	.286
Karros, LA	.206	.161	.343	.143	Yount, Mil	.248	.258	.308	.077
Kent, NYN	.291	.265	.238	.429	Zeile, StL	.298	.353	.267	.242
King, Pit	.286	.277	.349	.208	**MLB Avg**	**.284**	**.287**	**.279**	**.274**
Knoblauch, Min	.286	.224	.414	.313					
Kruk, Phi	.414	.424	.429	.364					

WHO'S ON TRACK FOR THE HALL OF FAME? (p. 82)

Both Leagues — Listed Alphabetically
(Minimum 7.5 Hall of Fame Points)

Player	HP	Player	HP	Player	HP	Player	HP
Nolan Ryan	189.5	Will Clark	41.5	Matt Williams	22.0	Tony Phillips	12.5
Wade Boggs	189.0	Bobby Thigpen	41.0	Edgar Martinez	21.5	Bip Roberts	12.5
George Brett	182.0	Brett Butler	40.0	Vince Coleman	21.0	Chris Sabo	12.5
Roger Clemens	140.0	John Candelaria	38.0	Mark Davis	21.0	Glenn Davis	12.0
Tony Gwynn	129.5	Fred McGriff	38.0	Teddy Higuera	21.0	Greg Gagne	12.0
Dave Winfield	123.0	Howard Johnson	37.0	Randy Johnson	21.0	Joe Magrane	12.0
Robin Yount	123.0	Rafael Palmeiro	36.5	Barry Larkin	21.0	Mike Mussina	12.0
Kirby Puckett	117.5	Jesse Orosco	36.0	Dan Plesac	21.0	Mickey Tettleton	12.0
Dennis Eckersley	116.0	Terry Pendleton	36.0	Juan Guzman	20.0	Mariano Duncan	11.5
Don Mattingly	115.5	Mark McGwire	35.5	Juan Samuel	20.0	Kevin Appier	11.0
Goose Gossage	114.0	Rick Aguilera	35.0	Tim Belcher	19.5	Rod Beck	11.0
Ryne Sandberg	113.5	Ken Griffey Jr	34.5	Rob Dibble	19.0	Kevin Brown	11.0
Lee Smith	112.0	Darryl Strawberry	34.0	Mike Henneman	19.0	Jim Gott	11.0
Rickey Hend'rs'n	110.0	Bobby Bonilla	33.0	Rick Honeycutt	19.0	Greg Olson	11.0
Cal Ripken	105.0	David Cone	33.0	Jay Howell	19.0	Mike Schooler	11.0
Jack Morris	104.5	Jeff Russell	33.0	Craig Lefferts	19.0	Terry Steinbach	11.0
Dale Murphy	102.5	Doug Jones	32.0	Darren Daulton	18.5	Kevin Tapani	11.0
Andre Dawson	101.5	Randy Myers	32.0	Dave Henderson	18.5	Kenny Lofton	10.5
Jeff Reardon	100.0	Todd Worrell	32.0	Eric Davis	18.0	Terry Mulholland	10.5
Eddie Murray	98.0	Lenny Dykstra	31.5	Mike Greenwell	18.0	Rafael Belliard	10.0
Paul Molitor	95.0	Juan Gonzalez	31.5	Charlie Leibrandt	18.0	Jeff Brantley	10.0
Carlton Fisk	94.5	Roberto Alomar	31.0	Kevin Seitzer	17.5	John Burkett	10.0
Alan Trammell	83.0	Jimmy Key	31.0	Larry Andersen	17.0	Alfredo Griffin	10.0
Barry Bonds	82.0	Gregg Olson	31.0	Bill Gullickson	17.0	Marquis Grissom	10.0
Ozzie Smith	81.5	Duane Ward	31.0	Brian Harper	17.0	Chuck Knobl'ch	10.0
Dwight Gooden	78.5	Tony Fernandez	30.0	Bobby Ojeda	17.0	Bryn Smith	10.0
Lance Parrish	72.0	Kevin Mitchell	30.0	Bill Swift	17.0	Mike Piazza	9.5
Willie McGee	66.5	Julio Franco	29.5	Tim Wallach	17.0	Benito Santiago	9.5
Dave Stewart	65.0	Bruce Hurst	28.5	Mike Witt	17.0	Robby Th'mps'n	9.5
Tim Raines	64.5	John Olerud	28.5	Chuck Finley	16.5	Robin Ventura	9.5
Tony Pena	63.5	Andy Van Slyke	28.5	Kent Hrbek	16.5	Pat Hentgen	9.0
Jose Canseco	62.5	Jeff Montgomery	28.0	Wally Joyner	16.5	Steve Howe	9.0
Bob Welch	62.0	John Smoltz	28.0	John Kruk	16.5	Dave Justice	9.0
Orel Hershiser	61.5	Devon White	28.0	Albert Belle	16.0	Curt Schilling	9.0
Frank Viola	60.0	Mitch Williams	27.0	Kirk Gibson	16.0	Bob Tewksbury	9.0
Cecil Fielder	59.0	Danny Jackson	26.5	Storm Davis	16.0	Wally Backman	8.5
Tom Henke	57.0	Danny Tartabull	26.5	Sid Fernandez	16.0	Chili Davis	8.5
Joe Carter	55.5	Carlos Baerga	26.0	Gary Sheffield	15.5	Chris Bosio	8.0
Willie Wilson	55.5	Harold Baines	26.0	Mark Grace	15.0	Norm Charlton	8.0
Greg Maddux	53.5	Steve Bedrosian	26.0	John Wetteland	15.0	Jose DeLeon	8.0
John Franco	53.0	Mike Boddicker	26.0	Jay Bell	14.5	Tommy Greene	8.0
Fernando V'lnz'la	50.5	Tom Browning	26.0	Ramon Martinez	14.5	Greg Harris	8.0
Dave Righetti	50.0	Doug Drabek	26.0	Harold Reynolds	14.5	Dave Hollins	8.0
Tom Glavine	49.5	Andres G'l'rr'ga	26.0	Pat Borders	14.0	Manuel Lee	8.0
Lou Whitaker	48.5	Bryan Harvey	26.0	Ken Dayley	14.0	Mark Portugal'	8.0
Steve Sax	47.5	Ron Gant	25.5	Mark Eichhorn	14.0	Dennis R'sm'ss'n	8.0
George Bell	47.0	Mike Moore	25.5	Kelly Gruber	14.0	Jody Reed	8.0
Charlie Hough	47.0	Ron Darling	25.0	Mark Gubicza	14.0	Todd Stottlemyre	8.0
Frank Tanana	47.0	Jack McDowell	25.0	Scott Sanderson	14.0	Bob Walk	8.0
Frank Thomas	46.0	Jose Rijo	24.0	John Smiley	14.0	Hal Morris	7.5
Bret Saberhagen	44.5	Steve Avery	23.0	Mike Stanton	14.0	Mike Pagliarulo	7.5
Dennis Martinez	44.0	Roger McD'w'll	23.0	Jeff Blauser	13.5		
Mark Langston	43.0	Gary Gaetti	22.5	Scott Erickson	13.0		
Rick Sutcliffe	43.0	Lonnie Smith	22.5	Gene Nelson	13.0		
Dave Stieb	42.5	Danny Cox	22.0	Walt Weiss	13.0		
Ruben Sierra	42.0	Steve Farr	22.0	Shane Mack	12.5		

CAN A SALMON SWIM UP A FENCE? (p. 86)

Both Leagues — Listed by Game Date
1993 Home Runs "Saved" by Outfielders

Date	Park	Batter	Pitcher	Outfielder
4/11	Cal	Gonzales R	Kiely	Gladden
4/14	SF	Destrade	Rogers Kev	McGee
4/22	Bal	Anderson	McDowell J	Johnson L
4/28	Cin	King	Reardon	Hernandez Csr
4/29	SD	Geren	West	Thompson M
4/30	ChA	Bell G	Stottlemyre	White Dev
5/2	SF	Benjamin	Wetteland	Frazier
5/3	NYA	O'Neill	Welch	Henderson R
5/10	Cal	Hrbek	Patterson K	Salmon
5/11	NYA	Williams B	Navarro	Brunansky
5/15	Cal	Gagne	Lewis S	Curtis
5/20	Bal	Martinez Crls	Moyer	McLemore
5/21	Bal	Surhoff	Mussina	McLemore
5/22	Cle	Kreuter	Mesa	Kirby
5/25	NYA	Hoiles	Wickman	Humphreys
5/25	Oak	Puckett	Davis S	Blankenship
5/26	NYA	Ripken C	Perez Mld	James D
5/31	Min	Davis B	Tapani	Puckett
6/1	Fla	Berroa	Black	Lewis D
6/5	ChA	Cooper	McDowell J	Burks
6/8	Cle	Belle	Clemens	Greenwell
6/10	Bos	Valentin John	Moyer	McLemore
6/10	Mil	Vaughn G	Wickman	James D
6/11	Cal	Vizquel	Finley	Polonia
6/12	Min	Steinbach	Trombley	Puckett
6/17	Oak	Ventura	Witt B	Sierra
6/20	Det	Fielder	Bones	Yount
6/21	SF	Bonds	Brocail	Bell D
6/22	Cle	Sorrento	Eldred	Hamilton
6/25	Bos	Whitaker	Darwin	Quintana
6/26	LA	Butler B	Castillo F	Sosa
6/27	Cle	Gaetti	Young Cliff	Lofton
7/2	Cal	Salmon	Young M	Lofton
7/8	Bal	Baines	Pall	Raines
7/9	NYN	Davis E	Tanana	Coleman
7/10	NYN	Bonilla	Nichols	Snyder
7/10	Fla	Sanders D	Armstrong	Whitmore
7/18	Bal	Mack	Valenzuela	Anderson
7/20	Bos	Dawson	Hathaway	Salmon
7/21	Bos	Riles	Finley	Salmon
7/27	NYN	Sheffield	Gooden	Thompson Ryan
7/28	ChA	Raines	Young M	Lofton
7/29	Cal	Gates	Leftwich	Salmon
7/31	Cal	Van Burkleo	Tapani	Mack
8/1	Cin	Larkin B	Harris Gene	Gwynn T
8/3	Bal	Yount	Mills	Devereaux
8/3	Bal	Baines	Maldonado	Yount
8/3	SD	Plantier	Burba	Lewis D
8/4	NYA	Stanley	Stewart	White Dev
8/8	Bal	Belle	Moyer	McLemore
8/10	SD	Gonzalez L	Ashby	Bell D
8/12	ChA	Burks	Appier	McReynolds
8/12	LA	Snyder	Blair	Boston
8/14	NYA	Stanley	O'Donoghue	Anderson
8/16	Cin	Morris	Fernandez S	Orsulak
8/18	Bos	Thomas	Darwin	Dawson
8/19	Bos	Greenwell	Tavarez	Hill
8/20	SF	Benzinger	Harvey	Carr
8/21	Tor	White Dev	Fleming	Buhner
8/31	NYA	Jackson B	Hitchcock	O'Neill
9/1	NYN	Anthony	Maddux M	Thompson Ryan
9/5	Min	Ducey	Banks	Mack
9/8	Cle	Kirby	Brummett	Winfield
9/9	SF	Pappas	Deshaies	Bonds
9/11	Bal	Ripken C	Welch	Henderson D
9/16	NYA	Stanley	Ryan K	Deer
9/28	Bal	Hoiles	Hitchcock	James D
10/3	Bal	Ripken C	Hentgen	Henderson R

ARE THERE TOO MANY OLD GUYS IN THE GAME? (p. 88)

Ten-Year Intervals — Number of Players 35 Years and Older

YEAR	35+	AVG	AB	R	H	2B	3B	HR	RBI	BB	K	SB	OBP	SLG
1993	31	.273	9520	1274	2602	465	63	218	1214	901	1278	186	.336	.404
1983	47	.272	13633	1709	3703	644	75	341	1821	1494	1886	204	.344	.405
1973	24	.260	7344	877	1911	273	27	230	979	817	966	46	.335	.399
1963	26	.248	6283	667	1561	205	33	134	682	579	815	53	.313	.356
1953	31	.275	5453	695	1500	245	48	124	786	667	574	23	.358	.406
1943	31	.260	6735	707	1754	268	34	65	723	744	479	88	.337	.339
1933	23	.266	4319	504	1149	176	34	41	475	442	306	32	.339	.351
1923	22	.305	6019	948	1837	302	69	95	825	604	280	155	.374	.426
1913	17	.289	2402	328	694	111	29	15	285	251	208	86	.364	.378
1903	13	.277	4105	517	1137	198	43	15	507	254	-	134	.323	.357

YEAR	35+	ERA	W	L	S	IP	H	R	ER	BB	K	HR
1993	44	4.41	218	261	219	3942.2	4104	2132	1933	1339	2495	443
1983	31	3.90	229	261	58	4422.0	4456	2153	1917	1543	2422	379
1973	19	3.53	127	117	100	1886.1	1878	838	740	608	1095	169
1963	22	3.24	143	142	127	2525.1	2331	1022	908	578	1513	237
1953	21	3.73	148	146	105	2547.1	2663	1196	1057	814	1095	257
1943	32	3.17	247	198	43	4113.0	3930	1697	1448	1418	1624	85
1933	28	3.75	157	150	58	2814.1	3071	1405	1173	827	754	3
1923	9	3.87	91	84	18	1528.1	1748	774	657	352	438	26
1913	5	2.90	33	37	13	606.0	555	258	195	165	266	12
1903	3	2.58	45	25	2	614.1	581	262	176	132	254	6

YEAR: 1993	AGE	YEAR: 1993	AGE	YEAR: 1993	AGE
Nolan RYAN	46	Eddie MURRAY	37	Bill LANDRUM	35
Carlton FISK	45	Dale MURPHY	37	Mike BODDICKER	35
Charlie HOUGH	45	Lance PARRISH	37	Tom CANDIOTTI	35
Goose GOSSAGE	41	Rick SUTCLIFFE	37	Tim WALLACH	35
Dave WINFIELD	41	Scott SANDERSON	36	Tony FOSSAS	35
Bob McCLURE	41	Paul MOLITOR	36	Craig LEFFERTS	35
Rick HONEYCUTT	41	Hubie BROOKS	36	Alfredo GRIFFIN	35
Larry ANDERSEN	40	Charlie LEIBRANDT	36	Chico WALKER	35
George BRETT	40	Frank DiPINO	36	Lee SMITH	35
Frank TANANA	39	Gary REDUS	36	Steve BEDROSIAN	35
John CANDELARIA	39	Bob WELCH	36	Bobby OJEDA	35
Terry LEACH	39	Bob WALK	36	Tom HENKE	35
Andre DAWSON	38	Steve FARR	36	Pete O'BRIEN	35
Dennis ECKERSLEY	38	Steve BALBONI	36	Alan TRAMMELL	35
Ozzie SMITH	38	Dave STEWART	36	Juan AGOSTO	35
Ted POWER	38	Skeeter BARNES	36	Steve HOWE	35
Dennis MARTINEZ	38	Steve LAKE	36	Tim LEARY	35
Jack MORRIS	38	Jesse OROSCO	36	Bruce HURST	35
Willie WILSON	37	Lou WHITAKER	36	Bill KRUEGER	35
Bryn SMITH	37	Kirk GIBSON	36	Bill DORAN	35
Robin YOUNT	37	Tony PENA	36	Wade BOGGS	35
Jeff REARDON	37	Brett BUTLER	36	Butch DAVIS	35
Danny DARWIN	37	Doug JONES	36	Dickie THON	35
Greg HARRIS	37	Bud BLACK	36		
Jay HOWELL	37	Dan GLADDEN	35		
Lonnie SMITH	37	Dave STIEB	35		

WHAT KIND OF TEAM GOES OFF ON A STREAK? (p. 92)

American League — Streaks of 3 or more games

Team	W/L	3	4	5	6	7	8	9	10	11	12	13	Tot
Orioles	W	4	0	0	1	0	2	0	1	0	0	0	8
	L	7	2	1	0	0	1	0	0	0	0	0	11
Red Sox	W	5	2	1	0	1	0	0	1	0	0	0	10
	L	3	1	1	3	1	0	0	0	0	0	0	9
Angels	W	5	1	0	1	0	0	0	0	0	0	0	7
	L	6	2	1	2	0	0	0	1	0	0	0	12
White Sox	W	6	2	3	2	0	0	0	0	0	0	0	13
	L	4	1	0	1	0	0	0	0	0	0	0	6
Indians	W	3	3	2	0	0	1	0	0	0	0	0	9
	L	4	8	1	0	0	0	0	0	0	0	0	13
Tigers	W	5	1	2	1	1	0	0	0	0	0	0	10
	L	6	0	1	1	0	0	0	1	0	0	0	9
Royals	W	4	4	1	0	0	0	0	0	0	0	0	9
	L	5	0	1	0	0	0	0	0	0	0	0	6
Brewers	W	5	0	0	0	1	0	0	0	0	0	0	6
	L	6	3	4	0	1	0	0	0	0	0	0	14
Twins	W	3	3	1	1	0	0	0	0	0	0	0	8
	L	7	1	0	1	0	2	1	0	0	0	0	12
Yankees	W	4	6	0	1	0	0	0	0	0	0	0	11
	L	7	1	1	0	0	0	0	0	0	0	0	9
Athletics	W	3	3	0	0	1	0	0	0	0	0	0	7
	L	3	5	2	1	0	0	1	0	0	0	0	12
Mariners	W	8	2	0	1	0	0	0	0	0	0	0	11
	L	5	4	1	0	0	0	0	0	0	0	0	10
Rangers	W	5	3	0	2	0	0	0	0	0	0	0	10
	L	2	4	0	1	0	0	0	0	0	0	0	7
Blue Jays	W	2	5	2	1	2	0	1	0	0	0	0	13
	L	2	2	2	1	0	0	0	0	0	0	0	7

National League — Streaks of 3 or more games

Team	W/L	3	4	5	6	7	8	9	10	11	12	13	Tot
Braves	W	9	4	2	1	0	0	1	0	0	0	0	17
	L	4	0	1	0	0	0	0	0	0	0	0	5
Cubs	W	4	2	1	1	0	0	0	0	0	0	0	8
	L	7	1	0	0	0	0	0	0	0	0	0	8
Reds	W	5	2	0	0	1	0	0	0	0	0	0	8
	L	4	1	2	0	1	0	0	0	0	1	0	9
Astros	W	12	4	2	0	0	0	0	0	0	0	0	18
	L	6	2	3	0	0	0	0	0	0	0	0	11
Dodgers	W	6	1	0	1	0	0	0	0	1	0	0	9
	L	4	4	0	1	1	0	0	0	0	0	0	10
Expos	W	7	2	1	1	1	0	1	0	0	0	0	13
	L	3	3	0	0	0	0	0	0	0	0	0	6
Mets	W	2	0	0	1	0	0	0	0	0	0	0	3
	L	5	1	3	2	1	1	0	0	0	0	0	13
Phillies	W	12	5	1	1	0	0	0	0	0	0	0	19
	L	5	1	0	0	0	0	0	0	0	0	0	6
Pirates	W	5	4	1	0	0	0	0	0	0	0	0	10
	L	7	2	2	0	1	0	0	0	0	0	0	12
Cardinals	W	5	4	1	0	0	0	0	0	0	0	0	10
	L	6	2	0	1	0	0	0	0	0	0	0	9
Padres	W	3	1	1	0	0	0	0	0	0	0	0	5
	L	5	6	2	1	1	0	0	0	0	0	0	15
Giants	W	5	6	0	2	2	0	0	0	0	0	0	15
	L	3	1	0	0	0	1	0	0	0	0	0	5
Rockies	W	5	1	2	1	0	0	0	0	0	0	0	9
	L	5	2	4	0	1	0	0	0	0	0	1	13
Marlins	W	1	3	0	0	0	0	0	0	0	0	0	4
	L	7	5	0	1	1	0	0	0	0	0	0	14

WHAT HAPPENS WHEN A PLAYER SWITCHES LEAGUES? (p. 98)

Both Leagues — Listed Alphabetically
(Batter Minimum: 250 PA in Year-1 and Year-2)
(Pitcher Minimum: 100 IP or 40 Games in Year-1 and Year-2)

Batter	Year-1	Lg	Avg/HR/RBI	Year-2	Lg	Avg/HR/RBI
BELL, George	1990	A	.265/21/86	1991	N	.285/25/86
BELL, George	1991	N	.285/25/86	1992	A	.255/25/112
BICHETTE, Dante	1992	A	.287/5/41	1993	N	.310/21/89
BROOKS, Hubie	1991	N	.238/16/50	1992	A	.216/8/36
CARREON, Mark	1991	N	.260/4/21	1992	A	.232/10/41
DAWSON, Andre	1992	N	.277/22/90	1993	A	.273/13/67
EISENREICH, Jim	1992	A	.269/2/28	1993	N	.318/7/54
FELDER, Mike	1992	N	.286/4/23	1993	A	.211/1/20
HAYES, Charlie	1991	N	.230/12/53	1992	A	.257/18/66
HAYES, Charlie	1992	A	.257/18/66	1993	N	.305/25/98
HAYES, Von	1982	A	.250/14/82	1983	N	.265/6/32
HAYES, Von	1991	N	.225/0/21	1992	A	.225/4/29
INCAVIGLIA, Pete	1991	A	.214/11/38	1992	N	.266/11/44
JEFFERIES, Gregg	1991	N	.272/9/62	1992	A	.285/10/75
JEFFERIES, Gregg	1992	A	.285/10/75	1993	N	.342/16/83
JOSE, Felix	1992	N	.295/14/75	1993	A	.253/6/43
KELLY, Roberto	1992	A	.272/10/66	1993	N	.319/9/35
LIND, Jose	1992	N	.235/0/39	1993	A	.248/0/37
McREYNOLDS, Kevin	1991	N	.259/16/74	1992	A	.247/13/49
MILLER, Keith	1991	N	.280/4/23	1992	A	.284/4/38
MITCHELL, Kevin	1991	N	.256/27/69	1992	A	.286/9/67
MITCHELL, Kevin	1992	A	.286/9/67	1993	N	.341/19/64
O'NEILL, Paul	1992	N	.246/14/66	1993	A	.311/20/75
ORSULAK, Joe	1992	A	.289/4/39	1993	N	.284/8/35
OWEN, Spike	1988	A	.249/5/18	1989	N	.233/6/41
OWEN, Spike	1992	N	.269/7/40	1993	A	.234/2/20
PECOTA, Bill	1991	A	.286/6/45	1992	N	.227/2/26
PLANTIER, Phil	1992	A	.246/7/30	1993	N	.240/34/100
RANDOLPH, Willie	1988	A	.230/2/34	1989	N	.282/2/36
RANDOLPH, Willie	1991	A	.327/0/54	1992	N	.252/2/15
REED, Jody	1992	A	.247/3/40	1993	N	.276/2/31
SOSA, Sammy	1991	A	.203/10/33	1992	N	.260/8/25
STILLWELL, Kurt	1987	N	.258/4/33	1988	A	.251/10/53
STILLWELL, Kurt	1991	A	.265/6/51	1992	N	.227/2/24
THON, Dickie	1991	N	.252/9/44	1992	A	.247/4/37
WEISS, Walt	1992	A	.212/0/21	1993	N	.266/1/39
WHITEN, Mark	1992	A	.254/9/43	1993	N	.253/25/99

Pitcher	Year-1	Lg	W-L	ERA	Year-2	Lg	W-L	ERA
ARMSTRONG, Jack	1991	N	7-13	5.48	1992	A	6-15	4.64
ARMSTRONG, Jack	1992	A	6-15	4.64	1993	N	9-17	4.49
BOEVER, Joe	1992	N	3-6	2.51	1993	A	6-3	3.61
CANDIOTTI, Tom	1991	A	13-13	2.65	1992	N	11-15	3.00
CLARK, Mark	1992	N	3-10	4.45	1993	A	7-5	4.28
GUZMAN, Jose	1992	A	16-11	3.66	1993	N	12-10	4.34
HIBBARD, Greg	1992	A	10-7	4.40	1993	N	15-11	3.96
HOUGH, Charlie	1992	A	7-12	3.93	1993	N	9-16	4.27
LEIBRANDT, Charlie	1989	A	5-11	5.14	1990	N	9-11	3.16
LEIBRANDT, Charlie	1992	N	15-7	3.36	1993	A	9-10	4.55
SCUDDER, Scott	1991	N	6-9	4.35	1992	A	6-10	5.28
SMILEY, John	1991	N	20-8	3.08	1992	A	16-9	3.21
SMILEY, John	1992	A	16-9	3.21	1993	N	3-9	5.62
SWINDELL, Greg	1991	A	9-16	3.48	1992	N	12-8	2.70
VIOLA, Frank	1991	N	13-15	3.97	1992	A	13-12	3.44

DOES GOOD PITCHING BEAT GOOD HITTING IN THE POSTSEASON? (p. 100)

The chart below lists all pennant winners since 1901: the league (**Lg**), the **Team** (* indicates World Series winner), the Pitching Index (**Pit**), Batting Index (**Bat**), and category (**Type**): **DP** = Dominant Pitching, **SP** = Stronger Pitching, **DH** = Dominant Hitting, **SH** = Strong Hitting, - = Neutral (Note: There was no World Series in 1901, 1902, or 1904)

Pennant Winners since 1901 — Listed by Season

Year	Lg	Team	Pit	Bat	Type	Year	Lg	Team	Pit	Bat	Type
1901	AL	Chicago	123.0	111.5	SP	1926	AL	New York	104.1	115.2	SH
1901	NL	Pittsburgh	128.6	119.8	SP	1926	NL	St. Louis*	104.3	115.5	SH
1902	AL	Philadelphia	108.7	115.5	SH	1927	AL	New York*	129.0	127.9	-
1902	NL	Pittsburgh	120.8	137.8	SH	1927	NL	Pittsburgh	107.1	114.3	SH
1903	AL	Boston*	115.0	122.3	SH	1928	AL	New York*	108.1	122.1	SH
1903	NL	Pittsburgh	112.1	117.3	SH	1928	NL	St. Louis	118.0	112.1	SP
1904	AL	Boston	122.6	109.4	SP	1929	AL	Philadelphia*	123.7	119.1	-
1904	NL	New York	125.6	121.0	-	1929	NL	Chicago	113.4	117.3	-
1905	AL	Philadelphia	120.8	110.2	SP	1930	AL	Philadelphia*	108.6	114.2	SH
1905	NL	New York*	125.1	122.7	-	1930	NL	St. Louis	113.9	114.7	-
1906	AL	Chicago*	126.0	100.3	SP	1931	AL	Philadelphia	126.2	109.3	SP
1906	NL	Chicago	150.1	128.1	SP	1931	NL	St. Louis*	112.0	118.1	SH
1907	AL	Detroit	109.0	124.2	SH	1932	AL	New York*	112.5	122.9	SH
1907	NL	Chicago*	142.4	108.7	SP	1932	NL	Chicago	112.6	101.8	SP
1908	AL	Detroit	99.4	121.8	DH	1933	AL	Washington	112.1	111.3	-
1908	NL	Chicago*	109.6	119.4	SH	1933	NL	New York*	123.1	102.8	SP
1909	AL	Detroit	109.3	122.5	SH	1934	AL	Detroit	110.8	121.2	SH
1909	NL	Pittsburgh*	125.3	124.5	-	1934	NL	St. Louis*	110.3	110.9	-
1910	AL	Philadelphia*	141.0	118.3	SP	1935	AL	Detroit*	116.6	118.8	-
1910	NL	Chicago	120.7	114.5	SP	1935	NL	Chicago	123.3	116.8	SP
1911	AL	Philadelphia*	111.1	123.5	SH	1936	AL	New York*	120.8	121.2	-
1911	NL	New York	126.1	111.1	SP	1936	NL	New York	116.4	102.1	SP
1912	AL	Boston*	121.1	117.1	-	1937	AL	New York*	126.6	119.3	SP
1912	NL	New York	131.6	115.7	SP	1937	NL	New York	114.2	106.7	SP
1913	AL	Philadelphia*	91.7	132.1	DH	1938	AL	New York*	122.3	114.6	SP
1913	NL	New York	131.9	105.4	SP	1938	NL	Chicago	112.3	104.9	SP
1914	AL	Philadelphia	98.5	130.2	DH	1939	AL	New York*	139.5	122.2	SP
1914	NL	Boston*	101.6	108.7	SH	1939	NL	Cincinnati	119.7	110.8	SP
1914	FL	Indianapolis	104.8	118.2	SH	1940	AL	Detroit	109.3	115.4	SH
1915	AL	Boston*	122.7	108.9	SP	1940	NL	Cincinnati*	126.3	103.8	SP
1915	NL	Philadelphia	126.2	106.5	SP	1941	AL	New York*	117.7	112.1	SP
1915	FL	Chicago	114.8	107.5	SP	1941	NL	Brooklyn	115.7	120.4	-
1916	AL	Boston*	113.9	95.5	DP	1942	AL	New York	125.9	122.0	-
1916	NL	Brooklyn	123.4	108.9	SP	1942	NL	St. Louis*	130.1	124.0	SP
1917	AL	Chicago*	123.1	115.9	SP	1943	AL	New York*	112.7	111.1	-
1917	NL	New York	118.9	113.6	SP	1943	NL	St. Louis	131.4	110.2	SP
1918	AL	Boston*	120.1	103.2	SP	1944	AL	St. Louis	108.2	108.7	-
1918	NL	Chicago	126.7	113.5	SP	1944	NL	St. Louis*	134.8	115.4	SP
1919	AL	Chicago	105.9	115.9	SH	1945	AL	Detroit*	112.4	104.7	SP
1919	NL	Cincinnati*	130.4	113.2	SP	1945	NL	Chicago	127.5	106.5	SP
1920	AL	Cleveland*	111.1	116.8	SH	1946	AL	Boston	103.7	123.6	SH
1920	NL	Brooklyn	119.5	107.3	SP	1946	NL	St. Louis*	113.6	115.3	-
1921	AL	New York	112.8	121.3	SH	1947	AL	New York*	109.3	123.7	SH
1921	NL	New York*	106.4	119.5	SH	1947	NL	Brooklyn	106.8	109.3	-
1922	AL	New York	118.9	103.9	SP	1948	AL	Cleveland*	132.9	114.0	SP
1922	NL	New York*	118.6	109.5	SP	1948	NL	Boston	117.2	108.5	SP
1923	AL	New York*	108.9	113.6	-	1949	AL	New York*	113.6	114.4	-
1923	NL	New York	102.5	114.9	SH	1949	NL	Brooklyn	106.3	124.1	SH
1924	AL	Washington*	125.7	97.4	DP	1950	AL	New York*	110.3	116.9	SH
1924	NL	New York	106.9	122.6	SH	1950	NL	Philadelphia	118.5	98.7	DP
1925	AL	Washington	119.7	105.0	SP	1951	AL	New York*	115.7	111.9	-
1925	NL	Pittsburgh*	110.1	117.8	SH	1951	NL	New York	113.7	111.5	-

Year	Lg	Team	Pit	Bat	Type	Year	Lg	Team	Pit	Bat	Type
1952	AL	New York*	116.9	112.9	-	1977	NL	Los Angeles	121.4	107.9	SP
1952	NL	Brooklyn	105.7	119.8	SH	1978	AL	New York*	118.9	107.3	SP
1953	AL	New York*	124.8	119.0	SP	1978	AL	Kansas City	109.9	109.1	-
1953	NL	Brooklyn	104.5	129.6	SH	1978	NL	Philadelphia	107.4	109.6	-
1954	AL	Cleveland	133.9	114.2	SP	1978	NL	Los Angeles	114.5	112.6	-
1954	NL	New York*	131.6	104.0	SP	1979	AL	Baltimore	129.3	101.9	SP
1955	AL	New York	122.5	111.2	SP	1979	AL	California	97.5	114.5	DH
1955	NL	Brooklyn*	109.6	122.9	SH	1979	NL	Pittsburgh*	109.3	112.8	-
1956	AL	New York*	114.6	119.5	-	1979	NL	Cincinnati	103.9	107.7	-
1956	NL	Brooklyn	105.5	110.1	-	1980	AL	New York	112.6	112.3	-
1957	AL	New York	126.2	111.0	SP	1980	AL	Kansas City	105.1	110.8	SH
1957	NL	Milwaukee*	111.9	113.6	-	1980	NL	Philadelphia*	104.3	111.4	SH
1958	AL	New York*	117.1	117.5	-	1980	NL	Houston	116.1	96.9	DP
1958	NL	Milwaukee	123.1	99.6	DP	1981	AL	New York	126.5	96.6	DP
1959	AL	Chicago	117.4	98.3	DP	1981	AL	Milwaukee	93.7	111.0	DH
1959	NL	Los Angeles*	104.1	102.6	-	1981	AL	Oakland	111.0	103.1	SP
1960	AL	New York	110.1	109.7	-	1981	AL	Kansas City	102.9	94.6	DP
1960	NL	Pittsburgh*	107.8	111.7	-	1981	NL	Philadelphia	86.3	117.4	DH
1961	AL	New York*	116.2	112.1	-	1981	NL	Montreal	105.9	104.9	-
1961	NL	Cincinnati	106.6	101.9	-	1981	NL	Los Angeles*	116.0	104.6	SP
1962	AL	New York*	107.3	113.6	SH	1981	NL	Houston	131.3	91.6	DP
1962	NL	San Francisco	103.9	118.7	SH	1982	AL	Milwaukee	102.4	122.1	SH
1963	AL	New York	118.0	108.6	SP	1982	AL	California	106.9	112.2	SH
1963	NL	Los Angeles*	115.2	103.0	SP	1982	NL	St. Louis*	107.0	103.4	-
1964	AL	New York	114.9	109.7	SP	1982	NL	Atlanta	94.5	111.6	DH
1964	NL	St. Louis*	103.0	110.0	SH	1983	AL	Baltimore*	111.9	110.0	-
1965	AL	Minnesota	110.3	121.2	SH	1983	AL	Chicago	110.6	110.1	-
1965	NL	Los Angeles*	125.9	93.1	DP	1983	NL	Philadelphia	108.6	104.1	-
1966	AL	Baltimore*	103.5	121.2	SH	1983	NL	Los Angeles	116.9	97.8	DP
1966	NL	Los Angeles	137.6	91.4	DP	1984	AL	Detroit*	114.5	115.7	-
1967	AL	Boston	96.2	120.5	DH	1984	AL	Kansas City	102.0	94.0	DP
1967	NL	St. Louis*	110.7	112.5	-	1984	NL	Chicago	95.7	116.4	DH
1968	AL	Detroit*	109.8	120.1	SH	1984	NL	San Diego	103.2	104.2	-
1968	NL	St. Louis	120.0	104.9	SP	1985	AL	Toronto	125.5	103.5	SP
1969	AL	Baltimore	128.1	117.6	SP	1985	AL	Kansas City*	119.0	93.1	DP
1969	AL	Minnesota	111.5	119.2	SH	1985	NL	St. Louis	115.7	113.4	-
1969	NL	New York*	120.5	96.2	DP	1985	NL	Los Angeles	119.8	103.5	SP
1969	NL	Atlanta	101.8	105.2	-	1986	AL	Boston	106.4	107.0	-
1970	AL	Baltimore*	118.2	117.3	-	1986	AL	California	108.9	105.3	-
1970	AL	Minnesota	115.0	110.2	-	1986	NL	New York*	119.7	115.7	-
1970	NL	Pittsburgh	109.4	99.6	DP	1986	NL	Houston	118.2	96.6	DP
1970	NL	Cincinnati	109.4	105.9	-	1987	AL	Detroit	111.1	112.9	-
1971	AL	Baltimore	115.5	121.4	SH	1987	AL	Minnesota*	95.8	99.0	-
1971	AL	Oakland	113.2	111.0	-	1987	NL	St. Louis	103.8	109.1	SH
1971	NL	Pittsburgh*	104.9	124.4	SH	1987	NL	San Francisco	110.6	107.0	-
1971	NL	San Francisco	104.1	111.5	SH	1988	AL	Boston	100.0	115.2	SH
1972	AL	Detroit	103.7	103.2	-	1988	AL	Oakland	115.6	113.3	-
1972	AL	Oakland*	119.1	112.4	SP	1988	NL	New York	118.8	113.2	SP
1972	NL	Pittsburgh	122.9	114.1	SP	1988	NL	Los Angeles*	116.5	99.9	DP
1972	NL	Cincinnati	107.6	117.5	SH	1989	AL	Toronto	108.5	105.1	-
1973	AL	Baltimore	124.0	108.8	SP	1989	AL	Oakland*	124.3	102.3	SP
1973	AL	Oakland*	116.4	109.4	SP	1989	NL	Chicago	102.2	109.9	SH
1973	NL	New York	112.1	91.0	DP	1989	NL	San Francisco	106.0	109.4	-
1973	NL	Cincinnati	106.9	110.2	-	1990	AL	Boston	105.3	100.3	-
1974	AL	Baltimore	110.3	99.2	DP	1990	AL	Oakland	123.3	105.2	SP
1974	AL	Oakland*	122.5	103.8	SP	1990	NL	Pittsburgh	111.8	107.6	-
1974	NL	Pittsburgh	103.4	111.7	SH	1990	NL	Cincinnati*	111.9	101.7	SP
1974	NL	Los Angeles	121.7	118.7	-	1991	AL	Toronto	117.1	94.1	DP
1975	AL	Boston	95.0	115.7	DH	1991	AL	Minnesota*	111.0	106.8	-
1975	AL	Oakland	115.1	108.8	SP	1991	NL	Pittsburgh	107.1	115.6	SH
1975	NL	Pittsburgh	120.5	107.2	SP	1991	NL	Atlanta	105.5	112.8	SH
1975	NL	Cincinnati*	107.9	125.7	SH	1992	AL	Toronto*	100.8	111.4	SH
1976	AL	New York	110.5	114.5	-	1992	AL	Oakland	106.0	106.4	-
1976	AL	Kansas City	109.8	109.8	-	1992	NL	Pittsburgh	104.7	110.3	SH
1976	NL	Philadelphia	113.4	119.4	SH	1992	NL	Atlanta	111.6	108.6	-
1976	NL	Cincinnati*	100.0	132.9	DH	1993	AL	Toronto*	102.7	111.1	SH
1977	AL	New York*	112.3	113.2	-	1993	AL	Chicago	116.5	101.8	SP
1977	AL	Kansas City	114.9	112.0	-	1993	NL	Philadelphia	102.0	120.6	SH
1977	NL	Philadelphia	105.4	118.8	SH	1993	NL	Atlanta	129.0	105.5	SP

DO THOSE 3-AND-2 FOULS PAY OFF? (p. 102)

The charts below summarize how major league batters have fared when fouling off two-strike pitches: Count/NF is the # of foul balls hit by the batter at that count.

Count/NF	AB	H	2B	3B	HR	BB	K	Avg	OBP	Slg
0-2 Count										
0	61295	10492	1726	237	753	1849	25906	.171	.201	.244
1	9637	1810	307	42	133	230	3807	.188	.212	.270
2	1755	294	48	8	17	31	673	.168	.188	.233
3	324	68	14	4	7	5	107	.210	.231	.343
4	74	15	2	0	0	0	25	.203	.211	.230
5	17	2	1	0	0	0	6	.118	.118	.176
6	1	0	0	0	0	0	0	.000	.000	.000
7	2	1	0	0	1	0	0	.500	.500	2.000
8	1	1	0	0	0	0	0	1.000	1.000	1.000
9	1	0	0	0	0	0	0	.000	.000	.000
1-2 Count										
0	89145	16456	2778	390	1253	4997	34936	.185	.231	.267
1	17912	3462	636	94	267	993	6460	.193	.239	.284
2	3797	796	138	19	66	185	1326	.210	.248	.308
3	857	165	37	3	14	33	318	.193	.225	.292
4	197	41	7	1	4	8	61	.208	.239	.315
5	54	12	3	0	1	1	16	.222	.246	.333
6	18	7	1	0	0	0	4	.389	.389	.444
7	2	1	1	0	0	0	1	.500	.500	1.000
8	2	0	0	0	0	0	1	.000	.000	.000
2-2 Count										
0	66336	13116	2358	319	1121	8769	23239	.198	.292	.294
1	15500	3340	581	79	290	2108	5122	.215	.310	.319
2	3812	814	137	20	83	463	1230	.214	.300	.325
3	939	194	37	9	21	102	296	.207	.283	.332
4	271	58	16	1	3	35	71	.214	.306	.314
5	77	18	3	0	5	8	22	.234	.306	.468
6	22	3	1	0	1	1	5	.136	.167	.318
7	4	1	0	0	0	0	1	.250	.250	.250
8	2	1	0	0	1	1	0	.500	.667	2.000
10	1	0	0	0	0	0	0	.000	.000	.000
3-2 Count										
0	28798	6327	1237	160	648	12538	8602	.220	.455	.341
1	7638	1793	328	51	200	3530	2090	.235	.475	.370
2	2154	502	102	11	62	987	576	.233	.472	.377
3	584	154	38	7	20	260	143	.264	.488	.455
4	186	39	8	3	6	78	50	.210	.444	.382
5	56	15	1	0	1	18	17	.268	.446	.339
6	14	6	1	0	0	8	2	.429	.636	.500
7	6	2	0	0	0	4	2	.333	.600	.333
8	3	2	0	0	1	0	0	.667	.667	1.667
9	0	0	0	0	0	1	0	-	1.000	-

Is THERE REALLY A "SOPHOMORE JINX"? (p. 104)

Batters: At Bats (**AB**) and Runs Created per 27 Outs (**RCp27**); Pitchers: Win-Loss record (**W-L**), Saves (**Sv**), and Earned Run Average (**ERA**).

Both Leagues — Listed Alphabetically
(Minimum 250 PA, 100 IP or 40 Games Pitched in Rookie Season: 1991)

Batter, Team	1991 AB	RC/27	1992 AB	RC/27	1993 AB	RC/27
Bagwell, Hou	554	6.38	586	5.73	535	7.17
Bordick, Oak	235	2.56	504	4.82	546	3.63
Cedeno A, Hou	251	3.71	220	2.22	505	4.69
Chamberlain, Phi	383	4.01	275	3.99	284	5.32
Cuyler, Det	475	4.36	291	2.83	249	3.15
Decker, Fla	233	2.48	43	2.06	15	0.10
Gilkey, StL	268	2.90	384	5.58	557	6.22
Gomez L, Bal	391	4.03	468	5.22	244	3.60
Gonzalez L, Hou	473	4.68	387	3.60	540	6.03
Grebeck, ChA	224	6.54	287	4.52	190	2.64
Hoiles, Bal	341	3.71	310	6.97	419	9.26
Howard D, KC	236	2.43	219	2.45	24	6.17
Howard T, Cin	281	3.66	361	3.64	319	3.65
Huff, ChA	243	4.51	115	2.22	44	3.87
Hunter, Atl	271	4.34	238	4.84	80	0.93
Kelly P, NYA	298	3.50	318	3.68	406	3.93
Knoblauch, Min	565	4.83	600	5.51	602	4.57
Lankford, StL	566	4.00	598	6.37	407	4.52
Lewis D, SF	222	4.22	320	2.98	522	3.51
Lewis M, Cle	314	2.91	413	3.49	52	2.99
Mayne, KC	231	3.29	213	2.09	205	3.44
Merced, Pit	411	5.66	405	4.52	447	7.18
Meulens, NYA	288	2.93	5	28.17	53	2.65
Morandini, Phi	325	3.57	422	3.78	425	3.95
Palmer, Tex	268	3.67	541	4.51	519	5.51
Reimer, Mil	394	5.32	494	5.11	437	3.85
Rodriguez I, Tex	280	2.95	420	3.42	473	4.07
Shumpert, KC	369	2.71	94	1.11	10	1.53
Sojo, Tor	364	2.98	368	3.11	47	1.26
Vaughn M, Bos	219	4.33	355	4.41	539	7.43
Whiten, StL	407	3.65	508	4.24	562	4.65
Williams B, NYA	320	4.30	261	4.99	567	4.38

Pitcher, Team	W-L	Sv	ERA	W-L	Sv	ERA	W-L	Sv	ERA
Barnes, Mon	5-8	0	4.22	6-6	0	2.97	2-6	3	4.41
Castillo F, ChN	6-7	0	4.35	10-11	0	3.46	5-8	0	4.84
DeLucia, Sea	12-13	0	5.09	3-6	1	5.49	3-6	0	4.64
Fassero, Mon	2-5	8	2.44	8-7	1	2.84	12-5	1	2.29
Gardiner, Det	9-10	0	4.85	4-10	0	4.75	2-3	0	4.93
Guzman Juan, Tor	10-3	0	2.99	16-5	0	2.64	14-3	0	3.99
Holmes, Col	1-4	3	4.72	4-4	6	2.55	3-3	25	4.05
Johnson J, NYA	6-11	0	5.88	2-3	0	6.66	0-2	0	30.38
Kile, Hou	7-11	0	3.69	5-10	0	3.95	15-8	0	3.51
Leiter M, Det	9-7	1	4.21	8-5	0	4.18	6-6	0	4.73
MacDonald, Det	3-3	0	2.85	1-0	0	4.37	3-3	3	5.35
McElroy, ChN	6-2	3	1.95	4-7	6	3.55	2-2	0	4.56
Nagy, Cle	10-15	0	4.13	17-10	0	2.96	2-6	0	6.29
Olivares, StL	11-7	1	3.71	9-9	0	3.84	5-3	1	4.17
Osuna, Hou	7-6	12	3.42	6-3	0	4.23	1-1	2	3.20
Otto, Pit	2-8	0	4.23	5-9	0	7.06	3-4	0	5.03
Rodriguez, Fla	3-1	0	3.26	6-3	0	2.37	2-4	3	3.79
Scanlan, ChN	7-8	1	3.89	3-6	14	2.89	4-5	0	4.54
Slocumb, Cle	2-1	1	3.45	0-3	1	6.50	4-1	0	4.03
Slusarski, Oak	5-7	0	5.27	5-5	0	5.45	0-0	0	5.19
Stanton, Atl	5-5	7	2.88	5-4	8	4.10	4-6	27	4.67
Timlin, Tor	11-6	3	3.16	0-2	1	4.12	4-2	1	4.69

ARE THESE THE GOOD OLD DAYS? (p. 107)

The statistics and averages are for each ten-year period beginning with the year in the column heading.

Stat	1900	1910	1920	1930	1940	1950	1960	1970	1980	1990
CG%	.788	.569	.497	.446	.426	.335	.252	.253	.156	.092
SV%	.057	.119	.147	.176	.196	.281	.385	.377	.466	.530
BB/9	2.5	3.0	3.0	3.3	3.6	3.6	3.1	3.3	3.2	3.3
K/9	3.6	3.7	2.8	3.4	3.6	4.4	5.7	5.2	5.4	5.7
ERA	2.79	2.96	4.03	4.28	3.75	3.97	3.56	3.70	3.87	3.93
Avg	.252	.255	.285	.279	.260	.259	.249	.256	.259	.259
OBP	.310	.322	.347	.342	.332	.331	.314	.323	.324	.326
Slg	.326	.338	.397	.399	.368	.391	.374	.377	.388	.388
R/Game	7.9	7.8	9.6	9.9	8.6	8.9	8.1	8.3	8.6	8.6
2B/Game	2.3	2.5	3.3	3.5	3.0	2.8	2.6	2.8	3.0	3.1
3B/Game	0.9	1.0	1.0	0.8	0.6	0.6	0.5	0.5	0.4	0.4
HR/Game	0.3	0.3	0.8	1.1	1.0	1.7	1.6	1.5	1.6	1.6
SB/Game	2.4	2.3	1.2	0.8	0.7	0.6	0.8	1.2	1.5	1.5
SB%	-	.576	.553	.602	.582	.579	.625	.642	.677	.671
FPct	.954	.961	.968	.971	.973	.977	.977	.977	.979	.980

CG% = Major League Complete Games/Major League Games Started

SV% = Major League Saves/Major League Games Played

FPct = Major League Fielding Percentage

WHO OUGHT TO BE A LEADOFF MAN? (p. 112)

The chart below lists the number of innings in which a batter led off (**#Inn**), the number of runs his team scored in those innings (**#RS**), the percentage of runs scored per inning lef off (**R/I**), the number of innings in which his team scored any runs (**#IwR**), and the percentage of run-scoring innings per inning led off (**IwR/I**).

Both Leagues — Listed Alphabetically
(Minimum 125 Innings led off in 1993)

Batter, Team	#Inn	#RS	R/I	#IwR	IwR/I	Batter, Team	#Inn	#RS	R/I	#IwR	IwR/I
Alomar, Tor	138	97	0.70	52	.377	Hollins, Phi	138	78	0.57	47	.341
Amaral, Sea	134	60	0.45	36	.269	Hulse, Tex	162	119	0.73	57	.352
Anderson, Bal	241	113	0.47	71	.295	Jaha, Mil	137	69	0.50	39	.285
Anthony, Hou	126	56	0.44	39	.310	Jose, KC	187	107	0.57	64	.342
Baerga, Cle	126	84	0.67	47	.373	Joyner, KC	133	72	0.54	40	.301
Baines, Bal	127	76	0.60	39	.307	Justice, Atl	150	77	0.51	44	.293
Bell D, SD	139	60	0.43	39	.281	Karros, LA	157	78	0.50	48	.306
Belle, Cle	150	66	0.44	37	.247	King, Pit	183	76	0.42	50	.273
Biggio, Hou	280	161	0.58	89	.318	Knoblauch, Min	206	93	0.45	56	.272
Boggs, NYA	180	112	0.62	56	.311	Lemke, Atl	128	66	0.52	35	.273
Bonds, SF	153	82	0.54	49	.320	Lewis D, SF	207	142	0.69	72	.348
Bonilla, NYN	156	81	0.52	47	.301	Listach, Mil	129	69	0.53	39	.302
Bordick, Oak	157	60	0.38	29	.185	Lofton, Cle	259	196	0.76	103	.398
Buhner, Sea	170	81	0.48	46	.271	Mack, Min	172	75	0.44	46	.267
Burks, ChA	125	53	0.42	30	.240	Manwaring, SF	126	61	0.48	29	.230
Butler B, LA	285	154	0.54	86	.302	Martin A, Pit	149	89	0.60	52	.349
Caminiti, Hou	137	58	0.42	37	.270	McGee, SF	133	71	0.53	37	.278
Carr, Fla	265	133	0.50	79	.298	McGriff F, Atl	168	97	0.58	57	.339
Carter, Tor	145	86	0.59	45	.310	McRae, KC	156	70	0.45	46	.295
Cedeno A, Hou	130	72	0.55	41	.315	Nixon, Atl	227	165	0.73	77	.339
Clayton, SF	141	71	0.50	38	.270	Olerud, Tor	177	85	0.48	57	.322
Coleman, NYN	163	91	0.56	59	.362	Palmeiro, Tex	142	100	0.70	53	.373
Conine, Fla	131	61	0.47	38	.290	Phillips T, Det	273	183	0.67	89	.326
Cora, ChA	141	82	0.58	41	.291	Polonia, Cal	265	130	0.49	78	.294
Cordero, Mon	127	38	0.30	25	.197	Raines, ChA	199	147	0.74	77	.387
Daulton, Phi	129	67	0.52	36	.279	Reynolds, Bal	145	58	0.40	31	.214
Davis C, Cal	144	64	0.44	38	.264	Ripken C, Bal	154	70	0.45	38	.247
DeShields, Mon	217	123	0.57	71	.327	Sabo, Cin	140	80	0.57	47	.336
Destrade, Fla	151	47	0.31	32	.212	Smith D, ChN	143	71	0.50	46	.322
Dykstra, Phi	312	235	0.75	117	.375	Sosa, ChN	154	61	0.40	44	.286
Fielder, Det	141	97	0.69	48	.340	Sprague, Tor	131	66	0.50	35	.267
Fletcher S, Bos	212	133	0.63	75	.354	Surhoff, Mil	129	61	0.47	36	.279
Franco, Tex	134	77	0.57	36	.269	Tartabull, NYA	138	88	0.64	46	.333
Fryman, Det	125	82	0.66	44	.352	Tettleton, Det	172	91	0.53	53	.308
Gagne, KC	143	59	0.41	40	.280	Vaughn G, Mil	152	91	0.60	54	.355
Galarraga, Col	130	80	0.62	41	.315	Vaughn M, Bos	162	83	0.51	56	.346
Gant, Atl	132	82	0.62	52	.394	Ventura, ChA	143	60	0.42	36	.252
Garcia, Pit	211	108	0.51	63	.299	Vizcaino, ChN	142	86	0.61	44	.310
Gardner, SD	130	79	0.61	45	.346	Vizquel, Sea	177	89	0.50	54	.305
Gilkey, StL	214	121	0.57	66	.308	Walker L, Mon	138	82	0.59	39	.283
Gonzalez J, Tex	143	90	0.63	52	.364	Wallach, LA	132	53	0.40	34	.258
Griffey Jr, Sea	131	91	0.69	50	.382	Weiss, Fla	139	46	0.33	29	.209
Grissom, Mon	156	113	0.72	64	.410	White Dev, Tor	223	161	0.72	90	.404
Gutierrez, SD	136	89	0.65	35	.257	Whiten, StL	147	63	0.43	38	.259
Gwynn T, SD	131	58	0.44	30	.229	Williams B, NYA	178	97	0.54	55	.309
Hamilton, Mil	183	95	0.52	52	.284	Williams M, SF	149	99	0.66	59	.396
Harper, Min	139	56	0.40	29	.209	Winfield, Min	133	54	0.41	33	.248
Hatcher, Bos	127	71	0.56	37	.291	Young E, Col	231	144	0.62	73	.316
Hayes, Col	138	53	0.38	33	.239	Zeile, StL	138	67	0.49	38	.275
Henderson R, Tor	231	151	0.65	84	.364						

HOW GOOD IS AVERAGE? (p. 116)

1993 Composite League Statistics — Per 600 Plate Appearances

American League

Pos	AVG	OBP	SLG	AB	H	2B	3B	HR	RBI	BB	K
As c	.255	.324	.396	532	62	136	26	1	15	70	49
As 1b	.282	.368	.469	518	79	146	30	1	21	83	70
As 2b	.270	.339	.370	527	72	142	25	3	7	58	53
As 3b	.266	.335	.400	535	68	142	28	2	13	66	52
As ss	.261	.318	.358	539	65	141	23	3	7	58	43
As lf	.269	.344	.429	529	78	142	28	4	16	69	59
As cf	.275	.339	.410	537	80	148	26	6	12	60	50
As rf	.263	.335	.417	532	73	140	26	3	17	73	57
All DH	.262	.332	.426	533	71	140	26	2	19	81	56
All PH	.240	.325	.350	523	54	125	25	2	9	85	65

National League

Pos	AVG	OBP	SLG	AB	H	2B	3B	HR	RBI	BB	K
As p	.151	.182	.185	514	28	78	10	1	2	28	18
As c	.255	.317	.400	540	57	138	26	2	16	71	46
As 1b	.287	.353	.449	536	74	154	27	3	18	79	54
As 2b	.268	.334	.386	535	72	144	27	5	9	52	50
As 3b	.273	.335	.431	537	73	146	29	2	17	79	50
As ss	.272	.338	.366	532	69	145	23	4	6	52	51
As lf	.277	.343	.451	535	80	148	27	5	19	79	53
As cf	.275	.341	.408	536	80	148	23	5	12	59	51
As rf	.274	.339	.441	539	77	148	26	4	19	77	52
All PH	.233	.304	.330	531	57	124	21	2	9	66	55

How Important Is the Go-Ahead RBI? (p. 118)

Both Leagues — Listed Alphabetically
(Minimum 50 RBI total in 1993)

Player, Team	GA RBI	Occ	RBI	%	Player, Team	GA RBI	Occ	RBI	%	Player, Team	GA RBI	Occ	RBI	%
Alomar, Tor	24	67	93	36	Gibson, Det	8	51	62	16	Palmer, Tex	9	65	96	14
Alou, Mon	17	67	85	25	Gilkey, StL	15	55	70	27	Pendleton, Atl	21	69	84	30
Anderson, Bal	9	57	66	16	Gladden, Det	8	39	56	21	Phillips T, Det	8	47	57	17
Anthony, Hou	19	49	66	39	Gonz'l'z J, Tex	24	80	118	30	Piazza, LA	23	89	112	26
Baerga, Cle	27	89	114	30	Gonz'l'z L, Hou	18	62	72	29	Plantier, SD	21	65	100	32
Bagwell, Hou	20	71	88	28	Grace, ChN	26	81	98	32	Puckett, Min	18	65	89	28
Baines, Bal	19	59	78	32	Greenwell, Bos	20	52	72	38	Raines, ChA	13	44	54	30
Bell D, SD	9	57	72	16	Griffey Jr, Sea	23	83	109	28	Reimer, Mil	14	47	60	30
Bell G, ChA	16	47	64	34	Grissom, Mon	27	75	95	36	Ripken C, Bal	20	71	90	28
Bell Jay, Pit	9	46	51	20	Guillen, ChA	8	43	50	19	Rodrig'z I, Tex	10	51	66	20
Belle, Cle	36	102	129	35	Gwynn T, SD	13	46	59	28	Sabo, Cin	17	58	82	29
Bichette, Col	26	71	89	37	Harper, Min	19	61	73	31	Salmon, Cal	24	70	95	34
Biggio, Hou	13	53	64	25	Hatcher, Bos	12	45	57	27	Sanders R, Cin	14	65	83	22
Blauser, Atl	23	60	73	38	Hayes, Col	21	71	98	30	Santiago, Fla	8	40	50	20
Blowers, Sea	15	41	57	37	H'nd's'n D,Oak	9	44	53	20	Segui, Bal	15	51	60	29
Boggs, NYA	11	52	59	21	H'nd's'n R, Tor	17	51	59	33	Seitzer, Mil	11	43	57	26
Bonds, SF	25	88	123	28	Hoiles, Bal	14	56	82	25	Sheffield, Fla	21	56	73	38
Bonilla, NYN	16	68	87	24	Hollins, Phi	20	71	93	28	Sierra, Oak	22	66	101	33
Borders, Tor	12	43	55	28	Hrbek, Min	21	60	83	35	Slaught, Pit	12	45	55	27
Brett, KC	28	63	75	44	Hundley, NYN	5	43	53	12	Smith O, StL	10	46	53	22
Buechele, ChN	11	53	65	21	Incaviglia, Phi	19	65	89	29	Snow, Cal	11	48	57	23
Buhner, Sea	28	76	98	37	Jaha, Mil	15	59	70	25	Snyder, LA	7	47	56	15
Burks, ChA	11	55	74	20	Jefferies, StL	27	67	83	40	Sorrento, Cle	12	50	65	24
Caminiti, Hou	16	56	75	29	Joyner, KC	13	58	65	22	Sosa, ChN	16	71	93	23
Carter, Tor	25	91	121	27	Justice, Atl	26	85	120	31	Sprague, Tor	6	58	73	10
Cedeno, Hou	11	48	56	23	Kark'v'ce, ChA	14	39	54	36	Stanley, NYA	18	57	84	32
Clark J, Col	14	49	67	29	Karros, LA	19	59	80	32	Strange, Tex	15	48	60	31
Clark W, SF	27	61	73	44	Kelly P, NYA	10	45	51	22	Surhoff, Mil	17	60	79	28
Clayton, SF	17	57	70	30	Kent, NYN	21	58	80	36	Tartabull, NYA	26	78	102	33
Conine, Fla	18	60	79	30	King, Pit	24	79	98	30	Tettleton, Det	22	75	110	29
Cooper, Bos	12	47	63	26	Kirby, Cle	13	49	60	27	Thomas, ChA	31	93	128	33
Cora, ChA	12	45	51	27	Kreuter, Det	6	41	51	15	Th'mpsn R, SF	12	55	65	22
Cordero, Mon	6	42	58	14	Kruk, Phi	26	69	85	38	Trammell, Det	13	47	60	28
Curtis, Cal	12	53	59	23	Larkin B, Cin	22	46	51	48	Valentin J, Bos	15	52	66	29
Daulton, Phi	26	72	105	36	Leyritz, NYA	10	34	53	29	Valle, Sea	8	49	63	16
Davis C, Cal	24	77	112	31	Macfarl'ne, KC	20	53	67	38	Van Slyke, Pit	17	40	50	43
Davis E, Det	14	49	68	29	Mack, Min	17	44	61	39	Vaughn G, Mil	22	78	97	28
Dawson, Bos	23	54	67	43	Magadan, Sea	10	43	50	23	Vaughn, Bos	17	76	101	22
Deer, Bos	11	43	55	26	Martin A, Pit	16	49	64	33	Ventura, ChA	26	72	94	36
Destrade, Fla	27	67	87	40	Martin'z T, Sea	13	43	60	30	Vizcaino, ChN	10	44	54	23
Dever'x, Bal	21	58	75	36	Mattingly, NYA	25	66	86	38	Walker L, Mon	28	64	86	44
Duncan, Phi	9	56	73	16	May, ChN	23	59	77	39	Wallach, LA	10	51	62	20
Dykstra, Phi	16	52	66	31	McGriff F, Atl	27	75	101	36	Whitaker, Det	11	52	67	21
Eisenreich, Phi	13	43	54	30	McLemore, Bal	15	56	72	27	White Dev, Tor	9	43	52	21
Fernand'z, Tor	10	52	64	19	McRae, KC	14	57	69	25	Whiten, StL	28	69	99	41
Fielder, Det	27	87	117	31	Merced, Pit	14	56	70	25	Wilkins, ChN	17	55	73	31
Fletcher, Mon	11	52	60	21	Mitchell, Cin	15	49	64	31	Will'ms B, NYA	14	53	68	26
Franco, Tex	23	69	84	33	Molitor, Tor	30	93	111	32	Williams M, SF	25	84	110	30
Fryman, Det	30	73	97	41	Murray, NYN	28	78	100	36	Winfield, Min	11	52	76	21
Gaetti, KC	11	41	50	27	Neel, Oak	14	51	63	27	Yount, Mil	16	46	51	35
Gagne, KC	7	41	57	17	O'Neill, NYA	14	63	75	22	Zeile, StL	30	72	103	42
Galarraga, Col	18	79	98	23	Offerman, LA	15	58	62	26					
Gallego, NYA	9	43	54	21	Olerud, Tor	24	87	107	28					
Gant, Atl	32	85	117	38	Oliver, Cin	12	53	75	23					
Gates, Oak	16	52	69	31	Palmeiro, Tex	23	79	105	29					

WHY WERE JOHN OLERUD'S 107 RBI LAST YEAR BETTER THAN ALBERT BELLE'S 129? (p. 121)

Both Leagues — Listed Alphabetically
(minimum 165 RBI Opportunities)

Player, Team	RBI	Opp	Pct	Player, Team	RBI	Opp	Pct
Alicea, StL	210	42	20.0	Deer, Bos	343	32	9.3
Alomar, Tor	344	76	22.1	DeShields, Mon	212	27	12.7
Alou, Mon	354	66	18.6	Destrade, Fla	407	67	16.5
Amaral, Sea	232	43	18.5	Devereaux, Bal	375	61	16.3
Anderson, Bal	315	50	15.9	DiSarcina, Cal	282	41	14.5
Anthony, Hou	329	51	15.5	Duncan, Phi	344	62	18.0
Baerga, Cle	409	93	22.7	Dykstra, Phi	295	46	15.6
Bagwell, Hou	326	66	20.2	Eisenreich, Phi	289	46	15.9
Baines, Bal	279	58	20.8	Espinoza, Cle	167	23	13.8
Barberie, Fla	203	26	12.8	Felder, Sea	219	19	8.7
Bell D, SD	348	48	13.8	Fermin, Cle	302	42	13.9
Bell G, ChA	307	51	16.6	Fernandez, Tor	368	57	15.5
Bell Jay, Pit	293	41	14.0	Fielder, Det	471	86	18.3
Bell Juan, Mil	218	31	14.2	Finley, Hou	304	36	11.8
Belle, Cle	406	90	22.2	Fletcher D, Mon	285	46	16.1
Berry, Mon	211	35	16.6	Fletcher S, Bos	227	40	17.6
Berryhill, Atl	226	35	15.5	Franco, Tex	322	70	21.7
Bichette, Col	317	68	21.5	Fryman, Det	452	74	16.4
Biggio, Hou	265	43	16.2	Gaetti, KC	221	35	15.8
Blankenship, Oak	173	19	11.0	Gagne, KC	303	46	15.2
Blauser, Atl	340	56	16.5	Galarraga, Col	281	75	26.7
Blowers, Sea	253	41	16.2	Gallego, NYA	291	41	14.1
Boggs, NYA	318	56	17.6	Gant, Atl	423	80	18.9
Bonds, SF	324	76	23.5	Garcia, Pit	285	35	12.3
Bonilla, NYN	285	52	18.2	Gardner, SD	198	23	11.6
Boone, Sea	169	26	15.4	Gates, Oak	395	62	15.7
Borders, Tor	305	45	14.8	Gibson, Det	307	48	15.6
Bordick, Oak	329	43	13.1	Gilkey, StL	321	54	16.8
Boston, Col	181	26	14.4	Girardi, Col	189	28	14.8
Branson, Cin	216	19	8.8	Gladden, Det	276	43	15.6
Bream, Atl	168	26	15.5	Gonzales R, Cal	202	27	13.4
Brett, KC	360	55	15.3	Gonzalez J, Tex	342	72	21.1
Buechele, ChN	287	49	17.1	Gonzalez L, Hou	355	56	15.8
Buhner, Sea	376	70	18.6	Grace, ChN	411	84	20.4
Burks, ChA	321	56	17.4	Greenwell, Bos	317	59	18.6
Burnitz, NYN	170	25	14.7	Griffey Jr, Sea	356	63	17.7
Butler B, LA	290	40	13.8	Grissom, Mon	390	76	19.5
Caminiti, Hou	377	61	16.2	Guillen, ChA	287	46	16.0
Carr, Fla	245	35	14.3	Gutierrez, SD	221	21	9.5
Carter, Tor	453	85	18.8	Gwynn C, KC	176	24	13.6
Castilla, Col	183	21	11.5	Gwynn T, SD	264	52	19.7
Cedeno A, Hou	319	45	14.1	Hamilton, Mil	284	36	12.7
Chamberlain, Phi	194	33	17.0	Harper, Min	312	61	19.6
Cianfrocco, SD	194	36	18.6	Hatcher, Bos	298	47	15.8
Clark D, Pit	198	35	17.7	Hayes, Col	362	72	19.9
Clark J, Col	300	53	17.7	Henderson D, Oak	279	31	11.1
Clark W, SF	321	58	18.1	Henderson R, Tor	262	37	14.1
Clayton, SF	408	63	15.4	Hill, ChN	191	31	16.2
Cole, Col	171	24	14.0	Hoiles, Bal	266	52	19.5
Conine, Fla	374	65	17.4	Hollins, Phi	432	75	17.4
Cooper, Bos	348	53	15.2	Howard T, Cin	181	29	16.0
Cora, ChA	343	48	14.0	Hrbek, Min	294	57	19.4
Cordero, Mon	274	46	16.8	Hulett, Bal	190	21	11.1
Curtis, Cal	344	53	15.4	Hulse, Tex	188	28	14.9
Cuyler, Det	175	19	10.9	Hundley, NYN	261	42	16.1
Daulton, Phi	400	75	18.8	Incaviglia, Phi	307	64	20.8
Davis C, Cal	386	85	22.0	Jackson B, ChA	190	28	14.7
Davis E, Det	300	47	15.7	Jaha, Mil	284	49	17.3
Dawson, Bos	309	54	17.5	James D, NYA	212	26	12.3

Player, Team	RBI	Opp	Pct	Player, Team	RBI	Opp	Pct
Jefferies, StL	356	67	18.8	Pena T, Bos	202	14	6.9
Jefferson, Cle	216	24	11.1	Pendleton, Atl	443	67	15.1
Johnson L, ChA	317	47	14.8	Phillips T, Det	302	45	14.9
Jose, KC	241	37	15.4	Piazza, LA	339	77	22.7
Joyner, KC	302	48	15.9	Plantier, SD	320	66	20.6
Justice, Atl	391	79	20.2	Polonia, Cal	268	31	11.6
Karkovice, ChA	260	34	13.1	Puckett, Min	425	66	15.5
Karros, LA	405	57	14.1	Quintana, Bos	203	16	7.9
Kelly P, NYA	316	43	13.6	Raines, ChA	183	37	20.2
Kelly R, Cin	197	26	13.2	Reed Jody, LA	290	29	10.0
Kent, NYN	312	57	18.3	Reimer, Mil	312	46	14.7
King, Pit	444	87	19.6	Reynolds, Bal	326	43	13.2
Kirby, Cle	296	52	17.6	Ripken C, Bal	391	65	16.6
Knoblauch, Min	315	38	12.1	Rodriguez I, Tex	317	55	17.4
Kreuter, Det	243	35	14.4	Sabo, Cin	372	61	16.4
Kruk, Phi	365	67	18.4	Salmon, Cal	317	61	19.2
Lankford, StL	258	38	14.7	Sandberg, ChN	281	36	12.8
Lansing, Mon	308	41	13.3	Sanders R, Cin	367	62	16.9
Larkin B, Cin	254	38	15.0	Santiago, Fla	289	36	12.5
Lemke, Atl	305	42	13.8	Segui, Bal	329	49	14.9
Lewis D, SF	266	46	17.3	Seitzer, Mil	273	45	16.5
Leyritz, NYA	190	39	20.5	Sheffield, Fla	297	51	17.2
Lind, KC	270	37	13.7	Sierra, Oak	446	77	17.3
Listach, Mil	211	25	11.8	Slaught, Pit	277	44	15.9
Livingstone, Det	213	37	17.4	Smith O, StL	344	52	15.1
Lofton, Cle	267	41	15.4	Snow, Cal	253	39	15.4
Lovullo, Cal	235	23	9.8	Snyder, LA	306	44	14.4
Macfarlane, KC	251	47	18.7	Sorrento, Cle	298	46	15.4
Mack, Min	270	50	18.5	Sosa, ChN	376	58	15.4
Magadan, Sea	315	45	14.3	Spiers, Mil	225	34	15.1
Maldonado, Cle	175	26	14.9	Sprague, Tor	401	61	15.2
Manwaring, SF	298	44	14.8	Stanley, NYA	288	55	19.1
Martin A, Pit	261	46	17.6	Steinbach, Oak	242	32	13.2
Martinez Crls, Cle	196	26	13.3	Stocker, Phi	189	27	14.3
Martinez T, Sea	259	42	16.2	Strange, Tex	309	49	15.9
Mattingly, NYA	357	68	19.0	Surhoff, Mil	328	70	21.3
May, ChN	325	67	20.6	Tartabull, NYA	376	67	17.8
McCarty, Min	227	19	8.4	Taubensee, Hou	201	33	16.4
McGee, SF	274	40	14.6	Tettleton, Det	356	73	20.5
McGriff F, Atl	365	64	17.5	Thomas, ChA	377	86	22.8
McLemore, Bal	378	66	17.5	Thompson M, Phi	246	39	15.9
McRae, KC	322	55	17.1	Thompson Rob, SF	298	46	15.4
McReynolds, KC	204	30	14.7	Thon, Mil	181	32	17.7
Meares, Min	197	33	16.8	Trammell, Det	313	48	15.3
Merced, Pit	329	62	18.8	Valentin John, Bos	333	55	16.5
Milligan, Cle	178	30	16.9	Valle, Sea	308	49	15.9
Mitchell, Cin	247	45	18.2	Van Slyke, Pit	221	42	19.0
Molitor, Tor	429	89	20.7	Vaughn G, Mil	378	65	17.2
Morandini, Phi	254	27	10.6	Vaughn M, Bos	337	71	21.1
Morris, Cin	225	42	18.7	Ventura, ChA	402	71	17.7
Munoz, Min	191	24	12.6	Vizcaino, ChN	316	50	15.8
Murray, NYN	339	72	21.2	Vizquel, Sea	338	29	8.6
Myers, Cal	200	33	16.5	Walker L, Mon	329	63	19.1
Neel, Oak	267	42	15.7	Wallach, LA	303	49	16.2
Nilsson, Mil	207	31	15.0	Weiss, Fla	307	37	12.1
Nixon, Atl	223	21	9.4	Whitaker, Det	320	56	17.5
O'Neill, NYA	379	52	13.7	White Dev, Tor	285	37	13.0
Offerman, LA	377	56	14.9	Whiten, StL	382	71	18.6
Olerud, Tor	351	81	23.1	Wilkins, ChN	257	43	16.7
Oliver, Cin	345	61	17.7	Williams B, NYA	377	55	14.6
Orsulak, NYN	195	27	13.8	Williams M, SF	377	71	18.8
Owen, NYA	211	17	8.1	Winfield, Min	374	55	14.7
Pagliarulo, Bal	245	32	13.1	Young E, Col	203	38	18.7
Pagnozzi, StL	225	34	15.1	Young K, Pit	292	37	12.7
Palmeiro, Tex	342	67	19.6	Yount, Mil	296	41	13.9
Palmer, Tex	328	61	18.6	Zeile, StL	434	86	19.8
Paquette, Oak	251	34	13.5	**MLB Avg**	**98346**	**15261**	**15.5**

WHICH HITTERS CAN HANDLE THE TOUGHEST PITCHERS? (p. 124)

How batters have fared against the game's top pitchers.

Both Leagues — Listed by On-Base + Slugging
(Minimum 100 PA and .700 OBP+Slg, 1989-1993)

Batter	OPS	AB	H	2B	3B	HR	BB	K	Avg	OBP	Slg
Frank Thomas	.969	385	118	27	0	21	86	76	.306	.429	.540
Kevin Mitchell	.925	546	158	28	0	42	53	103	.289	.353	.571
Barry Bonds	.919	692	204	39	5	35	121	118	.295	.401	.517
Rickey Henderson	.905	519	160	28	3	17	115	78	.308	.433	.472
Fred McGriff	.900	617	179	28	2	32	121	136	.290	.402	.498
Dave Hollins	.873	360	103	17	3	16	55	77	.286	.390	.483
Mike Piazza	.859	132	39	3	0	8	13	22	.295	.359	.500
Mark Grace	.857	783	251	50	5	20	83	62	.321	.383	.474
Paul Molitor	.850	614	201	26	4	18	55	85	.327	.379	.471
Harold Baines	.844	440	129	19	0	19	62	83	.293	.378	.466
Ken Griffey Jr	.842	489	138	27	2	22	61	69	.282	.362	.481
Alan Trammell	.842	364	113	26	3	9	33	28	.310	.369	.473
Mike Greenwell	.839	472	151	32	3	9	47	48	.320	.382	.458
Mike Stanley	.826	199	53	8	0	9	38	45	.266	.383	.442
Phil Plantier	.825	201	52	12	2	10	22	47	.259	.338	.488
Tony Gwynn	.823	714	239	34	9	9	51	31	.335	.377	.445
Al Martin	.819	113	34	5	3	2	12	28	.301	.368	.451
Gary Redus	.817	287	77	16	4	12	33	56	.268	.340	.477
Gregg Jefferies	.813	619	189	35	3	17	53	49	.305	.359	.454
Lloyd McClendon	.812	177	48	5	0	8	31	22	.271	.377	.435
Barry Larkin	.811	580	174	31	8	13	58	44	.300	.363	.448
Mike Sharperson	.811	205	65	19	2	0	22	22	.317	.382	.429
Sam Horn	.810	150	35	6	1	10	20	58	.233	.324	.487
Don Slaught	.809	311	91	20	2	8	29	46	.293	.362	.447
Dion James	.801	255	83	8	1	3	32	28	.325	.401	.400
Brett Butler	.801	745	235	18	14	5	107	89	.315	.403	.397
Lonnie Smith	.799	348	96	13	5	10	49	72	.276	.371	.428
Albert Belle	.796	420	104	24	2	24	40	94	.248	.311	.486
Will Clark	.795	752	216	39	2	24	84	136	.287	.355	.440
Cecil Fielder	.794	461	111	20	0	26	65	149	.241	.341	.453
John Olerud	.793	359	96	19	0	14	50	63	.267	.356	.437
Ryne Sandberg	.792	779	216	33	3	32	78	114	.277	.342	.451
Glenn Wilson	.792	196	56	9	0	8	15	31	.286	.338	.454
Kent Hrbek	.791	413	105	17	1	19	64	45	.254	.353	.438
Joe Carter	.791	650	170	30	3	35	40	114	.262	.312	.478
Shane Mack	.789	387	114	21	4	8	35	69	.295	.357	.432
John Kruk	.787	632	176	28	8	14	98	102	.278	.373	.415
Ron Gant	.783	629	160	31	6	30	53	126	.254	.317	.466
Gary Sheffield	.782	523	150	30	2	15	44	60	.287	.344	.438
Mike LaValliere	.781	319	100	14	0	3	44	24	.313	.395	.386
Cal Ripken	.781	582	167	34	1	16	56	59	.287	.349	.431
Darren Daulton	.776	540	124	29	5	21	105	101	.230	.357	.419
Ellis Burks	.774	403	115	21	7	9	28	86	.285	.335	.439
Terry Pendleton	.772	713	209	39	8	17	41	95	.293	.330	.442
Reggie Sanders	.772	229	64	10	2	8	15	62	.279	.327	.445
Dave Magadan	.771	473	137	29	2	5	70	56	.290	.380	.391
Chris Hoiles	.770	210	56	13	1	5	28	50	.267	.361	.410
Skeeter Barnes	.768	93	26	9	1	2	4	18	.280	.306	.462
Chad Kreuter	.767	132	31	6	1	6	21	49	.235	.335	.432
Danny Tartabull	.767	344	79	14	1	17	62	112	.230	.342	.424
Wally Joyner	.764	473	129	32	4	9	53	53	.273	.350	.414
Ricky Gutierrez	.762	101	28	2	2	3	8	22	.277	.336	.426
John Valentin	.762	136	37	12	0	3	13	33	.272	.336	.426
Edgar Martinez	.760	368	100	25	2	7	45	67	.272	.353	.408
Dave Winfield	.759	467	117	26	2	21	41	103	.251	.310	.450
Delino DeShields	.759	515	146	15	9	8	68	107	.283	.365	.394
Wade Boggs	.759	534	155	35	2	4	72	53	.290	.374	.386

Batter	OPS	AB	H	2B	3B	HR	BB	K	Avg	OBP	Slg
Brian Harper	.759	489	154	31	1	4	24	32	.315	.352	.407
Bob Zupcic	.758	116	33	11	1	1	9	23	.284	.336	.422
Deion Sanders	.758	271	72	11	9	6	20	45	.266	.319	.439
Larry Walker	.758	455	121	26	4	12	48	98	.266	.338	.420
Jeff Bagwell	.757	484	135	22	3	12	45	93	.279	.346	.411
Julio Franco	.757	439	131	25	1	4	49	76	.298	.369	.387
Juan Gonzalez	.756	362	84	13	2	23	23	95	.232	.287	.470
Ray Lankford	.756	488	135	24	7	10	45	113	.277	.340	.416
Lenny Dykstra	.756	602	158	34	6	11	93	78	.262	.362	.394
Howard Johnson	.755	536	134	38	4	18	57	114	.250	.319	.437
Bip Roberts	.755	541	158	30	4	4	62	92	.292	.370	.384
Dave Henderson	.754	438	113	20	1	18	39	123	.258	.323	.432
Eric Davis	.751	447	113	12	3	18	56	124	.253	.337	.414
Travis Fryman	.750	390	96	16	3	18	37	109	.246	.309	.441
Paul O'Neill	.750	559	135	31	2	23	64	106	.242	.322	.428
Dave Justice	.749	454	100	23	2	21	77	102	.220	.330	.419
Lou Whitaker	.748	431	105	20	2	14	75	58	.244	.351	.397
Kevin Bass	.747	397	102	23	4	12	37	70	.257	.321	.426
Tim Raines	.747	588	159	26	8	8	84	75	.270	.364	.383
Mark McGwire	.746	416	91	14	0	22	70	98	.219	.335	.411
Andy Van Slyke	.746	617	159	33	8	15	75	114	.258	.336	.410
Darryl Strawberry	.743	388	87	12	3	21	45	83	.224	.310	.433
Bobby Bonilla	.742	729	179	44	6	26	73	132	.246	.313	.429
Chris Sabo	.739	586	147	28	3	25	43	90	.251	.302	.437
Glenn Davis	.737	375	92	16	2	15	34	86	.245	.318	.419
Mo Vaughn	.736	219	52	8	0	10	28	53	.237	.325	.411
Tony Phillips	.735	564	150	25	4	7	95	116	.266	.373	.362
Carlos Baerga	.735	496	141	26	2	11	26	77	.284	.323	.411
Greg Briley	.734	296	82	17	3	4	27	66	.277	.338	.395
Joe Orsulak	.733	390	107	16	2	10	32	43	.274	.330	.403
Rick Wilkins	.733	236	58	11	0	9	25	45	.246	.326	.407
Rene Gonzales	.732	200	55	8	1	3	22	36	.275	.362	.370
Chad Curtis	.731	204	59	6	1	3	21	37	.289	.358	.373
Marquis Grissom	.729	534	153	32	4	7	32	76	.287	.329	.401
Leo Gomez	.729	211	52	9	0	8	25	49	.246	.326	.403
Jeff Treadway	.727	376	110	18	1	7	20	48	.293	.326	.402
Dwight Smith	.724	334	88	15	5	7	30	61	.263	.323	.401
Jeff Kent	.723	184	46	8	0	8	10	38	.250	.299	.424
Moises Alou	.723	163	43	9	2	4	12	29	.264	.306	.417
David Segui	.721	172	46	13	0	2	21	30	.267	.344	.378
Robin Ventura	.721	477	124	21	0	11	65	76	.260	.348	.373
Orlando Merced	.721	343	95	17	1	4	39	63	.277	.353	.367
Matt D. Williams	.720	723	175	37	6	32	30	176	.242	.277	.443
Roberto Alomar	.719	634	174	30	5	8	68	90	.274	.344	.375
Tino Martinez	.718	194	49	9	1	6	17	42	.253	.316	.402
Mariano Duncan	.718	519	139	34	10	9	17	101	.268	.294	.424
Randy Bush	.718	168	44	8	0	4	18	30	.262	.337	.381
Roberto Kelly	.716	474	123	28	2	14	27	102	.259	.300	.416
Ivan Rodriguez	.714	219	60	16	2	3	10	41	.274	.307	.406
Derrick May	.713	244	68	14	1	5	10	22	.279	.307	.406
Paul Sorrento	.713	251	53	12	0	14	27	57	.211	.287	.426
Rob Deer	.713	438	90	13	0	27	53	166	.205	.293	.420
Hal Morris	.712	368	103	21	2	4	29	45	.280	.332	.380
Steve Finley	.711	618	171	22	6	10	50	82	.277	.331	.380
Todd Benzinger	.710	428	114	16	2	12	27	83	.266	.313	.397
Carlton Fisk	.710	302	74	17	0	10	25	56	.245	.309	.401
Ivan Calderon	.710	518	134	29	2	13	39	85	.259	.312	.398
George Brett	.708	416	111	28	2	7	31	63	.267	.313	.394
Brady Anderson	.707	355	86	23	1	6	52	78	.242	.344	.363
Chuck Knoblauch	.705	384	106	13	4	1	52	41	.276	.367	.339
Kirby Puckett	.705	652	177	42	0	12	39	112	.271	.314	.391
Rafael Palmeiro	.703	547	143	28	4	10	50	78	.261	.321	.382
Tim Hulett	.702	171	48	10	0	2	11	43	.281	.328	.374
Scott Brosius	.702	104	27	5	0	2	10	21	.260	.336	.365
Chili Davis	.701	535	126	19	2	17	76	138	.236	.327	.374
Luis Gonzalez	.701	380	90	22	3	12	28	73	.237	.296	.405
Mike Devereaux	.701	489	119	23	7	12	47	78	.243	.308	.393
Chris James	.700	424	107	19	5	13	16	69	.252	.287	.413

WHO'S THE KING WHEN IT COMES TO CAUSING PITCHING SWITCHES? (p. 126)

The chart below lists the number of times a player was the scheduled first batter when a pitching change was made (#).

Both Leagues — Listed Alphabetically
(Minimum 25 Pitching Changes Caused)

Batter	#PC	Batter	#PC	Batter	#PC	Batter	#PC
King, Pit	62	Butler B, LA	40	Anthony, Hou	34	DeShields, Mon	29
Buhner, Sea	61	Garcia, Pit	40	Gates, Oak	34	DiSarcina, Cal	29
Belle, Cle	60	Hrbek, Min	40	Gilkey, StL	34	Guillen, ChA	29
McGriff F, Atl	59	Lansing, Mon	40	Hayes, Col	34	Jose, KC	29
Olerud, Tor	58	Offerman, LA	40	Orsulak, NYN	34	Kelly P, NYA	29
Bonds, SF	56	Valle, Sea	40	Reimer, Mil	34	Kent, NYN	29
Fryman, Det	53	Ventura, ChA	40	Reynolds, Bal	34	Kreuter, Det	29
Gonzalez J, Tex	53	Alou, Mon	39	Santiago, Fla	34	McLemore, Bal	29
Dykstra, Phi	52	Duncan, Phi	39	Wallach, LA	34	Neel, Oak	29
Incaviglia, Phi	52	Gwynn T, SD	39	Young E, Col	34	Paquette, Oak	29
Tartabull, NYA	52	Macfarlane, KC	39	Bagwell, Hou	33	Polonia, Cal	29
Greenwell, Bos	51	Magadan, Sea	39	Bell Jay, Pit	33	Raines, ChA	29
Thomas, ChA	51	Sprague, Tor	39	Boston, Col	33	Thon, Mil	29
Conine, Fla	50	Gonzalez L, Hou	38	Hamilton, Mil	33	Bordick, Oak	28
Bell D, SD	49	Lankford, StL	38	Lemke, Atl	33	Buechele, ChN	28
Ripken C, Bal	49	Lofton, Cle	38	May, ChN	33	Martinez T, Sea	28
Zeile, StL	48	Morris, Cin	38	Murray, NYN	33	Stanley, NYA	28
Blauser, Atl	47	Sosa, ChN	38	Snyder, LA	33	Dawson, Bos	27
Clark W, SF	47	Vaughn M, Bos	38	Surhoff, Mil	33	Destrade, Fla	27
Kruk, Phi	47	Carter, Tor	37	Williams B, NYA	33	Eisenreich, Phi	27
Anderson, Bal	46	Devereaux, Bal	37	Gutierrez, SD	32	Morandini, Phi	27
Clayton, SF	46	McRae, KC	37	Henderson R, Tor	32	Berryhill, Atl	26
Brett, KC	45	Oliver, Cin	37	Jaha, Mil	32	Blowers, Sea	26
Palmeiro, Tex	45	Phillips T, Det	37	McReynolds, KC	32	Davis C, Cal	26
Walker L, Mon	45	Puckett, Min	37	Sheffield, Fla	32	Gardner, SD	26
Yount, Mil	45	Sabo, Cin	37	Gibson, Det	31	Jefferies, StL	26
Griffey Jr, Sea	44	Smith O, StL	37	Gladden, Det	31	Jefferson, Cle	26
O'Neill, NYA	44	Sorrento, Cle	37	Lewis D, SF	31	Kirby, Cle	26
Cedeno A, Hou	43	Young K, Pit	37	Mack, Min	31	Mattingly, NYA	26
Cooper, Bos	43	Baines, Bal	36	Martin A, Pit	31	Nixon, Atl	26
Cordero, Mon	43	Merced, Pit	36	Reed Jody, LA	31	Slaught, Pit	26
Grissom, Mon	43	Sandberg, ChN	36	Salmon, Cal	31	Thompson M, Phi	26
Tettleton, Det	43	Williams M, SF	36	Vizcaino, ChN	31	White Dev, Tor	26
Whiten, StL	43	Biggio, Hou	35	Wilkins, ChN	31	Carr, Fla	25
Caminiti, Hou	42	Cora, ChA	35	Winfield, Min	31	Fernandez, Tor	25
Curtis, Cal	42	Davis E, Det	35	Bonilla, NYN	30	Gonzales R, Cal	25
Daulton, Phi	42	Fielder, Det	35	Branson, Cin	30	Johnson L, ChA	25
Deer, Bos	42	Finley, Hou	35	Joyner, KC	30	McCarty, Min	25
Justice, Atl	42	Franco, Tex	35	Pagliarulo, Bal	30	Rodriguez I, Tex	25
Grace, ChN	41	Gant, Atl	35	Sanders R, Cin	30	Seitzer, Mil	25
Karros, LA	41	Molitor, Tor	35	Strange, Tex	30	Valentin Jn, Bos	25
Pendleton, Atl	41	Piazza, LA	35	Thompson R, SF	30		
Sierra, Oak	41	Segui, Bal	35	Alomar, Tor	29		
Boggs, NYA	40	Vaughn G, Mil	35	Clark J, Col	29		

DO ROOKIES COOL OFF THE SECOND TIME AROUND THE LEAGUE? (p. 130)

Both Leagues — Listed Alphabetically
(Minimum 225 PA in the Rookie Season, 1991-1993)

Rookie	Year	First 75 PA			Second 75 PA			Rest of the Year		
		Avg	OBP	Slg	Avg	OBP	Slg	Avg	OBP	Slg
Alou, Moises	1992	.338	.392	.544	.266	.306	.422	.268	.314	.435
Amaral, Rich	1993	.324	.378	.426	.328	.384	.418	.269	.330	.336
Amaro, Ruben	1992	.133	.278	.333	.302	.389	.381	.219	.288	.343
Arias, Alex	1993	.246	.347	.377	.290	.371	.306	.270	.329	.302
Bagwell, Jeff	1991	.266	.351	.406	.297	.392	.406	.298	.391	.446
Bolick, Frank	1993	.246	.333	.415	.238	.338	.365	.165	.237	.235
Boone, Bret	1993	.242	.314	.500	.239	.292	.313	.261	.299	.479
Bordick, Mike	1991	.194	.216	.222	.270	.333	.333	.250	.309	.260
Branson, Jeff	1993	.348	.384	.420	.242	.278	.379	.211	.243	.260
Brumfield, Jacob	1993	.313	.397	.531	.269	.320	.418	.248	.284	.369
Burnitz, Jeromy	1993	.270	.365	.540	.215	.311	.369	.244	.340	.496
Carr, Chuck	1993	.242	.296	.318	.250	.375	.333	.273	.324	.332
Castilla, Vinny	1993	.362	.400	.536	.264	.284	.431	.214	.240	.347
Cedeno, Andujar	1991	.229	.250	.386	.243	.260	.371	.252	.288	.468
Chamberlain, Wes	1991	.300	.329	.400	.286	.315	.529	.210	.289	.362
Cianfrocco, Archi	1992	.250	.284	.471	.233	.253	.315	.242	.289	.308
Clark, Phil	1993	.329	.365	.486	.300	.347	.400	.310	.330	.570
Clayton, Royce	1992	.212	.274	.288	.210	.286	.355	.233	.282	.301
Conine, Jeff	1993	.338	.389	.369	.254	.389	.356	.291	.340	.414
Cooper, Scott	1992	.231	.307	.262	.250	.292	.353	.299	.376	.431
Cordero, Wil	1993	.254	.315	.478	.221	.270	.368	.253	.314	.374
Curtis, Chad	1992	.270	.347	.413	.273	.351	.364	.253	.337	.365
Cuyler, Milt	1991	.250	.338	.300	.231	.320	.323	.263	.338	.346
Decker, Steve	1991	.238	.319	.444	.171	.181	.243	.210	.277	.270
Destrade, Orestes	1993	.277	.365	.400	.242	.311	.303	.253	.320	.422
DiSarcina, Gary	1992	.318	.378	.364	.234	.296	.250	.237	.263	.299
Frye, Jeff	1992	.270	.338	.397	.206	.270	.279	.294	.351	.309
Garcia, Carlos	1993	.254	.301	.358	.246	.307	.420	.276	.321	.402
Gardner, Jeff	1993	.268	.307	.366	.300	.394	.417	.253	.331	.341
Gates, Brent	1993	.283	.366	.400	.300	.380	.383	.289	.351	.390
Gilkey, Bernard	1991	.262	.351	.354	.230	.373	.377	.190	.273	.268
Gomez, Leo	1991	.258	.343	.371	.246	.365	.443	.224	.277	.410
Gonzalez, Luis	1991	.188	.253	.377	.257	.293	.586	.266	.339	.413
Grebeck, Craig	1991	.250	.314	.469	.343	.400	.552	.258	.420	.387
Gutierrez, Ricky	1993	.297	.384	.313	.294	.351	.382	.232	.320	.324
Hansen, Dave	1992	.154	.257	.231	.239	.320	.433	.225	.284	.278
Hemond, Scott	1993	.206	.306	.270	.274	.343	.468	.278	.393	.478
Hiatt, Phil	1993	.250	.307	.412	.219	.324	.391	.198	.246	.321
Hoiles, Chris	1991	.231	.311	.369	.203	.292	.281	.259	.305	.420
Howard, Dave	1991	.138	.208	.138	.318	.333	.455	.200	.263	.210
Howard, Thomas	1991	.227	.288	.288	.294	.360	.397	.238	.296	.367
Huff, Michael	1991	.278	.429	.352	.230	.347	.328	.250	.336	.352
Hulse, David	1993	.273	.329	.333	.271	.301	.414	.299	.341	.365
Hundley, Todd	1992	.161	.268	.258	.188	.233	.348	.229	.259	.322
Hunter, Brian	1991	.314	.351	.571	.188	.243	.362	.250	.294	.432
Karros, Eric	1992	.265	.288	.485	.235	.278	.412	.259	.311	.418
Kelly, Pat	1991	.229	.280	.443	.261	.311	.290	.239	.281	.314
Kent, Jeff	1992	.246	.347	.508	.242	.320	.318	.236	.296	.444

Rookie	Year	First 75 PA			Second 75 PA			Rest of the Year		
		Avg	OBP	Slg	Avg	OBP	Slg	Avg	OBP	Slg
Kirby, Wayne	1993	.333	.338	.403	.306	.375	.403	.247	.310	.358
Knoblauch, Chuck	1991	.338	.405	.400	.288	.333	.409	.272	.345	.334
Lankford, Ray	1991	.254	.306	.328	.243	.253	.311	.252	.308	.416
Lansing, Mike	1993	.369	.406	.600	.250	.329	.344	.279	.347	.331
Leius, Scott	1991	.259	.403	.362	.317	.391	.500	.284	.348	.395
Lewis, Darren	1991	.339	.446	.435	.258	.329	.348	.181	.319	.202
Lewis, Mark	1991	.400	.444	.477	.282	.288	.324	.208	.238	.258
Listach, Pat	1992	.328	.384	.418	.303	.378	.318	.283	.343	.343
Livingstone, Scott	1992	.286	.324	.329	.262	.319	.308	.288	.318	.411
Lofton, Kenny	1992	.230	.329	.246	.318	.392	.394	.287	.362	.376
Martin, Al	1993	.275	.282	.478	.239	.288	.343	.291	.359	.509
Martinez, Chito	1991	.299	.333	.537	.343	.387	.657	.177	.198	.367
May, Derrick	1992	.206	.260	.235	.314	.333	.471	.282	.313	.385
Mayne, Brent	1991	.273	.333	.288	.284	.351	.373	.214	.279	.316
McCarty, Dave	1993	.371	.397	.529	.183	.227	.183	.172	.221	.239
Meares, Pat	1993	.300	.315	.371	.343	.378	.443	.204	.210	.243
Mejia, Roberto	1993	.262	.329	.492	.194	.229	.209	.237	.267	.474
Merced, Orlando	1991	.365	.459	.603	.226	.333	.306	.266	.363	.374
Meulens, Hensley	1991	.214	.257	.343	.246	.278	.319	.215	.283	.309
Morandini, Mickey	1991	.292	.347	.308	.194	.275	.242	.253	.313	.343
Neel, Troy	1993	.242	.315	.439	.224	.280	.403	.316	.398	.497
Palmer, Dean	1991	.206	.270	.353	.250	.342	.531	.147	.256	.368
Pappas, Erik	1993	.338	.403	.385	.267	.378	.350	.243	.342	.311
Paquette, Craig	1993	.286	.292	.543	.230	.240	.351	.197	.234	.345
Piazza, Mike	1993	.284	.329	.478	.379	.431	.591	.314	.368	.570
Reimer, Kevin	1991	.273	.338	.424	.308	.366	.400	.259	.322	.510
Renteria, Rich	1993	.309	.365	.353	.286	.333	.486	.208	.275	.224
Reyes, Gil	1991	.290	.347	.319	.147	.203	.191	.214	.304	.271
Rodriguez, Ivan	1991	.342	.338	.411	.250	.270	.306	.230	.246	.348
Salmon, Tim	1993	.254	.392	.559	.258	.360	.355	.292	.384	.561
Sanchez, Rey	1992	.221	.239	.353	.221	.284	.235	.286	.312	.395
Sanders, Reggie	1992	.333	.387	.536	.318	.378	.439	.240	.343	.448
Segui, David	1991	.264	.280	.361	.318	.375	.409	.257	.295	.257
Servais, Scott	1992	.250	.292	.324	.134	.205	.134	.329	.382	.386
Sheaffer, Danny	1993	.243	.250	.329	.300	.301	.457	.289	.337	.368
Shumpert, Terry	1991	.182	.222	.227	.231	.282	.415	.223	.299	.324
Snow, J.T.	1993	.343	.389	.687	.127	.219	.333	.242	.338	.360
Sojo, Luis	1991	.232	.254	.275	.188	.235	.250	.286	.324	.364
Stankiewicz, Andy	1992	.317	.414	.450	.303	.361	.394	.248	.315	.314
Stocker, Kevin	1993	.413	.493	.540	.313	.389	.484	.288	.379	.326
Taubensee, Eddie	1992	.197	.274	.242	.125	.219	.172	.269	.341	.413
Thompson, Ryan	1993	.229	.270	.400	.231	.296	.400	.268	.319	.484
VanderWal, John	1992	.231	.333	.323	.309	.373	.426	.188	.253	.313
Vaughn, Mo	1991	.239	.293	.388	.267	.387	.317	.272	.337	.391
Whiten, Mark	1991	.258	.297	.364	.217	.260	.304	.246	.305	.415
Whitmore, Darrell	1993	.232	.274	.391	.183	.216	.268	.200	.254	.264
Wilkins, Rick	1991	.270	.333	.492	.242	.315	.348	.162	.279	.243
Williams, Bernie	1991	.267	.392	.467	.210	.338	.258	.237	.317	.343
Young, Kevin	1993	.250	.324	.344	.210	.329	.371	.238	.289	.337
Zupcic, Bob	1992	.279	.329	.397	.385	.432	.523	.247	.291	.297
Average		.270	.331	.398	.255	.319	.370	.255	.317	.375

WHO ARE THE "HUMAN AIR CONDITIONERS"? (p. 132)

The table below shows swings missed (**Sw**) as a **%** of total pitches swung at (**Pit**).

Both Leagues — Listed Alphabetically
(minimum 350 plate appearances in 1993)

Player, Team	Sw	Pit	%	Player, Team	Sw	Pit	%	Player, Team	Sw	Pit	%
Alicea, StL	87	630	13.8	Castilla, Col	152	605	25.1	Galarraga, Col	234	944	24.8
Alomar, Tor	126	1145	11.0	Cedeno A, Hou	300	1066	28.1	Gallego, NYA	139	774	18.0
Alou, Mon	138	864	16.0	Clark J, Col	208	951	21.9	Gant, Atl	281	1150	24.4
Amaral, Sea	81	588	13.8	Clark W, SF	152	980	15.5	Garcia, Pit	135	988	13.7
Anderson, Bal	150	1024	14.6	Clayton, SF	237	1133	20.9	Gardner, SD	87	726	12.0
Anthony, Hou	191	861	22.2	Cole, Col	75	569	13.2	Gates, Oak	132	974	13.6
Baerga, Cle	171	1206	14.2	Coleman, NYN	132	761	17.3	Gibson, Det	174	768	22.7
Bagwell, Hou	189	998	18.9	Conine, Fla	252	1207	20.9	Gilkey, StL	140	941	14.9
Baines, Bal	105	718	14.6	Cooper, Bos	157	1008	15.6	Girardi, Col	101	554	18.2
Barberie, Fla	125	701	17.8	Cora, ChA	80	1027	7.8	Gladden, Det	102	650	15.7
Bell D, SD	337	1151	29.3	Cordero, Mon	146	877	16.6	Gonzales R, Cal	108	677	16.0
Bell G, ChA	135	786	17.2	Curtis, Cal	162	1045	15.5	Gonzalez J, Tex	276	1079	25.6
Bell Jay, Pit	184	1113	16.5	Daulton, Phi	214	957	22.4	Gonzalez L, Hou	189	1089	17.4
Bell Juan, Mil	105	612	17.2	Davis C, Cal	326	1171	27.8	Grace, ChN	90	959	9.4
Belle, Cle	248	1175	21.1	Davis E, Det	240	874	27.5	Greenwell, Bos	107	918	11.7
Berry, Mon	146	581	25.1	Dawson, Bos	193	959	20.1	Griffey Jr, Sea	218	1125	19.4
Berryhill, Atl	173	727	23.8	Deer, Bos	376	1047	35.9	Grissom, Mon	169	1084	15.6
Bichette, Col	262	1127	23.2	DeShields, Mon	85	792	10.7	Guillen, ChA	117	868	13.5
Biggio, Hou	178	1117	15.9	Destrade, Fla	246	1034	23.8	Gutierrez, SD	200	885	22.6
Blauser, Atl	198	1144	17.3	Devereaux, Bal	200	954	21.0	Gwynn T, SD	46	778	5.9
Blowers, Sea	192	738	26.0	DiSarcina, Cal	69	680	10.1	Hamilton, Mil	87	963	9.0
Boggs, NYA	58	1003	5.8	Duncan, Phi	210	969	21.7	Harper, Min	97	938	10.3
Bonds, SF	154	1004	15.3	Dykstra, Phi	94	1122	8.4	Hatcher, Bos	110	908	12.1
Bonilla, NYN	252	1074	23.5	Eisenreich, Phi	76	609	12.5	Hayes, Col	259	1131	22.9
Borders, Tor	140	893	15.7	Felder, Sea	64	584	11.0	Hend'rs'n D, Oak	236	825	28.6
Bordick, Oak	93	936	9.9	Fermin, Cle	53	770	6.9	Henderson R, Tor	93	796	11.7
Branson, Cin	152	775	19.6	Fernandez, Tor	86	962	8.9	Hoiles, Bal	228	905	25.2
Brett, KC	180	1090	16.5	Fielder, Det	378	1271	29.7	Hollins, Phi	191	1037	18.4
Buechele, ChN	192	823	23.3	Finley, Hou	121	929	13.0	Hrbek, Min	155	774	20.0
Buhner, Sea	363	1151	31.5	Fletcher D, Mon	80	699	11.4	Hulse, Tex	121	790	15.3
Burks, ChA	173	931	18.6	Fletcher S, Bos	61	793	7.7	Hundley, NYN	127	769	16.5
Butler B, LA	86	1082	7.9	Franco, Tex	190	1040	18.3	Incaviglia, Phi	233	751	31.0
Caminiti, Hou	194	1022	19.0	Fryman, Det	244	1182	20.6	Jaha, Mil	229	971	23.6
Carr, Fla	203	1076	18.9	Gaetti, KC	239	737	32.4	James D, NYA	55	591	9.3
Carter, Tor	305	1465	20.8	Gagne, KC	199	1076	18.5	Jefferies, StL	65	870	7.5

Player, Team	Sw	Pit	%	Player, Team	Sw	Pit	%	Player, Team	Sw	Pit	%
Jefferson, Cle	187	724	25.8	Munoz, Min	237	735	32.2	Spiers, Mil	117	579	20.2
Johnson L, ChA	68	853	8.0	Murray, NYN	217	1216	17.8	Sprague, Tor	213	1050	20.3
Jose, KC	205	968	21.2	Neel, Oak	218	824	26.5	Stanley, NYA	186	871	21.4
Joyner, KC	153	951	16.1	Nixon, Atl	108	789	13.7	Steinbach, Oak	165	746	22.1
Justice, Atl	241	1170	20.6	O'Neill, NYA	154	943	16.3	Strange, Tex	167	906	18.4
Karkovice, ChA	278	871	31.9	Offerman, LA	150	1090	13.8	Surhoff, Mil	98	927	10.6
Karros, LA	209	1153	18.1	Olerud, Tor	131	974	13.4	Tartabull, NYA	356	1038	34.3
Kelly P, NYA	161	815	19.8	Oliver, Cin	214	1000	21.4	Tettleton, Det	237	958	24.7
Kent, NYN	232	1005	23.1	Orsulak, NYN	77	717	10.7	Thomas, ChA	121	990	12.2
King, Pit	116	1016	11.4	Owen, NYA	52	511	10.2	Thompson M, Phi	99	602	16.4
Kirby, Cle	143	873	16.4	Pagliarulo, Bal	125	707	17.7	Thompson R, SF	192	957	20.1
Knoblauch, Min	70	1037	6.8	Pagnozzi, StL	90	632	14.2	Trammell, Det	82	651	12.6
Kreuter, Det	148	749	19.8	Palmeiro, Tex	154	1123	13.7	Valentin Jn, Bos	128	789	16.2
Kruk, Phi	229	1025	22.3	Palmer, Tex	330	1113	29.6	Valle, Sea	143	798	17.9
Lankford, StL	227	870	26.1	Paquette, Oak	233	778	29.9	Van Slyke, Pit	79	524	15.1
Lansing, Mon	97	797	12.2	Pendleton, Atl	227	1261	18.0	Vaughn G, Mil	297	1142	26.0
Larkin B, Cin	76	677	11.2	Phillips T, Det	191	1124	17.0	Vaughn M, Bos	291	1114	26.1
Lemke, Atl	100	814	12.3	Piazza, LA	230	1064	21.6	Ventura, ChA	172	1006	17.1
Lewis D, SF	73	841	8.7	Plantier, SD	260	960	27.1	Vizcaino, ChN	123	945	13.0
Lind, KC	75	737	10.2	Polonia, Cal	103	1085	9.5	Vizquel, Sea	126	1148	11.0
Listach, Mil	116	645	18.0	Puckett, Min	261	1212	21.5	Walker L, Mon	195	983	19.8
Lofton, Cle	98	904	10.8	Raines, ChA	71	749	9.5	Wallach, LA	193	929	20.8
Lovullo, Cal	115	653	17.6	Reed Jody, LA	57	695	8.2	Weiss, Fla	91	862	10.6
Macfarlane, KC	183	782	23.4	Reimer, Mil	204	865	23.6	Whitaker, Det	83	722	11.5
Mack, Min	190	983	19.3	Reynolds, Bal	92	837	11.0	White Dev, Tor	324	1251	25.9
Magadan, Sea	94	796	11.8	Ripken C, Bal	149	1088	13.7	Whiten, StL	228	990	23.0
Manwaring, SF	158	836	18.9	Rodriguez I, Tex	199	1015	19.6	Wilkins, ChN	251	927	27.1
Martin A, Pit	303	961	31.5	Sabo, Cin	213	1131	18.8	Williams B, NYA	209	1060	19.7
Martinez T, Sea	126	747	16.9	Salmon, Cal	269	995	27.0	Williams M, SF	266	1165	22.8
Mattingly, NYA	79	897	8.8	Sanchez, ChN	55	551	10.0	Winfield, Min	283	1070	26.4
May, ChN	126	822	15.3	Sandberg, ChN	151	856	17.6	Young E, Col	76	770	9.9
McCarty, Min	153	661	23.1	Sanders R, Cin	273	1016	26.9	Young K, Pit	174	983	17.7
McGee, SF	203	978	20.8	Santiago, Fla	235	967	24.3	Yount, Mil	203	940	21.6
McGriff F, Atl	244	1072	22.8	Segui, Bal	129	806	16.0	Zeile, StL	164	976	16.8
McLemore, Bal	162	1017	15.9	Seitzer, Mil	101	787	12.8	**MLB Average**			**18.8**
McRae, KC	225	1339	16.8	Sheffield, Fla	197	974	20.2				
McReynolds, KC	123	681	18.1	Sierra, Oak	203	1156	17.6				
Meares, Min	124	643	19.3	Slaught, Pit	119	749	15.9				
Merced, Pit	147	791	18.6	Smith O, StL	54	959	5.6				
Mitchell, Cin	122	605	20.2	Snow, Cal	139	768	18.1				
Molitor, Tor	181	1231	14.7	Snyder, LA	347	1095	31.7				
Morandini, Phi	122	810	15.1	Sorrento, Cle	225	896	25.1				
Morris, Cin	99	692	14.3	Sosa, ChN	391	1316	29.7				

DID FRANK THOMAS DESERVE THE MVP? (p. 135)

In the chart below, **RC** stands for Runs Created, and **OW%** stands for Offensive Winning Percentage.

Both Leagues — Listed Alphabetically
(minimum 250 plate appearances in 1993)

Player, Team	RC	OW%	Player, Team	RC	OW%	Player, Team	RC	OW%
Aldrete, Oak	39.7	.570	Caminiti, Hou	65.5	.462	Fryman, Det	117.1	.696
Alicea, StL	52.8	.563	Canseco J, Tex	29.8	.455	Gaetti, KC	44.6	.474
Alomar, Tor	125.4	.733	Carr, Fla	64.1	.431	Gagne, KC	67.2	.462
Alou, Mon	79.4	.626	Carter, Tor	93.1	.560	Galarraga, Col	110.2	.816
Amaral, Sea	49.4	.483	Castilla, Col	34.3	.367	Gallego, NYA	59.9	.544
Anderson, Bal	93.9	.599	Cedeno A, Hou	68.7	.522	Gant, Atl	106.8	.651
Anthony, Hou	61.1	.482	Chamberlain, Phi	43.2	.592	Garcia, Pit	68.0	.475
Arias, Fla	29.1	.453	Cianfrocco, SD	34.1	.421	Gardner, SD	50.0	.486
Baerga, Cle	105.5	.633	Clark D, Pit	43.6	.601	Gates, Oak	75.1	.520
Bagwell, Hou	104.9	.715	Clark J, Col	64.9	.534	Gibson, Det	62.2	.572
Baines, Bal	82.2	.702	Clark P, SD	41.8	.686	Gilkey, StL	96.3	.657
Barberie, Fla	48.4	.502	Clark W, SF	80.6	.630	Girardi, Col	42.0	.515
Bass, Hou	34.7	.598	Clayton, SF	64.7	.444	Gladden, Det	43.4	.431
Bell D, SD	70.9	.508	Cole, Col	39.1	.407	Gomez L, Bal	27.2	.369
Bell G, ChA	33.0	.231	Coleman, NYN	46.2	.480	Gonzales R, Cal	37.3	.383
Bell Jay, Pit	104.3	.653	Conine, Fla	84.5	.568	Gonzalez J, Tex	122.6	.771
Bell Juan, Mil	36.5	.350	Cooper, Bos	76.4	.551	Gonzalez L, Hou	91.3	.643
Belle, Cle	119.4	.683	Cora, ChA	75.3	.459	Grace, ChN	107.0	.681
Berry, Mon	52.3	.640	Cordero, Mon	55.7	.441	Greenwell, Bos	94.8	.654
Berryhill, Atl	36.8	.411	Cotto, Fla	23.5	.347	Griffey Jr, Sea	146.7	.792
Bichette, Col	97.5	.689	Curtis, Cal	79.3	.482	Grissom, Mon	103.1	.635
Biggio, Hou	107.3	.652	Cuyler, Det	23.9	.310	Guillen, ChA	49.0	.381
Blankenship, Oak	29.0	.353	Daulton, Phi	109.2	.740	Gutierrez, SD	50.7	.446
Blauser, Atl	111.9	.695	Davis C, Cal	80.3	.508	Gwynn C, KC	38.6	.519
Blowers, Sea	61.0	.586	Davis E, Det	62.2	.502	Gwynn T, SD	94.4	.735
Boggs, NYA	81.6	.563	Dawson, Bos	57.1	.451	Hamilton, Mil	76.9	.567
Bonds, SF	172.2	.877	Deer, Bos	57.6	.432	Harper, Min	74.4	.543
Bonilla, NYN	92.6	.669	DeShields, Mon	80.2	.642	Hatcher, Bos	66.3	.477
Boone, Sea	34.8	.447	Destrade, Fla	72.9	.487	Hayes, Col	97.6	.642
Borders, Tor	46.6	.316	Devereaux, Bal	63.0	.429	Hemond, Oak	34.5	.564
Bordick, Oak	59.8	.373	DiSarcina, Cal	32.0	.220	Henderson D, Oak	46.6	.426
Boston, Col	41.6	.548	Duncan, Phi	57.9	.457	Henderson R, Tor	118.4	.742
Branson, Cin	33.6	.304	Dykstra, Phi	142.3	.770	Hiatt, KC	23.6	.317
Bream, Atl	38.5	.534	Easley, Cal	37.4	.608	Hill, ChN	43.5	.503
Brett, KC	70.6	.452	Eisenreich, Phi	59.3	.657	Hoiles, Bal	104.9	.795
Browne, Oak	25.6	.333	Espinoza, Cle	28.1	.371	Hollins, Phi	91.7	.633
Brumfield, Cin	37.9	.534	Felder, Sea	24.9	.197	Howard T, Cin	35.2	.385
Brunansky, Mil	18.1	.221	Fermin, Cle	43.8	.307	Hrbek, Min	66.9	.593
Buechele, ChN	69.1	.578	Fernandez, Tor	71.1	.489	Hulett, Bal	36.1	.538
Buhner, Sea	105.0	.655	Fielder, Det	96.4	.604	Hulse, Tex	50.5	.460
Burks, ChA	77.2	.560	Finley, Hou	64.3	.456	Hundley, NYN	38.3	.316
Burnitz, NYN	42.8	.598	Fletcher D, Mon	49.6	.479	Incaviglia, Phi	60.4	.621
Butler B, LA	95.9	.602	Fletcher S, Bos	66.9	.522	Jackson B, ChA	34.4	.433
Calderon, ChA	17.0	.196	Franco, Tex	84.6	.585	Jackson D, NYN	16.9	.159

Player, Team	RC	OW%	Player, Team	RC	OW%	Player, Team	RC	OW%
Jaha, Mil	74.0	.527	Morris, Cin	60.7	.643	Smith D, ChN	54.4	.670
James D, NYA	63.6	.705	Munoz, Min	36.3	.393	Smith L, Bal	47.4	.729
Javier, Cal	36.4	.571	Murray, NYN	85.6	.544	Smith O, StL	67.4	.481
Jefferies, StL	112.6	.755	Myers, Cal	29.7	.348	Snow, Cal	58.4	.492
Jefferson, Cle	41.1	.400	Neel, Oak	74.3	.644	Snyder, LA	69.4	.533
Johnson H, NYN	34.0	.542	Nilsson, Mil	35.9	.420	Sorrento, Cle	69.3	.551
Johnson L, ChA	78.4	.569	Nixon, Atl	58.2	.474	Sosa, ChN	86.5	.554
Jose, KC	53.8	.380	O'Neill, NYA	88.9	.664	Spiers, Mil	30.5	.266
Joyner, KC	87.8	.645	Offerman, LA	72.8	.445	Sprague, Tor	61.1	.394
Justice, Atl	107.8	.679	Olerud, Tor	161.2	.861	Stanley, NYA	89.7	.733
Karkovice, ChA	47.1	.387	Oliver, Cin	49.3	.365	Steinbach, Oak	50.3	.489
Karros, LA	68.5	.417	Olson, Atl	24.0	.307	Stocker, Phi	45.4	.678
Kelly P, NYA	48.2	.411	Orsulak, NYN	53.7	.529	Strange, Tex	55.3	.400
Kelly R, Cin	52.5	.642	Ortiz J, Cle	16.9	.178	Surhoff, Mil	68.0	.456
Kent, NYN	68.6	.532	Owen, NYA	31.2	.311	Tartabull, NYA	98.8	.671
King, Pit	87.7	.565	Pagliarulo, Bal	60.2	.600	Taubensee, Hou	32.2	.421
Kirby, Cle	57.4	.454	Pagnozzi, StL	35.8	.413	Tettleton, Det	101.3	.666
Knoblauch, Min	78.9	.485	Palmeiro, Tex	128.5	.735	Thomas, ChA	149.2	.821
Kreuter, Det	70.0	.676	Palmer, Tex	84.0	.578	Thompson M, Phi	41.5	.464
Kruk, Phi	117.7	.774	Pappas, StL	29.3	.496	Th'mps'n Rob, SF	94.4	.709
Lankford, StL	55.8	.504	Paquette, Oak	34.8	.282	Th'mps'n Ryan, NYN	35.5	.454
Lansing, Mon	65.5	.513	Pena G, StL	35.8	.530	Thon, Mil	26.8	.381
Larkin B, Cin	69.5	.689	Pena T, Bos	18.1	.121	Trammell, Det	76.7	.697
Lemke, Atl	55.1	.405	Pendleton, Atl	77.3	.474	Valentin John, Bos	72.8	.559
Lewis D, SF	54.9	.380	Phillips T, Det	111.1	.701	Valle, Sea	59.2	.493
Leyritz, NYA	54.6	.727	Piazza, LA	112.1	.746	Van Slyke, Pit	49.8	.605
Lind, KC	33.8	.234	Plantier, SD	81.2	.640	Vaughn G, Mil	105.5	.661
Listach, Mil	37.6	.353	Polonia, Cal	64.1	.388	Vaughn M, Bos	111.0	.714
Livingstone, Det	36.1	.449	Puckett, Min	100.1	.604	Velarde, NYA	34.5	.556
Lofton, Cle	108.6	.696	Quintana, Bos	25.8	.261	Ventura, ChA	93.0	.598
Lovullo, Cal	40.9	.390	Raines, ChA	84.6	.715	Vizcaino, ChN	68.7	.482
Macfarlane, KC	69.9	.638	Reboulet, Min	27.5	.395	Vizquel, Sea	54.5	.322
Mack, Min	68.7	.509	Reed Jody, LA	48.9	.399	Walker L, Mon	91.6	.677
Magadan, Sea	66.3	.541	Reimer, Mil	49.7	.400	Wallach, LA	44.0	.313
Manwaring, SF	50.3	.446	Renteria, Fla	25.9	.355	Weiss, Fla	63.1	.494
Martin A, Pit	78.2	.625	Reynolds, Bal	60.1	.435	Whitaker, Det	77.6	.700
Martinez Crls, Cle	26.1	.344	Ripken C, Bal	85.7	.489	White Dev, Tor	98.5	.614
Martinez Dave, SF	27.7	.432	Roberts, Cin	34.2	.438	Whiten, StL	76.3	.518
Martinez T, Sea	63.7	.572	Rodriguez I, Tex	57.2	.428	Whitmore, Fla	17.2	.194
Mattingly, NYA	83.6	.592	Sabo, Cin	76.5	.531	Wilkins, ChN	94.8	.762
May, ChN	63.4	.540	Salmon, Cal	110.2	.725	Williams B, NYA	72.1	.464
McCarty, Min	21.9	.153	Samuel, Cin	27.1	.371	Williams M, SF	101.3	.665
McGee, SF	62.4	.524	Sanchez, ChN	34.4	.375	Winfield, Min	75.2	.515
McGriff F, Atl	115.7	.724	Sandberg, ChN	68.2	.597	Young E, Col	65.3	.498
McLemore, Bal	73.0	.444	Sanders D, Atl	39.6	.563	Young K, Pit	47.7	.378
McRae, KC	83.0	.487	Sanders R, Cin	77.1	.585	Yount, Mil	57.3	.452
McReynolds, KC	46.5	.478	Santiago, Fla	50.9	.392	Zeile, StL	87.1	.589
Meares, Min	25.1	.207	Segui, Bal	62.7	.504	Zupcic, Bos	32.3	.380
Merced, Pit	85.3	.719	Seitzer, Mil	54.1	.456			
Milligan, Cle	57.6	.705	Servais, Hou	33.7	.489			
Mitchell, Cin	69.9	.768	Sheffield, Fla	86.5	.659			
Molitor, Tor	136.1	.750	Sierra, Oak	70.0	.378			
Morandini, Phi	49.3	.441	Slaught, Pit	57.4	.593			

IS BARRY STILL BEST IN THE SECONDARY? (p. 138)

Both Leagues — Listed Alphabetically
(minimum 350 plate appearances in 1993)

Player, Team	SA	Player, Team	SA	Player, Team	SA	Player, Team	SA
Alicea, StL	.251	Dykstra, Phi	.419	King, Pit	.211	Reimer, Mil	.215
Alomar, Tor	.370	Eisenreich, Phi	.213	Kirby, Cle	.210	Reynolds, Bal	.221
Alou, Mon	.299	Felder, Sea	.140	Knoblauch, Min	.206	Ripken C, Bal	.259
Amaral, Sea	.188	Fermin, Cle	.102	Kreuter, Det	.332	Rodriguez I, Tex	.203
Anderson, Bal	.330	Fernandez, Tor	.241	Kruk, Phi	.374	Sabo, Cin	.263
Anthony, Hou	.245	Fielder, Det	.353	Lankford, StL	.307	Salmon, Cal	.410
Baerga, Cle	.237	Finley, Hou	.194	Lansing, Mon	.212	Sanchez, ChN	.087
Bagwell, Hou	.329	Fletcher D, Mon	.210	Larkin B, Cin	.297	Sandberg, ChN	.200
Baines, Bal	.334	Fletcher S, Bos	.221	Lemke, Atl	.219	Sanders R, Cin	.306
Barberie, Fla	.176	Franco, Tex	.276	Lewis D, SF	.188	Santiago, Fla	.235
Bell D, SD	.236	Fryman, Det	.321	Lind, KC	.072	Segui, Bal	.258
Bell G, ChA	.178	Gaetti, KC	.251	Listach, Mil	.202	Seitzer, Mil	.233
Bell Jay, Pit	.265	Gagne, KC	.183	Lofton, Cle	.323	Sheffield, Fla	.302
Bell Juan, Mil	.208	Galarraga, Col	.279	Lovullo, Cal	.204	Sierra, Oak	.271
Belle, Cle	.409	Gallego, NYA	.256	Macfarlane, KC	.320	Slaught, Pit	.220
Berry, Mon	.375	Gant, Atl	.375	Mack, Min	.237	Smith O, StL	.171
Berryhill, Atl	.200	Garcia, Pit	.200	Magadan, Sea	.262	Snow, Cal	.305
Bichette, Col	.279	Gardner, SD	.196	Manwaring, SF	.164	Snyder, LA	.229
Biggio, Hou	.310	Gates, Oak	.213	Martin A, Pit	.302	Sorrento, Cle	.307
Blauser, Atl	.290	Gibson, Det	.303	Martinez T, Sea	.294	Sosa, ChN	.329
Blowers, Sea	.301	Gilkey, StL	.285	Mattingly, NYA	.270	Spiers, Mil	.153
Boggs, NYA	.191	Girardi, Col	.184	May, ChN	.209	Sprague, Tor	.187
Bonds, SF	.607	Gladden, Det	.233	McCarty, Min	.114	Stanley, NYA	.364
Bonilla, NYN	.400	Gonzales R, Cal	.215	McGee, SF	.171	Steinbach, Oak	.195
Borders, Tor	.158	Gonzalez J, Tex	.397	McGriff F, Atl	.399	Strange, Tex	.196
Bordick, Oak	.172	Gonzalez L, Hou	.265	McLemore, Bal	.205	Surhoff, Mil	.188
Branson, Cin	.126	Grace, ChN	.276	McRae, KC	.204	Tartabull, NYA	.433
Brett, KC	.241	Greenwell, Bos	.267	McReynolds, KC	.285	Tettleton, Det	.448
Buechele, ChN	.270	Griffey Jr, Sea	.486	Meares, Min	.075	Thomas, ChA	.497
Buhner, Sea	.377	Grissom, Mon	.290	Merced, Pit	.302	Thompson M, Phi	.221
Burks, ChA	.281	Guillen, ChA	.118	Mitchell, Cin	.341	Thompson R, SF	.287
Butler B, LA	.247	Gutierrez, SD	.196	Molitor, Tor	.327	Trammell, Det	.272
Caminiti, Hou	.225	Gwynn T, SD	.239	Morandini, Phi	.214	Valentin John, Bos	.271
Carr, Fla	.218	Hamilton, Mil	.198	Morris, Cin	.193	Valle, Sea	.253
Carter, Tor	.322	Harper, Min	.172	Munoz, Min	.233	Van Slyke, Pit	.241
Castilla, Col	.178	Hatcher, Bos	.181	Murray, NYN	.248	Vaughn G, Mil	.376
Cedeno A, Hou	.228	Hayes, Col	.300	Neel, Oak	.293	Vaughn M, Bos	.377
Clark J, Col	.209	Henderson D, Oak	.283	Nixon, Atl	.252	Ventura, ChA	.352
Clark W, SF	.277	Henderson R, Tor	.528	O'Neill, NYA	.277	Vizcaino, ChN	.160
Clayton, SF	.160	Hoiles, Bal	.439	Offerman, LA	.210	Vizquel, Sea	.129
Cole, Col	.221	Hollins, Phi	.324	Olerud, Tor	.439	Walker L, Mon	.412
Coleman, NYN	.220	Hrbek, Min	.411	Oliver, Cin	.201	Wallach, LA	.182
Conine, Fla	.198	Hulse, Tex	.192	Orsulak, NYN	.186	Weiss, Fla	.208
Cooper, Bos	.234	Hundley, NYN	.185	Owen, NYA	.168	Whitaker, Det	.363
Cora, ChA	.218	Incaviglia, Phi	.313	Pagliarulo, Bal	.232	White Dev, Tor	.311
Cordero, Mon	.229	Jaha, Mil	.258	Pagnozzi, StL	.176	Whiten, StL	.286
Curtis, Cal	.245	James D, NYA	.224	Palmeiro, Tex	.414	Wilkins, ChN	.372
Daulton, Phi	.465	Jefferies, StL	.325	Palmer, Tex	.362	Williams B, NYA	.226
Davis C, Cal	.326	Jefferson, Cle	.194	Paquette, Oak	.204	Williams M, SF	.311
Davis E, Det	.361	Johnson L, ChA	.204	Pendleton, Atl	.199	Winfield, Min	.252
Dawson, Bos	.191	Jose, KC	.204	Phillips T, Det	.327	Young E, Col	.259
Deer, Bos	.307	Joyner, KC	.300	Piazza, LA	.325	Young K, Pit	.187
DeShields, Mon	.295	Justice, Atl	.374	Plantier, SD	.398	Yount, Mil	.233
Destrade, Fla	.250	Karkovice, ChA	.268	Polonia, Cal	.193	Zeile, StL	.280
Devereaux, Bal	.231	Karros, LA	.215	Puckett, Min	.257	**MLB Average**	.254
DiSarcina, Cal	.106	Kelly P, NYA	.182	Raines, ChA	.361		
Duncan, Phi	.161	Kent, NYN	.236	Reed Jody, LA	.151		

ARE GALARRAGA AND OLERUD FOR REAL? (p. 140)

Both Leagues — Listed Alphabetically
(Minimum 350 PA in 1992 and 1993)

Player, Team	92	93	+/-	Player, Team	92	93	+/-	Player, Team	92	93	+/-
Alomar, Tor	.310	.326	+16	Griffey Jr, Sea	.308	.309	+1	Orsulak, NYN	.289	.284	-5
Alou, Mon	.282	.286	+4	Grissom, Mon	.276	.298	+22	Owen, NYA	.269	.234	-35
Anderson, Bal	.271	.263	-8	Gwynn T, SD	.317	.358	+41	Pagnozzi, StL	.249	.258	+9
Anthony, Hou	.239	.249	+10	Hamilton, Mil	.298	.310	+12	Palmeiro, Tex	.268	.295	+27
Baerga, Cle	.312	.321	+9	Harper, Min	.307	.304	-3	Palmer, Tex	.229	.245	+16
Bagwell, Hou	.273	.320	+47	Hatcher, Bos	.249	.287	+38	Pendleton, Atl	.311	.272	-39
Baines, Bal	.253	.313	+60	Hayes, Col	.257	.305	+48	Phillips T, Det	.276	.313	+37
Bell G, ChA	.255	.217	-38	Henderson R, Tor	.283	.289	+6	Plantier, SD	.246	.240	-6
Bell Jay, Pit	.264	.310	+46	Hoiles, Bal	.274	.310	+36	Polonia, Cal	.286	.271	-15
Belle, Cle	.260	.290	+30	Hollins, Phi	.270	.273	+3	Puckett, Min	.329	.296	-33
Bichette, Col	.287	.310	+23	Hrbek, Min	.244	.242	-2	Raines, ChA	.294	.306	+12
Biggio, Hou	.277	.287	+10	Hundley, NYN	.209	.228	+19	Reed Jody, LA	.247	.276	+29
Blauser, Atl	.262	.305	+43	Incaviglia, Phi	.266	.274	+8	Reimer, Mil	.267	.249	-18
Boggs, NYA	.259	.302	+43	Jefferies, StL	.285	.342	+57	Reynolds, Bal	.247	.252	+5
Bonds, SF	.311	.336	+25	Johnson L, ChA	.279	.311	+32	Ripken C, Bal	.251	.257	+6
Bonilla, NYN	.249	.265	+16	Jose, KC	.295	.253	-42	Rodriguez I, Tex	.260	.273	+13
Borders, Tor	.242	.254	+12	Joyner, KC	.269	.292	+23	Sabo, Cin	.244	.259	+15
Bordick, Oak	.300	.249	-51	Justice, Atl	.256	.270	+14	Sandberg, ChN	.304	.309	+5
Brett, KC	.285	.266	-19	Karkovice, ChA	.237	.228	-9	Sanders R, Cin	.270	.274	+4
Buechele, ChN	.261	.272	+11	Karros, LA	.257	.247	-10	Santiago, Fla	.251	.230	-21
Buhner, Sea	.243	.272	+29	Kelly P, NYA	.226	.273	+47	Seitzer, Mil	.270	.269	-1
Butler B, LA	.309	.298	-11	King, Pit	.231	.295	+64	Sheffield, Fla	.330	.294	-36
Caminiti, Hou	.294	.262	-32	Knoblauch, Min	.297	.277	-20	Sierra, Oak	.278	.233	-45
Carter, Tor	.264	.254	-10	Kruk, Phi	.323	.316	-7	Smith O, StL	.295	.288	-7
Clark J, Col	.242	.282	+40	Lankford, StL	.293	.238	-55	Snyder, LA	.269	.266	-3
Clark W, SF	.300	.283	-17	Larkin B, Cin	.304	.315	+11	Sorrento, Cle	.269	.257	-12
Clayton, SF	.224	.282	+58	Lemke, Atl	.227	.252	+25	Steinbach, Oak	.279	.285	+6
Cooper, Bos	.276	.279	+3	Lewis D, SF	.231	.253	+22	Surhoff, Mil	.252	.274	+22
Curtis, Cal	.259	.285	+26	Lind, KC	.235	.248	+13	Tartabull, NYA	.266	.250	-16
Daulton, Phi	.270	.257	-13	Listach, Mil	.290	.244	-46	Tettleton, Det	.238	.245	+7
Davis C, Cal	.288	.243	-45	Lofton, Cle	.285	.325	+40	Thomas, ChA	.323	.317	-6
Dawson, Bos	.277	.273	-4	Macfarlane, KC	.234	.273	+39	Thompson R, SF	.260	.312	+52
Deer, Bos	.247	.210	-37	Mack, Min	.315	.276	-39	Valle, Sea	.240	.258	+18
DeShields, Mon	.292	.295	+3	Magadan, Sea	.283	.273	-10	Van Slyke, Pit	.324	.310	-14
Devereaux, Bal	.276	.250	-26	Manwaring, SF	.244	.275	+31	Vaughn G, Mil	.228	.267	+39
DiSarcina, Cal	.247	.238	-9	Martinez T, Sea	.257	.265	+8	Vaughn M, Bos	.234	.297	+63
Duncan, Phi	.267	.282	+15	Mattingly, NYA	.288	.291	+3	Ventura, ChA	.282	.262	-20
Dykstra, Phi	.301	.305	+4	May, ChN	.274	.295	+21	Vizquel, Sea	.294	.255	-39
Eisenreich, Phi	.269	.318	+49	McGee, SF	.297	.301	+4	Walker L, Mon	.301	.265	-36
Felder, Sea	.286	.211	-75	McGriff F, Atl	.286	.291	+5	Wallach, LA	.223	.222	-1
Fernandez, Tor	.275	.279	+4	McRae, KC	.223	.282	+59	Weiss, Fla	.212	.266	+54
Fielder, Det	.244	.267	+23	McReynolds, KC	.247	.245	-2	Whitaker, Det	.278	.290	+12
Finley, Hou	.292	.266	-26	Merced, Pit	.247	.313	+66	White Dev, Tor	.248	.273	+25
Fletcher S, Bos	.275	.285	+10	Mitchell, Cin	.286	.341	+55	Whiten, StL	.254	.253	-1
Fryman, Det	.266	.300	+34	Molitor, Tor	.320	.332	+12	Williams M, SF	.227	.294	+67
Gaetti, KC	.226	.245	+19	Morandini, Phi	.265	.247	-18	Winfield, Min	.290	.271	-19
Gagne, KC	.246	.280	+34	Morris, Cin	.271	.317	+46	Yount, Mil	.264	.258	-6
Gant, Atl	.259	.274	+15	Munoz, Min	.270	.233	-37	Zeile, StL	.257	.277	+20
Gilkey, StL	.302	.305	+3	Murray, NYN	.261	.285	+24	**AL Avg**	**.259**	**.267**	**+8**
Gladden, Det	.254	.267	+13	Nixon, Atl	.294	.269	-25	**NL Avg**	**.252**	**.264**	**+12**
Gonzales R, Cal	.277	.251	-26	O'Neill, NYA	.246	.311	+65				
Gonzalez J, Tex	.260	.310	+50	Offerman, LA	.260	.269	+9				
Gonzalez L, Hou	.243	.300	+57	Olerud, Tor	.284	.363	+79				
Grace, ChN	.307	.325	+18	Oliver, Cin	.270	.239	-31				

WHAT ARE THE BEST COUNTS TO STEAL ON? (p. 142)

Both Leagues — Listed Alphabetically
(Minimum 100 Stolen Base Attempts, 1991-1993)

Roberto Alomar

B-S	SB-CS	Pct
Tot	157-35	.818
0-0	50-6	.893
0-1	18-3	.857
0-2	14-4	.778
1-0	19-10	.655
1-1	11-1	.917
1-2	16-4	.800
2-0	6-3	.667
2-1	7-2	.778
2-2	5-1	.833
3-0	6-0	1.000
3-1	1-0	1.000
3-2	4-1	.800

Brett Butler

B-S	SB-CS	Pct
Tot	118-68	.634
0-0	40-23	.635
0-1	10-7	.588
0-2	4-1	.800
1-0	28-13	.683
1-1	8-11	.421
1-2	4-3	.571
2-0	4-1	.800
2-1	4-3	.571
2-2	12-4	.750
3-0	0-0	-
3-1	0-2	.000
3-2	4-0	1.000

Delino DeShields

B-S	SB-CS	Pct
Tot	145-48	.751
0-0	51-11	.823
0-1	10-1	.909
0-2	6-1	.857
1-0	33-11	.750
1-1	8-7	.533
1-2	6-2	.750
2-0	6-3	.667
2-1	10-2	.833
2-2	12-5	.706
3-0	0-0	-
3-1	1-1	.500
3-2	2-4	.333

Ron Gant

B-S	SB-CS	Pct
Tot	92-34	.730
0-0	36-10	.783
0-1	1-5	.167
0-2	0-1	.000
1-0	19-9	.679
1-1	8-3	.727
1-2	7-3	.700
2-0	1-0	1.000
2-1	7-1	.875
2-2	8-1	.889
3-0	0-0	-
3-1	2-0	1.000
3-2	3-1	.750

Brady Anderson

B-S	SB-CS	Pct
Tot	89-33	.730
0-0	33-9	.786
0-1	8-5	.615
0-2	2-3	.400
1-0	10-6	.625
1-1	10-2	.833
1-2	4-1	.800
2-0	7-1	.875
2-1	8-2	.800
2-2	5-2	.714
3-0	0-0	-
3-1	1-1	.500
3-2	1-1	.500

Alex Cole

B-S	SB-CS	Pct
Tot	73-36	.670
0-0	28-11	.718
0-1	8-7	.533
0-2	1-0	1.000
1-0	16-5	.762
1-1	4-2	.667
1-2	2-1	.667
2-0	3-2	.600
2-1	4-2	.667
2-2	4-1	.800
3-0	0-0	-
3-1	2-2	.500
3-2	1-3	.250

Lenny Dykstra

B-S	SB-CS	Pct
Tot	91-21	.813
0-0	31-8	.795
0-1	8-3	.727
0-2	1-1	.500
1-0	6-1	.857
1-1	11-4	.733
1-2	11-1	.917
2-0	4-0	1.000
2-1	8-1	.889
2-2	7-0	1.000
3-0	1-0	1.000
3-1	2-1	.667
3-2	1-1	.500

Marquis Grissom

B-S	SB-CS	Pct
Tot	207-40	.838
0-0	72-9	.889
0-1	24-5	.828
0-2	6-1	.857
1-0	39-7	.848
1-1	20-5	.800
1-2	11-3	.786
2-0	8-2	.800
2-1	9-3	.750
2-2	13-2	.867
3-0	1-0	1.000
3-1	1-1	.500
3-2	3-2	.600

Craig Biggio

B-S	SB-CS	Pct
Tot	72-38	.655
0-0	24-12	.667
0-1	6-3	.667
0-2	1-1	.500
1-0	9-8	.529
1-1	10-6	.625
1-2	2-1	.667
2-0	2-0	1.000
2-1	6-4	.600
2-2	8-1	.889
3-0	0-0	-
3-1	1-2	.333
3-2	3-0	1.000

Vince Coleman

B-S	SB-CS	Pct
Tot	99-36	.733
0-0	43-12	.782
0-1	12-3	.800
0-2	2-0	1.000
1-0	10-7	.588
1-1	13-3	.813
1-2	5-3	.625
2-0	4-1	.800
2-1	7-4	.636
2-2	2-2	.500
3-0	1-1	.500
3-1	0-0	-
3-2	0-0	-

Tony Fernandez

B-S	SB-CS	Pct
Tot	64-39	.621
0-0	12-13	.480
0-1	10-2	.833
0-2	3-0	1.000
1-0	10-6	.625
1-1	5-5	.500
1-2	9-1	.900
2-0	4-3	.571
2-1	3-3	.500
2-2	5-5	.500
3-0	0-0	-
3-1	2-1	.667
3-2	1-0	1.000

Darryl Hamilton

B-S	SB-CS	Pct
Tot	78-33	.703
0-0	19-11	.633
0-1	10-0	1.000
0-2	2-0	1.000
1-0	13-6	.684
1-1	12-5	.706
1-2	3-0	1.000
2-0	2-1	.667
2-1	6-2	.750
2-2	4-4	.500
3-0	0-0	-
3-1	4-1	.800
3-2	3-3	.500

Barry Bonds

B-S	SB-CS	Pct
Tot	111-33	.771
0-0	34-8	.810
0-1	21-4	.840
0-2	4-2	.667
1-0	13-7	.650
1-1	15-5	.750
1-2	8-2	.800
2-0	2-0	1.000
2-1	8-0	1.000
2-2	3-4	.429
3-0	1-0	1.000
3-1	0-0	-
3-2	2-1	.667

Chad Curtis

B-S	SB-CS	Pct
Tot	91-42	.684
0-0	16-9	.640
0-1	14-4	.778
0-2	6-2	.750
1-0	10-7	.588
1-1	14-3	.824
1-2	9-3	.750
2-0	6-2	.750
2-1	4-3	.571
2-2	6-6	.500
3-0	0-0	-
3-1	2-3	.400
3-2	4-0	1.000

Steve Finley

B-S	SB-CS	Pct
Tot	97-33	.746
0-0	19-9	.679
0-1	10-4	.714
0-2	5-1	.833
1-0	16-6	.727
1-1	9-3	.750
1-2	15-2	.882
2-0	2-1	.667
2-1	5-4	.556
2-2	11-1	.917
3-0	0-0	-
3-1	2-0	1.000
3-2	3-2	.600

Rickey Henderson

B-S	SB-CS	Pct
Tot	159-37	.811
0-0	39-7	.848
0-1	17-4	.810
0-2	17-1	.944
1-0	19-5	.792
1-1	22-4	.846
1-2	17-4	.810
2-0	4-3	.571
2-1	12-3	.800
2-2	7-2	.778
3-0	0-0	-
3-1	2-1	.667
3-2	3-3	.500

B-S	SB-CS	Pct	B-S	SB-CS	Pct	B-S	SB-CS	Pct	B-S	SB-CS	Pct
Gregg Jefferies			**Chuck Knoblauch**			**Otis Nixon**			**Ozzie Smith**		
Tot	91-23	.798	Tot	88-29	.752	Tot	160-52	.755	Tot	99-26	.792
0-0	25-10	.714	0-0	22-8	.733	0-0	46-13	.780	0-0	23-1	.958
0-1	8-2	.800	0-1	10-2	.833	0-1	21-3	.875	0-1	11-5	.688
0-2	3-1	.750	0-2	5-0	1.000	0-2	5-4	.556	0-2	6-0	1.000
1-0	12-3	.800	1-0	10-2	.833	1-0	24-8	.750	1-0	4-3	.571
1-1	16-1	.941	1-1	11-6	.647	1-1	18-8	.692	1-1	11-3	.786
1-2	7-1	.875	1-2	4-2	.667	1-2	8-3	.727	1-2	16-5	.762
2-0	1-0	1.000	2-0	3-1	.750	2-0	10-3	.769	2-0	5-1	.833
2-1	7-2	.778	2-1	3-4	.429	2-1	11-7	.611	2-1	13-4	.765
2-2	5-1	.833	2-2	16-0	1.000	2-2	10-1	.909	2-2	7-2	.778
3-0	0-0	-	3-0	0-0	-	3-0	0-0	-	3-0	0-0	-
3-1	2-0	1.000	3-1	1-0	1.000	3-1	5-1	.833	3-1	1-1	.500
3-2	5-2	.714	3-2	3-4	.429	3-2	2-1	.667	3-2	2-1	.667
Lance Johnson			**Ray Lankford**			**Luis Polonia**			**Devon White**		
Tot	102-32	.761	Tot	100-58	.633	Tot	154-68	.694	Tot	104-18	.852
0-0	30-5	.857	0-0	34-12	.739	0-0	40-12	.769	0-0	30-5	.857
0-1	7-2	.778	0-1	10-5	.667	0-1	19-10	.655	0-1	13-2	.867
0-2	1-1	.500	0-2	4-2	.667	0-2	3-3	.500	0-2	3-0	1.000
1-0	17-6	.739	1-0	18-9	.667	1-0	20-13	.606	1-0	21-2	.913
1-1	15-8	.652	1-1	9-9	.500	1-1	17-9	.654	1-1	9-2	.818
1-2	7-0	1.000	1-2	6-3	.667	1-2	16-7	.696	1-2	5-2	.714
2-0	5-2	.714	2-0	4-7	.364	2-0	12-3	.800	2-0	6-0	1.000
2-1	6-2	.750	2-1	8-8	.500	2-1	8-4	.667	2-1	5-4	.556
2-2	8-3	.727	2-2	6-1	.857	2-2	11-4	.733	2-2	6-1	.857
3-0	0-0	-	3-0	0-0	-	3-0	1-1	.500	3-0	0-0	-
3-1	2-1	.667	3-1	1-1	.500	3-1	2-0	1.000	3-1	3-0	1.000
3-2	4-2	.667	3-2	0-1	.000	3-2	5-2	.714	3-2	3-0	1.000
Felix Jose			**Darren Lewis**			**Tim Raines**					
Tot	79-37	.681	Tot	87-30	.744	Tot	117-28	.807			
0-0	18-2	.900	0-0	40-9	.816	0-0	39-7	.848			
0-1	11-6	.647	0-1	7-4	.636	0-1	12-5	.706			
0-2	6-2	.750	0-2	3-0	1.000	0-2	4-1	.800			
1-0	14-6	.700	1-0	10-7	.588	1-0	25-1	.962			
1-1	9-9	.500	1-1	9-3	.750	1-1	12-5	.706			
1-2	9-4	.692	1-2	3-2	.600	1-2	2-3	.400			
2-0	2-1	.667	2-0	4-0	1.000	2-0	5-0	1.000			
2-1	4-2	.667	2-1	3-2	.600	2-1	8-2	.800			
2-2	4-4	.500	2-2	6-2	.750	2-2	5-2	.714			
3-0	0-0	-	3-0	0-0	-	3-0	1-0	1.000			
3-1	1-1	.500	3-1	0-1	.000	3-1	1-2	.333			
3-2	1-0	1.000	3-2	2-0	1.000	3-2	3-0	1.000			
Roberto Kelly			**Kenny Lofton**			**Bip Roberts**					
Tot	81-19	.810	Tot	138-27	.836	Tot	96-33	.744			
0-0	11-1	.917	0-0	48-8	.857	0-0	46-13	.780			
0-1	7-4	.636	0-1	10-2	.833	0-1	12-4	.750			
0-2	6-0	1.000	0-2	3-2	.600	0-2	3-0	1.000			
1-0	12-3	.800	1-0	30-6	.833	1-0	10-4	.714			
1-1	8-2	.800	1-1	12-4	.750	1-1	8-3	.727			
1-2	14-2	.875	1-2	4-1	.800	1-2	1-3	.250			
2-0	3-1	.750	2-0	13-1	.929	2-0	2-2	.500			
2-1	9-2	.818	2-1	10-3	.769	2-1	6-2	.750			
2-2	9-1	.900	2-2	4-0	1.000	2-2	3-1	.750			
3-0	0-0	-	3-0	1-0	1.000	3-0	0-0	-			
3-1	2-0	1.000	3-1	1-0	1.000	3-1	3-0	1.000			
3-2	0-3	.000	3-2	2-0	1.000	3-2	2-1	.667			

WILL THE GIANTS STILL HAVE THE BEST "HEART OF THE ORDER" IN 1994? (p. 144)

Team total statistics for the Number 3, 4, and 5 hitters

American League — Listed by Most RBI

Team	Avg	HR	RBI	Slg	Main 3-4-5 Hitters
Toronto	.313	78	350	.519	Molitor, Carter, Olerud
New York	.292	91	344	.499	Mattingly, Tartabull, O'Neill
Cleveland	.290	81	335	.483	Baerga, Belle, Sorrento
Texas	.290	104	330	.526	Palmeiro, Gonzalez J, Franco
Detroit	.280	78	325	.466	Fryman, Fielder, Gibson
Chicago	.261	88	322	.458	Thomas, Ventura, Bell
Minnesota	.277	81	305	.463	Puckett, Hrbek, Winfield
California	.256	78	304	.437	Salmon, Davis C, Lovullo
Seattle	.280	94	303	.493	Griffey Jr, Buhner, Martinez T
Baltimore	.259	72	287	.422	Ripken C, Baines, Devereaux
Milwaukee	.273	61	283	.435	Surhoff, Vaughn G, Reimer
Oakland	.251	72	281	.418	Sierra, Neel, Steinbach
Boston	.273	56	270	.433	Greenwell, Dawson, Vaughn M
Kansas City	.266	60	249	.433	Brett, Macfarlane, Joyner
AL Average	**.276**	**78**	**306**	**.463**	

National League — Listed by Most RBI

Team	Avg	HR	RBI	Slg	Main 3-4-5 Hitters
San Francisco	.302	107	344	.548	Clark W, Williams M, Bonds
Colorado	.310	83	336	.523	Bichette, Galarraga, Hayes
Atlanta	.272	96	326	.477	Gant, McGriff F, Justice
Philadelphia	.280	65	323	.458	Kruk, Hollins, Daulton
San Diego	.277	84	307	.466	Sheffield, McGriff F, Bell D
Chicago	.291	58	306	.445	Grace, May, Sosa
St. Louis	.291	60	296	.448	Jefferies, Zeile, Whiten
Los Angeles	.244	75	293	.417	Davis E, Karros, Piazza
Pittsburgh	.289	41	287	.419	Van Slyke, King, Clark D
Montreal	.259	55	286	.410	Grissom, Walker L, Alou
Cincinnati	.285	63	279	.448	Larkin B, Mitchell, Sabo
New York	.267	80	275	.450	Murray, Bonilla, Johnson H
Houston	.286	56	272	.444	Bagwell, Anthony, Caminiti
Florida	.262	46	242	.387	Conine, Destrade, Sheffield
NL Average	**.280**	**69**	**298**	**.453**	

WHO GETS THE "SLIDIN' BILLY" TROPHY ? (p. 146)

Both Leagues — Listed Alphabetically
(Players with 100+ Plate Appearances Batting Leadoff in 1993)

Player, Team	OBP	AB	R	H	BB	HBP	SB
Alicea, StL	.308	143	16	37	10	2	3
Amaral, Sea	.408	158	23	56	15	0	5
Anderson, Bal	.365	542	83	143	80	10	24
Bell Juan, Mil	.330	90	13	22	11	1	3
Biggio, Hou	.373	610	98	175	77	10	15
Boggs, NYA	.397	253	44	80	35	0	0
Bordick, Oak	.343	94	11	23	12	2	1
Brown, SD	.360	118	18	29	15	6	3
Butler B, LA	.385	584	79	176	78	4	38
Carr, Fla	.328	549	75	147	49	2	58
Cole, Col	.319	118	13	27	16	0	10
Coleman, NYN	.316	369	63	103	21	0	38
Cora, ChA	.345	159	28	43	18	0	0
DeShields, Mon	.388	423	66	127	59	2	34
Dykstra, Phi	.420	637	143	194	129	2	37
Felder, Sea	.210	119	7	21	4	1	2
Fletcher S, Bos	.344	472	80	136	37	5	16
Garcia, Pit	.314	377	55	104	16	7	17
Gardner, SD	.366	166	22	50	16	1	1
Gilkey, StL	.380	395	78	123	42	3	11
Grissom, Mon	.411	138	30	51	11	0	20
Gutierrez, SD	.346	144	21	38	17	1	1
Gwynn T, SD	.376	111	14	34	13	0	4
Hamilton, Mil	.387	304	42	99	30	1	15
Hatcher, Bos	.277	122	10	28	4	4	6
Henderson R, Tor	.432	466	111	137	112	4	50
Howard T, Cin	.375	132	22	42	12	0	3
Hulse, Tex	.331	381	64	110	24	1	29
Jose, KC	.307	347	48	91	22	1	18
Knoblauch, Min	.358	320	46	87	38	6	14
Lewis D, SF	.299	429	68	108	23	6	34
Listach, Mil	.320	240	35	57	28	2	11
Lofton, Cle	.408	566	114	184	81	1	69
Mack, Min	.324	253	35	70	16	2	6
Martin A, Pit	.281	162	29	41	7	0	0
McGee, SF	.322	163	17	46	10	0	4
McRae, KC	.343	190	22	59	8	2	7
Nixon, Atl	.357	447	75	122	61	0	44
Pena G, StL	.345	121	17	32	14	2	6
Phillips T, Det	.443	559	111	174	131	4	16
Polonia, Cal	.328	567	75	154	47	2	54
Raines, ChA	.400	413	75	127	62	3	21
Redus, Tex	.330	102	15	28	9	0	2
Reynolds, Bal	.339	107	16	27	14	1	0
Roberts, Cin	.329	249	37	58	35	2	22
Sanchez, ChN	.324	105	14	30	5	1	0
Sanders D, Atl	.303	228	32	60	13	1	17
Smith D, ChN	.349	247	40	74	17	3	6
Th'mp'n Ryan, NYN	.293	186	22	47	8	3	1
Vizcaino, ChN	.310	129	19	32	12	1	4
Vizquel, Sea	.325	283	35	72	29	1	10
White Dev, Tor	.343	434	87	120	38	6	24
Williams B, NYA	.306	289	36	69	27	2	1
Wilson W, ChN	.273	145	17	36	4	1	5
Young E, Col	.339	414	63	105	51	4	30
AL Team Avg	.356	671	107	187	79	5	32
NL Team Avg	.343	676	104	185	69	5	37

WHO'S THE BEST BUNTER? (p. 148)

The following table shows: **SH** = Sac Hits, **FSH** = Failed Sac Hits; and **BH** = Bunt Hits, **FBH** = Failed Bunt Hits

Both Leagues — Listed Alphabetically
(minimum 10 bunts in play)

Batter, Team	SH	FSH	%	BH	FBH	%
Alomar, Tor	4	1	80	7	3	70
Amaral, Sea	7	4	64	3	4	43
Arocha, StL	7	2	78	0	1	0
Astacio, LA	7	2	78	1	1	50
Avery, Atl	8	4	67	2	0	100
Baerga, Cle	3	0	100	7	2	78
Bell Jay, Pit	13	1	93	1	0	100
Bell Juan, Mil	5	0	100	3	2	60
Benes, SD	14	0	100	0	0	0
Benjamin, SF	6	3	67	1	1	50
Biggio, Hou	4	0	100	5	5	50
Borders, Tor	7	3	70	1	0	100
Bordick, Oak	10	2	83	1	0	100
Branson, Cin	8	0	100	2	3	40
Brocail, SD	11	5	69	0	0	0
Brumfield, Cin	3	1	75	2	4	33
Burkett, SF	12	3	80	0	0	0
Butler B, LA	14	3	82	26	39	40
Calderon, ChA	2	1	67	4	3	57
Candiotti, LA	9	4	69	0	0	0
Carr, Fla	7	1	87	16	18	47
Castillo F, ChN	8	2	80	0	0	0
Clayton, SF	8	1	89	9	5	64
Cole, Col	4	1	80	7	6	54
Coleman, NYN	3	3	50	12	11	52
Cora, ChA	19	2	90	10	16	38
Cuyler, Det	4	2	67	2	9	18
DeShields, Mon	4	2	67	2	3	40
Drabek, Hou	9	1	90	0	0	0
Duncan, Phi	4	1	80	5	1	83
Espinoza, Cle	8	2	80	0	1	0
Felder, Sea	7	0	100	1	4	20
Fernandez, Tor	8	1	89	8	9	47
Fernandez S, NYN	8	2	80	0	0	0
Finley, Hou	6	3	67	6	8	43
Franco, Tex	5	0	100	3	3	50
Gagne, KC	4	2	67	3	4	43
Gallagher, NYN	7	0	100	3	2	60
Garcia, Pit	6	0	100	6	5	55
Girardi, Col	12	1	92	1	0	100
Glavine, Atl	11	1	92	0	0	0
Grebeck, ChA	7	0	100	2	1	67
Gross Kev, LA	8	2	80	0	0	0
Guillen, ChA	13	3	81	1	2	33
Guzman Jose, ChN	9	2	82	0	0	0
Hamilton, Mil	4	2	67	6	9	40
Harkey, ChN	5	5	50	1	0	100
Harnisch, Hou	10	3	77	0	0	0
Hatcher, Bos	11	1	92	4	1	80
Hemond, Oak	6	1	86	3	5	37
Hershiser, LA	8	2	80	7	0	100
Hill K, Mon	14	2	87	0	0	0
Hulse, Tex	5	2	71	8	6	57
Jackson D, Phi	12	4	75	0	0	0
Johnson L, ChA	3	2	60	6	8	43
Jose, KC	1	5	17	3	9	25
Karkovice, ChA	11	1	92	4	2	67
Kelly P, NYA	10	2	83	11	13	46
King, Pit	1	0	100	5	4	56
Kirby, Cle	7	4	64	11	9	55
Lansing, Mon	10	2	83	1	2	33
Lee M, Tex	9	4	69	0	0	0
Lewis D, SF	12	1	92	6	25	19
Lind, KC	13	0	100	1	0	100
Listach, Mil	5	0	100	4	11	27
Lofton, Cle	2	1	67	19	13	59
Maddux G, Atl	10	3	77	0	0	0
Martinez D, Mon	9	1	90	0	0	0
Martinez R, LA	7	2	78	0	2	0
McLemore, Bal	11	1	92	5	4	56
McRae, KC	14	4	78	11	16	41
Mejia, Col	4	1	80	3	3	50
Morandini, Phi	4	1	80	4	2	67
Mulholland, Phi	8	3	73	0	0	0
Nilsson, Mil	4	0	100	3	3	50
Nixon, Atl	5	0	100	8	14	36
Offerman, LA	25	2	93	6	6	50
Pena T, Bos	13	2	87	0	3	0
Polonia, Cal	8	1	89	12	4	75
Portugal, Hou	10	4	71	0	0	0
Puckett, Min	1	0	100	9	4	69
Raines, ChA	2	0	100	3	5	37
Reed Jody, LA	17	1	94	4	4	50
Reynolds, Bal	10	2	83	8	3	73
Rijo, Cin	12	3	80	1	1	50
Rivera, Phi	13	2	87	0	0	0
Rodriguez I, Tex	5	1	83	1	5	17
Rueter, Mon	8	2	80	0	1	0
Saberhagen, NYN	8	1	89	1	0	100
Sanchez, ChN	9	2	82	1	1	50
Schilling, Phi	13	5	72	0	0	0
Slaught, Pit	4	0	100	2	5	29
Smith O, StL	7	0	100	9	3	75
Smoltz, Atl	11	3	79	0	0	0
Spiers, Mil	9	1	90	5	3	62
Stocker, Phi	4	0	100	6	4	60
Strange, Tex	8	2	80	3	3	50
Surhoff, Mil	4	2	67	4	2	67
Swift, SF	10	1	91	0	0	0
Swindell, Hou	10	0	100	0	0	0
Thompson Rob, SF	9	0	100	1	0	100
Valentin John, Bos	16	0	100	2	2	50
Valle, Sea	8	2	80	0	0	0
Vizcaino, ChN	8	1	89	4	3	57
Vizquel, Sea	13	2	87	19	1	95
Whitaker, Det	7	0	100	2	2	50
White Dev, Tor	3	1	75	4	3	57
Whitehurst, SD	10	2	83	0	0	0
Wilson T, SF	8	1	89	0	1	0
Young E, Col	4	1	80	3	8	27
MLB Avg.	1811	388	82	625	577	52

WHY WAS 1993 THE "YEAR OF THE MOON SHOT"? (p. 150)

Both Leagues — 1993 Home Runs Listed by Distance (450+ Feet)

Dir	Dis	Batter	Pitcher	When?	Where?
G	480	Fielder, Det	Whiteside, Tex	7/2	@Det
Q	470	Kreuter, Det	Gardner, KC	5/4	@Det
C	470	Fielder, Det	Bielecki, Cle	6/14	@Det
K	470	Tartabull, NYA	Guardado, Min	6/18	@NYA
N	470	Jackson B, ChA	Hanson, Sea	7/31	@Sea
P	470	Hrbek, Min	Leary, Sea	10/3	@Min
P	460	Galarraga, Col	Bautista, ChN	4/27	@Col
H	460	Gonzalez J, Tex	Pichardo, KC	5/7	@KC
D	460	Mitchell, Cin	Eiland, SD	5/13	@Cin
V	460	Nokes, NYA	Aguilera, Min	5/19	@Min
P	460	Hrbek, Min	Bielecki, Cle	5/29	@Min
J	460	Deer, Det	Slocumb, Cle	6/17	@Det
T	460	Whiten, StL	Drabek, Hou	7/15	@StL
M	460	Fielder, Det	Aguilera, Min	7/20	@Det
O	460	Tartabull, NYA	Sanderson, Cal	7/24	@NYA
X	460	Whiten, StL	Minor, Pit	8/11	@Pit
S	460	Brett, KC	Guardado, Min	8/19	@Min
I	460	Galarraga, Col	Petkovsek, Pit	9/4	@Col
K	460	Sosa, ChN	Hershiser, LA	9/27	@LA
L	450	Fielder, Det	Gardner, KC	5/4	@Det
U	450	Justice, Atl	Ashby, Col	5/9	@Col
H	450	Kelly P, NYA	Moyer, Bal	5/25	@NYA
Q	450	Baerga, Cle	Banks, Min	5/29	@Min
H	450	Mitchell, Cin	Maddux G, Atl	6/11	@Atl
I	450	Stanley, NYA	Deshaies, Min	6/17	@NYA
M	450	Galarraga, Col	Ayala, Cin	6/22	@Col
K	450	Thomas, ChA	Leary, Sea	6/25	@ChA
O	450	Davis C, Cal	Banks, Min	6/26	@Min
C	450	Incaviglia, Phi	Cormier, StL	6/28	@StL
O	450	Buhner, Sea	Bankhead, Bos	7/2	@Sea
T	450	Tettleton, Det	Trombley, Min	7/6	@Min
E	450	Hiatt, KC	Knudsen, Det	7/10	@KC
G	450	Galarraga, Col	Hammond, Fla	7/20	@Fla
R	450	Stanley, NYA	Fleming, Sea	7/20	@NYA
R	450	Griffey Jr, Sea	Gibson, NYA	7/20	@NYA
L	450	Buhner, Sea	Farr, NYA	7/21	@NYA
J	450	Thomas, ChA	Miranda, Mil	7/23	@ChA
V	450	Bonds, SF	Leskanic, Col	7/30	@Col
E	450	Williams M, SF	Myers, ChN	8/15	@ChN
U	450	Jackson B, ChA	Deshaies, Min	8/27	@ChA
Q	450	Gibson, Det	Nelson J, Sea	8/30	@Sea
G	450	Jordan B, StL	Deshaies, SF	9/3	@StL
N	450	Baines, Bal	Darwin, Bos	9/14	@Bos
E	450	Leyritz, NYA	Maysey, Mil	9/15	@Mil
S	450	Rodriguez H, LA	Reynoso, Col	9/19	@Col
N	450	Horn, Cle	Johnson D, Det	9/19	@Det
P	450	Davis E, Det	Rhodes, Bal	9/26	@Bal
I	450	Pena T, Bos	Bones, Mil	10/2	@Bos

IS JACK MCDOWELL A QUALITY STARTER? (p. 156)

Both leagues — Listed Alphabetically
(minimum 15 games started in 1993)

Player,Team	GS	QS	%	Player,Team	GS	QS	%	Player,Team	GS	QS	%
Abbott J, NYA	32	20	62.5	Guardado, Min	16	5	31.3	Portugal, Hou	33	21	63.6
Alvarez, ChA	31	20	64.5	Gullickson, Det	28	11	39.3	Pugh, Cin	27	12	44.4
Appier, KC	34	29	85.3	G'zm'n Jose, ChN	30	16	53.3	Rapp, Fla	16	8	50.0
Armstrong, Fla	33	17	51.5	G'zm'n Juan, Tor	33	20	60.6	Reynoso, Col	30	13	43.3
Arocha, StL	29	16	55.2	Hammond, Fla	32	16	50.0	Rhodes, Bal	17	2	11.8
Ashby, SD	21	7	33.3	Haney, KC	23	8	34.8	Rijo, Cin	36	28	77.8
Astacio, LA	31	16	51.6	Hanson, Sea	30	22	73.3	Rivera, Phi	28	11	39.3
Avery, Atl	35	25	71.4	Harkey, ChN	28	13	46.4	Rogers Ken, Tex	33	22	66.7
Banks, Min	30	12	40.0	Harnisch, Hou	33	24	72.7	Roper, Cin	15	5	33.3
Belcher, ChA	33	16	48.5	Harris GW, Col	35	18	51.4	Saberhagen, NYN	19	12	63.2
Benes, SD	34	20	58.8	Henry B, Mon	16	5	31.3	Sanderson, SF	29	16	55.2
Bere, ChA	24	16	66.7	Hentgen, Tor	32	16	50.0	Schilling, Phi	34	23	67.6
Black, SF	16	6	37.5	Hershiser, LA	33	21	63.6	Schourek, NYN	18	6	33.3
Blair, Col	18	9	50.0	Hibbard, ChN	31	16	51.6	Sele, Bos	18	12	66.7
Bones, Mil	31	14	45.2	Hickerson, SF	15	6	40.0	Smiley, Cin	18	8	44.4
Bosio, Sea	24	12	50.0	Hill K, Mon	28	16	57.1	Smoltz, Atl	35	19	54.3
Bottenfield, Col	25	11	44.0	Hillman, NYN	22	13	59.1	Stewart, Tor	26	11	42.3
Bowen, Fla	27	13	48.1	Hough, Fla	34	21	61.8	Stottlemyre, Tor	28	9	32.1
Brocail, SD	24	7	29.2	Jackson D, Phi	32	22	68.8	Sutcliffe, Bal	28	12	42.9
Brown, Tex	34	20	58.8	Johnson R, Sea	34	23	67.6	Swift, SF	34	23	67.6
Browning, Cin	20	11	55.0	Kamieniecki, NYA	20	11	55.0	Swindell, Hou	30	16	53.3
Burkett, SF	34	24	70.6	Key, NYA	34	25	73.5	Tanana, NYA	32	20	62.5
Candiotti, LA	32	22	68.8	Kile, Hou	26	14	53.8	Tapani, Min	35	20	57.1
Castillo F, ChN	25	13	52.0	Kramer, Cle	16	6	37.5	Tewksbury, StL	32	22	68.8
Clark, Cle	15	8	53.3	Langston, Cal	35	23	65.7	Tomlin, Pit	18	9	50.0
Clemens, Bos	29	14	48.3	Leary, Sea	27	13	48.1	Valenzuela, Bal	31	15	48.4
Cone, KC	34	24	70.6	Leibrandt, Tex	26	12	46.2	Van Poppel, Oak	16	4	25.0
Cooke, Pit	32	20	62.5	Maddux G, Atl	36	29	80.6	Viola, Bos	29	16	55.2
Cormier, StL	21	11	52.4	Magrane, Cal	28	14	50.0	Wagner, Pit	17	11	64.7
Darling, Oak	29	12	41.4	Martinez D, Mon	34	22	64.7	Wakefield, Pit	20	8	40.0
Darwin, Bos	34	23	67.6	Martinez R, LA	32	20	62.5	Walk, Pit	32	10	31.3
Deshaies, SF	31	16	51.6	McDonald, Bal	34	23	67.6	Watson, StL	15	8	53.3
Doherty, Det	31	14	45.2	McDowell J, ChA	34	21	61.8	Wegman, Mil	18	10	55.6
Dopson, Bos	28	9	32.1	Mesa, Cle	33	14	42.4	Welch, Oak	28	12	42.9
Drabek, Hou	34	22	64.7	Miranda, Mil	17	11	64.7	Wells, Det	30	17	56.7
Eldred, Mil	36	21	58.3	Moore Mike, Det	36	15	41.7	Whitehurst, SD	19	7	36.8
Erickson, Min	34	12	35.3	Morgan, ChN	32	19	59.4	Wickman, NYA	19	6	31.6
Farrell, Cal	17	5	29.4	Morris, Tor	27	8	29.6	Wilson T, SF	18	8	44.4
Fassero, Mon	15	9	60.0	Moyer, Bal	25	16	64.0	Witt B, Oak	33	18	54.5
F'rn'nd'z A, ChA	34	23	67.6	Mulholland, Phi	28	18	64.3	Worrell Tim, SD	16	6	37.5
F'rn'nd'z S, NYN	18	12	66.7	Mussina, Bal	25	14	56.0	**MLB Avg**	4538		50.4
Finley, Cal	35	25	71.4	Nabholz, Mon	21	10	47.6			2285	
Fleming, Sea	26	14	53.8	Navarro, Mil	34	15	44.1				
Gardner, KC	16	5	31.3	Nied, Col	16	3	18.8				
Glavine, Atl	36	28	77.8	Osborne, StL	26	17	65.4				
Gooden, NYN	29	18	62.1	Pavlik, Tex	26	18	69.2				
Greene, Phi	30	17	56.7	Perez Mld, NYA	25	8	32.0				
Gross Kev, LA	32	16	50.0	Pichardo, KC	25	8	32.0				

WHO GETS THE EASY SAVES? (p. 158)

Both Leagues — Listed Alphabetically
(1993 Relievers with a minimum of 4 Save Opportunities)

Reliever	Easy	Regular	Tough	Reliever	Easy	Regular	Tough
Aguilera, Min	19/20	12/16	3/4	Maddux M, NYN	0/0	5/6	0/5
Andersen, Phi	0/0	0/1	0/3	McMichael, Atl	6/6	12/13	1/2
Assenmacher, NYA	0/0	0/1	0/4	Mills, Bal	1/1	2/3	1/3
Ayala, Cin	1/1	1/2	1/2	Montgomery, KC	13/14	27/30	5/7
Barnes, Mon	0/1	3/4	0/0	Murphy, StL	0/0	1/3	0/1
Beck, SF	22/22	18/21	8/9	Myers, ChN	31/33	18/20	4/6
Belinda, KC	7/8	11/12	1/3	Nelson G, Tex	1/2	3/5	1/1
Boever, Det	1/1	1/3	1/1	Nelson J, Sea	0/0	1/4	0/7
Burns, StL	0/0	0/2	0/3	Nunez, Oak	0/0	1/2	0/2
Butcher, Cal	0/1	6/6	2/3	Olivares, StL	0/1	1/2	0/2
Carpenter, Tex	0/0	1/1	0/3	Olson, Bal	20/20	8/11	1/4
Charlton, Sea	10/11	8/10	0/0	Orosco, Mil	4/4	3/6	1/3
Cox, Tor	0/0	2/5	0/1	Parrett, Col	0/0	1/2	0/2
Davis M, SD	0/0	3/4	1/3	Pennington, Bal	0/0	2/2	2/5
Davis S, Det	1/1	2/2	1/2	Perez Mike, StL	4/4	3/6	0/0
DeLucia, Sea	0/0	0/1	0/3	Plunk, Cle	4/5	8/10	3/3
Dewey, Pit	2/2	5/6	0/4	Power, Sea	5/5	6/7	2/4
Dibble, Cin	15/16	3/9	1/3	Radinsky, ChA	2/2	2/3	0/0
DiPoto, Cle	7/8	2/6	2/3	Reardon, Cin	3/4	4/7	1/1
Eckersley, Oak	21/23	9/14	6/9	Reed S, Col	0/0	1/2	2/4
Farr, NYA	14/14	10/12	1/5	Rodriguez, Fla	1/1	0/1	2/5
Franco, NYN	5/5	3/8	2/4	Rojas, Mon	2/2	7/11	1/6
Frey, Cal	2/2	8/9	3/5	Russell, Bos	19/21	12/13	2/3
Frohwirth, Bal	0/0	3/3	0/4	Ryan K, Bos	0/0	1/1	0/3
Gordon, KC	0/0	1/4	0/2	Sampen, KC	0/0	0/3	0/1
Gossage, Oak	0/0	1/4	0/0	Scott T, Mon	0/0	0/1	1/3
Gott, LA	3/4	15/16	7/9	Smith L, NYA	30/31	13/18	3/4
Grahe, Cal	2/2	7/9	2/2	Smithberg, Oak	0/0	3/4	0/0
Guetterman, StL	0/0	1/2	0/2	Stanton, Atl	17/18	8/11	2/4
Harris Gene, SD	9/9	12/15	2/7	Thigpen, Phi	0/0	1/2	0/2
Harris GA, Bos	0/2	7/10	1/6	Timlin, Tor	0/0	0/1	1/3
Harvey, Fla	18/18	25/28	2/3	Trombley, Min	0/0	2/3	0/2
Henke, Tex	15/15	16/23	9/9	Valera, Cal	0/1	1/2	3/4
Henneman, Det	9/9	14/17	1/3	Wagner, Pit	2/2	0/1	0/2
Henry Doug, Mil	9/10	7/9	1/5	Ward, Tor	29/29	14/14	2/8
Hernandez J, Cle	1/1	6/8	1/4	West, Phi	0/1	1/3	2/5
Hernandez R, ChA	16/17	16/19	6/8	Wetteland, Mon	15/15	18/24	10/10
Hernandez X, Hou	1/1	7/13	1/3	Whiteside, Tex	0/1	1/2	0/2
Hoffman, SD	1/1	3/4	1/3	Wickman, NYA	1/1	2/4	1/3
Holmes, Col	10/10	12/15	3/4	Williams B, Hou	0/0	3/6	0/0
Howe, NYA	0/0	3/4	1/3	Williams Mtch, Phi	31/32	12/17	0/0
Innis, NYN	0/0	2/3	1/2	Willis, Min	0/0	3/4	2/5
Jackson M, SF	1/2	0/2	0/2	Worrell Todd, LA	2/2	3/6	0/0
Jones D, Hou	11/12	11/16	4/6	Young A, NYN	1/1	2/3	0/1
Knudsen, Det	0/0	2/2	0/2	**AL Average**	**234/258**	**273/379**	**86/231**
Lilliquist, Cle	2/2	4/5	4/6	**NL Average**	**256/271**	**269/399**	**74/190**
Lloyd, Mil	0/0	0/0	0/4	**MLB Totals**	**490/529**	**542/778**	**160/421**
MacDonald, Det	1/1	0/1	2/4				

WHICH STARTING STAFFS STAR, AND WHICH RELIEF STAFFS REEK? (p. 161)

AL Starters	ERA	W	L	IP	H	R	ER	HR	BB	K	BA
Baltimore	4.57	62	56	977.33	993	522	496	108	373	589	.266
Boston	3.81	55	56	1001.00	966	476	424	98	332	623	.253
California	4.32	57	71	1039.33	1080	553	499	111	371	612	.271
Chicago	3.72	76	55	1067.33	1006	486	441	97	425	708	.252
Cleveland	5.25	42	54	884.33	1002	552	516	119	341	481	.288
Detroit	4.78	64	51	940.33	1012	552	499	128	304	473	.275
Kansas City	4.03	59	55	1040.00	979	504	466	81	404	682	.251
Milwaukee	4.63	50	70	1036.00	1100	580	533	122	349	554	.273
Minnesota	4.92	50	78	966.00	1086	573	528	104	338	581	.287
New York	4.26	60	55	1011.67	1038	529	479	117	358	627	.266
Oakland	5.19	41	63	904.00	987	549	521	113	415	476	.280
Seattle	3.99	62	54	1043.67	1023	505	463	98	381	754	.259
Texas	4.39	63	59	968.67	992	524	472	92	378	623	.265
Toronto	4.63	70	50	999.33	1023	569	514	103	432	649	.265

NL Starters	ERA	W	L	IP	H	R	ER	HR	BB	K	BA
Atlanta	3.13	79	42	1083.00	997	413	377	82	327	719	.247
Chicago	4.45	58	62	981.33	1051	529	485	106	304	566	.278
Cincinnati	4.50	49	62	969.00	1042	519	484	104	314	652	.277
Houston	3.48	72	53	1049.33	997	456	406	87	339	764	.251
Los Angeles	3.55	57	59	1033.67	990	472	408	72	390	700	.253
Montreal	3.61	64	44	944.33	909	444	379	73	319	540	.254
New York	3.88	45	76	1064.33	1069	523	459	108	281	634	.263
Philadelphia	3.95	69	42	1040.67	1027	519	457	88	346	749	.256
Pittsburgh	4.78	46	64	954.00	1046	538	507	101	323	483	.284
St. Louis	4.03	61	49	973.33	1051	492	436	99	226	475	.277
San Diego	4.53	42	72	939.00	973	534	473	111	341	559	.268
San Francisco	3.72	82	43	980.67	972	441	405	111	277	583	.262
Colorado	5.49	37	73	878.67	1072	594	536	113	348	492	.305
Florida	4.33	47	72	959.67	997	504	462	92	372	586	.269

AL Relievers	ERA	W	L	IP	H	R	ER	HR	BB	K	BA
Baltimore	3.81	23	21	465.33	434	223	197	45	206	311	.250
Boston	3.79	25	26	451.33	413	222	190	29	220	374	.247
California	4.47	14	20	391.00	402	217	194	42	179	231	.268
Chicago	3.72	18	13	386.67	392	178	160	28	141	266	.264
Cleveland	3.51	34	32	561.33	589	261	219	63	250	407	.270
Detroit	4.57	21	26	496.33	535	285	252	60	238	355	.278
Kansas City	4.06	25	23	405.33	400	190	183	24	167	303	.261
Milwaukee	4.05	19	23	411.00	411	212	185	31	173	256	.264
Minnesota	4.35	21	13	478.33	505	257	231	44	176	320	.276
New York	4.62	28	19	426.67	429	232	219	53	194	272	.265
Oakland	4.43	27	31	548.33	564	297	270	44	265	388	.269
Seattle	4.74	20	26	410.00	398	226	216	37	224	329	.260
Texas	4.06	23	17	469.67	484	227	212	52	184	334	.270
Toronto	3.30	25	17	442.00	418	173	162	31	188	374	.251

NL Relievers	ERA	W	L	IP	H	R	ER	HR	BB	K	BA
Atlanta	3.15	25	16	372.00	300	146	130	19	153	317	.222
Chicago	3.61	26	16	468.33	463	210	188	47	166	339	.262
Cincinnati	4.55	24	27	465.00	468	266	235	54	194	344	.262
Houston	3.51	13	24	392.00	366	174	153	30	137	292	.250
Los Angeles	3.38	24	22	439.00	416	190	165	31	177	343	.254
Montreal	3.43	30	24	512.33	460	238	195	46	202	394	.240
New York	4.53	14	27	373.67	414	221	188	31	153	233	.285
Philadelphia	4.00	28	23	432.00	392	221	192	41	227	368	.240
Pittsburgh	4.74	29	23	491.67	511	268	259	52	162	349	.272
St. Louis	4.24	26	26	479.67	502	252	226	53	157	300	.273
San Diego	3.65	19	29	498.67	497	238	202	37	217	398	.262
San Francisco	3.44	21	16	476.00	413	195	182	57	165	399	.234
Colorado	5.36	30	22	552.67	592	373	329	68	261	421	.277
Florida	3.78	17	26	480.67	440	220	202	43	226	359	.245

DO HIT-BY-PITCHES INTIMIDATE HITTERS . . . OR PITCHERS? (p. 164)

Both Leagues — Listed Alphabetically
(Minimum 2000 Career BFP)

Pitcher	BFP	HB	BFP/HB	Pitcher	BFP	HB	BFP/HB	Pitcher	BFP	HB	BFP/HB
Abbott J	4495	21	214.0	Gott	4509	19	237.3	Murphy	2427	5	485.4
Agosto	2713	30	90.4	Grant	2743	10	274.3	Myers	2573	9	285.9
Aguilera	3414	23	148.4	Greene	2319	7	331.3	Nabholz	2230	17	131.2
Andersen	4024	17	236.7	Gross Kev	8600	64	134.4	Nagy	2363	11	214.8
Appier	3576	11	325.1	Gubicza	7486	45	166.4	Navarro	4085	28	145.9
Aquino	2489	19	131.0	Guetterman	2701	13	207.8	Nelson G	4652	33	141.0
Armstrong	3409	18	189.4	Gullickson	10223	30	340.8	Nunez	2786	19	146.6
Assenmacher	2586	11	235.1	Guzman Jose	5149	25	206.0	Ojeda	7952	24	331.3
Avery	3194	5	638.8	Guzm'n Juan	2270	8	283.8	Olivares	2244	20	112.2
Ballard	3245	17	190.9	Hanson	4048	22	184.0	Orosco	3888	21	185.1
Bankhead	3483	15	232.2	Harnisch	4005	22	182.0	Parrett	2510	7	358.6
Bedrosian	4719	24	196.6	Harris GA	5849	50	117.0	Perez Mld	4816	14	344.0
Belcher	5133	24	213.9	Harris GW	3118	16	194.9	Plesac	2462	12	205.2
Benes	3928	15	261.9	Heaton	6481	32	202.5	Plunk	3191	12	265.9
Bielecki	4313	14	308.1	Henke	2817	9	313.0	Portugal	4294	16	268.4
Black	8181	46	177.8	Henneman	2558	15	170.5	Power	4982	17	293.1
Boddicker	8999	87	103.4	Hershiser	8359	52	160.8	Rasmussen	6143	26	236.3
Boever	2421	10	242.1	Hesketh	3618	7	516.9	Reardon	4672	27	173.0
Bolton T	2317	17	136.3	Hibbard	3813	20	190.6	Righetti	5665	20	283.3
Bosio	5635	30	187.8	Higuera	5472	23	237.9	Rijo	6419	23	279.1
Brantley	2159	21	102.8	Hill K	3698	21	176.1	Rogers Ken	2475	15	165.0
Brown	4727	46	102.8	Hillegas	2265	13	174.2	Ruffin B	4783	9	531.4
Browning	7848	31	253.2	Honeycutt	8638	47	183.8	Russell	4127	23	179.4
Burkett	3516	30	117.2	Hough	15655	164	95.5	Ryan N	22575	158	142.9
Burns	2045	8	255.6	Howe	2065	13	158.8	Saberhagen	7678	34	225.8
Cadaret	2751	11	250.1	Howell	3375	18	187.5	Sanderson	10052	37	271.7
Candelaria	10366	37	280.2	Hurst	10028	28	358.1	Schilling	2518	6	419.7
Candiotti	7670	45	170.4	Jackson D	7289	36	202.5	Smiley	4941	20	247.1
Charlton	2222	17	130.7	Jackson M	2729	28	97.5	Smith B	7434	48	154.9
Clemens	9037	64	141.2	Johnson R	4622	54	85.6	Smith L	4673	7	667.6
Cone	6315	42	150.4	Jones D	2607	22	118.5	Smith P	2844	3	948.0
Cook D	2219	8	277.4	Jones J	3260	19	171.6	Smith Z	6580	26	253.1
Cox	5174	17	304.4	Key	7931	25	317.2	Smoltz	5106	19	268.7
Crim	2686	19	141.4	Kilgus	2348	22	106.7	Stewart	10268	56	183.4
Darling	8866	48	184.7	Knudson	2108	8	263.5	Stieb	11844	124	95.5
Darwin	9889	59	167.6	Krueger	4844	22	220.2	Stottlemyre	4316	42	102.8
Davis M	4802	27	177.9	Lancaster	3032	11	275.6	Sutcliffe	11229	44	255.2
Davis S	7411	20	370.5	Langston	9788	40	244.7	Swift	4849	39	124.3
Dayley	2450	8	306.3	Leach	2928	13	225.2	Swindell	6001	10	600.1
DeLeon	7364	49	150.3	Leary	6337	51	124.3	Tanana	17641	129	136.8
Deshaies	5804	25	232.2	Lefferts	4596	11	417.8	Tapani	3677	15	245.1
DiPino	2981	10	298.1	Leibrandt	9774	37	264.2	Tewksbury	4158	25	166.3
Dopson	2861	7	408.7	Maddux G	7100	50	142.0	Thigpen	2408	23	104.7
Downs	4122	25	164.9	Maddux M	2120	16	132.5	Tomlin	2310	17	135.9
Drabek	7063	27	261.6	Magrane	4076	33	123.5	Valenzuela	10661	20	533.0
Eckersley	12489	65	192.1	Martinez D	14135	91	155.3	Viola	11583	46	251.8
Eichhorn	3277	33	99.3	Martinez R	4007	25	160.3	Walk	7127	40	178.2
Erickson	3200	29	110.3	McCaskill	6566	27	243.2	Ward	2758	16	172.4
Farr	3344	30	111.5	McClure	5005	34	147.2	Wegman	5440	35	155.4
Farrell	2925	29	100.9	McDonald	2909	15	193.9	Welch	12631	78	161.9
Fernandez A	3013	19	158.6	McDowell J	4830	30	161.0	Wells	3638	21	173.2
Fernandez S	6489	37	175.4	McDowell R	3700	19	194.7	Williams Mtch	2910	49	59.4
Finley	6128	31	197.7	Mesa	2508	15	167.2	Williamson	2636	7	376.6
Franco	3030	7	432.9	Milacki	3064	5	612.8	Wilson T	2677	22	121.7
Gardner	2616	28	93.4	Montgomery	2179	16	136.2	Witt B	6184	19	325.5
Gibson	2274	12	189.5	Moore Mike	10892	50	217.8	Witt M	8927	55	162.3
Glavine	5699	20	285.0	Morgan	7761	35	221.7	Young Curt	4731	33	143.4
Gooden	8716	40	217.9	Morris	15484	54	286.7	Young M	5236	37	141.5
Gordon	3453	13	265.6	Moyer	3705	25	148.2				
Gossage	7309	44	166.1	Mulholland	4374	17	257.3				

WHO ARE THE HIDDEN RELIEF STARS? (p. 166)

The table below lists a relievers Holds (**H**), Saves (**Sv**), Blown Saves (**BS**), and Hold + Save Percentage (**%**), which is Holds plus Saves divided by Holds plus Saves plus Blown Saves.

Both Leagues — Listed Alphabetically
(minimum 5 Holds+Saves+Blown Saves in 1993)

Pitcher	H	Sv	BS	%	Pitcher	H	Sv	BS	%	Pitcher	H	Sv	BS	%
Aguilera, Min	0	34	6	85	Henke, Tex	0	40	7	85	Patterson B, Tex	6	1	1	88
Andersen, Phi	25	0	4	86	Henneman, Det	2	24	5	84	Patterson K, Cal	4	1	1	83
Assenmacher, NYA	17	0	5	77	Henry Doug, Mil	0	17	7	71	Pennington, Bal	5	4	3	75
Austin, Mil	4	0	2	67	Hernandez J, Cle	9	8	5	77	Perez Mike, StL	13	7	3	87
Ayala, Cin	6	3	2	82	Hernandez R, ChA	0	38	6	86	Plantenberg, Sea	6	1	0	100
Bankhead, Bos	4	0	2	67	Hernandez X, Hou	22	9	8	79	Plesac, ChN	12	0	2	86
Barnes, Mon	1	3	2	67	Hickerson, SF	6	0	0	100	Plunk, Cle	16	15	3	91
Bautista, ChN	7	2	0	100	Hoffman, SD	15	5	3	87	Poole, Bal	14	2	1	94
Beck, SF	0	48	4	92	Holman, Sea	2	3	0	100	Powell D, Sea	11	0	0	100
Belinda, KC	8	19	4	87	Holmes, Col	2	25	4	87	Power, Sea	6	13	3	86
Boever, Det	9	3	2	86	Honeycutt, Oak	20	1	2	91	Quantrill, Bos	3	1	1	80
Boskie, ChN	6	0	3	67	Horsman, Oak	10	0	0	100	Radinsky, ChA	12	4	1	94
Brantley, SF	10	0	3	77	Howe, NYA	10	4	3	82	Reardon, Cin	9	8	4	81
Brewer, KC	5	0	2	71	Howell, Atl	7	0	3	70	Reed S, Col	9	3	3	80
Bronkey, Tex	2	1	2	60	Ignasiak, Mil	3	0	2	60	Righetti, SF	6	1	2	78
Burba, SF	10	0	0	100	Innis, NYN	6	3	2	82	Rodriguez, Fla	10	3	4	76
Burns, StL	8	0	5	62	Jackson M, SF	34	1	5	88	Rogers Kev, SF	17	0	2	89
Butcher, Cal	3	8	2	85	Johnston, Pit	5	2	1	88	Rojas, Mon	14	10	9	73
Cadaret, KC	5	1	0	100	Jones D, Hou	1	26	8	77	Ruffin B, Col	3	2	1	83
Candelaria, Pit	4	1	2	71	Jones T, Hou	6	2	1	89	Ruffin J, Cin	2	2	1	80
Carpenter, Tex	14	1	3	83	Kilgus, StL	7	1	0	100	Russell, Bos	1	33	4	89
Casian, Min	15	1	2	89	King, Sea	4	0	1	80	Ryan A, Bos	3	1	3	57
Castillo T, Tor	13	0	1	93	Klink, Fla	9	0	0	100	Sampen, KC	3	0	4	43
Charlton, Sea	1	18	3	86	Knudsen, Det	6	2	2	80	Scanlan, ChN	25	0	3	89
Cox, Tor	10	2	4	75	Kramer, Cle	3	0	2	60	Schwarz, ChA	6	0	0	100
Daal, LA	7	0	1	88	Krueger, Det	6	0	3	67	Scott T, Mon	3	1	3	57
Davis M, SD	5	4	3	75	Lancaster, StL	5	0	0	100	Service, Cin	3	2	0	100
Davis S, Det	3	4	1	88	Lefferts, Tex	11	0	0	100	Shaw, Mon	4	0	1	80
DeLeon, ChA	7	0	2	78	Leiter A, Tor	3	2	1	83	Slocumb, Cle	3	0	2	60
DeLucia, Sea	6	0	4	60	Lewis R, Fla	3	0	2	60	Smith L, NYA	0	46	7	87
Dewey, Pit	0	7	5	58	Lilliquist, Cle	11	10	3	88	Stanton, Atl	5	27	6	84
Dibble, Cin	0	19	9	68	Lloyd, Mil	6	0	4	60	Swan, Sea	5	0	0	100
DiPoto, Cle	6	11	6	74	MacDonald, Det	16	3	3	86	Thigpen, Phi	1	1	3	40
Eckersley, Oak	0	36	10	78	Maddux M, NYN	3	5	6	57	Timlin, Tor	9	1	3	77
Eichhorn, Tor	5	0	2	71	Martinez P, LA	14	2	1	94	Trombley, Min	8	2	3	77
Farr, NYA	1	25	6	81	Mason, Phi	10	0	3	77	Turner, Fla	9	0	1	90
Fassero, Mon	6	1	2	78	McDowell R, LA	3	2	1	83	Valera, Cal	2	4	3	67
Fetters, Mil	8	0	0	100	McMichael, Atl	12	19	2	94	Wagner, Pit	4	2	3	67
Fossas, Bos	13	0	2	87	Mercker, Atl	4	0	3	57	Ward, Tor	0	45	6	88
Foster S, Cin	5	0	0	100	Mills, Bal	4	4	3	73	Wayne, Col	3	1	2	67
Franco, NYN	0	10	7	59	Minor, Pit	7	2	1	90	Wertz, Cle	3	0	2	60
Frey, Cal	7	13	3	87	Montgomery, KC	0	45	6	88	West, Phi	21	3	6	80
Frohwirth, Bal	14	3	4	81	Moore Mrcs, Col	3	0	2	60	Wetteland, Mon	0	43	6	88
Gardiner, Det	4	0	2	67	Munoz B, NYA	6	0	2	75	Whiteside, Tex	14	1	4	79
Gordon, KC	2	1	5	38	Murphy, StL	24	1	3	89	Wickman, NYA	2	4	4	60
Gossage, Oak	8	1	3	75	Myers, ChN	0	53	6	90	Williams B, Hou	2	3	3	63
Gott, LA	7	25	4	89	Neagle, Pit	6	1	0	100	Williams Mtch, Phi	1	43	6	88
Grahe, Cal	3	11	2	88	Nelson G, Tex	9	5	3	82	Williams W, Tor	4	0	2	67
Gubicza, KC	8	2	1	91	Nelson J, Sea	17	1	10	64	Williamson, Bal	10	0	2	83
Guetterman, StL	4	1	3	63	Nunez, Oak	16	1	3	85	Willis, Min	14	5	4	83
Guthrie, Min	8	0	1	89	Olivares, StL	2	1	4	43	Wohlers, Atl	12	0	0	100
Habyan, KC	7	1	2	80	Olson, Bal	0	29	6	83	Worrell Todd, LA	4	5	3	75
Harris GA, Bos	17	8	10	71	Orosco, Mil	11	8	5	79	Young A, NYN	2	3	2	71
Harris Gene, SD	1	23	8	75	Osuna, Hou	11	2	0	100	**MLB Average**				65
Hartley, Min	6	1	2	78	Pall, Phi	9	1	1	91					
Harvey, Fla	0	45	4	92	Parrett, Col	1	1	3	40					

DID STEVE FARR INHERIT A TICKET OUT OF TOWN? (p. 168)

The table below shows the percentage (%) of Inherited Runners (IR) each relief pitcher allowed to score (SC)

Both Leagues — Listed Alphabetically
(minimum 20 inherited runners in 1993)

Pitcher, Team	IR	SC	%	Pitcher, Team	IR	SC	%	Pitcher, Team	IR	SC	%
Aguilera, Min	21	6	28.6	Henke, Tex	36	9	25.0	Patterson K, Cal	53	10	18.9
Andersen, Phi	48	14	29.2	Henneman, Det	42	9	21.4	Pennington, Bal	45	13	28.9
Assenmacher, NYA	63	15	23.8	Henry Doug, Mil	27	10	37.0	Perez Mike, StL	22	7	31.8
Austin, Mil	26	6	23.1	Henry Dw, Sea	23	6	26.1	Petkovsek, Pit	20	9	45.0
Ayala, Cin	23	6	26.1	Hernandez J, Cle	50	18	36.0	Plantenberg, Sea	21	5	23.8
Ayrault, LA	28	11	39.3	Hernandez R, ChA	39	13	33.3	Plesac, ChN	38	19	50.0
Bankhead, Bos	28	11	39.3	Hernandez X, Hou	48	14	29.2	Plunk, Cle	56	14	25.0
Barnes, Mon	32	13	40.6	Hoffman, SD	45	6	13.3	Poole, Bal	65	14	21.5
Bautista, ChN	38	15	39.5	Holman, Sea	23	3	13.0	Powell D, Sea	30	9	30.0
Beck, SF	35	7	20.0	Honeycutt, Oak	35	8	22.9	Power, Sea	42	13	31.0
Bedrosian, Atl	36	16	44.4	Horsman, Oak	35	7	20.0	Quantrill, Bos	36	5	13.9
Belinda, KC	29	9	31.0	Howe, NYA	59	13	22.0	Radinsky, ChA	50	13	26.0
Boever, Det	36	14	38.9	Howell, Atl	25	11	44.0	Reardon, Cin	28	1	3.6
Bohanon, Tex	33	11	33.3	Ignasiak, Mil	26	8	30.8	Reed S, Col	44	9	20.5
Bolton T, Det	33	15	45.5	Innis, NYN	34	9	26.5	Righetti, SF	23	9	39.1
Boskie, ChN	28	6	21.4	Jackson M, SF	58	17	29.3	Rodriguez, Fla	51	14	27.5
Brewer, KC	39	4	10.3	Jones D, Hou	20	9	45.0	Rogers Kev, SF	41	11	26.8
Bronkey, Tex	24	8	33.3	Klink, Fla	56	14	25.0	Rojas, Mon	37	19	51.4
Burba, SF	35	12	34.3	Knudsen, Det	27	11	40.7	Ruffin B, Col	25	6	24.0
Burns, StL	45	16	35.6	Krueger, Det	25	6	24.0	Russell, Bos	24	10	41.7
Butcher, Cal	21	5	23.8	Lancaster, StL	49	19	38.8	Ryan K, Bos	41	16	39.0
Cadaret, KC	22	7	31.8	Lefferts, Tex	38	8	21.1	Scanlan, ChN	59	19	32.2
Carpenter, Tex	45	14	31.1	Leiter A, Tor	22	5	22.7	Schooler, Tex	23	7	30.4
Casian, Min	47	10	21.3	Lewis R, Fla	55	20	36.4	Schwarz, ChA	22	7	31.8
Castillo T, Tor	45	11	24.4	Lilliquist, Cle	42	8	19.0	Scott T, Mon	31	17	54.8
Cox, Tor	27	10	37.0	Lloyd, Mil	65	21	32.3	Shaw, Mon	32	7	21.9
Daal, LA	48	13	27.1	MacDonald, Det	56	18	32.1	Slocumb, Cle	32	13	40.6
Davis M, SD	38	13	34.2	Maddux M, NYN	36	12	33.3	Smith L, NYA	25	5	20.0
Davis S, Det	28	6	21.4	Martinez P, LA	33	7	21.2	Spradlin, Cin	22	10	45.5
DeLucia, Sea	26	12	46.2	Martinez PA, SD	22	5	22.7	Stanton, Atl	25	10	40.0
DiPoto, Cle	30	10	33.3	Mason, Phi	41	12	29.3	Swan, Sea	20	1	5.0
Downs, Oak	26	3	11.5	Mauser, StL	34	14	41.2	Timlin, Tor	32	12	37.5
Eckersley, Oak	32	13	40.6	McDowell R, LA	30	9	30.0	Trlicek, LA	37	11	29.7
Edens, Hou	27	10	37.0	McElroy, ChN	23	8	34.8	Trombley, Min	29	11	37.9
Eichhorn, Tor	48	20	41.7	McMichael, Atl	22	6	27.3	Tsamis, Min	39	13	33.3
Farr, NYA	28	17	60.7	Mercker, Atl	20	7	35.0	Turner, Fla	40	14	35.0
Fassero, Mon	24	10	41.7	Mills, Bal	53	20	37.7	Wagner, Pit	21	11	52.4
Fetters, Mil	41	19	46.3	Minor, Pit	37	15	40.5	Ward, Tor	26	9	34.6
Fossas, Bos	60	11	18.3	Mohler, Oak	38	9	23.7	Wayne, Col	58	20	34.5
Fredrickson, Col	20	5	25.0	Monteleone, NYA	41	10	24.4	Wertz, Cle	29	8	27.6
Frey, Cal	49	14	28.6	Montgomery, KC	30	8	26.7	West, Phi	52	18	34.6
Frohwirth, Bal	79	20	25.3	Moore Mrcs, Col	22	8	36.4	Wetteland, Mon	33	6	18.2
Gardiner, Det	27	4	14.8	Munoz B, NYA	33	6	18.2	Whiteside, Tex	59	15	25.4
Gibson, NYA	30	14	46.7	Munoz M, Col	21	9	42.9	Wickander, Cin	46	15	32.6
Gomez, SD	21	8	38.1	Murphy, StL	33	4	12.1	Wickman, NYA	24	6	25.0
Gordon, KC	23	11	47.8	Myers, ChN	24	4	16.7	Williams B, Hou	22	5	22.7
Gossage, Oak	29	13	44.8	Neagle, Pit	28	11	39.3	Williams W, Tor	20	9	45.0
Gott, LA	35	12	34.3	Nelson G, Tex	40	10	25.0	Williamson, Bal	43	10	23.3
Grahe, Cal	38	12	31.6	Nelson J, Sea	95	32	33.7	Willis, Min	59	22	37.3
Gubicza, KC	33	15	45.5	Nunez, Oak	43	15	34.9	Wilson S, LA	25	5	20.0
Guetterman, StL	30	11	36.7	Olivares, StL	38	18	47.4	Wohlers, Atl	21	8	38.1
Guthrie, Min	21	9	42.9	Olson, Bal	31	15	48.4	Young Cliff, Cle	23	10	43.5
Habyan, KC	33	9	27.3	Orosco, Mil	41	11	26.8	**MLB Average**			**32.2**
Harris GA, Bos	75	18	24.0	Osuna, Hou	44	5	11.4				
Harris Gene, SD	31	9	29.0	Pall, Phi	34	15	44.1				
Hartley, Min	54	19	35.2	Parrett, Col	20	13	65.0				
Harvey, Fla	28	9	32.1	Patterson B, Tex	29	12	41.4				

WHO HOLDS THE FORT? (p. 171)

A Hold (**H**) is a Save Opportunity passed on to the next pitcher. If a pitcher comes into the game in a Save Situation and leaves the game having gotten at least one out and without having blown the lead, this is a "passed on" Save Opportunity and the pitcher is credited with a Hold.

Both Leagues — Listed By Most Holds
(minumum 1 Hold in 1993)

Pitcher, Team	H	Pitcher, Team	H	Pitcher, Team	H	Pitcher, Team	H
Jackson M, SF	34	Gossage, Oak	8	Wagner, Pit	4	Shepherd, Col	2
Andersen, Phi	25	Gubicza, KC	8	Williams W, Tor	4	Taylor S, Bos	2
Scanlan, ChN	25	Guthrie, Min	8	Worrell Todd, LA	4	Tsamis, Min	2
Murphy, StL	24	Trombley, Min	8	Aquino, Fla	3	Valera, Cal	2
Hernandez X, Hou	22	Bautista, ChN	7	Ballard, Pit	3	Wickander, Cin	2
West, Phi	21	Daal, LA	7	Blair, Col	3	Wickman, NYA	2
Honeycutt, Oak	20	DeLeon, ChA	7	Bullinger, ChN	3	Williams B, Hou	2
Assenmacher, NYA	17	Frey, Cal	7	Butcher, Cal	3	Young A, NYN	2
Harris GA, Bos	17	Gott, LA	7	Davis S, Det	3	Agosto, Hou	1
Nelson J, Sea	17	Habyan, KC	7	Edens, Hou	3	Ayrault, LA	1
Rogers Kev, SF	17	Howell, Atl	7	Grahe, Cal	3	Barnes, Mon	1
MacDonald, Det	16	Kilgus, StL	7	Gross Kip, LA	3	Batchelor, StL	1
Nunez, Oak	16	Minor, Pit	7	Ignasiak, Mil	3	Bell, Hou	1
Plunk, Cle	16	Ayala, Cin	6	Kramer, Cle	3	Bohanon, Tex	1
Casian, Min	15	Boskie, ChN	6	Leiter A, Tor	3	Bosio, Sea	1
Hoffman, SD	15	DeLucia, Sea	6	Lewis R, Fla	3	Cary, ChA	1
Carpenter, Tex	14	DiPoto, Cle	6	Maddux M, NYN	3	Charlton, Sea	1
Frohwirth, Bal	14	Fassero, Mon	6	Martinez PA, SD	3	Corsi, Fla	1
Martinez P, LA	14	Hartley, Min	6	McDowell R, LA	3	Dopson, Bos	1
Poole, Bal	14	Hickerson, SF	6	Moore Mrcs, Col	3	Downs, Oak	1
Rojas, Mon	14	Innis, NYN	6	Quantrill, Bos	3	Ettles, SD	1
Whiteside, Tex	14	Jones T, Hou	6	Ruffin B, Col	3	Farr, NYA	1
Willis, Min	14	Knudsen, Det	6	Ryan K, Bos	3	Freeman, Atl	1
Castillo T, Tor	13	Krueger, Det	6	Sampen, KC	3	Gibson, NYA	1
Fossas, Bos	13	Lloyd, Mil	6	Scott T, Mon	3	Gohr, Det	1
Perez Mike, StL	13	Munoz B, NYA	6	Service, Cin	3	Gomez, SD	1
McMichael, Atl	12	Neagle, Pit	6	Slocumb, Cle	3	Grater, Det	1
Plesac, ChN	12	Patterson B, Tex	6	Wayne, Col	3	Grimsley, Cle	1
Radinsky, ChA	12	Plantenberg, Sea	6	Wertz, Cle	3	Groom, Det	1
Wohlers, Atl	12	Power, Sea	6	Bolton T, Det	2	Harris Gene, SD	1
Lefferts, Tex	11	Righetti, SF	6	Bronkey, Tex	2	Heredia, Mon	1
Lilliquist, Cle	11	Schwarz, ChA	6	Clark, Cle	2	Jones Bar, ChA	1
Orosco, Mil	11	Brewer, KC	5	Cook D, Cle	2	Jones D, Hou	1
Osuna, Hou	11	Cadaret, KC	5	Crim, Cal	2	Leiter M, Det	1
Powell D, Sea	11	Davis M, SD	5	Draper, NYN	2	Meacham, KC	1
Brantley, SF	10	Eichhorn, Tor	5	Flener, Tor	2	Merriman, Min	1
Burba, SF	10	Foster S, Cin	5	Fredrickson, Col	2	Minutelli, SF	1
Cox, Tor	10	Johnston, Pit	5	Gordon, KC	2	Mohler, Oak	1
Horsman, Oak	10	Lancaster, StL	5	Gozzo, NYN	2	Monteleone, NYA	1
Howe, NYA	10	Pennington, Bal	5	Haas, Det	2	Nabholz, Mon	1
Mason, Phi	10	Stanton, Atl	5	Hampton, Sea	2	Otto, Pit	1
Rodriguez, Fla	10	Swan, Sea	5	Heaton, NYA	2	Parrett, Col	1
Williamson, Bal	10	Austin, Mil	4	Henneman, Det	2	Pichardo, KC	1
Boever, Det	9	Bankhead, Bos	4	Holman, Sea	2	Rasmussen, KC	1
Hernandez J, Cle	9	Bedrosian, Atl	4	Holmes, Col	2	Rogers Ken, Tex	1
Klink, Fla	9	Candelaria, Pit	4	Landrum, Cin	2	Russell, Bos	1
Nelson G, Tex	9	Gardiner, Det	4	Leach, ChA	2	Seminara, SD	1
Pall, Phi	9	Guetterman, StL	4	Lewis S, Cal	2	Telgheder, NYN	1
Reardon, Cin	9	King, Sea	4	Maldonado, Mil	2	Thigpen, Phi	1
Reed S, Col	9	McElroy, ChN	4	McCaskill, ChA	2	Toliver, Pit	1
Timlin, Tor	9	Mercker, Atl	4	Munoz M, Col	2	Trlicek, LA	1
Turner, Fla	9	Mills, Bal	4	Olivares, StL	2	Wells, Det	1
Belinda, KC	8	Patterson K, Cal	4	Ruffin J, Cin	2	Williams Mtch, Phi	1
Burns, StL	8	Schooler, Tex	4	Schourek, NYN	2	Wilson S, LA	1
Fetters, Mil	8	Shaw, Mon	4	Scott D, Cal	2	Worrell Tim, SD	1

Is Randy Johnson the "Leading Scorer" Among Pitchers? (p. 174)

The formula for determing a Game Score (starting pitchers only):

50 + Thirds of an inning + K - BB - 2*Hits - 4*ER - 2*(R-ER) + two points for each inning the pitcher completes after the fourth inning

Both Leagues — Listed by Game Score
(Minimum Game Score of 92, 1989-1993)

Pitcher, Team	Date	Opp	IP	H	R	ER	BB	K	Score
DeLEON J, StL	8/30/89	Cin	11.0	1	0	0	0	8	103
RYAN N, Tex	8/17/90	ChA	10.0	3	0	0	0	15	101
RYAN N, Tex	5/1/91	Tor	9.0	0	0	0	2	16	101
RYAN N, Tex	4/26/90	ChA	9.0	1	0	0	2	16	99
RYAN N, Tex	6/11/90	Oak	9.0	0	0	0	2	14	99
HANSON E, Sea	8/1/90	Oak	10.0	2	0	0	0	11	99
CONE D, NYN	10/6/91	Phi	9.0	3	0	0	1	19	99
MARTINEZ R, LA	6/4/90	Atl	9.0	3	0	0	1	18	98
JOHNSON R, Sea	9/16/92	Cal	9.0	1	1	0	1	15	97
SCOTT M, Hou	6/8/90	Cin	10.0	3	1	1	1	15	96
STEWART D, Oak	6/29/90	Tor	9.0	0	0	0	3	12	96
JOHNSON R, Sea	5/16/93	Oak	9.0	1	0	0	3	14	96
MULHOLLAND T, Phi	8/15/90	SF	9.0	0	0	0	0	8	95
CONE D, NYN	9/20/91	StL	9.0	1	0	0	1	11	95
CLEMENS R, Bos	6/16/89	ChA	9.0	2	0	0	1	12	94
RYAN N, Tex	9/30/89	Cal	9.0	3	0	0	0	13	94
WILSON T, SF	6/13/90	SD	9.0	1	0	0	0	9	94
JOHNSON R, Sea	8/14/91	Oak	9.0	1	0	0	3	12	94
GROSS K, LA	5/12/92	Mon	9.0	3	0	0	0	13	94
MUSSINA M, Bal	7/17/92	Tex	9.0	1	0	0	1	10	94
RYAN N, Tex	4/12/89	Mil	8.0	1	0	0	2	15	93
RIJO J, Cin	9/17/90	SF	9.0	2	0	0	2	12	93
MULHOLLAND T, Phi	9/18/91	Mon	9.0	2	0	0	0	10	93
TAPANI K, Min	6/24/92	Cal	9.0	2	0	0	0	10	93
KILE D, Hou	9/8/93	NYN	9.0	0	1	0	1	9	93
RIJO J, Cin	9/25/93	Col	9.0	1	0	0	0	8	93
McCASKILL K, Cal	4/28/89	Tor	9.0	1	0	0	2	9	92
RYAN N, Tex	6/3/89	Sea	9.0	1	1	0	2	11	92
FERNANDEZ S, NYN	9/21/89	StL	9.0	2	1	1	0	13	92
STIEB D, Tor	9/2/90	Cle	9.0	0	0	0	4	9	92
CLEMENS R, Bos	4/13/91	Cle	9.0	3	0	0	0	11	92
RYAN N, Tex	7/7/91	Cal	8.1	2	0	0	1	14	92
MARTINEZ D, Mon	7/28/91	LA	9.0	0	0	0	0	5	92
BENES A, SD	8/29/91	StL	9.0	2	0	0	1	10	92
CLEMENS R, Bos	4/12/92	Cle	9.0	2	0	0	3	12	92
KEY J, NYA	4/27/93	Cal	9.0	1	0	0	1	8	92
BELCHER T, Cin	5/26/93	Atl	9.0	1	0	0	3	10	92
HARNISCH P, Hou	7/10/93	ChN	9.0	1	0	0	3	10	92

HOW MANY PITCHES SHOULD YOU THROW? (p. 176)

Most Pitches In a Game By Starting Pitchers in 1993

Date	Opp	Score	Pitcher	W/L	IP	H	R	ER	BB	SO	#Pit	Time
4/27	@Atl	6-2	Wakefield, Pit	W	10.0	6	2	2	10	1	172	2:54
9/2	Bal	3-4	Finley, Cal	L	9.0	13	4	4	3	8	158	3:01
6/24	Oak	2-3	Johnson R, Sea	L	9.0	4	3	2	8	14	157	3:04
8/30	KC	2-1	Eldred, Mil	W	9.0	4	1	1	2	7	156	2:36
6/26	@SF	5-1	Reynoso, Col	W	9.0	7	1	1	2	8	152	3:19
8/14	@Oak	5-1	Banks, Min		8.0	6	1	1	4	13	151	3:38
10/1	@Min	8-2	Johnson R, Sea	W	9.0	9	2	2	2	7	150	2:59
10/3	Cal	3-7	Witt B, Oak	L	9.0	11	7	7	6	7	150	2:43
5/28	Cin	2-5	Gooden, NYN		9.0	8	2	2	5	4	149	3:03
8/20	@Cal	7-2	Eldred, Mil	W	10.0	6	2	1	2	9	149	3:01
8/3	@Oak	5-4	Johnson R, Sea	W	8.0	7	4	4	4	12	148	2:51
9/21	Tex	8-0	Johnson R, Sea	W	9.0	3	0	0	1	11	147	2:37
7/5	NYA	3-6	Johnson R, Sea	L	9.0	6	6	6	4	7	146	2:29
8/14	Cal	7-2	Johnson R, Sea	W	8.0	8	2	2	2	10	146	2:45
6/9	@Mil	6-1	Johnson R, Sea	W	8.0	7	1	1	4	11	145	2:40
5/18	Det	1-5	Eldred, Mil	L	8.0	10	5	5	2	4	144	3:00
8/15	Det	6-4	Eldred, Mil	W	8.0	6	4	4	4	3	144	2:54
10/1	@Cin	2-0	Swindell, Hou	W	9.0	8	0	0	1	10	144	2:34
5/11	@Bal	4-0	Clemens, Bos	W	9.0	5	0	0	2	13	143	3:27
6/6	@LA	2-0	Smoltz, Atl	W	9.0	5	0	0	4	12	143	2:48
7/25	@Det	0-3	Cone, KC	L	7.2	4	3	3	6	6	143	2:37
8/26	Tor	6-3	Johnson R, Sea	W	8.0	9	3	3	1	8	143	2:35
9/15	ChA	6-10	Cone, KC		7.2	8	5	4	5	5	143	4:05
9/18	Tor	1-5	Erickson, Min	L	8.2	8	5	4	3	4	143	2:48
9/27	Tor	0-2	Eldred, Mil	L	9.0	7	2	2	2	7	143	2:53
5/15	@Cin	3-5	Reynoso, Col	L	6.2	9	5	5	2	2	142	2:52
5/24	NYN	6-3	Greene, Phi	W	9.0	5	3	2	3	7	142	2:47
7/11	NYA	3-2	Finley, Cal		9.0	6	2	2	2	9	142	4:51
7/16	ChA	3-4	Eldred, Mil	L	9.0	8	4	4	2	8	142	2:59
8/17	Mon	7-2	Guzman Jose, ChN	W	9.0	5	2	1	2	12	142	2:57
9/24	Atl	3-0	Greene, Phi	W	8.1	3	0	0	8	6	142	2:50

Fewest Pitches In a 9-Inning Complete Game By Starting Pitchers in 1993

Date	Opp	Score	Pitcher	W/L	IP	H	R	ER	BB	SO	#Pit	Time
6/15	NYN	2-1	Glavine, Atl	W	9.0	6	1	1	0	0	79	2:09
4/12	KC	4-1	Abbott J, NYA	W	9.0	8	1	1	0	4	85	2:16
7/26	@SF	15-1	Hershiser, LA	W	9.0	5	1	1	0	2	85	2:31
9/17	@Cin	13-0	Swift, SF	W	9.0	7	0	0	0	4	85	2:24
9/8	NYN	7-1	Kile, Hou	W	9.0	0	1	0	1	9	88	2:11
5/7	Bos	0-1	Wegman, Mil	L	9.0	4	1	0	3	2	90	2:06
6/22	ChN	7-2	Walk, Pit	W	9.0	3	2	2	0	4	90	2:09
8/28	ChN	5-1	Avery, Atl	W	9.0	6	1	0	0	3	91	2:27
7/1	Col	4-0	Glavine, Atl	W	9.0	4	0	0	0	2	93	2:31
9/24	@Bal	2-0	Doherty, Det	W	9.0	7	0	0	0	4	93	2:12
8/19	@ChN	10-2	Fassero, Mon	W	9.0	6	2	2	3	9	94	2:49
8/23	Oak	9-0	Moore Mike, Det	W	9.0	1	0	0	0	5	94	2:34
5/19	Mon	1-0	Glavine, Atl	W	9.0	4	0	0	1	3	95	2:12
8/18	ChA	5-0	Darwin, Bos	W	9.0	1	0	0	2	2	95	2:20
8/29	@NYN	6-1	Painter, Col	W	9.0	5	1	1	0	2	95	2:05
5/27	Col	8-0	Drabek, Hou	W	9.0	7	0	0	1	3	96	2:38
6/12	@Cal	2-0	Fleming, Sea	W	9.0	3	0	0	0	2	96	2:04
8/13	Bal	4-1	Abbott J, NYA	W	9.0	8	1	1	3	1	96	2:27
4/22	Bos	7-0	Bosio, Sea	W	9.0	0	0	0	2	4	97	2:12
7/6	@KC	8-0	Moyer, Bal	W	9.0	4	0	0	0	4	97	2:25
8/15	@Cin	1-0	Maddux G, Atl	W	9.0	4	0	0	2	6	97	2:16
9/25	@Col	6-0	Rijo, Cin	W	9.0	1	0	0	0	8	97	1:59
6/7	@SD	4-0	Avery, Atl	W	9.0	4	0	0	0	4	98	2:04
8/11	@NYN	4-2	Maddux G, Atl	W	9.0	6	2	2	0	3	98	2:18
5/21	@NYN	4-2	Maddux G, Atl	W	9.0	6	2	2	0	5	99	2:44
5/29	@Col	6-0	Mulholland, Phi	W	9.0	6	0	0	1	2	99	2:13
6/27	Oak	4-0	Brown, Tex	W	9.0	5	0	0	1	5	99	2:10
7/9	@Cal	3-2	Key, NYA	W	9.0	5	2	2	1	6	99	2:26
7/15	Col	1-0	Morgan, ChN	W	9.0	5	0	0	0	5	99	2:19
9/14	@SF	8-1	Bautista, ChN	W	9.0	5	1	1	2	5	99	2:47

WHOSE HEATER IS HOTTEST? (p. 178)

Both Leagues — Listed Alphabetically
(minimum 81 innings pitched or 50 relief games)

Pitcher, Team	IP	K	K/9	Pitcher, Team	IP	K	K/9
Abbott J, NYA	214.0	95	4.0	Erickson, Min	218.2	116	4.8
Aguilera, Min	72.1	59	7.3	Farrell, Cal	90.2	45	4.5
Alvarez, ChA	207.2	155	6.7	Fassero, Mon	149.2	140	8.4
Andersen, Phi	61.2	67	9.8	Fernandez A, ChA	247.1	169	6.1
Appier, KC	238.2	186	7.0	Fernandez S, NYN	119.2	81	6.1
Aquino, Fla	110.2	67	5.4	Finley, Cal	251.1	187	6.7
Armstrong, Fla	196.1	118	5.4	Fleming, Sea	167.1	75	4.0
Arocha, StL	188.0	96	4.6	Fossas, Bos	40.0	39	8.8
Ashby, SD	123.0	77	5.6	Frey, Cal	48.1	22	4.1
Assenmacher, NYA	56.0	45	7.2	Frohwirth, Bal	96.1	50	4.7
Astacio, LA	186.1	122	5.9	Gardner, KC	91.2	54	5.3
Avery, Atl	223.1	125	5.0	Glavine, Atl	239.1	120	4.5
Ayala, Cin	98.0	65	6.0	Gooden, NYN	208.2	149	6.4
Banks, Min	171.1	138	7.2	Gordon, KC	155.2	143	8.3
Barnes, Mon	100.0	60	5.4	Gott, LA	77.2	67	7.8
Bautista, ChN	111.2	63	5.1	Greene, Phi	200.0	167	7.5
Beck, SF	79.1	86	9.8	Gross Kev, LA	202.1	150	6.7
Belcher, ChA	208.2	135	5.8	Guardado, Min	94.2	46	4.4
Belinda, KC	69.2	55	7.1	Gubicza, KC	104.1	80	6.9
Benes, SD	230.2	179	7.0	Gullickson, Det	159.1	70	4.0
Bere, ChA	142.2	129	8.1	Guzman Jose, ChN	191.0	163	7.7
Black, SF	93.2	45	4.3	Guzman Juan, Tor	221.0	194	7.9
Blair, Col	146.0	84	5.2	Hammond, Fla	191.0	108	5.1
Boever, Det	102.1	63	5.5	Haney, KC	124.0	65	4.7
Bohanon, Tex	92.2	45	4.4	Hanson, Sea	215.0	163	6.8
Bolton T, Det	102.2	66	5.8	Harkey, ChN	157.1	67	3.8
Bones, Mil	203.2	63	2.8	Harnisch, Hou	217.2	185	7.6
Bosio, Sea	164.1	119	6.5	Harris GA, Bos	112.1	103	8.3
Bottenfield, Col	159.2	63	3.6	Harris Gene, SD	59.1	39	5.9
Bowen, Fla	156.2	98	5.6	Harris GW, Col	225.1	123	4.9
Brantley, SF	113.2	76	6.0	Hartley, Min	81.0	57	6.3
Brocail, SD	128.1	70	4.9	Harvey, Fla	69.0	73	9.5
Brown, Tex	233.0	142	5.5	Henke, Tex	74.1	79	9.6
Browning, Cin	114.0	53	4.2	Henneman, Det	71.2	58	7.3
Burba, SF	95.1	88	8.3	Henry B, Mon	103.0	47	4.1
Burkett, SF	231.2	145	5.6	Henry Doug, Mil	55.0	38	6.2
Burns, StL	95.2	45	4.2	Hentgen, Tor	216.1	122	5.1
Candiotti, LA	213.2	155	6.5	Hernandez J, Cle	111.2	70	5.6
Carpenter, Tex	69.1	53	6.9	Hernandez R, ChA	78.2	71	8.1
Casian, Min	56.2	31	4.9	Hernandez X, Hou	96.2	101	9.4
Castillo F, ChN	141.1	84	5.3	Hershiser, LA	215.2	141	5.9
Castillo T, Tor	50.2	28	5.0	Hibbard, ChN	191.0	82	3.9
Clark, Cle	109.1	57	4.7	Hickerson, SF	120.1	69	5.2
Clemens, Bos	191.2	160	7.5	Hill K, Mon	183.2	90	4.4
Cone, KC	254.0	191	6.8	Hillman, NYN	145.0	60	3.7
Cooke, Pit	210.2	132	5.6	Hoffman, SD	90.0	79	7.9
Cormier, StL	145.1	75	4.6	Holmes, Col	66.2	60	8.1
Cox, Tor	83.2	84	9.0	Honeycutt, Oak	41.2	21	4.5
Darling, Oak	178.0	95	4.8	Hough, Fla	204.1	126	5.5
Darwin, Bos	229.1	130	5.1	Howe, NYA	50.2	19	3.4
Davis M, SD	69.2	70	9.0	Howell, Atl	58.1	37	5.7
Davis S, Det	98.0	73	6.7	Innis, NYN	76.2	36	4.2
Deshaies, SF	184.1	85	4.2	Jackson D, Phi	210.1	120	5.1
Doherty, Det	184.2	63	3.1	Jackson M, SF	77.1	70	8.1
Dopson, Bos	155.2	89	5.1	Johnson R, Sea	255.1	308	10.9
Downs, Oak	119.2	66	5.0	Jones D, Hou	85.1	66	7.0
Drabek, Hou	237.2	157	5.9	Kamieniecki, NYA	154.1	72	4.2
Eckersley, Oak	67.0	80	10.7	Key, NYA	236.2	173	6.6
Eichhorn, Tor	72.2	47	5.8	Kile, Hou	171.2	141	7.4
Eldred, Mil	258.0	180	6.3	Klink, Fla	37.2	22	5.3

Pitcher,Team	IP	K	K/9	Pitcher,Team	IP	K	K/9
Kramer, Cle	121.0	71	5.3	Reynoso, Col	189.0	117	5.6
Krueger, Det	82.0	60	6.6	Rhodes, Bal	85.2	49	5.1
Lancaster, StL	61.1	36	5.3	Righetti, SF	47.1	31	5.9
Langston, Cal	256.1	196	6.9	Rijo, Cin	257.1	227	7.9
Leary, Sea	169.1	68	3.6	Rivera, Phi	163.0	123	6.8
Lefferts, Tex	83.1	58	6.3	Rodriguez, Fla	76.0	43	5.1
Leibrandt, Tex	150.1	89	5.3	Rogers Ken, Tex	208.1	140	6.0
Leiter A, Tor	105.0	66	5.7	Rogers Kev, SF	80.2	62	6.9
Leiter M, Det	106.2	70	5.9	Rojas, Mon	88.1	48	4.9
Lewis R, Fla	77.1	65	7.6	Rueter, Mon	85.2	31	3.3
Lilliquist, Cle	64.0	40	5.6	Ruffin B, Col	139.2	126	8.1
Lloyd, Mil	63.2	31	4.4	Russell, Bos	46.2	45	8.7
MacDonald, Det	65.2	39	5.3	Saberhagen, NYN	139.1	93	6.0
Maddux G, Atl	267.0	197	6.6	Sanderson, SF	184.0	102	5.0
Maddux M, NYN	75.0	57	6.8	Scanlan, ChN	75.1	44	5.3
Magrane, Cal	164.0	62	3.4	Schilling, Phi	235.1	186	7.1
Martinez D, Mon	224.2	138	5.5	Schourek, NYN	128.1	72	5.0
Martinez P, LA	107.0	119	10.0	Scott T, Mon	71.2	65	8.2
Martinez R, LA	211.2	127	5.4	Sele, Bos	111.2	93	7.5
Mason, Phi	99.2	71	6.4	Shaw, Mon	95.2	50	4.7
McCaskill, ChA	113.2	65	5.1	Smiley, Cin	105.2	60	5.1
McDonald, Bal	220.1	171	7.0	Smith L, NYA	58.0	60	9.3
McDowell J, ChA	256.2	158	5.5	Smith P, Atl	90.2	53	5.3
McDowell R, LA	68.0	27	3.6	Smith Z, Pit	83.0	32	3.5
McMichael, Atl	91.2	89	8.7	Smoltz, Atl	243.2	208	7.7
Mesa, Cle	208.2	118	5.1	Stanton, Atl	52.0	43	7.4
Mills, Bal	100.1	68	6.1	Stewart, Tor	162.0	96	5.3
Minor, Pit	94.1	84	8.0	Stottlemyre, Tor	176.2	98	5.0
Miranda, Mil	120.0	88	6.6	Sutcliffe, Bal	166.0	80	4.3
Monteleone, NYA	85.2	50	5.3	Swift, SF	232.2	157	6.1
Montgomery, KC	87.1	66	6.8	Swindell, Hou	190.1	124	5.9
Moore Mike, Det	213.2	89	3.7	Tanana, NYA	202.2	116	5.2
Morgan, ChN	207.2	111	4.8	Tapani, Min	225.2	150	6.0
Morris, Tor	152.2	103	6.1	Tewksbury, StL	213.2	97	4.1
Moyer, Bal	152.0	90	5.3	Timlin, Tor	55.2	49	7.9
Mulholland, Phi	191.0	116	5.5	Tomlin, Pit	98.1	44	4.0
Murphy, StL	64.2	41	5.7	Trombley, Min	114.1	85	6.7
Mussina, Bal	167.2	117	6.3	Turner, Fla	68.0	59	7.8
Mutis, Cle	81.0	29	3.2	Valenzuela, Bal	178.2	78	3.9
Myers, ChN	75.1	86	10.3	Van Poppel, Oak	84.0	47	5.0
Nabholz, Mon	116.2	74	5.7	Viola, Bos	183.2	91	4.5
Navarro, Mil	214.1	114	4.8	Wagner, Pit	141.1	114	7.3
Neagle, Pit	81.1	73	8.1	Wakefield, Pit	128.1	59	4.1
Nelson G, Tex	60.2	35	5.2	Walk, Pit	187.0	80	3.9
Nelson J, Sea	60.0	61	9.1	Ward, Tor	71.2	97	12.2
Nied, Col	87.0	46	4.8	Watson, StL	86.0	49	5.1
Nunez, Oak	75.2	58	6.9	Wayne, Col	62.1	49	7.1
Olivares, StL	118.2	63	4.8	Wegman, Mil	120.2	50	3.7
Olson, Bal	45.0	44	8.8	Welch, Oak	166.2	63	3.4
Orosco, Mil	56.2	67	10.6	Wells, Det	187.0	139	6.7
Osborne, StL	155.2	83	4.8	West, Phi	86.1	87	9.1
Patterson B, Tex	52.2	46	7.9	Wetteland, Mon	85.1	113	11.9
Pavlik, Tex	166.1	131	7.1	Whitehurst, SD	105.2	57	4.9
Perez Mike, StL	72.2	58	7.2	Whiteside, Tex	73.0	39	4.8
Perez Mld, NYA	163.0	148	8.2	Wickman, NYA	140.0	70	4.5
Pichardo, KC	165.0	70	3.8	Williams B, Hou	82.0	56	6.1
Plesac, ChN	62.2	47	6.8	Williams Mtch, Phi	62.0	60	8.7
Plunk, Cle	71.0	77	9.8	Williamson, Bal	88.0	45	4.6
Poole, Bal	50.1	29	5.2	Willis, Min	58.0	44	6.8
Portugal, Hou	208.0	131	5.7	Wilson T, SF	110.0	57	4.7
Pugh, Cin	164.1	94	5.1	Witt B, Oak	220.0	131	5.4
Quantrill, Bos	138.0	66	4.3	Worrell Tim, SD	100.2	52	4.6
Radinsky, ChA	54.2	44	7.2	Young A, NYN	100.1	62	5.6
Rapp, Fla	94.0	57	5.5	**MLB Avg**			**5.8**
Reardon, Cin	61.2	35	5.1				
Reed S, Col	84.1	51	5.4				

WHO'S AFRAID OF THE DARK? (p. 180)

Both Leagues — Listed Alphabetically
(Active Pitchers with 150 IP Day/150 IP Night, 1989-93)

Pitcher	Day				Night			
	W	L	ERA	K/9	W	L	ERA	K/9
Abbott J	20	18	3.38	5.41	38	48	3.77	5.00
Aguilera	11	6	2.23	8.00	13	22	3.13	7.93
Appier	18	11	2.54	6.65	41	27	3.12	6.56
Armstrong	12	14	4.03	7.00	24	43	4.62	5.42
Assenmacher	16	5	3.19	9.52	9	16	3.73	8.23
Avery	16	10	3.52	5.73	34	26	3.48	5.38
Belcher	12	16	3.93	6.15	49	39	3.38	6.62
Benes	20	9	2.71	7.88	39	45	3.74	6.46
Bielecki	21	20	4.57	5.40	24	18	3.66	5.47
Black	21	12	2.98	4.74	34	40	4.02	3.93
Boddicker	13	13	4.15	5.51	35	27	4.02	5.06
Boever	5	9	4.15	6.60	14	22	3.07	6.82
Bosio	16	16	3.10	6.13	42	28	3.56	5.37
Boskie	12	14	4.16	4.20	7	15	4.91	4.74
Brantley	17	5	2.69	6.75	12	14	3.46	7.05
Brown	12	13	4.69	4.25	57	41	3.36	5.23
Browning	17	17	3.71	4.22	40	30	4.16	4.11
Burkett	29	16	3.33	5.36	32	18	4.35	5.47
Cadaret	11	12	4.51	6.67	14	13	3.74	6.14
Candiotti	24	16	3.25	6.61	36	43	3.02	5.95
Castillo F	13	13	3.71	5.88	8	13	4.56	5.57
Clemens	28	14	2.42	7.75	57	38	3.06	8.00
Cone	20	21	3.48	8.77	50	35	3.11	8.53
Cook D	11	10	3.72	5.05	16	14	4.04	4.59
Darling	14	18	4.02	5.14	35	39	4.21	5.80
Darwin	18	11	3.15	6.67	31	23	3.24	5.91
Davis S	13	16	5.40	5.01	25	21	4.04	5.19
DeLeon	11	15	3.70	7.35	22	33	3.42	6.96
Deshaies	14	12	3.74	5.75	30	44	3.89	4.92
Dopson	11	8	4.11	3.83	15	22	4.37	4.98
Downs	9	8	3.93	4.66	19	23	4.52	4.91
Drabek	25	14	2.97	5.46	50	47	3.06	5.45
Erickson	21	15	3.24	4.59	28	28	4.11	4.52
Fernandez A	8	11	4.66	6.78	32	27	3.64	5.65
Fernandez S	10	12	3.38	8.04	33	27	2.80	7.88
Finley	19	18	3.79	6.50	56	35	2.92	6.58
Gardner	7	18	4.76	7.20	25	21	4.10	6.26
Glavine	20	14	4.19	5.76	66	31	2.94	5.20
Gooden	21	19	3.60	7.03	42	27	3.52	7.34
Gordon	21	16	3.38	8.26	35	34	4.04	8.44
Gross Kev	13	12	3.17	6.70	38	49	4.26	6.86
Gubicza	11	12	3.84	6.38	29	32	4.19	6.37
Gullickson	17	15	4.33	3.22	40	30	4.28	3.42
Guzman Jose	12	5	2.95	7.79	29	23	4.00	6.96
Guzman Juan	14	4	3.31	8.19	26	7	3.26	7.94
Hanson	13	12	3.57	6.28	41	39	3.76	7.02
Harnisch	12	10	3.76	7.06	41	38	3.46	6.82
Harris GA	16	12	3.53	7.58	22	29	3.61	6.10
Harris GW	18	14	3.34	5.61	22	33	3.35	6.21
Hershiser	17	17	3.38	5.64	28	30	3.13	6.04
Hesketh	14	9	3.36	6.15	16	18	4.88	6.79
Hibbard	16	14	4.56	3.99	40	31	3.51	3.51
Hill K	18	17	2.91	5.54	30	30	3.85	5.58
Hough	12	11	3.09	4.91	35	52	4.49	4.69
Hurst	9	9	3.31	5.96	46	30	3.28	6.12

Pitcher	Day				Night			
	W	L	ERA	K/9	W	L	ERA	K/9
Jackson D	11	19	4.37	4.83	22	27	4.34	5.04
Johnson R	17	8	4.03	9.85	48	48	3.74	9.33
Key	17	19	4.13	5.48	56	33	3.22	5.38
Lancaster	15	9	4.02	6.52	14	10	3.75	4.56
Langston	16	19	4.00	8.16	58	45	3.16	7.08
Leary	12	17	5.59	5.20	28	45	4.31	4.73
Lefferts	10	12	3.27	6.05	17	24	3.99	5.58
Leibrandt	12	18	4.49	4.83	41	34	3.65	4.68
Maddux G	37	25	3.03	6.21	52	34	2.71	6.14
Magrane	15	6	4.19	5.77	25	34	3.44	3.90
Martinez D	17	19	3.67	5.81	54	30	2.68	5.54
Martinez R	18	14	2.90	6.57	43	32	3.50	6.87
McCaskill	10	8	2.50	4.69	43	53	4.17	4.29
McDonald	5	12	5.02	6.38	36	28	3.49	6.15
McDowell J	21	13	3.62	6.40	52	26	3.33	6.37
Mesa	5	16	5.76	4.73	21	21	4.62	4.36
Milacki	8	8	3.91	4.52	28	30	4.41	4.36
Moore Mike	35	19	3.80	5.17	44	36	3.92	4.89
Morgan	29	21	2.54	4.58	30	38	3.59	4.87
Morris	27	19	4.19	5.47	40	43	4.57	5.85
Mulholland	15	21	3.85	5.31	39	29	3.62	4.83
Mussina	11	5	3.01	5.36	25	11	3.35	5.45
Nagy	9	15	4.37	6.34	22	20	3.71	4.89
Navarro	21	16	3.84	4.46	37	34	4.19	4.27
Ojeda	11	14	3.87	4.43	29	22	3.36	5.34
Perez Mld	15	18	4.66	7.44	36	47	3.90	7.85
Portugal	18	12	3.60	5.78	34	18	3.22	6.32
Rasmussen	9	14	4.67	3.80	23	27	4.06	4.30
Rijo	21	12	2.27	7.42	44	27	2.73	7.41
Ruffin B	8	11	5.15	6.17	15	30	4.39	6.16
Saberhagen	10	16	3.28	6.88	41	19	2.74	6.18
Sanderson	20	21	3.96	5.70	47	33	4.27	5.02
Schilling	6	10	4.42	7.25	28	16	2.85	6.53
Smiley	22	14	3.58	4.89	38	30	3.62	5.87
Smith B	11	12	3.88	4.89	26	22	3.82	4.66
Smith Z	10	14	3.34	4.14	30	33	3.15	4.97
Smoltz	17	14	2.95	7.74	53	44	3.56	6.84
Stewart	35	15	3.33	5.77	43	34	3.98	5.49
Stieb	15	11	4.21	4.75	29	15	3.19	4.70
Stottlemyre	16	18	4.59	4.75	42	37	4.13	4.96
Sutcliffe	14	19	4.33	5.39	34	24	4.60	4.46
Swift	25	9	2.68	4.24	20	12	2.82	4.60
Swindell	18	14	3.56	5.80	40	38	3.63	6.09
Tanana	18	27	4.10	4.68	34	35	4.30	5.40
Tapani	19	10	3.24	6.09	39	35	4.06	5.31
Tewksbury	18	12	3.17	3.82	37	24	3.11	3.58
Tomlin	6	11	3.81	4.18	24	17	3.23	4.64
Viola	30	20	3.00	5.83	40	44	3.59	5.63
Walk	15	8	4.46	4.29	37	29	4.20	4.28
Ward	10	10	2.86	10.50	12	21	2.93	9.38
Wegman	12	17	4.09	4.24	24	26	3.44	4.32
Welch	33	16	3.31	4.99	43	29	4.08	4.14
Wells	12	14	4.92	5.04	39	24	3.36	6.05
Wilson S	7	10	4.72	7.30	6	8	4.06	6.14
Wilson T	20	10	3.32	6.03	18	30	4.20	5.07
Witt B	11	15	4.44	6.55	45	42	4.39	7.27
Witt M	10	8	3.64	5.34	7	19	5.16	5.32
Young Curt	12	5	3.90	3.74	11	15	4.75	3.80
Young M	7	14	4.04	7.38	6	25	4.67	7.03
MLB Totals	**3298**	**7388**	**3.94**	**5.79**	**7388**	**7388**	**3.87**	**5.70**

ARE PITCHERS LEARNING TO HIT AGAIN? (p. 182)

1993 Active Pitchers — Listed Alphabetically
(minimum 50 plate appearances lifetime)

Pitcher, Team	AVG	AB	H	HR	RBI
Aguilera, Min	.203	138	28	3	11
Armstrong, Fla	.114	185	21	0	8
Arocha, StL	.103	58	6	0	3
Ashby, SD	.119	59	7	0	2
Astacio, LA	.151	86	13	0	3
Avery, Atl	.177	260	46	0	11
Barnes, Mon	.140	107	15	0	4
Bedrosian, Atl	.093	151	14	0	2
Belcher, ChA	.124	372	46	2	25
Benes, SD	.116	285	33	4	14
Black, SF	.154	162	25	0	11
Blair, Col	.094	53	5	0	4
Boskie, ChN	.200	115	23	1	6
Bottenfield, Col	.241	58	14	0	3
Bowen, Fla	.134	82	11	0	3
Brantley, SF	.131	61	8	0	5
Browning, Cin	.153	607	93	2	32
Burkett, SF	.072	250	18	0	10
Candelaria, Pit	.174	596	104	1	48
Candiotti, LA	.121	116	14	0	3
Castillo F, ChN	.126	143	18	0	5
Charlton, Sea	.082	85	7	0	0
Cooke, Pit	.162	74	12	0	6
Cormier, StL	.173	127	22	0	7
Darling, Oak	.145	525	76	2	21
Davis M, SD	.156	167	26	1	9
DeLeon, ChA	.091	419	38	0	9
Deshaies, SF	.089	372	33	0	12
Drabek, Hou	.150	540	81	2	29
Eckersley, Oak	.133	180	24	3	12
Fassero, Mon	.071	42	3	0	0
Fernandez S, NYN	.192	496	95	1	31
Glavine, Atl	.183	437	80	0	30
Gooden, NYN	.198	718	142	7	63
Gossage, Oak	.106	85	9	0	2
Gott, LA	.181	72	13	4	5
Grant, Col	.067	104	7	0	2
Greene, Phi	.217	189	41	4	17
Gross Kev, LA	.162	612	99	5	33
Guzman Jose, ChN	.111	63	7	0	2
Hammond, Fla	.208	144	30	3	9
Harkey, ChN	.184	141	26	0	4
Harnisch, Hou	.122	196	24	0	14
Harris GW, Col	.107	178	19	0	7
Henry B, Mon	.128	78	10	1	9
Hershiser, LA	.215	628	135	0	42
Hibbard, ChN	.092	65	6	0	3
Hickerson, SF	.091	44	4	0	4
Hill K, Mon	.143	245	35	1	14
Hillman, NYN	.140	57	8	0	0
Hough, Fla	.150	193	29	1	13
Hurst, Col	.113	274	31	0	8
Jackson D, Phi	.113	311	35	0	15
Jones J, Mon	.166	193	32	2	11
Kile, Hou	.081	123	10	1	4
Kilgus, StL	.087	46	4	0	2
Lancaster, StL	.098	132	13	0	5
Leary, Sea	.221	163	36	1	19
Maddux G, Atl	.181	581	105	2	33
Maddux M, NYN	.071	85	6	0	4
Magrane, Cal	.139	280	39	4	13
Martinez D, Mon	.143	509	73	0	30
Martinez R, LA	.125	321	40	1	22
Mason, Phi	.071	56	4	0	0
McDowell R, LA	.225	71	16	0	6
Morgan, ChN	.093	323	30	0	12
Mulholland, Phi	.079	356	28	0	6
Myers, ChN	.190	58	11	0	6
Nabholz, Mon	.107	177	19	0	4
Olivares, StL	.232	164	38	2	16
Orosco, Mil	.169	59	10	0	4
Osborne, StL	.159	107	17	0	3
Portugal, Hou	.180	239	43	2	18
Power, Sea	.089	157	14	1	7
Pugh, Cin	.194	67	13	0	1
Reardon, Cin	.088	57	5	0	2
Reynoso, Col	.111	72	8	2	4
Rijo, Cin	.196	358	70	2	23
Rivera, Phi	.095	84	8	0	2
Ruffin B, Col	.080	288	23	0	6
Saberhagen, NYN	.110	73	8	0	0
Sanderson, SF	.097	474	46	2	26
Schilling, Phi	.155	142	22	0	6
Schourek, NYN	.125	96	12	0	8
Smiley, Cin	.126	286	36	0	20
Smith B, Col	.153	496	76	3	37
Smith L, NYA	.047	64	3	1	2
Smith P, Atl	.114	193	22	0	10
Smith Z, Pit	.152	468	71	0	27
Smoltz, Atl	.146	364	53	2	21
Swift, SF	.221	131	29	0	7
Swindell, Hou	.150	140	21	0	8
Tanana, NYA	.153	59	9	0	5
Tewksbury, StL	.146	254	37	0	13
Tomlin, Pit	.149	175	26	0	4
Wagner, Pit	.200	45	9	0	1
Wakefield, Pit	.127	71	9	1	3
Walk, Pit	.145	510	74	1	48
Whitehurst, SD	.159	88	14	0	3
Williams B, Hou	.140	43	6	0	4
Wilson S, LA	.133	60	8	0	3
Wilson T, SF	.166	163	27	2	11
Young A, NYN	.127	55	7	0	0

IS THAT LEFTY YOU'RE BRINGING IN JUST GOING TO PITCH TO A RIGHTY? (p. 184)

The chart below lists left-handed relievers, and the number of times they were scheduled to face a left- or right-handed batter coming in to the game, and how many times they actually faced a left- or right-handed batter.

Both Leagues — Listed Alphabetically
(Left-handed relievers with 30 Relief games in 1993)

Reliever, Team	G	Scheduled Batter LHB	RHB	LHB%	Actually Batted LHB	RHB	LHB%
Assenmacher, NYA	72	53	19	.736	43	29	.597
Barnes, Mon	44	20	24	.455	16	28	.364
Bolton T, Det	35	14	21	.400	12	23	.343
Brewer, KC	46	30	16	.652	29	17	.630
Cadaret, KC	47	18	29	.383	15	32	.319
Casian, Min	54	32	22	.593	27	27	.500
Castillo T, Tor	51	25	26	.490	16	35	.314
Charlton, Sea	34	11	23	.324	8	26	.235
Daal, LA	47	40	7	.851	34	13	.723
Davis M, SD	60	36	24	.600	33	27	.550
Fassero, Mon	41	15	26	.366	15	26	.366
Fossas, Bos	71	54	17	.761	47	24	.662
Franco, NYN	35	13	22	.371	9	26	.257
Frey, Cal	55	34	21	.618	29	26	.527
Guetterman, StL	40	15	25	.375	11	29	.275
Hickerson, SF	32	13	19	.406	11	21	.344
Honeycutt, Oak	52	34	18	.654	25	27	.481
Horsman, Oak	40	26	14	.650	22	18	.550
Howe, NYA	51	36	15	.706	28	23	.549
Klink, Fla	59	47	12	.797	38	21	.644
Lefferts, Tex	44	29	15	.659	25	19	.568
Lilliquist, Cle	54	26	28	.481	17	37	.315
Lloyd, Mil	55	31	24	.564	24	31	.436
MacDonald, Det	68	36	32	.529	31	37	.456
Martinez PA, SD	32	21	11	.656	18	14	.563
McElroy, ChN	49	31	18	.633	29	20	.592
Mercker, Atl	37	18	19	.486	16	21	.432
Mohler, Oak	33	21	12	.636	18	15	.545
Murphy, StL	73	41	32	.562	34	39	.466
Myers, ChN	73	27	46	.370	18	55	.247
Neagle, Pit	43	30	13	.698	27	16	.628
Orosco, Mil	57	33	24	.579	24	33	.421
Osuna, Hou	44	34	10	.773	24	20	.545
Patterson B, Tex	52	30	22	.577	28	24	.538
Patterson K, Cal	46	25	21	.543	25	21	.543
Pennington, Bal	34	24	10	.706	16	18	.471
Plesac, ChN	57	32	25	.561	29	28	.509
Poole, Bal	55	43	12	.782	36	19	.655
Powell D, Sea	31	21	10	.677	17	14	.548
Radinsky, ChA	73	49	24	.671	42	31	.575
Righetti, SF	51	29	22	.569	23	28	.451
Rodriguez, Fla	70	41	29	.586	32	38	.457
Rogers Kev, SF	64	32	32	.500	25	39	.391
Ruffin B, Col	47	31	16	.660	27	20	.574
Stanton, Atl	63	36	27	.571	25	38	.397
Tsamis, Min	41	16	25	.390	12	29	.293
Wayne, Col	65	54	11	.831	48	17	.738
West, Phi	76	39	37	.513	30	46	.395
Wickander, Cin	44	29	15	.659	25	19	.568
Williams Mtch, Phi	65	16	49	.246	9	56	.138
MLB Avg	**3173**	**1855**	**1318**	**.585**	**1542**	**1631**	**.486**

WHICH PITCHERS CAN REST IN PEACE? (p. 186)

The following table lists the Percentage (%) of baserunners that a pitcher "bequeathed" to his bullpen (**Left**), and those that subsequently scored (**Sc**).

Both Leagues — Listed Alphabetically
(minimum 15 runners bequeathed)

Pitcher	Left	Sc	%	Pitcher	Left	Sc	%	Pitcher	Left	Sc	%
Abbott J, NYA	20	6	30.0	Harkey, ChN	23	12	52.2	Nelson J, Sea	48	11	22.9
Alvarez, ChA	22	6	27.3	Harris GA, Bos	43	17	39.5	Nunez, Oak	22	7	31.8
Andersen, Phi	23	7	30.4	Harris GW, Col	24	7	29.2	Olivares, StL	27	7	25.9
Aquino, Fla	21	7	33.3	Hartley, Min	28	6	21.4	Orosco, Mil	24	8	33.3
Armstrong, Fla	23	3	13.0	Henry B, Mon	21	5	23.8	Osborne, StL	26	8	30.8
Assenmacher, NYA	53	9	17.0	Hentgen, Tor	23	4	17.4	Osuna, Hou	35	5	14.3
Astacio, LA	32	12	37.5	Hernandez J, Cle	23	7	30.4	Patterson B, Tex	25	6	24.0
Austin, Mil	22	4	18.2	Hesketh, Bos	21	7	33.3	Patterson K, Cal	35	9	25.7
Ayala, Cin	29	7	24.1	Hibbard, ChN	24	7	29.2	Pavlik, Tex	27	5	18.5
Bankhead, Bos	28	3	10.7	Hickerson, SF	30	8	26.7	Perez Mike, StL	22	4	18.2
Banks, Min	31	9	29.0	Hoffman, SD	24	5	20.8	Perez Mld, NYA	21	13	61.9
Barnes, Mon	23	5	21.7	Honeycutt, Oak	28	10	35.7	Plantenberg, Sea	23	5	21.7
Belcher, ChA	26	12	46.2	Horsman, Oak	29	6	20.7	Plesac, ChN	31	7	22.6
Benes, SD	29	15	51.7	Hough, Fla	23	11	47.8	Plunk, Cle	23	8	34.8
Blair, Col	22	4	18.2	Howe, NYA	35	12	34.3	Poole, Bal	50	10	20.0
Boever, Det	26	7	26.9	Innis, NYN	21	10	47.6	Portugal, Hou	32	4	12.5
Bohanon, Tex	31	6	19.4	Jackson D, Phi	27	9	33.3	Powell D, Sea	31	7	22.6
Bolton T, Det	34	15	44.1	Jackson M, SF	25	5	20.0	Power, Sea	21	8	38.1
Bones, Mil	29	17	58.6	Kamieniecki, NYA	23	7	30.4	Pugh, Cin	25	7	28.0
Bottenfield, Col	23	8	34.8	Kile, Hou	23	3	13.0	Quantrill, Bos	35	10	28.6
Bowen, Fla	23	8	34.8	Klink, Fla	45	12	26.7	Radinsky, ChA	44	13	29.5
Brantley, SF	27	12	44.4	Knudsen, Det	21	3	14.3	Reed S, Col	25	13	52.0
Brewer, KC	20	3	15.0	Kramer, Cle	22	8	36.4	Rodriguez, Fla	44	9	20.5
Brown, Tex	25	9	36.0	Krueger, Det	24	4	16.7	Rogers Ken, Tex	25	10	40.0
Burba, SF	24	6	25.0	Leary, Sea	32	14	43.8	Rogers Kev, SF	31	10	32.3
Burkett, SF	25	7	28.0	Lefferts, Tex	42	4	9.5	Rojas, Mon	23	5	21.7
Burns, StL	21	6	28.6	Leiter A, Tor	29	11	37.9	Ruffin B, Col	31	6	19.4
Carpenter, Tex	22	7	31.8	Lewis R, Fla	24	9	37.5	Ryan K, Bos	23	6	26.1
Casian, Min	40	9	22.5	Lilliquist, Cle	33	3	9.1	Scanlan, ChN	26	6	23.1
Castillo T, Tor	24	6	25.0	Lloyd, Mil	24	8	33.3	Schourek, NYN	31	11	35.5
Cook D, Cle	22	6	27.3	MacDonald, Det	27	7	25.9	Sutcliffe, Bal	30	8	26.7
Cormier, StL	24	7	29.2	Martinez P, LA	26	8	30.8	Swan, Sea	22	7	31.8
Daal, LA	29	6	20.7	Martinez PA, SD	20	5	25.0	Tapani, Min	26	8	30.8
Davis M, SD	26	3	11.5	Martinez R, LA	25	8	32.0	Taylor K, SD	25	12	48.0
Deshaies, SF	23	11	47.8	McCaskill, ChA	20	4	20.0	Tewksbury, StL	20	5	25.0
Doherty, Det	27	10	37.0	McDonald, Bal	35	10	28.6	Tsamis, Min	25	12	48.0
Dopson, Bos	28	13	46.4	McElroy, ChN	34	13	38.2	Valenzuela, Bal	32	11	34.4
Eldred, Mil	26	9	34.6	Mercker, Atl	23	4	17.4	Viola, Bos	26	8	30.8
Erickson, Min	29	15	51.7	Mesa, Cle	26	13	50.0	Wagner, Pit	22	8	36.4
Fassero, Mon	23	4	17.4	Mills, Bal	26	7	26.9	Wayne, Col	22	10	45.5
Fleming, Sea	27	7	25.9	Minor, Pit	25	12	48.0	Welch, Oak	24	6	25.0
Fossas, Bos	50	17	34.0	Mohler, Oak	32	8	25.0	West, Phi	26	6	23.1
Frey, Cal	27	8	29.6	Monteleone, NYA	26	10	38.5	Whiteside, Tex	35	15	42.9
Frohwirth, Bal	48	19	39.6	Moore Mike, Det	27	5	18.5	Wickander, Cin	35	7	20.0
Greene, Phi	20	6	30.0	Morgan, ChN	20	9	45.0	Wickman, NYA	27	8	29.6
Gross Kev, LA	25	8	32.0	Morris, Tor	20	10	50.0	Williamson, Bal	32	12	37.5
Gubicza, KC	29	11	37.9	Moyer, Bal	22	8	36.4	Witt B, Oak	27	5	18.5
Gullickson, Det	20	11	55.0	Munoz B, NYA	32	13	40.6	Young M, Tor	29	13	44.8
Guzman Jose, ChN	22	7	31.8	Murphy, StL	32	12	37.5	**MLB Avg**			**32.2**
Guzman Juan, Tor	29	13	44.8	Navarro, Mil	32	12	37.5				
Hammond, Fla	27	8	29.6	Neagle, Pit	20	6	30.0				
Haney, KC	22	9	40.9	Nelson G, Tex	26	5	19.2				

WHICH TEAMS DO DOMINANT PITCHER DOMINATE? (p. 188)

The following chart lists how pitchers have fared against three different types of teams: **Singles** (HR 10% <rest of the League Average), **Home Run** (HR 10% > rest of the league average), and **Regular**.

Both Leagues — Listed Alphabetically
(Minimum 400 IP/OppAvg <.246, 1989-1993)

Pitcher	Opp Avg	Singles W-L	ERA	Neutral W-L	ERA	Home Runs W-L	ERA
RYAN, Nolan	.197	14-13	3.54	18-16	3.69	19-10	2.97
FERNANDEZ, Sid	.202	17-17	2.76	13-15	3.15	13-7	3.04
WARD, Duane	.214	8-9	4.44	9-10	2.13	5-12	2.57
JOHNSON, Randy	.215	21-12	3.37	32-22	3.56	12-22	4.76
MONTGOMERY, Jeff	.217	11-4	1.69	9-9	1.80	5-10	3.17
JACKSON, Mike	.222	9-13	3.10	9-10	3.51	10-9	4.13
GUZMAN, Juan	.224	9-1	3.21	16-2	2.55	15-8	4.03
CONE, David	.225	18-21	3.26	29-19	3.17	23-16	3.28
AGUILERA, Rick	.225	8-8	2.66	9-11	2.63	7-9	3.06
CHARLTON, Norm	.227	8-10	3.27	7-4	1.91	13-8	3.42
DeLEON, Jose	.228	13-21	3.77	9-11	3.18	11-16	3.46
RIJO, Jose	.228	26-17	2.69	18-4	2.13	21-18	2.82
CLEMENS, Roger	.229	29-21	3.43	27-12	1.92	29-19	3.08
SMOLTZ, John	.230	35-21	3.25	18-19	3.34	17-18	3.79
SCOTT, Mike	.231	11-7	3.09	9-11	3.99	9-7	3.74
MYERS, Randy	.231	9-16	3.84	5-10	2.64	8-7	2.61
NABHOLZ, Chris	.232	17-10	3.72	8-5	3.78	9-14	3.10
HARNISCH, Pete	.232	18-14	3.27	11-19	4.68	24-15	2.88
LANGSTON, Mark	.233	20-15	3.07	28-24	3.26	26-25	3.69
GORDON, Tom	.234	16-17	4.24	19-14	3.43	21-19	3.89
MARTINEZ, Dennis	.234	29-24	2.61	15-10	2.90	27-15	3.49
MARTINEZ, Ramon	.235	24-12	2.71	18-9	3.24	19-25	4.01
DARWIN, Danny	.235	12-6	3.93	17-9	2.79	20-19	3.12
BELCHER, Tim	.237	15-21	3.39	20-17	4.08	26-17	3.19
McDONALD, Ben	.237	5-10	3.72	17-13	3.60	19-17	4.08
APPIER, Kevin	.237	13-9	3.18	21-16	3.17	25-13	2.62
SCHILLING, Curt	.237	13-9	3.30	11-7	3.26	10-10	3.24
SABERHAGEN, Bret	.238	31-12	2.62	11-9	2.71	9-14	3.65
STIEB, Dave	.238	16-12	3.72	22-9	3.02	6-5	4.45
MADDUX, Greg	.238	28-22	3.05	33-19	2.40	28-18	3.13
HILL, Ken	.239	20-14	2.78	11-14	3.33	17-19	4.42
HARRIS, Greg	.241	9-10	3.14	11-19	3.56	18-12	3.93
BENES, Andy	.241	22-22	3.43	20-14	3.72	17-18	3.22
PLUNK, Eric	.241	8-8	3.06	14-8	3.47	7-9	4.14
GREENE, Tommy	.242	14-7	3.89	12-8	3.64	10-4	3.95
CANDIOTTI, Tom	.242	19-26	3.62	18-17	2.90	23-16	2.66
HOUGH, Charlie	.242	13-21	4.68	15-20	4.31	19-22	3.52
BRANTLEY, Jeff	.242	13-12	3.46	9-1	2.16	7-6	3.83
HARRIS, Greg W.	.243	13-16	3.52	10-14	3.28	17-17	3.22
HURST, Bruce	.244	13-13	3.84	26-12	2.51	16-14	3.73
PORTUGAL, Mark	.244	18-15	3.68	14-3	2.59	20-12	3.40
MORGAN, Mike	.245	25-20	2.70	14-20	3.40	20-19	3.44
WILSON, Trevor	.245	15-14	3.50	10-16	3.88	13-10	4.30
MUSSINA, Mike	.245	5-4	3.45	18-6	3.33	13-6	3.04

HOW IMPORTANT IS RUN SUPPORT? (p. 190)

In the table below, **Sup** stands for Run Support Per Nine Innigs. **RS** is the total Runs In Support for that pitcher while he was in the game.

Both Leagues — Listed Alphabetically
(minimum 20 games started in 1993)

Pitcher, Team	W/L	ERA	Sup	IP	RS	Pitcher, Team	W/L	ERA	Sup	IP	RS
Abbott J, NYA	11-14	4.37	5.00	214.0	119	Hough, Fla	9-16	4.27	3.22	204.1	73
Alvarez, ChA	15-8	2.95	4.25	207.2	98	Jackson D, Phi	12-11	3.77	5.52	210.1	129
Appier, KC	18-8	2.56	4.49	238.2	119	Johnson R, Sea	19-8	3.26	5.46	254.0	154
Armstrong, Fla	8-17	4.59	3.52	192.0	75	Kamieniecki, NYA	10-6	3.80	4.97	130.1	72
Arocha, StL	11-7	3.68	4.92	181.0	99	Key, NYA	18-6	3.00	6.01	236.2	158
Ashby, SD	3-10	6.53	5.48	111.2	68	Kile, Hou	14-8	3.60	6.27	165.0	115
Astacio, LA	14-9	3.57	4.73	186.1	98	Langston, Cal	16-11	3.20	4.00	256.1	114
Avery, Atl	18-6	2.94	5.04	223.1	125	Leary, Sea	11-8	4.90	6.31	159.2	112
Banks, Min	11-12	3.83	4.62	169.1	87	Leibrandt, Tex	9-10	4.55	5.93	150.1	99
Belcher, ChA	12-11	4.46	4.98	207.2	115	Maddux G, Atl	20-10	2.36	4.28	267.0	127
Benes, SD	15-15	3.78	4.10	230.2	105	Magrane, Cal	11-11	4.49	4.49	162.1	81
Bere, ChA	12-5	3.47	6.06	142.2	96	Martinez D, Mon	15-9	3.85	4.61	224.1	115
Bones, Mil	11-11	4.91	5.85	201.2	131	Martinez R, LA	10-12	3.44	3.49	211.2	82
Bosio, Sea	8-9	3.40	4.26	156.1	74	McDonald, Bal	13-14	3.39	3.96	220.1	97
Bottenfield, Col	5-9	5.32	3.66	135.1	55	McDowell J, ChA	22-10	3.37	5.40	256.2	154
Bowen, Fla	8-12	4.42	4.08	156.2	71	Mesa, Cle	10-12	4.94	4.81	207.2	111
Brocail, SD	4-13	4.56	4.00	128.1	57	Moore Mike, Det	13-9	5.22	6.32	213.2	150
Brown, Tex	15-12	3.59	4.67	233.0	121	Morgan, ChN	10-15	4.03	3.42	207.2	79
Browning, Cin	7-7	4.70	5.42	113.0	68	Morris, Tor	7-12	6.19	4.78	152.2	81
Burkett, SF	22-7	3.65	5.52	231.2	142	Moyer, Bal	12-9	3.43	4.32	152.0	73
Candiotti, LA	8-10	2.97	2.50	212.1	59	Mulholland, Phi	12-9	3.27	5.02	190.0	106
Castillo F, ChN	5-8	4.82	5.02	136.1	76	Mussina, Bal	14-6	4.46	6.12	167.2	114
Clemens, Bos	11-14	4.46	3.66	191.2	78	Nabholz, Mon	9-8	4.04	5.58	111.1	69
Cone, KC	11-14	3.33	2.94	254.0	83	Navarro, Mil	11-12	5.30	5.21	212.1	123
Cooke, Pit	10-10	3.89	4.87	210.2	114	Osborne, StL	10-7	3.76	4.45	155.2	77
Cormier, StL	6-5	4.22	5.40	121.2	73	Pavlik, Tex	12-6	3.41	4.55	166.1	84
Darling, Oak	5-9	5.16	4.11	171.0	78	Perez Mld, NYA	6-14	5.19	3.48	163.0	63
Darwin, Bos	15-11	3.26	4.55	229.1	116	Pichardo, KC	7-7	4.00	4.98	155.1	86
Deshaies, SF	13-15	4.36	4.31	183.2	88	Portugal, Hou	18-4	2.77	4.98	208.0	115
Doherty, Det	14-11	4.47	5.89	183.1	120	Pugh, Cin	10-14	5.28	5.52	155.0	95
Dopson, Bos	7-9	4.83	5.32	149.0	88	Reynoso, Col	12-11	4.00	4.76	189.0	100
Drabek, Hou	9-18	3.79	3.64	237.2	96	Rijo, Cin	14-9	2.48	4.23	257.1	121
Eldred, Mil	16-16	4.01	4.74	258.0	136	Rivera, Phi	13-9	5.12	7.03	160.0	125
Erickson, Min	8-19	5.19	4.94	218.2	120	Rogers Ken, Tex	16-10	4.14	6.14	206.2	141
Fernandez A, ChA	18-9	3.13	5.57	247.1	153	Sanderson, SF	11-13	4.28	4.23	178.2	84
Finley, Cal	16-14	3.15	4.37	251.1	122	Schilling, Phi	16-7	4.02	4.97	235.1	130
Fleming, Sea	12-5	4.36	5.16	167.1	96	Smoltz, Atl	15-11	3.62	5.28	243.2	143
Glavine, Atl	22-6	3.20	5.72	239.1	152	Stewart, Tor	12-8	4.44	5.83	162.0	105
Gooden, NYN	12-15	3.45	4.57	208.2	106	Stottlemyre, Tor	11-12	4.93	5.19	171.2	99
Greene, Phi	16-4	3.47	6.89	197.1	151	Sutcliffe, Bal	10-10	5.66	5.33	163.2	97
Gross Kev, LA	13-12	4.09	5.93	200.1	132	Swift, SF	21-8	2.82	5.88	232.2	152
Gullickson, Det	13-9	5.37	6.95	159.1	123	Swindell, Hou	12-13	4.23	4.42	187.1	92
Guzman Jose, Ch	12-10	4.34	5.09	191.0	108	Tanana, NYA	7-17	4.35	4.09	202.2	92
Guzman Juan, Tor	14-3	3.99	6.19	221.0	152	Tapani, Min	12-15	4.47	4.27	223.2	106
Hammond, Fla	11-12	4.66	4.38	191.0	93	Tewksbury, StL	17-10	3.83	5.85	213.2	139
Haney, KC	9-9	6.02	5.37	124.0	74	Valenzuela, Bal	8-10	4.96	4.61	177.2	91
Hanson, Sea	11-11	3.32	4.48	209.0	104	Viola, Bos	11-8	3.14	4.80	183.2	98
Harkey, ChN	10-10	5.26	5.43	157.1	95	Wakefield, Pit	5-11	5.66	4.34	122.1	59
Harnisch, Hou	16-9	2.98	5.17	217.2	125	Walk, Pit	13-14	5.68	5.05	187.0	105
Harris GW, Col	11-17	4.59	3.91	225.1	98	Welch, Oak	8-11	5.34	3.84	161.2	69
Hentgen, Tor	19-8	3.88	6.00	208.2	139	Wells, Det	11-9	4.17	5.10	183.2	104
Hershiser, LA	12-14	3.59	5.05	215.2	121	Witt B, Oak	14-13	4.29	4.25	212.0	100
Hibbard, ChN	15-11	3.96	4.76	191.0	101	**MLB Average**		4.26	4.83		
Hill K, Mon	9-7	3.23	4.56	183.2	93						
Hillman, NYN	2-8	3.91	3.91	138.0	60						

WHICH FIREMEN AREN'T THE SAME WITHOUT A GREAT BIG BLAZE? (p. 194)

The chart below divides relief appearances between Regular and Tough Save Situations and games which are close (pitcher's team is behind by 1 run or tied) (**Crucial**) and all other relief situations (**Non-Crucial**).

Both Leagues — Listed Alphabetically
(Minimum 30 Save Opportunities 1991-1993)

Reliever	Crucial			Non-Crucial		
	IP	ER	ERA	IP	ER	ERA
Rick Aguilera	110.0	34	2.78	98.0	30	2.76
Paul Assenmacher	109.0	45	3.72	117.2	44	3.37
Rod Beck	105.2	22	1.87	118.0	37	2.82
Stan Belinda	135.0	53	3.53	84.1	32	3.42
Jeff Brantley	102.0	38	3.35	115.0	37	2.90
Norm Charlton	94.1	19	1.81	64.1	21	2.94
Rob Dibble	108.0	52	4.33	86.1	31	3.23
Dennis Eckersley	142.1	46	2.91	80.2	27	3.01
Steve Farr	92.0	28	2.74	77.0	20	2.34
John Franco	75.1	26	3.11	49.1	19	3.47
Jim Gott	112.1	33	2.64	129.1	36	2.51
Joe Grahe	72.0	16	2.00	59.0	20	3.05
Gene Harris	48.0	19	3.56	51.1	17	2.98
Greg Harris	117.1	37	2.84	142.0	51	3.23
Bryan Harvey	117.0	31	2.38	59.1	5	0.76
Tom Henke	90.1	22	2.19	90.0	29	2.90
Mike Henneman	145.1	48	2.97	88.0	34	3.48
Doug Henry	78.0	29	3.35	78.0	38	4.38
Roberto Hernandez	87.1	20	2.06	66.0	18	2.45
Xavier Hernandez	102.1	35	3.08	137.1	31	2.03
Darren Holmes	82.0	32	3.51	103.1	50	4.35
Mike Jackson	106.1	48	4.06	141.2	44	2.80
Doug Jones	146.2	55	3.38	82.2	37	4.03
Craig Lefferts	56.1	21	3.36	57.0	28	4.42
Roger McDowell	145.0	46	2.86	108.0	42	3.50
Jeff Montgomery	169.0	48	2.56	91.0	23	2.27
Randy Myers	120.2	47	3.51	96.0	42	3.94
Gregg Olson	94.2	38	3.61	85.1	10	1.05
Ted Power	94.2	38	3.61	137.0	52	3.42
Scott Radinsky	97.0	27	2.51	88.1	33	3.36
Jeff Reardon	90.1	38	3.79	88.2	32	3.25
Dave Righetti	83.0	30	3.25	95.2	53	4.99
Mel Rojas	109.2	29	2.38	127.1	36	2.54
Jeff Russell	117.1	25	1.92	75.0	30	3.60
Lee Smith	122.1	46	3.38	83.2	24	2.58
Mike Stanton	91.2	40	3.93	102.0	41	3.62
Bobby Thigpen	101.0	40	3.56	77.2	51	5.91
Duane Ward	123.1	39	2.85	157.0	33	1.89
John Wetteland	126.2	32	2.27	51.0	8	1.41
Mitch Williams	143.0	56	3.52	88.1	24	2.45
MLB Totals	4264.1	1428	3.01	3727.2	1270	3.07

HOW IMPORTANT IS A GOOD-THROWING CATCHER? (p. 202)

The chart below lists the Stolen Bases (**SB**) while this catcher was behind the plate, the runners he caught stealing (**CCS**), that percentage (**CS%**), the runners he picked off (**CPk**), the SB allowed per 9 innings (**SB/9**), the runners caught stealing (**PCS**) and picked off (**PPk**) by his pitchers.

Both Leagues — Listed Alphabetically
(Minimum 250 Innings Caught)

Catcher, Team	SB	CCS	CS%	CPk	SB/9	PCS	PPk
Alomar Jr, Cle	41	15	26.8	1	0.71	1	0
Ausmus, SD	31	18	36.7	0	0.69	1	0
Berryhill, Atl	62	25	28.7	0	0.72	3	6
Borders, Tor	108	52	32.5	1	0.82	1	2
Daulton, Phi	89	40	31.0	0	0.62	5	4
Fletcher D, Mon	99	14	12.4	0	0.97	12	3
Geren, SD	39	17	30.4	1	0.98	2	1
Girardi, Col	64	25	28.1	0	0.81	4	10
Harper, Min	114	41	26.5	2	0.91	14	4
Haselman, Sea	35	9	20.5	0	1.03	1	1
Hemond, Oak	50	26	34.2	0	0.75	1	1
Higgins, SD	43	16	27.1	1	0.94	0	1
Hoiles, Bal	67	31	31.6	0	0.58	15	3
Hundley, NYN	101	28	21.7	0	0.96	5	2
Karkovice, ChA	48	48	50.0	2	0.42	8	6
Kmak, Mil	27	13	32.5	0	0.77	2	4
Knorr, Tor	28	8	22.2	0	0.98	3	1
Kreuter, Det	57	35	38.0	1	0.57	10	2
Lake, ChN	10	12	54.5	0	0.30	0	2
Lampkin, Mil	28	13	31.7	1	0.63	0	0
LaValliere, ChA	9	21	70.0	0	0.30	3	1
Macfarlane, KC	70	42	37.5	1	0.69	11	3
Manwaring, SF	60	44	42.3	0	0.50	7	7
Mayne, KC	48	15	23.8	0	0.86	3	1
Melvin, Bos	31	8	20.5	0	0.61	0	2
Myers, Cal	67	23	25.6	0	0.94	4	2
Natal, Fla	23	8	25.8	1	0.73	3	2
Nilsson, Mil	60	18	23.1	1	0.75	4	2
Nokes, NYA	46	14	23.3	0	1.04	3	2
O'Brien C, NYN	42	22	34.4	2	0.76	1	1
Oliver, Cin	100	43	30.1	2	0.82	7	2
Olson, Atl	56	14	20.0	0	0.79	9	4
Ortiz J, Cle	47	37	44.0	0	0.60	2	1
Orton, Cal	17	6	26.1	0	0.57	3	3
Pagnozzi, StL	58	25	30.1	0	0.66	5	0
Pappas, StL	37	15	28.8	1	0.68	4	0
Pena T, Bos	52	31	37.3	1	0.51	0	6
Petralli, Tex	30	5	14.3	0	0.94	10	4
Piazza, LA	108	58	34.9	1	0.78	1	6
Prince, Pit	54	12	18.2	0	1.06	5	1
Rodriguez I, Tex	64	40	38.5	4	0.52	11	9
Santiago, Fla	90	29	24.4	7	0.74	10	1
Servais, Hou	56	15	21.1	0	0.77	3	2
Sheaffer, Col	36	13	26.5	1	0.66	2	9
Slaught, Pit	86	20	18.9	1	0.88	10	2
Stanley, NYA	65	22	25.3	0	0.58	7	2
Steinbach, Oak	62	30	32.6	0	0.79	4	0
Tackett, Bal	22	13	37.1	0	0.76	4	0
Taubensee, Hou	51	20	28.2	2	0.63	2	2
Tettleton, Det	36	5	12.2	0	0.75	4	0
Tingley, Cal	15	7	31.8	0	0.42	4	1
Valle, Sea	68	49	41.9	2	0.54	8	1
Webster L, Min	19	7	26.9	1	0.63	4	1
Wilkins, ChN	66	50	43.1	0	0.55	6	5

WHO LED THE LEAGUE IN FUMBLES? (p. 206)

Both Leagues — Listed by Fewest Games per Error (G/E) — 1993
(minimum 600 defensive innings played)

Name	Inn	E	G/E
Catchers			
Nilsson, Mil	719.0	9	8.9
Macfarlane, KC	917.1	11	9.3
Borders, Tor	1182.0	13	10.1
Santiago, Fla	1095.0	11	11.1
Olson, Atl	641.0	6	11.9
Myers, Cal	644.1	6	11.9
Harper, Min	1124.2	10	12.5
Piazza, LA	1243.1	11	12.6
Fletcher D, Mon	918.1	8	12.8
Hundley, NYN	942.2	8	13.1
Girardi, Col	707.2	6	13.1
Kreuter, Det	897.0	7	14.2
Berryhill, Atl	774.0	6	14.3
Rodriguez I, Tex	1117.0	8	15.5
Ortiz J, Cle	707.2	5	15.7
Steinbach, Oak	708.1	5	15.7
Daulton, Phi	1278.0	9	15.8
Taubensee, Hou	727.2	5	16.2
Hemond, Oak	600.0	4	16.7
Oliver, Cin	1102.2	7	17.5
Pagnozzi, StL	787.0	4	21.9
Karkovice, ChA	1038.2	5	23.1
Hoiles, Bal	1040.0	5	23.1
Slaught, Pit	874.2	4	24.3
Valle, Sea	1131.1	5	25.1
Pena T, Bos	915.1	4	25.4
Servais, Hou	653.2	2	36.3
Stanley, NYA	1001.2	3	37.1
Wilkins, ChN	1077.1	3	39.9
Manwaring, SF	1090.2	2	60.6
First Basemen			
Destrade, Fla	1281.2	19	7.5
Vaughn M, Bos	1129.1	16	7.8
Murray, NYN	1321.0	18	8.2
McGriff F, Atl	1281.2	17	8.4
Clark W, SF	1113.1	14	8.8
Thomas, ChA	1300.2	15	9.6
Galarraga, Col	1007.1	11	10.2
Fielder, Det	962.1	10	10.7
Karros, LA	1373.2	12	12.7
Olerud, Tor	1205.1	10	13.4
Jaha, Mil	1281.1	10	14.2
Jefferies, StL	1184.2	9	14.6
Bagwell, Hou	1229.2	9	15.2
Kruk, Phi	1243.1	8	17.3
Morris, Cin	834.1	5	18.5
Joyner, KC	1194.0	7	19.0
Snow, Cal	1059.0	6	19.6
Sorrento, Cle	1083.0	6	20.1
Hrbek, Min	944.2	5	21.0
Milligan, Cle	603.2	3	22.4
Bream, Atl	638.0	3	23.6
Segui, Bal	1155.1	5	25.7
Grace, ChN	1350.1	5	30.0
Palmeiro, Tex	1395.1	5	31.0
Martinez T, Sea	909.2	3	33.7
Young K, Pit	1056.2	3	39.1
Mattingly, NYA	1118.1	3	41.4
Second Basemen			
Young E, Col	650.1	15	4.8
Kent, NYN	1070.2	18	6.6
Spiers, Mil	804.0	13	6.9
Cora, ChA	1299.0	19	7.6
Amaral, Sea	617.2	9	7.6
Alicea, StL	779.2	11	7.9
Kelly P, NYA	1051.2	14	8.3
Baerga, Cle	1303.2	17	8.5
Whitaker, Det	864.0	11	8.7
Strange, Tex	1101.1	13	9.4
Gates, Oak	1211.0	14	9.6
Fletcher S, Bos	982.1	11	9.9
Lovullo, Cal	723.0	8	10.0
Lemke, Atl	1299.2	14	10.3
Alomar, Tor	1305.1	14	10.4
Barberie, Fla	844.1	9	10.4
Biggio, Hou	1352.2	14	10.7
DeShields, Mon	1073.2	11	10.8
Gardner, SD	907.2	9	11.2
Garcia, Pit	1186.0	11	12.0
Reynolds, Bal	1226.0	10	13.6
Thompson Rob, SF	1094.2	8	15.2
Sandberg, ChN	989.0	7	15.7
Knoblauch, Min	1273.0	9	15.7
Morandini, Phi	928.0	5	20.6
Boone, Sea	622.1	3	23.0
Reed Jody, LA	1134.2	5	25.2
Lind, KC	1152.2	4	32.0
Third Basemen			
Sheffield, Fla	1129.2	34	3.7
Zeile, StL	1299.2	33	4.4
Palmer, Tex	1259.1	29	4.8
Hollins, Phi	1214.2	27	5.0
Berry, Mon	686.1	15	5.1
Lansing, Mon	617.0	13	5.3
Caminiti, Hou	1237.0	24	5.7
Cooper, Bos	1304.1	24	6.0
Seitzer, Mil	660.0	12	6.1
Surhoff, Mil	1013.2	17	6.6
Blowers, Sea	928.2	15	6.9
Gonzales R, Cal	646.2	10	7.2
Hayes, Col	1301.1	20	7.2
Paquette, Oak	888.2	13	7.6
Wallach, LA	1084.2	15	8.0
Pendleton, Atl	1392.2	19	8.1
Sprague, Tor	1291.1	17	8.4

| Name | Inn | E | G/E |

Name	Inn	E	G/E
King, Pit	1366.2	17	8.9
Magadan, Sea	757.1	9	9.3
Boggs, NYA	1122.2	12	10.4
Ventura, ChA	1367.0	14	10.8
Gaetti, KC	600.2	6	11.1
Williams M, SF	1275.2	12	11.8
Pagliarulo, Bal	861.0	8	12.0
Sabo, Cin	1265.1	11	12.8
Buechele, ChN	1082.0	8	15.0

Shortstops

Name	Inn	E	G/E
Cordero, Mon	1114.0	33	3.8
Fryman, Det	721.1	19	4.2
Offerman, LA	1406.2	37	4.2
Stocker, Phi	639.2	14	5.1
Meares, Min	890.1	19	5.2
Cedeno A, Hou	1224.2	25	5.4
Clayton, SF	1328.2	27	5.5
Sanchez, ChN	762.1	15	5.6
Fermin, Cle	1186.1	23	5.7
Vizcaino, ChN	680.1	13	5.8
Larkin B, Cin	845.2	16	5.9
Owen, NYA	797.1	14	6.3
Smith O, StL	1138.1	19	6.7
Valentin John, Bos	1221.2	20	6.8
Gutierrez, SD	939.0	14	7.5
Blauser, Atl	1321.2	19	7.7
Guillen, ChA	1131.0	16	7.9
Castilla, Col	810.0	11	8.2
DiSarcina, Cal	1072.1	14	8.5
Listach, Mil	791.0	10	8.8
Ripken C, Bal	1425.2	17	9.3
Weiss, Fla	1322.1	15	9.8
Vizquel, Sea	1330.2	15	9.9
Fernandez, Tor	1235.1	13	10.6
Bordick, Oak	1374.2	13	11.7
Bell Jay, Pit	1349.0	11	13.6
Gagne, KC	1331.0	10	14.8

Left Fielders

Name	Inn	E	G/E
Mitchell, Cin	640.2	7	10.2
Clark J, Col	660.0	7	10.5
Gant, Atl	1384.1	11	14.0
Incaviglia, Phi	690.2	5	15.3
May, ChN	993.1	7	15.8
Gilkey, StL	1141.1	8	15.9
Henderson R, Tor	1006.2	7	16.0
Gonzalez L, Hou	1248.0	8	17.3
James D, NYA	608.0	3	22.5
Polonia, Cal	1181.0	5	26.2
Coleman, NYN	744.1	3	27.6
Belle, Cle	1324.2	5	29.4
Vaughn G, Mil	813.0	3	30.1
Bonds, SF	1370.0	5	30.4
Gonzalez J, Tex	1100.1	4	30.6
Felder, Sea	656.1	2	36.5
Plantier, SD	1103.0	3	40.9
Alou, Mon	796.1	2	44.2
McReynolds, KC	812.1	2	45.1
Davis E, Det	849.1	2	47.2

Name	Inn	E	G/E
Anderson, Bal	1080.0	2	60.0
Greenwell, Bos	1125.0	2	62.5
Conine, Fla	1212.1	2	67.4
Thompson M, Phi	754.0	1	83.8
Raines, ChA	913.2	0	-

Center Fielders

Name	Inn	E	G/E
Cuyler, Det	616.2	7	9.8
Bell D, SD	1011.0	8	14.0
Johnson L, ChA	1238.0	9	15.3
Lofton, Cle	1245.0	9	15.4
Dykstra, Phi	1422.1	10	15.8
Lankford, StL	1011.2	7	16.1
Curtis, Cal	1314.1	9	16.2
Cole, Col	749.2	4	20.8
McRae, KC	1345.1	7	21.4
Grissom, Mon	1357.0	7	21.5
Carr, Fla	1180.2	6	21.9
Thompson Ry, NYN	656.2	3	24.3
Devereaux, Bal	1130.1	4	31.4
Hulse, Tex	851.2	3	31.5
Finley, Hou	1167.0	4	32.4
Williams B, NYA	1225.1	4	34.0
Nixon, Atl	994.2	3	36.8
Griffey Jr, Sea	1208.1	3	44.8
Puckett, Min	807.0	2	44.8
White Dev, Tor	1265.2	3	46.9
Hatcher, Bos	1098.1	2	61.0
Kelly R, Cin	663.1	1	73.7
Van Slyke, Pit	675.0	1	75.0
Yount, Mil	949.1	1	105.5
Lewis D, SF	1080.2	0	-
Butler B, LA	1381.2	0	-

Right Fielders

Name	Inn	E	G/E
Merced, Pit	766.0	8	10.6
Bichette, Col	1122.0	9	13.9
Whiten, StL	1149.2	9	14.2
Deer, Bos	1030.1	8	14.3
Bonilla, NYN	712.2	5	15.8
Jose, KC	1027.0	7	16.3
Sierra, Oak	1150.2	7	18.3
Sanders R, Cin	1161.1	7	18.4
Kirby, Cle	859.1	5	19.1
Salmon, Cal	1219.2	7	19.4
Burks, ChA	1046.0	6	19.4
Walker L, Mon	1145.0	6	21.2
Gwynn T, SD	1012.1	5	22.5
Carter, Tor	825.2	4	22.9
McGee, SF	1041.2	5	23.1
Sosa, ChN	836.1	4	23.2
Buhner, Sea	1286.1	6	23.8
Snyder, LA	926.1	4	25.7
McLemore, Bal	1065.0	4	29.6
Justice, Atl	1394.1	5	31.0
O'Neill, NYA	759.1	2	42.2
Anthony, Hou	948.0	2	52.7
Eisenreich, Phi	809.0	1	89.9

WHO ARE THE PRIME PIVOT MEN? (p. 208)

Both Leagues — Listed Alphabetically
1993 Active Players with 10 or more DP Opportunities (1989-1993)

Player, Team	DP Opp	DP	Pct.	Player, Team	DP Opp	DP	Pct.
Alicea	95	56	.589	Liriano	134	71	.530
Alomar	397	223	.562	Litton	42	33	.786
Amaral	52	34	.654	Lovullo	62	35	.565
Arias	21	10	.476	Lyons	62	39	.629
Backman	72	37	.514	McKnight	15	6	.400
Baerga	261	181	.693	McLemore	82	59	.720
Barberie	71	38	.535	Mejia	31	14	.452
Bell Juan	65	43	.662	Miller	109	59	.541
Belliard	21	14	.667	Molitor	51	23	.451
Benavides	22	10	.455	Morandini	168	91	.542
Benjamin	16	12	.750	Naehring	26	12	.462
Biggio	149	81	.544	Oquendo	230	130	.565
Blankenship	88	59	.670	Pecota	52	26	.500
Blauser	47	25	.532	Pena G	109	74	.679
Boone	58	43	.741	Phillips T	188	109	.580
Bordick	62	40	.645	Polidor	12	4	.333
Branson	42	28	.667	Ready	60	28	.467
Browne	179	86	.480	Reboulet	11	4	.364
Brumley	19	17	.895	Reed Jody	372	237	.637
Buechele	12	5	.417	Renteria	17	8	.471
Candaele	76	47	.618	Reynolds	520	302	.581
Cora	136	90	.662	Riles	25	8	.320
DeShields	265	158	.596	Ripken B	292	189	.647
Doran	201	113	.562	Rivera	13	7	.538
Duncan	140	73	.521	Roberts	101	50	.495
Easley	28	15	.536	Rossy	11	7	.636
Faries	22	11	.500	Samuel	217	94	.433
Fletcher S	306	204	.667	Sandberg	373	205	.550
Foley	82	41	.500	Saunders	12	8	.667
Franco	239	122	.510	Sax	371	212	.571
Gallego	172	102	.593	Scarsone	14	7	.500
Garcia	90	50	.556	Sharperson	42	27	.643
Gardner	55	27	.491	Shipley	10	6	.600
Gates	72	47	.653	Shumpert	106	66	.623
Gonzales R	79	53	.671	Sojo	147	95	.646
Grebeck	21	14	.667	Spiers	57	32	.561
Hale	16	10	.625	Stankiewicz	21	14	.667
Harris L	116	55	.474	Stillwell	67	34	.507
Howard D	12	6	.500	Strange	93	54	.581
Hulett	38	21	.553	Sveum	10	7	.700
Huson	27	16	.593	Teufel	91	42	.462
Jefferies	121	47	.388	Thompson Rob	388	242	.624
Jones T	19	10	.526	Thon	10	6	.600
Kelly P	157	95	.605	Treadway	205	116	.566
Kent	70	43	.614	Vizcaino	20	14	.700
King	19	11	.579	Walker C	19	8	.421
Knoblauch	269	172	.639	Whitaker	426	238	.559
Lansing	12	8	.667	Wilkerson	58	31	.534
Lee M	93	45	.484	Yelding	21	12	.571
Lemke	229	131	.572	Young E	48	26	.542
Lewis M	29	19	.655	**MLB Avg**	**12905**	**7553**	**.585**
Lind	414	221	.534				

WHICH OUTFIELDERS HAVE THE CANNONS? (p. 210)

Both Leagues — 1993 — Listed by Hold Percentage
(minimum 25 baserunner opportunities to advance)

Left Field Player, Team	Opp	XB	Pct	Center Field Player, Team	Opp	XB	Pct	Right Field Player, Team	Opp	XB	Pct
Hamilton, Mil	32	6	18.8	Carr, Fla	142	60	42.3	Anthony, Hou	79	27	34.2
Vaughn G, Mil	48	10	20.8	Lewis D, SF	99	42	42.4	Puckett, Min	29	10	34.5
O'Neill, NYA	28	6	21.4	Grissom, Mon	145	64	44.1	Bass, Hou	31	11	35.5
Bonds, SF	124	28	22.6	Jackson D, NYN	29	13	44.8	Walker L, Mon	90	33	36.7
Felder, Sea	83	19	22.9	Brumfield, Cin	61	28	45.9	Felix, Fla	38	14	36.8
Martin A, Pit	56	13	23.2	Williams B, NYA	204	94	46.1	Whiten, StL	113	42	37.2
Incaviglia, Phi	64	16	25.0	Finley, Hou	142	66	46.5	Gwynn T, SD	111	43	38.7
Young E, Col	28	7	25.0	Smith D, ChN	51	24	47.1	McCarty, Min	38	15	39.5
Gonzalez L, Hou	149	40	26.8	Gallagher, NYN	31	15	48.4	Sanders R, Cin	107	43	40.2
Voigt, Bal	32	9	28.1	Lofton, Cle	190	92	48.4	Munoz, Min	27	11	40.7
Hill, ChN	35	10	28.6	Devereaux, Bal	125	61	48.8	Merced, Pit	61	25	41.0
Boston, Col	52	15	28.8	Van Slyke, Pit	79	40	50.6	Hamilton, Mil	65	27	41.5
Javier, Cal	31	9	29.0	Butler B, LA	163	83	50.9	Chamberlain, Phi	49	21	42.9
Gwynn C, KC	55	16	29.1	Harris D, Tex	25	13	52.0	Whitmore, Fla	58	25	43.1
Davis E, Det	84	25	29.8	Lankford, StL	123	64	52.0	Calderon, ChA	51	22	43.1
Orsulak, NYN	50	15	30.0	Hamilton, Mil	46	24	52.2	Clark D, Pit	39	17	43.6
Smith L, Bal	43	13	30.2	Dykstra, Phi	198	105	53.0	Deer, Bos	85	38	44.7
Conine, Fla	120	37	30.8	Griffey Jr, Sea	176	95	54.0	Snyder, LA	102	47	46.1
Alou, Mon	61	19	31.1	Hulse, Tex	124	67	54.0	Salmon, Cal	126	59	46.8
Greenwell, Bos	109	35	32.1	McRae, KC	156	86	55.1	Pasqua, ChA	34	16	47.1
Thompson M, Phi	65	21	32.3	Gibson, Det	27	15	55.6	Bean, SD	34	16	47.1
Gladden, Det	68	22	32.4	Thompson R, NY	75	42	56.0	Howard T, Cin	27	13	48.1
Belle, Cle	155	51	32.9	Curtis, Cal	162	91	56.2	Bichette, Col	118	57	48.3
Gilkey, StL	124	41	33.1	Martinez D, SF	32	18	56.3	Maldonado, Cle	31	15	48.4
Munoz, Min	54	18	33.3	Jordan B, StL	32	18	56.3	Bonilla, NYN	62	30	48.4
Frazier, Mon	27	9	33.3	Martin A, Pit	63	36	57.1	Kirby, Cle	74	36	48.6
Clark J, Col	109	37	33.9	Puckett, Min	117	67	57.3	Jackson D, NYN	42	21	50.0
Plantier, SD	114	39	34.2	Cuyler, Det	82	47	57.3	O'Neill, NYA	62	31	50.0
James D, NYA	73	25	34.2	Sanders D, Atl	50	29	58.0	Buhner, Sea	120	60	50.0
Mitchell, Cin	55	19	34.5	White Dev, Tor	175	102	58.3	Peltier, Tex	32	16	50.0
May, ChN	103	36	35.0	Hatcher, Bos	130	76	58.5	Hill, ChN	37	19	51.4
Polonia, Cal	163	58	35.6	Jones Chr, Col	73	43	58.9	Eisenreich, Phi	74	39	52.7
Mack, Min	59	21	35.6	Yount, Mil	127	75	59.1	Carter, Tor	83	44	53.0
Gonzalez J, Tex	125	45	36.0	Wilson W, ChN	44	26	59.1	Redus, Tex	30	16	53.3
Henderson R, Tor	122	44	36.1	Kelly R, Cin	81	48	59.3	Alou, Mon	30	16	53.3
McCarty, Min	36	13	36.1	Sosa, ChN	65	39	60.0	Burks, ChA	110	59	53.6
Raines, ChA	87	32	36.8	Mack, Min	83	51	61.4	Justice, Atl	118	64	54.2
Gant, Atl	102	38	37.3	Johnson L, ChA	142	88	62.0	Sosa, ChN	77	42	54.5
Anderson, Bal	117	44	37.6	Burks, ChA	29	18	62.1	Brunansky, Mil	51	28	54.9
McReynolds, KC	79	30	38.0	Bell D, SD	117	74	63.2	McGee, SF	93	52	55.9
Coleman, NYN	88	34	38.6	Nixon, Atl	102	65	63.7	Burnitz, NYN	39	22	56.4
Carter, Tor	54	21	38.9	Cole, Col	130	83	63.8	Quintana, Bos	44	25	56.8
Clark D, Pit	32	13	40.6	Anderson, Bal	31	20	64.5	Tettleton, Det	40	23	57.5
Phillips T, Det	59	25	42.4	Henders'n D, Oak	54	35	64.8	Strawberry, LA	26	15	57.7
VanderWal, Mon	28	14	50.0	Brown, SD	40	26	65.0	Jose, KC	115	67	58.3
MLB Avg			**32.5**	Browne, Oak	26	17	65.4	Tartabull, NYA	29	17	58.6
				Orsulak, NYN	38	25	65.8	Sierra, Oak	122	73	59.8
				Brosius, Oak	35	24	68.6	Brooks H, KC	25	15	60.0
				Boston, Col	39	27	69.2	Winfield, Min	31	19	61.3
				Blankenship, Oak	53	40	75.5	McLemore, Bal	119	75	63.0
				MLB Avg			**54.6**	Roberson, ChN	38	24	63.2
								Carreon, SF	26	17	65.4
								Canseco J, Tex	43	29	67.4
								MLB Avg			**50.0**

Can They "Zone In" Better on Turf? (p. 213)

The charts below show the zone ratings (**Rating**) of each player on grass (**Grass**), on artificial turf (**Turf**), and the total (**Overall**) for the last three seasons, 1991-1993.

Both Leagues — Listed Alphabetically
(First and Third Base: Minimum 500 Balls in Zone, 1991-1993)
(Second base and Shortstop: Minimum 500 Balls in Zone, 1991- 1993)

FIRST BASE	Grass			Turf			Overall		
Player, Team	In Zone	Outs	Zone Rating	In Zone	Outs	Zone Rating	In Zone	Outs	Zone Rating
Olerud, John	272	249	.915	419	370	.883	691	619	.896
Joyner, Wally	406	364	.897	358	320	.894	764	684	.895
McGwire, Mark	462	407	.881	72	69	.958	534	476	.891
Mattingly, Don	562	509	.906	108	87	.806	670	596	.890
Grace, Mark	714	625	.875	277	249	.899	991	874	.882
Hrbek, Kent	232	210	.905	325	280	.862	557	490	.880
Bagwell, Jeff	264	212	.803	581	514	.885	845	726	.859
Morris, Hal	157	135	.860	373	317	.850	530	452	.853
Palmeiro, Rafael	727	611	.840	138	125	.906	865	736	.851
Murray, Eddie	561	472	.841	207	178	.860	768	650	.846
Bream, Sid	251	213	.849	103	86	.835	354	299	.845
Martinez, Tino	148	128	.865	205	170	.829	353	298	.844
Kruk, John	159	136	.855	377	316	.838	536	452	.843
McGriff, Fred	530	443	.836	182	154	.846	712	597	.838
Milligan, Randy	375	315	.840	141	116	.823	516	431	.835
O'Brien, Pete	136	116	.853	208	171	.822	344	287	.834
Fielder, Cecil	451	375	.831	84	70	.833	535	445	.832
Vaughn, Mo	367	305	.831	68	56	.824	435	361	.830
Clark, Will	506	415	.820	192	164	.854	698	579	.830
Karros, Eric	477	395	.828	139	115	.827	616	510	.828
Galarraga, Andres	239	193	.808	319	267	.837	558	460	.824
Jaha, John	303	251	.828	56	43	.768	359	294	.819
Merced, Orlando	85	67	.788	287	235	.819	372	302	.812
Sorrento, Paul	366	299	.817	86	66	.767	452	365	.808
Segui, David	322	260	.807	57	42	.737	379	302	.797
Thomas, Frank	496	373	.752	95	80	.842	591	453	.766
			.842			.846			.843

SECOND BASE	Grass			Turf			Overall		
Player, Team	In Zone	Outs	Zone Rating	In Zone	Outs	Zone Rating	In Zone	Outs	Zone Rating
Sandberg, Ryne	1076	1021	.949	430	402	.935	1506	1423	.945
Reed, Jody	1131	1046	.925	303	263	.868	1434	1309	.913
Baerga, Carlos	1033	934	.904	224	210	.938	1257	1144	.910
Lemke, Mark	806	735	.912	264	237	.898	1070	972	.908
Kelly, Pat	656	596	.909	115	101	.878	771	697	.904
Knoblauch, Chuck	605	538	.889	835	759	.909	1440	1297	.901
Fletcher, Scott	824	741	.899	146	131	.897	970	872	.899
Thompson, Robby	899	810	.901	384	341	.888	1283	1151	.897
Whitaker, Lou	930	841	.904	187	161	.861	1117	1002	.897
Ripken, Billy	636	569	.895	102	93	.912	738	662	.897
Reynolds, Harold	700	614	.877	627	568	.906	1327	1182	.891
Morandini, Mickey	282	255	.904	697	613	.879	979	868	.887
Biggio, Craig	307	273	.889	704	620	.881	1011	893	.883
DeShields, Delino	392	328	.837	909	815	.897	1301	1143	.879
Lind, Jose	442	401	.907	952	822	.863	1394	1223	.877
Alomar, Roberto	581	493	.849	877	783	.893	1458	1276	.875
Sax, Steve	792	701	.885	179	148	.827	971	849	.874
Samuel, Juan	507	446	.880	337	285	.846	844	731	.866
Cora, Joey	634	552	.871	131	108	.824	765	660	.863
			.895			.887			.892

THIRD BASE

Player, Team	Grass In Zone	Outs	Zone Rating	Turf In Zone	Outs	Zone Rating	Overall In Zone	Outs	Zone Rating
Hulett, Tim	312	290	.929	50	42	.840	362	332	.917
Boggs, Wade	835	751	.899	171	152	.889	1006	903	.898
Gaetti, Gary	635	563	.887	172	153	.890	807	716	.887
Williams, Matt	747	655	.877	264	240	.909	1011	895	.885
Ventura, Robin	927	817	.881	209	186	.890	1136	1003	.883
Pagliarulo, Mike	274	253	.923	353	299	.847	627	552	.880
Livingstone, Scott	353	311	.881	73	63	.863	426	374	.878
Caminiti, Ken	289	258	.893	687	587	.854	976	845	.866
Pendleton, Terry	960	834	.869	314	261	.831	1274	1095	.859
Buechele, Steve	656	576	.878	380	313	.824	1036	889	.858
Wallach, Tim	360	306	.850	547	471	.861	907	777	.857
Gruber, Kelly	268	226	.843	360	311	.864	628	537	.855
Leius, Scott	184	157	.853	256	218	.852	440	375	.852
King, Jeff	241	199	.826	480	414	.863	721	613	.850
Gonzales, Rene	294	250	.850	95	79	.832	389	329	.846
Martinez, Edgar	272	225	.827	422	360	.853	694	585	.843
Sabo, Chris	251	219	.873	561	465	.829	812	684	.842
Hayes, Charlie	635	538	.847	391	320	.818	1026	858	.836
Fryman, Travis	335	278	.830	66	57	.864	401	335	.835
Magadan, Dave	271	224	.827	133	112	.842	404	336	.832
Jefferies, Gregg	228	192	.842	309	251	.812	537	443	.825
Seitzer, Kevin	530	433	.817	164	138	.841	694	571	.823
Berry, Sean	105	88	.838	204	166	.814	309	254	.822
Bonilla, Bobby	149	117	.785	152	129	.849	301	246	.817
Hollins, Dave	215	180	.837	502	405	.807	717	585	.816
Zeile, Todd	368	310	.842	738	592	.802	1106	902	.816
Gomez, Leo	636	514	.808	135	114	.844	771	628	.815
Blowers, Mike	160	130	.813	221	180	.814	381	310	.814
Sprague, Ed	151	120	.795	237	195	.823	388	315	.812
Cooper, Scott	438	354	.808	60	48	.800	498	402	.807
Palmer, Dean	666	533	.800	137	109	.796	803	642	.800
Sheffield, Gary	619	475	.767	192	158	.823	811	633	.781
Johnson, Howard	335	264	.788	84	60	.714	419	324	.773
			.848			.837			.843

SHORTSTOP

Player, Team	Grass In Zone	Outs	Zone Rating	Turf In Zone	Outs	Zone Rating	Overall In Zone	Outs	Zone Rating
Ripken, Cal	1385	1288	.930	248	242	.976	1633	1530	.937
DiSarcina, Gary	827	765	.925	162	159	.981	989	924	.934
Guillen, Ozzie	810	756	.933	136	127	.934	946	883	.933
Schofield, Dick	758	708	.934	263	238	.905	1021	946	.927
Smith, Ozzie	460	434	.943	980	900	.918	1440	1334	.926
Vizquel, Omar	601	543	.903	913	843	.923	1514	1386	.915
Fryman, Travis	901	820	.910	142	133	.937	1043	953	.914
Lee, Manuel	580	522	.900	495	457	.923	1075	979	.911
Belliard, Rafael	633	562	.888	181	177	.978	814	739	.908
Bordick, Mike	815	730	.896	161	143	.888	976	873	.894
Gagne, Greg	584	521	.892	864	773	.895	1448	1294	.894
Rivera, Luis	716	653	.912	144	114	.792	860	767	.892
Valentin, John	608	539	.887	113	102	.903	721	641	.889
Listach, Pat	733	653	.891	117	102	.872	850	755	.888
Larkin, Barry	356	322	.904	884	768	.869	1240	1090	.879
Fernandez, Tony	981	855	.872	506	448	.885	1487	1303	.876
Fermin, Felix	874	765	.875	172	150	.872	1046	915	.875
Blauser, Jeff	650	580	.892	243	196	.807	893	776	.869
Offerman, Jose	924	801	.867	300	262	.873	1224	1063	.868
Weiss, Walt	717	624	.870	213	182	.854	930	806	.867
Owen, Spike	516	438	.849	690	605	.877	1206	1043	.865
Thon, Dickie	406	348	.857	413	357	.864	819	705	.861
Bell, Jay	571	465	.814	1358	1186	.873	1929	1651	.856
Clayton, Royce	671	577	.860	201	163	.811	872	740	.849
Cedeno, Andujar	288	227	.788	583	471	.808	871	698	.801
			.888			**.880**			**.885**

WHO'S BEST IN THE INFIELD ZONE? (p. 216)

Zone Ratings — Infielders
(minimum 600 defensive innings in 1993)

| FIRST BASE | | 1993 | | | 1991-93 | | |
Player, Team	Innings	In Zone	Outs	Zone Rating	In Zone	Outs	Zone Rating
Bagwell, Hou	1229.2	241	217	.900	845	726	.859
Mattingly, NYA	1118.1	195	174	.892	670	596	.890
Young K, Pit	1056.2	203	180	.887	203	180	.887
Olerud, Tor	1205.1	257	225	.875	691	619	.896
Joyner, KC	1194.0	276	241	.873	764	684	.895
Grace, ChN	1350.1	268	232	.866	991	874	.882
Morris, Cin	834.1	170	145	.853	530	452	.853
McGriff F, Atl	1281.2	231	197	.853	712	597	.839
Kruk, Phi	1243.1	215	183	.851	536	452	.843
Hrbek, Min	944.2	188	160	.851	557	490	.880
Bream, Atl	638.0	106	90	.849	354	299	.845
Martinez T, Sea	909.2	178	151	.848	353	298	.844
Palmeiro, Tex	1395.1	295	249	.844	865	736	.851
Murray, NYN	1321.0	243	205	.844	768	650	.846
Destrade, Fla	1281.2	278	232	.835	278	232	.835
Milligan, Cle	603.2	120	100	.833	516	431	.835
Karros, LA	1373.2	314	261	.831	616	510	.828
Jaha, Mil	1281.1	296	246	.831	359	294	.819
Galarraga, Col	1007.1	215	178	.828	558	460	.824
Vaughn M, Bos	1129.1	240	196	.817	435	361	.830
Jefferies, StL	1184.2	215	173	.805	215	173	.805
Sorrento, Cle	1083.0	229	184	.803	452	365	.808
Clark W, SF	1113.1	207	165	.797	698	579	.830
Segui, Bal	1155.1	232	179	.772	379	302	.797
Snow, Cal	1059.0	198	151	.763	206	158	.767
Fielder, Det	962.1	160	120	.750	535	445	.832
Thomas, ChA	1300.2	234	175	.748	591	453	.767
				.834			.843

| SECOND BASE | | 1993 | | | 1991-93 | | |
Player, Team	Innings	In Zone	Outs	Zone Rating	In Zone	Outs	Zone Rating
Sandberg, ChN	989.0	368	347	.943	1506	1423	.945
Gardner, SD	907.2	322	301	.935	352	330	.938
Biggio, Hou	1352.2	496	460	.927	1011	893	.883
Lovullo, Cal	723.0	234	217	.927	234	217	.927
Kelly P, NYA	1051.2	399	370	.927	771	697	.904
Thompson Rob, SF	1094.2	409	379	.927	1283	1151	.897
Barberie, Fla	844.1	330	303	.918	424	393	.927
DeShields, Mon	1073.2	420	384	.914	1301	1143	.879
Lemke, Atl	1299.2	466	424	.910	1070	972	.908
Alicea, StL	779.2	313	284	.907	589	538	.913
Reynolds, Bal	1226.0	422	382	.905	1327	1182	.891
Fletcher S, Bos	982.1	419	379	.905	970	872	.899
Lind, KC	1152.2	407	368	.904	1394	1223	.877
Reed Jody, LA	1134.2	461	416	.902	1434	1309	.913
Whitaker, Det	864.0	360	323	.897	1117	1002	.897
Morandini, Phi	928.0	324	290	.895	979	868	.887
Young E, Col	650.1	268	239	.892	406	357	.879
Kent, NYN	1070.2	371	330	.889	517	456	.882
Strange, Tex	1101.1	388	345	.889	402	358	.891
Baerga, Cle	1303.2	501	445	.888	1257	1144	.910
Boone, Sea	622.1	205	180	.878	304	275	.905
Knoblauch, Min	1273.0	486	424	.872	1440	1297	.901
Spiers, Mil	804.0	265	229	.864	270	234	.867
Alomar, Tor	1305.1	511	441	.863	1458	1276	.875
Cora, ChA	1299.0	474	408	.861	765	660	.863
Gates, Oak	1211.0	522	440	.843	522	440	.843
Amaral, Sea	617.2	229	192	.838	243	207	.852
Garcia, Pit	1186.0	403	331	.821	428	358	.836
				.895			.892

THIRD BASE

Player, Team	Innings	1993			1991-93		
		In Zone	Outs	Zone Rating	In Zone	Outs	Zone Rating
Williams M, SF	1275.2	316	287	.908	1011	895	.885
Lansing, Mon	617.0	200	181	.905	200	181	.905
Gaetti, KC	600.2	163	144	.883	807	716	.887
Boggs, NYA	1122.2	388	342	.881	1006	903	.898
Ventura, ChA	1367.0	345	303	.878	1136	1003	.883
Surhoff, Mil	1013.2	277	243	.877	285	250	.877
Buechele, ChN	1082.0	295	257	.871	1036	889	.858
Gonzales R, Cal	646.2	200	173	.865	389	329	.846
King, Pit	1366.2	467	394	.844	721	613	.850
Paquette, Oak	888.2	216	182	.843	216	182	.843
Sabo, Cin	1265.1	303	255	.842	812	684	.842
Pendleton, Atl	1392.2	427	359	.841	1274	1095	.860
Caminiti, Hou	1237.0	352	295	.838	976	845	.866
Sprague, Tor	1291.1	300	250	.833	388	315	.812
Magadan, Sea	757.1	236	196	.831	404	336	.832
Wallach, LA	1084.2	294	244	.830	907	777	.857
Hayes, Col	1301.1	376	312	.830	1026	858	.836
Pagliarulo, Bal	861.0	251	208	.829	627	552	.880
Berry, Mon	686.1	217	179	.825	309	254	.822
Blowers, Sea	928.2	305	247	.810	381	310	.814
Seitzer, Mil	660.0	178	143	.803	694	571	.823
Palmer, Tex	1259.1	348	279	.802	803	642	.800
Zeile, StL	1299.2	414	328	.792	1106	902	.816
Hollins, Phi	1214.2	293	231	.788	717	585	.816
Cooper, Bos	1304.1	340	268	.788	498	402	.807
Sheffield, Fla	1129.2	329	237	.720	811	633	.781
				.834			**.843**

SHORTSTOP

Player, Team	Innings	1993			1991-93		
		In Zone	Outs	Zone Rating	In Zone	Outs	Zone Rating
Guillen, ChA	1131.0	397	379	.955	946	883	.933
Sanchez, ChN	762.1	326	308	.945	560	532	.950
Smith O, StL	1138.1	514	483	.940	1440	1334	.926
Vizquel, Sea	1330.2	558	519	.930	1514	1386	.915
Vizcaino, ChN	680.1	294	272	.925	546	509	.932
DiSarcina, Cal	1072.1	417	382	.916	989	924	.934
Gagne, KC	1331.0	507	462	.911	1448	1294	.894
Blauser, Atl	1321.2	510	460	.902	893	776	.869
Castilla, Col	810.0	314	279	.889	330	293	.888
Ripken C, Bal	1425.2	571	507	.888	1633	1530	.937
Weiss, Fla	1322.1	477	423	.887	930	806	.867
Valentin John, Bos	1221.2	507	449	.886	721	641	.889
Larkin B, Cin	845.2	335	295	.881	1240	1090	.879
Listach, Mil	791.0	319	280	.878	850	755	.888
Fernandez, Tor	1235.1	489	429	.877	1487	1303	.876
Offerman, LA	1406.2	564	494	.876	1224	1063	.868
Gutierrez, SD	939.0	352	307	.872	352	307	.872
Bordick, Oak	1374.2	505	435	.861	976	873	.894
Stocker, Phi	639.2	259	223	.861	259	223	.861
Fryman, Det	721.1	319	274	.859	1043	953	.914
Owen, NYA	797.1	387	332	.858	1206	1043	.865
Bell Jay, Pit	1349.0	651	555	.853	1929	1651	.856
Meares, Min	890.1	394	333	.845	394	333	.845
Cordero, Mon	1114.0	462	390	.844	546	463	.848
Clayton, SF	1328.2	546	458	.839	872	740	.849
Fermin, Cle	1186.1	446	372	.834	1046	915	.875
Cedeno A, Hou	1224.2	451	365	.809	871	698	.801
				.880			**.885**

WHO'S BEST IN THE OUTFIELD ZONE? (p. 220)

Zone Ratings — Outfielders
(minimum 600 defensive innings in 1993)

LEFT FIELD

Player, Team	Innings	1993 In Zone	Outs	Zone Rating	1991-93 In Zone	Outs	Zone Rating
Plantier, SD	1103.0	295	260	.881	365	309	.847
Vaughn G, Mil	813.0	236	206	.873	918	787	.857
Henderson R, Tor	1006.2	291	252	.866	863	716	.830
Davis E, Det	849.1	244	211	.865	380	324	.853
Mitchell, Cin	640.2	165	140	.848	555	445	.802
Bonds, SF	1370.0	340	287	.844	1069	888	.831
Thompson M, Phi	754.0	181	152	.840	436	371	.851
Alou, Mon	796.1	205	172	.839	336	291	.866
Gant, Atl	1384.1	314	263	.838	581	492	.847
Raines, ChA	913.2	228	189	.829	925	756	.817
McReynolds, KC	812.1	220	182	.827	708	590	.833
Gonzalez L, Hou	1248.0	383	316	.825	983	839	.854
May, ChN	993.1	258	210	.814	433	354	.818
Coleman, NYN	744.1	192	156	.813	263	209	.795
Gonzalez J, Tex	1100.1	302	245	.811	510	419	.822
Belle, Cle	1324.2	395	319	.808	745	583	.783
Greenwell, Bos	1125.0	315	254	.806	785	587	.748
Anderson, Bal	1080.0	291	234	.804	802	657	.819
Incaviglia, Phi	690.2	178	143	.803	414	338	.816
James D, NYA	608.0	152	122	.803	160	129	.806
Felder, Sea	656.1	164	130	.793	284	232	.817
Polonia, Cal	1181.0	346	271	.783	884	698	.790
Clark J, Col	660.0	196	152	.776	635	524	.825
Gilkey, StL	1141.1	285	213	.747	688	575	.836
Conine, Fla	1212.1	323	233	.721	367	267	.728
				.818			**.818**

CENTER FIELD

Player, Team	Innings	1993 In Zone	Outs	Zone Rating	1991-93 In Zone	Outs	Zone Rating
Lewis D, SF	1080.2	371	329	.887	820	701	.855
Curtis, Cal	1314.1	471	412	.875	563	486	.863
Cuyler, Det	616.2	245	214	.873	1023	854	.835
Lofton, Cle	1245.0	446	389	.872	963	841	.873
Johnson L, ChA	1238.0	465	405	.871	1422	1230	.865
Thompson R, NYN	656.2	254	220	.866	324	283	.873
White Dev, Tor	1265.2	444	383	.863	1408	1241	.881
Nixon, Atl	994.2	333	286	.859	712	613	.861
Bell D, SD	1011.0	365	312	.855	416	355	.853
Butler B, LA	1381.2	424	361	.851	1272	1075	.845
Dykstra, Phi	1422.1	530	449	.847	1025	862	.841
Williams B, NYA	1225.1	423	355	.839	893	745	.834
Grissom, Mon	1357.0	491	412	.839	1356	1143	.843
Lankford, StL	1011.2	369	308	.835	1344	1086	.808
McRae, KC	1345.1	468	386	.825	1435	1192	.831

Player, Team	Innings	In Zone	Outs	Zone Rating	In Zone	Outs	Zone Rating
Yount, Mil	949.1	354	291	.822	1181	962	.815
Finley, Hou	1167.0	380	312	.821	1181	977	.827
Hulse, Tex	851.2	284	233	.820	345	290	.841
Carr, Fla	1180.2	458	374	.817	488	400	.820
Kelly R, Cin	663.1	230	186	.809	746	626	.839
Devereaux, Bal	1130.1	376	303	.806	1328	1122	.845
Cole, Col	749.2	274	218	.796	579	465	.803
Hatcher, Bos	1098.1	353	278	.788	532	422	.793
Puckett, Min	807.0	266	208	.782	1162	933	.803
Griffey Jr, Sea	1208.1	396	307	.775	1275	1010	.792
Van Slyke, Pit	675.0	255	193	.757	1099	858	.781
				.829			**.832**

RIGHT FIELD		1993				1991-93	
Player, Team	Innings	In Zone	Outs	Zone Rating	In Zone	Outs	Zone Rating
Gwynn T, SD	1012.1	264	234	.886	920	780	.848
Kirby, Cle	859.1	242	213	.880	292	251	.860
Eisenreich, Phi	809.0	241	212	.880	426	369	.866
Salmon, Cal	1219.2	362	314	.867	411	353	.859
Deer, Bos	1030.1	330	286	.867	979	809	.826
Walker L, Mon	1145.0	299	259	.866	854	734	.860
Merced, Pit	766.0	214	185	.864	253	214	.846
McGee, SF	1041.2	247	213	.862	507	438	.864
Sosa, ChN	836.1	222	191	.860	445	377	.847
O'Neill, NYA	759.1	190	160	.842	869	731	.841
Sanders R, Cin	1161.1	336	281	.836	336	281	.836
Whiten, StL	1149.2	317	264	.833	960	799	.832
Anthony, Hou	948.0	236	196	.831	520	424	.815
Bonilla, NYN	712.2	171	142	.830	644	531	.825
Justice, Atl	1394.1	371	308	.830	981	816	.832
Burks, ChA	1046.0	307	253	.824	307	253	.824
Snyder, LA	926.1	198	163	.823	333	272	.817
Jose, KC	1027.0	265	213	.804	857	720	.840
Sierra, Oak	1150.2	351	280	.798	1024	853	.833
Bichette, Col	1122.0	336	268	.798	862	692	.803
McLemore, Bal	1065.0	340	271	.797	340	271	.797
Carter, Tor	825.2	224	175	.781	718	598	.833
Buhner, Sea	1286.1	336	256	.762	999	773	.774
				.826			**.821**

DO THE BRAVES HAVE THE MOST EFFICIENT DEFENSE? (p. 222)

The first section of the tables below lists the team's 1993 Defensive Efficiency Rating **(DER)**, which is the division of the Plays Made **(PM)** by the Balls in Play **(BIP)**. The second section shows that team's traditional defensive statistics: Total Chances **(TC)**, Errors **(R)**, and Fielding Percentage **(Pct)**, the latter being the division of (Total Chances minus Errors) by Total Chances.

American League

Team	BIP	PM	DER	TC	E	Pct
Kansas City Royals	4545	3114	.685	6142	97	.984
Chicago White Sox	4593	3126	.681	6139	112	.982
Boston Red Sox	4606	3132	.680	6171	122	.980
Baltimore Orioles	4668	3169	.679	6217	100	.984
Milwaukee Brewers	4895	3303	.675	6104	131	.979
New York Yankees	4721	3179	.673	6309	105	.983
California Angels	4759	3201	.673	6105	120	.980
Toronto Blue Jays	4596	3088	.672	6013	107	.982
Seattle Mariners	4503	3016	.670	6177	90	.985
Oakland Athletics	4864	3248	.668	6093	111	.982
Detroit Tigers	4890	3259	.666	6219	132	.979
Texas Rangers	4669	3110	.666	6227	132	.979
Minnesota Twins	4828	3165	.656	6188	100	.984
Cleveland Indians	4868	3184	.654	6146	148	.976
AL Totals	**66005**	**44294**	**.671**	**86250**	**1607**	**.981**

National League

Team	BIP	PM	DER	TC	E	Pct
Atlanta Braves	4474	3116	.696	6242	108	.983
Montreal Expos	4689	3207	.684	6356	159	.975
San Francisco Giants	4603	3139	.682	6204	101	.984
Houston Astros	4505	3057	.679	6101	126	.979
Los Angeles Dodgers	4626	3133	.677	6389	133	.979
Florida Marlins	4689	3168	.676	6149	125	.980
Philadelphia Phillies	4633	3113	.672	6095	141	.977
Pittsburgh Pirates	4884	3267	.669	6258	105	.983
St. Louis Cardinals	4998	3342	.669	6408	159	.975
New York Mets	4801	3208	.668	6251	156	.975
Chicago Cubs	4761	3179	.668	6353	115	.982
San Diego Padres	4717	3132	.664	6089	160	.974
Cincinnati Reds	4675	3093	.662	6056	121	.980
Colorado Rockies	4909	3134	.638	6221	167	.973
NL Average	**65964**	**44288**	**.671**	**87172**	**1876**	**.978**

WHO ARE THE "ALL-AMERICAN FIELDERS"? (p. 225)

Each chart summarizes, by position, the STATS All-Around Fielding Rating: a player's zone rating (**ZR**), his fielding percentage (**FP**), his pivot rating (**PR**) if he was a secondbaseman, and, if he was an outfielder, his outfield arm rating (**OA**). A weighting system (see article on page 224) was used to determine a player's all-around fielding rating (**Rtng**).

Both Leagues — Sorted by Fielding Rating
(Minimum 600 Innings Played in 1993)

First Base	ZR	FP	PR	OA	Rtng
Mattingly, NYA	.319	.318	-	-	.319
Young K, Pit	.315	.316	-	-	.315
Bagwell, Hou	.325	.281	-	-	.314
Grace, ChN	.301	.310	-	-	.303
Joyner, KC	.306	.291	-	-	.302
Olerud, Tor	.307	.272	-	-	.299
Martinez T, Sea	.289	.312	-	-	.294
Bream, Atl	.289	.301	-	-	.292
Hrbek, Min	.290	.297	-	-	.292
Palmeiro, Tex	.286	.310	-	-	.292
Morris, Cin	.292	.287	-	-	.291
Kruk, Phi	.291	.283	-	-	.289
Milligan, Cle	.278	.298	-	-	.283
McGriff F, Atl	.292	.231	-	-	.277
Jaha, Mil	.277	.275	-	-	.276
Karros, LA	.277	.271	-	-	.275
Murray, NYN	.285	.235	-	-	.273
Galarraga, Col	.274	.257	-	-	.270
Sorrento, Cle	.257	.292	-	-	.266
Destrade, Fla	.279	.227	-	-	.266
Jefferies, StL	.258	.282	-	-	.264
Vaughn M, Bos	.267	.227	-	-	.257
Segui, Bal	.235	.304	-	-	.252
Clark W, SF	.253	.240	-	-	.250
Snow, Cal	.229	.292	-	-	.245
Fielder, Det	.220	.259	-	-	.230
Thomas, ChA	.219	.244	-	-	.225

Second Base	ZR	FP	PR	OA	Rtng
Thompson Rob, SF	.308	.305	.310	-	.308
Sandberg, ChN	.323	.303	.246	-	.301
Kelly P, NYA	.309	.263	.288	-	.297
DeShields, Mon	.297	.283	.291	-	.293
Biggio, Hou	.309	.279	.262	-	.293
Lovullo, Cal	.309	.275	.265	-	.293
Lemke, Atl	.293	.281	.300	-	.293
Reynolds, Bal	.288	.296	.301	-	.293
Reed Jody, LA	.286	.324	.277	-	.289
Boone, Sea	.263	.315	.336	-	.289
Barberie, Fla	.300	.282	.264	-	.289
Gardner, SD	.316	.283	.225	-	.288
Fletcher S, Bos	.288	.279	.280	-	.284
Lind, KC	.287	.328	.251	-	.284

Second Base	ZR	FP	PR	OA	Rtng
Alicea, StL	.290	.263	.270	-	.281
Baerga, Cle	.272	.268	.302	-	.279
Knoblauch, Min	.258	.303	.316	-	.279
Kent, NYN	.273	.228	.306	-	.275
Strange, Tex	.273	.272	.273	-	.273
Morandini, Phi	.279	.313	.228	-	.271
Whitaker, Det	.281	.275	.242	-	.270
Cora, ChA	.247	.247	.308	-	.262
Young E, Col	.276	.200	.252	-	.258
Gates, Oak	.230	.275	.302	-	.255
Spiers, Mil	.250	.236	.269	-	.252
Alomar, Tor	.249	.273	.247	-	.252
Amaral, Sea	.226	.254	.308	-	.251
Garcia, Pit	.210	.285	.269	-	.236

Third Base	ZR	FP	PR	OA	Rtng
Williams M, SF	.327	.307	-	-	.319
Gaetti, KC	.310	.307	-	-	.309
Boggs, NYA	.309	.308	-	-	.308
Buechele, ChN	.302	.315	-	-	.307
Ventura, ChA	.307	.301	-	-	.304
Lansing, Mon	.325	.267	-	-	.302
Surhoff, Mil	.306	.277	-	-	.294
Gonzales R, Cal	.297	.287	-	-	.293
Sabo, Cin	.281	.303	-	-	.290
King, Pit	.283	.299	-	-	.289
Pagliarulo, Bal	.273	.307	-	-	.286
Pendleton, Atl	.281	.292	-	-	.285
Magadan, Sea	.274	.299	-	-	.284
Paquette, Oak	.282	.278	-	-	.280
Wallach, LA	.273	.290	-	-	.280
Sprague, Tor	.276	.285	-	-	.280
Hayes, Col	.273	.284	-	-	.278
Caminiti, Hou	.279	.266	-	-	.274
Blowers, Sea	.260	.279	-	-	.268
Berry, Mon	.270	.258	-	-	.265
Seitzer, Mil	.255	.259	-	-	.257
Cooper, Bos	.245	.259	-	-	.250
Palmer, Tex	.254	.237	-	-	.247
Zeile, StL	.248	.238	-	-	.244
Hollins, Phi	.245	.226	-	-	.237
Sheffield, Fla	.198	.204	-	-	.200

Shortstop	ZR	FP	PR	OA	Rtng
Guillen, ChA	.335	.285	-	-	.325
Sanchez, ChN	.327	.279	-	-	.317
Smith O, StL	.323	.290	-	-	.316
Vizquel, Sea	.316	.305	-	-	.314
Gagne, KC	.301	.322	-	-	.305
Vizcaino, ChN	.312	.275	-	-	.304
DiSarcina, Cal	.305	.295	-	-	.303
Blauser, Atl	.294	.281	-	-	.291
Ripken C, Bal	.283	.298	-	-	.286
Weiss, Fla	.282	.299	-	-	.285
Castilla, Col	.283	.292	-	-	.285
Fernandez, Tor	.274	.310	-	-	.281
Valentin John, Bos	.281	.283	-	-	.281
Listach, Mil	.275	.294	-	-	.278
Larkin B, Cin	.277	.268	-	-	.275
Gutierrez, SD	.270	.284	-	-	.273
Bordick, Oak	.262	.311	-	-	.272
Bell Jay, Pit	.255	.322	-	-	.268
Offerman, LA	.273	.230	-	-	.264
Owen, NYA	.259	.276	-	-	.262
Stocker, Phi	.262	.250	-	-	.259
Fryman, Det	.260	.238	-	-	.255
Meares, Min	.249	.258	-	-	.251
Clayton, SF	.244	.262	-	-	.248
Fermin, Cle	.240	.255	-	-	.243
Cordero, Mon	.248	.207	-	-	.240
Cedeno A, Hou	.221	.241	-	-	.225

Left Field	ZR	FP	PR	OA	Rtng
Vaughn G, Mil	.320	.290	-	.343	.320
Plantier, SD	.326	.298	-	.267	.310
Davis E, Det	.313	.301	-	.293	.307
Bonds, SF	.298	.285	-	.333	.303
Henderson R, Tor	.314	.261	-	.257	.295
Thompson M, Phi	.294	.308	-	.278	.293
Alou, Mon	.294	.297	-	.285	.293
Gonzalez L, Hou	.283	.270	-	.309	.286
Raines, ChA	.286	.322	-	.253	.285
Mitchell, Cin	.301	.214	-	.266	.281
McReynolds, KC	.285	.298	-	.246	.279
Felder, Sea	.259	.289	-	.331	.278
Greenwell, Bos	.269	.305	-	.279	.276
Gant, Atl	.293	.230	-	.250	.275
Incaviglia, Phi	.267	.248	-	.319	.274
Belle, Cle	.270	.289	-	.275	.274
Gonzalez J, Tex	.273	.288	-	.257	.272
Anderson, Bal	.267	.304	-	.248	.269
May, ChN	.275	.250	-	.263	.269
Coleman, NYN	.274	.280	-	.243	.268
James D, NYA	.266	.268	-	.267	.267
Polonia, Cal	.251	.283	-	.260	.258
Clark J, Col	.246	.226	-	.269	.247
Gilkey, StL	.224	.246	-	.274	.237
Conine, Fla	.204	.304	-	.287	.236

Center Field	ZR	FP	PR	OA	Rtng
Lewis D, SF	.322	.326	-	.329	.325
Lofton, Cle	.311	.248	-	.303	.299
Butler B, LA	.293	.326	-	.292	.298
Williams B, NYA	.284	.287	-	.313	.293
Grissom, Mon	.283	.267	-	.322	.292
Thompson R, NYN	.306	.280	-	.269	.291
Curtis, Cal	.313	.253	-	.268	.290
White Dev, Tor	.303	.299	-	.259	.289
Carr, Fla	.265	.272	-	.330	.286
Finley, Hou	.269	.283	-	.311	.284
Cuyler, Det	.312	.210	-	.263	.282
Dykstra, Phi	.290	.250	-	.282	.282
Johnson L, ChA	.310	.251	-	.243	.281
Nixon, Atl	.300	.291	-	.235	.279
Lankford, StL	.280	.247	-	.287	.277
Devereaux, Bal	.256	.281	-	.301	.273
Hulse, Tex	.268	.282	-	.278	.273
Yount, Mil	.269	.314	-	.256	.272
McRae, KC	.272	.263	-	.273	.271
Bell D, SD	.296	.238	-	.237	.270
Kelly R, Cin	.259	.308	-	.255	.265
Hatcher, Bos	.241	.301	-	.258	.255
Griffey Jr, Sea	.231	.292	-	.278	.254
Puckett, Min	.237	.294	-	.263	.253
Van Slyke, Pit	.216	.308	-	.293	.253
Cole, Col	.248	.262	-	.234	.246

Right Field	ZR	FP	PR	OA	Rtng
Gwynn T, SD	.320	.284	-	.314	.313
Walker L, Mon	.303	.281	-	.321	.306
Anthony, Hou	.274	.323	-	.330	.301
Eisenreich, Phi	.315	.343	-	.263	.301
Kirby, Cle	.315	.281	-	.278	.297
Salmon, Cal	.304	.283	-	.284	.294
Deer, Bos	.304	.258	-	.292	.293
Merced, Pit	.302	.225	-	.306	.292
Sanders R, Cin	.279	.274	-	.308	.288
Whiten, StL	.276	.242	-	.319	.286
O'Neill, NYA	.283	.315	-	.273	.284
Sosa, ChN	.299	.289	-	.256	.282
McGee, SF	.300	.279	-	.251	.280
Snyder, LA	.268	.276	-	.287	.276
Justice, Atl	.273	.303	-	.257	.272
Bonilla, NYN	.274	.239	-	.279	.270
Burks, ChA	.268	.276	-	.259	.266
Bichette, Col	.246	.247	-	.279	.258
Carter, Tor	.233	.280	-	.262	.250
McLemore, Bal	.246	.309	-	.225	.248
Jose, KC	.251	.242	-	.243	.247
Sierra, Oak	.246	.272	-	.237	.247
Buhner, Sea	.217	.276	-	.273	.245

WAS LA RUSSA'S "50-PITCH STRATEGY" A GOOD IDEA? (p. 230)

The chart below lists the Opponent On-Base plus Slugging Percentage for each pitcher at differnt pitch levels: 1-45, 46-75, and 76+.

Both Leagues — Listed Alphabetically
(Minimum 100 BFP at 1-45 and 75 BFP at 46-75 in 1993)

Pitcher	Pitch 1-45	Pitch 46-75	Pitch 76+	Pitcher	Pitch 1-45	Pitch 46-75	Pitch 76+
Abbott J, NYA	.676	.765	.794	Doherty, Det	.705	.807	.800
Alvarez, ChA	.669	.630	.705	Dopson, Bos	.707	.785	1.074
Appier, KC	.572	.457	.652	Downs, Oak	.788	.785	.775
Aquino, Fla	.746	.757	.614	Drabek, Hou	.662	.781	.641
Armstrong, Fla	.845	.720	.739	Eldred, Mil	.744	.682	.696
Arocha, StL	.635	.885	.687	Erickson, Min	.800	.663	.915
Ashby, SD	.975	.748	1.007	Farrell, Cal	.873	1.011	1.066
Astacio, LA	.655	.705	.610	Fassero, Mon	.550	.610	.645
Avery, Atl	.708	.593	.633	Fernandez A, ChA	.646	.675	.710
Banks, Min	.747	.800	.790	Fernandez S, NYN	.650	.542	.560
Belcher, ChA	.615	.765	.769	Finley, Cal	.711	.699	.628
Benes, SD	.505	.723	.844	Fleming, Sea	.727	.829	.790
Bere, ChA	.594	.613	.693	Gardner, KC	.797	.822	1.037
Bielecki, Bal	.737	.814	1.024	Glavine, Atl	.682	.786	.644
Black, SF	.828	.537	.780	Gooden, NYN	.758	.592	.590
Blair, Col	.758	.894	.932	Gordon, KC	.646	.642	.696
Bohanon, Tex	.839	.788	.478	Greene, Phi	.672	.560	.634
Bolton T, Det	.797	.568	.814	Gross Kev, LA	.758	.717	.668
Bones, Mil	.786	.906	.689	Guardado, Min	.777	1.069	.992
Bosio, Sea	.569	.648	.802	Gullickson, Det	.801	.856	.874
Bottenfield, Col	.809	.939	.826	Guzman Jose, ChN	.676	.845	.779
Bowen, Fla	.730	.685	.805	Guzman Juan, Tor	.681	.680	.722
Brantley, SF	.690	.718	1.385	Hammond, Fla	.753	.654	.855
Brocail, SD	.706	.744	1.035	Haney, KC	.723	.887	.739
Brown, Tex	.769	.626	.594	Hanson, Sea	.641	.802	.741
Browning, Cin	.850	.886	.868	Harkey, ChN	.817	.850	.602
Brummett, Min	.856	.864	.684	Harnisch, Hou	.712	.561	.578
Burkett, SF	.581	.704	.745	Harris GW, Col	.816	.681	.841
Candiotti, LA	.701	.684	.534	Hathaway, Cal	.916	.808	.805
Castillo F, ChN	.820	.871	.730	Henry B, Mon	.824	.885	.878
Clark, Cle	.803	.680	.922	Hentgen, Tor	.768	.728	.697
Clemens, Bos	.612	.778	.694	Hershiser, LA	.734	.561	.746
Cone, KC	.684	.575	.682	Hibbard, ChN	.759	.846	.664
Cooke, Pit	.659	.710	.875	Hickerson, SF	.768	.710	1.042
Cormier, StL	.752	.845	.739	Hill K, Mon	.583	.618	.799
Darling, Oak	.857	.819	.637	Hillman, NYN	.746	.725	.810
Darwin, Bos	.624	.690	.756	Hough, Fla	.805	.614	.709
Deshaies, SF	.832	.721	.702	Jackson D, Phi	.677	.662	.775

Pitcher	Pitch 1-45	Pitch 46-75	Pitch 76+	Pitcher	Pitch 1-45	Pitch 46-75	Pitch 76+
Johnson R, Sea	.512	.740	.619	Rogers Ken, Tex	.717	.842	.629
Jones Bob, NYN	.732	.650	.871	Roper, Cin	.837	.673	1.025
Kamieniecki, NYA	.855	.763	.605	Rueter, Mon	.606	.804	.640
Key, NYA	.597	.693	.714	Ruffin B, Col	.746	.701	.654
Kile, Hou	.674	.654	.661	Ryan N, Tex	.861	.504	.511
Kramer, Cle	.818	.728	.843	Saberhagen, NYN	.528	.656	.785
Langston, Cal	.586	.670	.685	Sanders, SD	.475	.787	1.090
Leary, Sea	.864	.820	.740	Sanderson, SF	.732	.734	.880
Leftwich, Cal	.654	.667	.772	Schilling, Phi	.719	.635	.716
Leibrandt, Tex	.667	.898	.815	Schourek, NYN	.833	.757	1.041
Leiter A, Tor	.650	.745	.517	Sele, Bos	.597	.595	.778
Leiter M, Det	.775	.903	.559	Smiley, Cin	.746	.993	.578
Luebbers, Cin	.701	.649	.882	Smith P, Atl	.815	.787	.816
Maddux G, Atl	.555	.592	.645	Smith Z, Pit	.755	.932	.686
Magrane, Cal	.813	.687	.815	Smoltz, Atl	.667	.565	.800
Martinez D, Mon	.677	.659	.820	Springer, Cal	1.088	.709	.680
Martinez R, LA	.757	.605	.736	Stewart, Tor	.717	.705	.811
McCaskill, ChA	.768	.832	1.004	Stottlemyre, Tor	.757	.824	.759
McDonald, Bal	.656	.611	.667	Sutcliffe, Bal	.954	.877	.776
McDowell J, ChA	.813	.650	.602	Swift, SF	.558	.627	.668
Mesa, Cle	.735	.654	.900	Swindell, Hou	.778	.757	.781
Mills, Bal	.747	.544	-	Tanana, NYA	.751	.773	.782
Miranda, Mil	.636	.679	.759	Tapani, Min	.727	.761	.728
Moore Mike, Det	.826	.799	.734	Tewksbury, StL	.708	.801	.676
Morgan, ChN	.668	.806	.634	Tomlin, Pit	.859	.863	.429
Morris, Tor	.836	.860	.768	Trombley, Min	.810	.871	1.012
Moyer, Bal	.671	.757	.651	Urbani, StL	.814	.573	1.113
Mulholland, Phi	.705	.547	.709	Valenzuela, Bal	.955	.664	.594
Mussina, Bal	.689	.713	.756	Van Poppel, Oak	.789	.716	.823
Mutis, Cle	.763	.884	1.048	Viola, Bos	.734	.738	.611
Nabholz, Mon	.703	.786	.509	Wagner, Pit	.674	.581	.990
Navarro, Mil	.806	.783	.795	Wakefield, Pit	.805	.806	.947
Nied, Col	.742	.771	.954	Walk, Pit	.781	.855	.797
Olivares, StL	.799	.738	.833	Watson, StL	.765	.755	.828
Osborne, StL	.772	.710	.668	Wegman, Mil	.739	.948	.764
Pavlik, Tex	.742	.699	.699	Welch, Oak	.888	.957	.653
Perez Mld, NYA	.811	.634	.808	Wells, Det	.667	.739	.794
Pichardo, KC	.723	.807	.679	Whitehurst, SD	.669	.856	.822
Portugal, Hou	.515	.703	.784	Wickman, NYA	.747	.840	.864
Pugh, Cin	.822	.689	.936	Wilson T, SF	.747	.641	.840
Quantrill, Bos	.776	.711	.761	Witt B, Oak	.830	.697	.629
Rapp, Fla	.694	.730	.974	Worrell Tim, SD	.699	.831	.728
Reynoso, Col	.735	.786	.831	Young A, NYN	.673	.686	.849
Rhodes, Bal	.848	.737	1.119	Young M, Tor	.649	1.043	.991
Rijo, Cin	.624	.626	.610	**MLB Avg (1993)**	**.740**	**.748**	**.755**
Rivera, Phi	.751	.750	.816				

About STATS, Inc.

From our humble beginnings less than a decade ago in a bedroom-slash-office—okay, maybe it was only for a month—STATS, Inc. has become the unchallenged leader in the field of statistical collection, analysis and publishing.

You want **baseball**? STATS publishes or co-publishes a number of invaluable baseball books. In addition to the book now in your hands, HarperPerennial and STATS publish *The Scouting Report: 1994*, now available at just about any bookstore. In addition, STATS Publishing produces reference books that major league teams and baseball fans everywhere order by the bushelful every fall (that's right, you don't have to wait until spring training). *STATS 1994 Major League Handbook* is a complete statistical record of every player who saw action in the majors last season, along with platoon splits, ballpark data, Bill James' and John Dewan's infamous projections, and assorted other goodies. *STATS 1994 Minor League Handbook* contains a complete statistical record for everyone who played Double- or Triple-A ball last year but didn't make it to the majors. Also included: Triple-A lefty-righty splits, ballpark effects, 1993 stats for those who only played A-ball, and Bill James' infamous Major League Equivalencies. *STATS 1994 Player Profiles* is full of various breakdowns and situational stats in one- and five-season formats, for every major league player. And new this season: *STATS 1994 Batter Versus Pitcher Match-Ups!*, in which you can look up any major league pitcher, and see how every batter who's faced him five times or more has done.

You want **basketball**? Last fall, HarperPerennial published the *STATS Basketball Scoreboard 1993-1994*, "The Thinking Fan's Guide to the NBA." Do you want to know "Which teams come from (way way) behind?" Or "How did Shaq stack up against the best?" Those are just two of the 60 questions that the *Basketball Scoreboard* asked and answered. If you like this book, go out and pick up the basketball book in time for the playoffs.

You want **football**? No books yet (they're coming, though), but if you have a computer, we have football data coming out the kazoo on STATS On-Line. By the time the Cowboys-49ers game starts on Monday night, everything you want to know about the previous day's games is at your fingertips, via STATS On-Line. What about **hockey**, you ask? As you read this, our intrepid STATS staff is busily expanding our hockey data base. Write HarperPerennial and tell them you want more books, then stay tuned.

You want games? We started in 1989 with *Bill James Fantasy Baseball*, the most realistic fantasy baseball game ever. Then in 1990, *STATS Fantasy Football* crashed into the end zone. The close of 1992 brought a new baby, *Bill James Fantasy Baseball: The Winter Game*, in which your roster is composed of your favorite players from the yellowing pages of baseball history. And finally, last fall marked the inaugural tip-off for *STATS Fantasy Hoops*.

What's that? You have a computer, and you'd like access to most of the information in the various books, along with plenty of other stuff, updated constantly—In-Progress box scores updated every few minutes by STATS' own press-box scorers, the next three days of probable starting pitchers, injury information, and lots more? Hook up with STATS On-Line, and the world is yours.

Believe it or not, the above barely scratches the surface of what STATS, Inc. can do for the sports fan or professional. For more information, write us at:

STATS, Inc.
8131 N. Monticello Ave.
Skokie, IL 60076-3325

. . . or call us at 1-800-63-STATS (outside the U.S., make that 1-708-676-3322). You'll be glad you did.

Index